501
low-carb recipes

501 low-carb recipes

Pamela Clark

THE AUSTRALIAN
Women's Weekly

Test Kitchen
Food director *Pamela Clark*
Food editors *Nancy Duran, Amira Georgy*
Test Kitchen manager *Cathie Lonnie*
Home economists *Sammie Coryton,*
Nancy Duran, Benjamin Haslam,
Elizabeth Macri, Christina Martignago,
Sharon Reeve, Susie Riggall,
Jessica Sly, Kirrily Smith, Kate Tait
Editorial coordinator *Rebecca Steyns*
Nutritional information *Laila Ibram*

ACP Books
Editorial director *Susan Tomnay*
Creative director *Hieu Chi Nguyen*
Editor *Stephanie Kistner*
Designer *Karen Lai*
Studio manager *Caryl Wiggins*
Editorial/sales coordinator *Caroline Lowry*
Publishing manager (sales) *Brian Cearnes*
Publishing manager (rights & new projects)
 Jane Hazell
Brand manager *Donna Gianniotis*
Pre-press *Harry Palmer*
Production manager *Carol Currie*
Business manager *Seymour Cohen*
Assistant business analyst *Martin Howes*
Chief executive officer *John Alexander*
Group publisher *Pat Ingram*
Publisher *Sue Wannan*
Editor-in-chief *Deborah Thomas*

Produced by ACP Books, Sydney.

Printed by Bookbuilders, China.

Published by ACP Publishing Pty Limited,
54 Park St, Sydney; GPO Box 4088,
Sydney, NSW 2001.
Ph: (02) 9282 8618 Fax: (02) 9267 9438.
acpbooks@acp.com.au
www.acpbooks.com.au

To order books, phone 136 116.
Send recipe enquiries to:
recipeenquiries@acp.com.au

AUSTRALIA: Distributed by Network Services,
GPO Box 4088, Sydney, NSW 2001.
Ph: (02) 9282 8777 Fax: (02) 9264 3278.

UNITED KINGDOM: Distributed by Australian
Consolidated Press (UK), Moulton Park Business
Centre, Red House Rd,
Moulton Park, Northampton, NN3 6AQ.
Ph: (01604) 497531 Fax: (01604) 497533
acpukltd@aol.com

CANADA: Distributed by Whitecap Books Ltd,
351 Lynn Ave, North Vancouver, BC, V7J 2C4.
Ph: (604) 980 9852 Fax: (604) 980 8197
customerservice@whitecap.ca
www.whitecap.ca

NEW ZEALAND: Distributed by Netlink Distribution
Company, ACP Media Centre,
Cnr Fanshawe and Beaumont Streets, Westhaven,
Auckland.
PO Box 47906, Ponsonby, Auckland, NZ.
Ph: (09) 366 9966 ask@ndcnz.co.nz

Clark, Pamela.
The Australian women's weekly 501 low-carb
recipes.

Includes index.
ISBN 1 86396 395 2.

1. Low-carbohydrate diet – Recipes. I. Title:
II. Title: Australian women's weekly.

641.56383

Photographer *Prue Ruscoe*
Stylist *Julz Beresford*

Front cover Grilled prawns and tropical fruit salad, page 216
Back cover clockwise from top left Cajun chicken with chunky
salsa, page 135; Sang choy bow, page 124; Barbecue sweet
and sour blue-eye, page 209; Tom yum goong, page 41;
Salade niçoise, page 34; Hot and sour steamed fish with thai
salad, page 222
Page 1 Cioppino, page 212
Page 2 Baked ricotta with roasted tomatoes, page 14

contents

LOW-CARB FOODS

	Carb (g)
almonds, with skin, 1 tablespoon	0.6
apple, granny smith, raw, unpeeled, small, 130g	10.8
artichoke, canned, in brine, drained, 100g	1.2
asparagus, canned in brine, drained, 100g	1.5
asparagus, raw, 100g	1
avocado, raw, small, 200g	0.6
bean, green, frozen, boiled, 100g	2.8
berries, mixed, frozen, 100g	8.7
bok choy, cooked, 100g	0.9
broccoli, boiled, 100g	0.4
brussels sprouts, boiled, 100g	1.9
cabbage, chinese, raw, 1 cup shredded, 80g	0.7
cabbage, red, raw, 1 cup shredded, 80g	2.5
capsicum, green, raw, small, 150g	2.3
carrot, raw, small, 70g	3.2
cashews, 1 tablespoon	2
cauliflower, boiled, 100g	2
celery, raw, 1 trimmed stalk, 100g	2.2
cheese, cheddar, 30g	0
cheese, fetta, 30g	0.1
cheese, parmesan, 30g	0
chilli, red, raw, 1 teaspoon chopped	0.2
coconut milk, canned, ¼ cup	2.3
coconut, desiccated, 1 tablespoon	0.4
cream, pure, ¼ cup	1.7
cream, sour, ¼ cup	1.7
cream, thickened, ¼ cup	3.1
cucumber, lebanese, raw, 1, 130g	2.3
curry paste, 1 tablespoon	1.8
egg, fried, 1, 60g	0.2
egg, hard-boiled, 1, 60g	0.2
eggplant, raw, small, 230g	6
fennel, raw, small, 200g	3.6
fig, raw, medium, 60g	4.9
gai larn, cooked, 100g	1.1
garlic, raw, 1 clove	0.3
ginger, raw, 1cm piece, 5g	0.2
honeydew, raw, 100g	6.5
kiwi fruit, raw, medium, 85g	7.1
leek, raw, small, 200g	4.7
lemon, raw, medium, 140g	2.5
lettuce, iceberg, raw, 100g	0.4
lime, raw, 1, 80g	0.8
mayonnaise, whole egg, 1 tablespoon	0.2
meat (beef, veal, lamb, pork)	0
milk, ¼ cup	2.9
mushroom, button, raw, 100g	1.5
mustard, all types, 1 teaspoon	0.2
oil, olive, 1 tablespoon	0

oil, peanut, 1 tablespoon	0
olives, black, pickled in brine, seeded, ¼ cup	9
onion, green, raw, 1, 10g	0.5
onion, raw, small, 80g	2.8
parsnip, boiled, small, 120g	9.7
passionfruit pulp, canned, 1 tablespoon	1
passionfruit, raw, 1, 1 tablespoon pulp	1.1
peach, raw, small, 115g	6.3
peanut butter, added sugar, unsalted, 1 tablespoon	2.5
peanuts, unsalted, 1 tablespoon	1.6
peas, green, frozen, boiled, 100g	5.8
pine nuts, 1 tablespoon	0.7
pistachios, shelled, 1 tablespoon	1.5
poultry (chicken, turkey)	0
prosciutto, 1 slice, 15g	0.1
pumpkin, baked, 100g	2.8
radish, red, raw, 1, 35g	0.7
rocket, raw, 100g	2.2
rockmelon, raw, 100g	4.7
sauce, barbecue, 1 tablespoon	9.4
sauce, soy, 1 tablespoon	0.6
sauce, tomato, 1 tablespoon	5.4
seafood, salmon, smoked, 1 slice, 30g	0
seafood, tuna, canned in oil, drained, 100g	0
silverbeet, boiled, 100g	1.3
snow peas, raw, 100g	4.7
spinach, boiled, 100g	0.8
squash, boiled, 100g	3.6
strawberry, raw, 100g	2.7
tofu, raw, 100g	1.3
tomato paste, 1 tablespoon	2.3
tomato, crushed, canned, 100g	3.2
tomato, raw, small, 90g	1.7
watermelon, raw, 100g	5
wine, dry red, ½ cup	0
wine, dry white, ½ cup	0.4
yogurt, plain, ½ cup, 140g	6.6
zucchini, raw, small, 90g	1.4

HIGH-CARB FOODS

honey, 1 tablespoon	23.5
ice-cream, chocolate, 1 scoop, 125g	25
kumara, boiled, small, 250g	30
lemonade, soft drink, 1 cup	27.1
mango, raw, small, 300g	25.5
milk, condensed, sweetened, 100g	55.3
pawpaw, raw, small, 650g	31
potato, baked, small, 120g	50.5
raisins, ¼ cup	28.6
yogurt, frozen, soft serve, fruit, 1 scoop, 125g	30.9

Low-carb eating

WHAT FOODS CONTAIN CARBS?

Carbohydrates are found in starchy foods and sugars. So all grains (flour, bread, pasta, rice, breakfast cereals), most fruits and many vegetables (especially root crops such as potatoes and carrots) fall into this category.

When starch is combined with sugar – in chocolate bars for example – this results in a very high carb count with almost no nutritive value.

Carbohydrates are used in the body as fuel. They give you energy. That's why athletes eat high-carbohydrate diets. However, if your life is sedimentary, you don't need a intake of carbs. When your grandmother wanted to lose weight, she'd cut out bread and potatoes for a couple of weeks – there's nothing new about a low-carb diet.

HOW TO USE THIS BOOK

Each of the three sections in this book – losing weight fast, losing weight slower, and maintaining weight – contains recipes for breakfast, lunch, dinner, and appetisers/snacks.

LOSING WEIGHT FAST

The first section is made up of recipes which have no more than 12g carb per serving. At three meals a day, that gives you a total of 36g carbohydrate. If some of the dishes contain much less than 12g, you can add a snack or two, to make up the 36g total. The limit of 12g per serving is not as restrictive as some low-carb diets, but you will lose weight on this diet without ever feeling hungry.

This diet contains plenty of vegetables, as well as protein, with a good balance of nutrients to keep you healthy. You won't suffer some of the common side-effects of the more restrictive diets, such as constipation and tiredness.

Unlike many low-carb diets, this section is full of interesting food ideas, so it's possible to stay on the 12g regime for longer and not get bored – and boredom is the reason most people come off their low-carb diet.

LOSING WEIGHT SLOWER

The second section contains recipes which have no more than 25g carb per serving. This increases the choice of foods considerably. Much more fruit is introduced and you can even have a piece of toast for breakfast.

This diet is suitable if you've already lost weight and wish to lose more, but at a slower rate.

There's a huge variety of delicious recipes to choose from, so many in fact that you could easily follow the recipes in this section all your life.

If you find you need to lose a bit more weight in a hurry, go back to the 12g section for a week or so.

MAINTAINING WEIGHT

The third section contains recipes with no more than 43g carb per serving. This is food for life. There are enough carbs to keep your diet balanced, but not so many that you gain weight.

With such a huge variety of recipes, all the family can enjoy the food in this chapter without ever knowing they're on a reduced-carb regimen.

A NEW WAY OF EATING

· Re-think your snacks. Don't go near the junk food aisle in the supermarket. Junk food is very high in carbs.

· Steer clear of carbs that put on weight without giving you any nutritive benefit. The worst offenders are potato chips, chocolate bars or any other sweets (very high in sugar), ice-cream (high in sugar), soft drinks, and any snack food made from flour, such as cookies.

· To lose weight you have to be prepared to spend more time cooking.

· The enemy of the diet is hunger. It's when you feel hungry that you reach for the quick fix – french fries, chocolate bars, cookies. Prevent hunger by eating enough food at each meal to satisfy yourself. Don't eat until you can eat no more, but eat enough to last you until the next meal.

· Be prepared. Take some berries to work with you, or a few slices of ham and a tomato. Eat these if the craving for 'a little something' comes upon you.

· Forget cakes, pastries, donuts. On a low-carb or reduced-carb diet, these are not for you.

Losing Weight Fast (no more than 12g carbs per serving)

rocket, speck and poached egg salad

PREPARATION TIME 15 MINUTES   COOKING TIME 15 MINUTES

Speck, a German salted and smoked pork product not dissimilar to some bacons, can be found at most delicatessens. Pecorino cheese, the generic Italian name for cheeses made from sheep milk, is a hard, white-to-pale-yellow cheese, traditionally produced when the sheep are grazing on summer pastures.

300g speck, sliced thinly

200g rocket

¼ cup coarsely chopped fresh basil

50g pecorino cheese, shaved

4 eggs

GARLIC VINAIGRETTE

2 cloves garlic, crushed

1 teaspoon dijon mustard

⅓ cup (80ml) extra virgin olive oil

¼ cup (60ml) balsamic vinegar

1 Cook speck in large non-stick frying pan, stirring occasionally, until crisp. Drain on absorbent paper; cool.

2 Meanwhile, make garlic vinaigrette.

3 Place speck in medium bowl with rocket, basil and cheese; toss gently to combine.

4 Half-fill a large frying pan with water; bring to a boil. One at a time, break eggs into cup then slide into pan. When all eggs are in pan, allow water to return to a boil. Cover pan, turn off heat; stand about 4 minutes or until a light film of egg white sets over yolks. Using egg slide, remove eggs, one at a time, and place on absorbent-paper-lined saucer to blot up poaching water.

5 Divide salad among serving plates; top each with an egg then drizzle with vinaigrette.

GARLIC VINAIGRETTE Place ingredients in screw-top jar; shake well.

SERVES 4
per serving 0.70g carbohydrate; 37.7g fat; 1877kJ (449 cal); 28.2g protein

mushroom and zucchini omelette

PREPARATION TIME 10 MINUTES   COOKING TIME 25 MINUTES

2 tablespoons butter

2 cloves garlic, crushed

125g button mushrooms,
**   sliced thinly**

1 cup (200g) coarsely
**   grated zucchini**

4 green onions, chopped finely

8 eggs

⅓ cup (80ml) water

1 cup (120g) coarsely grated
**   cheddar cheese**

1 Heat half of the butter in small non-stick frying pan; cook garlic and mushrooms, stirring, over medium heat about 2 minutes or until mushrooms are just browned. Add zucchini and onion; cook, stirring, about 1 minute or until zucchini begins to soften. Remove vegetable mixture from pan; cover to keep warm.

2 Break eggs into medium bowl, whisk lightly; whisk in the water and cheese.

3 Heat 1 teaspoon butter in same pan; swirl pan so butter covers base. Pour a quarter of the egg mixture into pan; cook over medium heat, tilting pan, until omelette is almost set.

4 Place a quarter of the vegetable mixture evenly over half of the omelette; using egg slide, flip other half over vegetable mixture. Using egg slide, slide omelette gently onto serving plate. Repeat steps 3 and 4 three more times with remaining ingredients.

SERVES 4

per serving 2.3g carbohydrate; 28.8g fat; 1492kJ (357 cal); 22.8g protein

tips Assemble and prepare all of the ingredients before beginning to cook. The frying pan and butter should be quite hot when the egg mixture is added, so the omelette base sets almost immediately. You can use any type of cheese in place of the cheddar, or substitute the mushrooms and zucchini with baby spinach leaves and chopped fried bacon, or finely chopped raw tomato and onion. Two tablespoons of your favourite chopped herbs will enliven almost every omelette.

egg-white omelette

PREPARATION TIME 25 MINUTES   COOKING TIME 20 MINUTES

12 egg whites

4 green onions, chopped finely

⅓ cup finely chopped fresh chives

½ cup finely chopped fresh flat-leaf parsley

½ cup (60g) coarsely grated cheddar cheese

½ cup (50g) coarsely grated mozzarella cheese

1   Using electric mixer, beat three of the egg whites in small bowl until soft peaks form; fold in a quarter of the combined onion and herbs.

2   Pour mixture into 20cm heated lightly oiled non-stick frying pan; cook, uncovered, over low heat until just browned on the bottom.

3   Sprinkle a quarter of the combined cheeses on half of the omelette. Place omelette under preheated grill until cheese begins to melt. Fold omelette in half to enclose. Carefully slide onto serving plate; cover to keep warm.

4   Repeat process with remaining egg whites, onion and herb mixture and combined cheeses.

SERVES 4
per serving 1.1g carbohydrate; 7.9g fat; 619kJ (148 cal); 18.2g protein

smoked salmon and roasted vegetables

PREPARATION TIME 10 MINUTES   COOKING TIME 15 MINUTES

2 large red capsicums (700g)

6 baby eggplants (360g)

4 medium zucchini (480g)

250g rocket leaves

200g sliced smoked salmon

1 teaspoon finely grated lemon rind

2 teaspoons lemon juice

1   Quarter capsicums, remove and discard seeds and membranes. Roast under grill or in very hot oven, skin-side up, until skin blisters and blackens. Cover capsicum pieces in plastic or paper for 5 minutes, peel away skin; slice capsicum thinly.

2   Meanwhile, slice eggplants and zucchini lengthways. Place eggplant and zucchini, in single layer, on oiled oven trays. Place under hot grill or in hot oven until browned lightly both sides.

3   Serve roasted vegetables and rocket with salmon. Sprinkle with lemon rind; drizzle with juice.

SERVES 4
per serving 11g carbohydrate; 3.6g fat; 614kJ (147 cal); 17.6g protein

breakfast fry-up

PREPARATION TIME 10 MINUTES   COOKING TIME 20 MINUTES

4 medium egg tomatoes (300g)

2 tablespoons balsamic vinegar

cooking-oil spray

300g mushrooms, sliced thickly

½ cup loosely packed fresh basil
leaves, torn

¼ cup loosely packed fresh
coriander leaves

¼ cup loosely packed fresh flat-leaf
parsley leaves

200g shaved ham

1 Preheat oven to moderately hot.

2 Cut each tomato into four wedges; toss in small bowl with half of the vinegar. Place tomato mixture, in single layer, in shallow oiled baking dish; spray with oil. Roast, uncovered, in moderately hot oven 20 minutes.

3 Meanwhile, toss mushrooms in same bowl with remaining vinegar; cook mushroom mixture, stirring, in medium oiled frying pan until tender. Add herbs; toss to combine.

4 Place ham in same pan; heat, stirring gently. Divide mushrooms, tomato and ham among serving plates.

SERVES 4
per serving 2.6g carbohydrate; 2.9g fat; 380kJ (91 cal); 13g protein

florentine eggs with bacon, spinach and pecorino

PREPARATION TIME 5 MINUTES   COOKING TIME 10 MINUTES

600g spinach, trimmed,
chopped coarsely

4 bacon rashers (280g),
rind removed

4 eggs

⅓ cup (40g) shaved
pecorino cheese

1 Boil, steam or microwave spinach until just wilted; drain. Cover to keep warm.

2 Meanwhile, heat large non-stick frying pan; cook bacon until crisp. Drain on absorbent paper; cover to keep warm.

3 Half-fill a large shallow frying pan with water; bring to a boil. Break eggs into cup, one at a time, then slide into pan. When all eggs are in pan, allow water to return to a boil. Cover pan, turn off heat; stand about 4 minutes or until a light film of egg white sets over yolks. Remove eggs, one at a time, using slotted spoon, and place on absorbent-paper-lined saucer to blot up poaching liquid.

4 Divide spinach among serving plates; top each with bacon, egg then cheese.

SERVES 4
per serving 0.8g carbohydrate; 13.1g fat; 811kJ (194 cal); 18.5g protein

bacon and asparagus frittata

PREPARATION TIME 15 MINUTES   COOKING TIME 45 MINUTES

**4 bacon rashers (280g), rind
   removed, sliced thickly**

1 large red onion (300g), sliced thinly

170g asparagus, trimmed

4 eggs

4 egg whites

1 cup (250ml) buttermilk

1 Preheat oven to moderate. Lightly oil deep 20cm-square cake pan; line
   base and sides with baking paper.

2 Cook bacon, stirring, in small heated non-stick frying pan until crisp.
   Remove bacon with slotted spoon; drain on absorbent paper. Add onion
   to same pan; cook, stirring, until soft and browned lightly. Layer bacon,
   onion and asparagus in prepared pan.

3 Whisk eggs, egg whites and buttermilk in medium jug; pour over
   mixture in pan. Bake frittata mixture, uncovered, in moderate oven about
   35 minutes or until set. Stand 10 minutes before serving.

SERVES 4
per serving 8.5g carbohydrate; 11.6g fat; 1346kJ (322 cal); 45.6g protein

zucchini, pumpkin and red capsicum frittata

PREPARATION TIME 10 MINUTES   COOKING TIME 1 HOUR 10 MINUTES

500g pumpkin, chopped coarsely

**2 large zucchini (300g),
   chopped coarsely**

**1 medium red capsicum (200g),
   chopped coarsely**

1 tablespoon olive oil

200g fetta, crumbled

8 eggs

½ cup (125ml) cream

1 Preheat oven to moderately hot. Oil and line base and side of deep
   22cm-round cake pan with baking paper.

2 Combine pumpkin, zucchini and capsicum in single layer, in large baking
   dish; drizzle with oil. Roast, uncovered, in moderately hot oven about
   30 minutes or until vegetables are browned and tender.

3 Reduce oven temperature to moderately slow.

4 Place pumpkin, zucchini, capsicum and cheese in prepared pan. Whisk
   eggs in medium bowl until frothy. Whisk in cream; pour over vegetables
   and cheese. Bake, uncovered, in moderately slow oven about 40 minutes
   or until frittata sets and is just cooked through.

SERVES 4
per serving 10.7g carbohydrate; 40.3g fat; 2149kJ (514 cal); 28.3g protein

cucumber, celery, apple and spinach juice

PREPARATION TIME 10 MINUTES (PLUS REFRIGERATION TIME)

1 telegraph cucumber (400g)

2 trimmed celery stalks (200g),

   chopped finely

2 large granny smith apples (400g)

50g baby spinach leaves,

   stems removed

⅓ cup firmly packed fresh

   mint leaves

1   Blend or process ingredients, in batches, until smooth; strain through fine sieve into large jug. Refrigerate, covered, until cold.

MAKES 1 LITRE
per 250ml   11.1g carbohydrate; 0.3g fat; 228kJ (55 cal); 2g protein

tomato and red capsicum juice

PREPARATION TIME 10 MINUTES (PLUS REFRIGERATION TIME)

1 medium red capsicum (300g),

   chopped coarsely

4 medium tomatoes (300g),

   chopped coarsely

2 medium carrots (240g),

   chopped coarsely

⅓ cup firmly packed fresh flat-leaf

   parsley leaves

1 cup (250ml) water

1   Blend or process ingredients, in batches, until smooth; strain through fine sieve into large jug. Refrigerate, covered, until cold.

MAKES 1 LITRE
per 250ml   6.3g carbohydrate; 0.2g fat; 153kJ (37 cal); 2.1g protein

baked ricotta with roasted tomatoes (see page 2)

PREPARATION TIME 10 MINUTES   COOKING TIME 15 MINUTES

1 teaspoon olive oil

1 clove garlic, crushed

1 tablespoon pine nuts

100g baby spinach leaves

1¼ cups (250g) low-fat
   ricotta cheese

1 egg, beaten lightly

2 tablespoons coarsely chopped
   fresh chives

500g baby vine-ripened
   truss tomatoes

1 tablespoon balsamic vinegar

1 teaspoon olive oil, extra

1 clove garlic, crushed, extra

1 Preheat oven to hot. Lightly oil four holes of a six-hole ⅓-cup (80ml) muffin pan.

2 Heat oil in medium frying pan; cook garlic and nuts, stirring, over low heat until nuts are just browned lightly. Add spinach; cook, stirring, until spinach just wilts. Cool 10 minutes.

3 Combine cheese, egg and chives in medium bowl with spinach mixture; divide mixture among prepared muffin pan holes. Bake, uncovered, in hot oven about 15 minutes or until cheese is just firm and browned lightly.

4 Meanwhile, toss tomatoes with vinegar, extra oil and extra garlic in medium bowl; place, in single layer, in small shallow baking dish. Roast, uncovered, in hot oven 10 minutes. Serve baked ricotta with roasted tomatoes.

SERVES 4

per serving 4g carbohydrate; 11.8g fat; 686kJ (164 cal); 10.5g protein

baked eggs with pancetta

PREPARATION TIME 15 MINUTES   COOKING TIME 20 MINUTES

2 teaspoons olive oil

**1 small red capsicum (150g),
    chopped finely**

100g pancetta, chopped finely

100g mushrooms, chopped finely

4 green onions, chopped finely

**⅔ cup (50g) finely grated
    parmesan cheese**

8 eggs

**2 teaspoons coarsely chopped
    fresh flat-leaf parsley**

1 Preheat oven to moderately hot. Lightly oil four ¾-cup (180ml) shallow ovenproof dishes.

2 Heat oil in medium frying pan; cook capsicum and pancetta, stirring, until capsicum is just tender. Add mushrooms and onion; cook, stirring, until onion softens. Remove pan from heat; stir in half of the cheese.

3 Divide capsicum mixture among dishes; carefully break two eggs into each dish. Bake eggs, uncovered, in moderately hot oven 5 minutes. Sprinkle remaining cheese over eggs; bake, uncovered, in moderately hot oven about 5 minutes or until eggs are just set. Sprinkle parsley over eggs just before serving.

SERVES 4

per serving 2.5g carbohydrate; 20g fat; 1187kJ (284 cal); 23.9g protein

scrambled eggs with chorizo

PREPARATION TIME 5 MINUTES   COOKING TIME 10 MINUTES

250g chorizo, sliced thickly

8 eggs

¾ cup (180ml) cream

2 tablespoons coarsely chopped fresh chives

10g butter

1 Cook chorizo, in batches, on heated grill plate (or grill or barbecue) until browned both sides; cover to keep warm.

2 Break eggs into medium bowl, whisk lightly; whisk in cream and half of the chives.

3 Melt butter in medium frying pan over low heat; cook egg mixture, stirring gently constantly, until egg mixture just begins to set.

4 Serve scrambled eggs sprinkled with remaining chives and chorizo.

SERVES 4
per serving 3.8g carbohydrate; 42.6g fat; 1998kJ (478 cal); 21.2g protein

scrambled eggs with dill and smoked salmon

PREPARATION TIME 10 MINUTES   COOKING TIME 5 MINUTES

8 eggs

½ cup (125ml) buttermilk

1 tablespoon finely chopped fresh dill

10g butter

300g sliced smoked salmon

1 Whisk eggs in medium bowl; add buttermilk and dill, whisking until mixture is frothy.

2 Melt butter in medium frying pan over low heat; cook egg mixture, stirring constantly, until egg mixture is just set.

3 Divide eggs among serving plates; top with salmon.

SERVES 4
per serving 1.8g carbohydrate; 16.8g fat; 1179kJ (282 cal); 31.1g protein

tomato and eggs on corn tortilla

PREPARATION TIME 10 MINUTES   COOKING TIME 30 MINUTES

1 small red onion (100g),
   chopped finely

4 medium tomatoes (600g),
   quartered lengthways

1 tablespoon balsamic vinegar

1 medium red capsicum (200g),
   chopped finely

4 eggs

4 x 15cm corn tortillas

1 Cook onion in lightly oiled large non-stick frying pan, stirring, until onion softens. Add tomato and vinegar; bring to a boil. Reduce heat; simmer, uncovered, 15 minutes, stirring occasionally. Add capsicum; cook, uncovered, 5 minutes.

2 Break eggs into cup, one at a time, then slide into same pan. When all eggs are in pan, return tomato mixture to a boil. Cover; cook about 10 minutes or until eggs are firm.

3 Warm tortillas according to instructions on packet. Place tortillas on serving plates; top with egg and tomato mixture. Serve immediately with Tabasco, if desired.

SERVES 4
per serving 8.5g carbohydrate; 5.7g fat; 518kJ (124 cal); 9.4g protein

fennel fritters with poached eggs

PREPARATION TIME 15 MINUTES   COOKING TIME 20 MINUTES

1 tablespoon finely chopped fresh
   fennel fronds

1 medium fennel bulb (500g),
   chopped finely

3 green onions, chopped finely

1 small carrot (70g), grated finely

2 bacon rashers (140g), rind
   removed, chopped finely

2 eggs, beaten lightly

75g ricotta cheese

¼ cup (35g) plain flour

2 teaspoons baking powder

vegetable oil, for shallow-frying

4 eggs

1 Combine fennel fronds, fennel bulb, onion, carrot, bacon, egg, cheese, flour and baking powder in medium bowl.

2 Heat the oil in large frying pan; shallow-fry heaped tablespoons of mixture in hot oil until golden brown and cooked through, flattening slightly during cooking. Drain on absorbent paper.

3 Meanwhile, half-fill a large shallow frying pan with water; bring to a boil. Break eggs into cup, one at a time, then slide into pan. When all eggs are in pan, allow water to return to a boil. Cover pan, turn off heat; stand about 4 minutes or until a light film of egg white sets over yolks. Remove eggs, one at a time, using slotted spoon, and place on absorbent-paper-lined saucer to blot up poaching liquid.

4 Serve eggs with fritters.

SERVES 4
per serving 10.9g carbohydrate; 29.5g fat; 1572kJ (376 cal); 17.4g protein

smoked salmon omelette

PREPARATION TIME 10 MINUTES   COOKING TIME 15 MINUTES

6 eggs

⅔ cup (160ml) cream

1 tablespoon warm water

⅔ cup (160g) sour cream

2 tablespoons coarsely chopped
   fresh dill

1 tablespoon lemon juice

250g sliced smoked salmon

30g baby rocket leaves

1 Break eggs into medium bowl, whisk lightly; whisk in cream.

2 Pour one-quarter of the egg mixture into heated lightly oiled 22cm non-stick frying pan; cook over medium heat, tilting pan, until omelette is almost set. Run spatula around edge of pan to loosen omelette, turn onto plate; cover to keep warm. Repeat process with remaining egg mixture to make four omelettes.

3 Combine the water with sour cream, dill and juice in small bowl. Fold omelettes into quarters; place on serving plates. Top each with equal amounts of the salmon, sour cream mixture and rocket.

SERVES 4
per serving 2.9g carbohydrate; 41.1g fat; 2011kJ (481 cal); 25.9g protein

smoked salmon omelette

grilled vegetable and ricotta stack

grilled vegetable and ricotta stack

PREPARATION TIME 20 MINUTES   COOKING TIME 30 MINUTES

2 baby eggplants (120g), sliced
   thickly lengthways

1 medium green capsicum (200g),
   sliced thickly lengthways

1 medium red capsicum (200g),
   sliced thickly lengthways

2 large zucchini (300g), sliced
   thickly lengthways

4 x 175g flat mushrooms

2 cups (400g) ricotta cheese

2 cloves garlic, crushed

½ cup finely chopped fresh basil

2 tablespoons finely chopped
   fresh chives

1 tablespoon finely chopped
   fresh oregano

1 tablespoon finely grated
   lemon rind

2 tablespoons toasted pine nuts

TOMATO PESTO

¼ cup (35g) drained semi-dried
   tomatoes, halved

½ cup firmly packed fresh
   basil leaves

2 tablespoons balsamic vinegar

2 tablespoons water

1   Cook eggplant, capsicums, zucchini and mushrooms, in batches, on heated oiled grill plate (or grill or barbecue) until browned and tender.

2   Meanwhile, combine cheese, garlic, herbs and rind in medium bowl.

3   Make tomato pesto.

4   Divide mushrooms, stem-side up, among serving plates; layer with cheese mixture then random slices of eggplant, zucchini and capsicums. Drizzle stack with pesto; sprinkle with nuts.

TOMATO PESTO   Blend or process tomato and basil until mixture forms a paste. With motor operating, gradually add combined vinegar and water in thin, steady stream until pesto is smooth.

SERVES 4
per serving 10.9g carbohydrate; 17.6g fat; 1204kJ (288 cal); 21g protein

grilled haloumi, asparagus and rocket salad

PREPARATION TIME 20 MINUTES   COOKING TIME 15 MINUTES

150g baby green beans, trimmed

1 tablespoon olive oil

500g asparagus, halved crossways

500g haloumi cheese, sliced thinly

1 large avocado (320g), sliced thinly

½ cup (75g) toasted macadamia nuts,
**   chopped coarsely**

200g rocket leaves

MACADAMIA DRESSING

1 teaspoon mild english mustard

¼ cup (60ml) macadamia oil

¼ cup (60ml) sherry vinegar

1   Make macadamia dressing.

2   Boil, steam or microwave beans until just tender; drain. Rinse under cold water; drain.

3   Meanwhile, heat half of the oil in large frying pan; cook asparagus, in batches, until just tender.

4   Heat remaining oil in same pan; cook cheese, in batches, until browned both sides. Drain on absorbent paper.

5   Place beans, asparagus and cheese in large bowl with avocado, nuts, rocket and dressing; toss gently to combine.

MACADAMIA DRESSING   Place ingredients in screw-top jar; shake well.

SERVES 4
per serving 6.5g carbohydrate; 67.4g fat; 3168kJ (758 cal); 33.4g protein
tip Haloumi must be browned just before serving or it becomes leathery and unpalatable.

avocado caesar salad

PREPARATION TIME 20 MINUTES   COOKING TIME 5 MINUTES

2 baby cos lettuce, torn

1 large red onion (300g), sliced thinly

2 medium avocados (500g),
**   chopped coarsely**

⅓ cup (50g) drained sun-dried
**   tomatoes, sliced thinly**

60g parmesan cheese, shaved

DRESSING

1 clove garlic, crushed

2 egg yolks

2 teaspoons dijon mustard

2 tablespoons white vinegar

1 cup (250ml) extra light olive oil

1   Make dressing.

2   Place ingredients and dressing in large bowl; toss gently to combine.

DRESSING   Blend or process garlic, yolks, mustard and vinegar until smooth. With motor operating, gradually add oil in thin, steady stream; process until mixture thickens.

SERVES 4
per serving 9.6g carbohydrate; 86.6g fat; 3591kJ (859 cal); 13g protein

sweet chilli and lime mixed vegetable salad

PREPARATION TIME 20 MINUTES   COOKING TIME 5 MINUTES

200g asparagus, trimmed, chopped coarsely

100g fresh baby corn, sliced lengthways

1 medium red capsicum (200g), sliced thinly

100g shiitake mushrooms, sliced thinly

1 lebanese cucumber (130g), seeded,

   sliced thinly

12 green onions, sliced thinly

1¼ cups (100g) bean sprouts

1 fresh small red thai chilli, sliced thinly

2 tablespoons finely chopped fresh coriander

2 tablespoons lime juice

1 tablespoon sweet chilli sauce

2 teaspoons sesame oil

2 teaspoons fish sauce

1 clove garlic, crushed

1 Boil, steam or microwave asparagus and corn, separately, until just tender; drain. Cool 10 minutes.

2 Combine asparagus and corn in large serving bowl with capsicum, mushrooms, cucumber, onion, sprouts, chilli and coriander.

3 Place remaining ingredients in screw-top jar; shake well. Drizzle salad with dressing; toss gently to combine.

SERVES 4

per serving 0.3g carbohydrate; 3.09g fat; 385kJ (92 cal); 5.2g protein

greek salad with taramasalata dressing

PREPARATION TIME 20 MINUTES

1 small red onion (100g), cut into wedges

2 medium egg tomatoes (300g), quartered

2 lebanese cucumbers (260g), sliced thickly

1 medium green capsicum (200g),

   sliced thickly

1 small cos lettuce, torn

¼ cup (40g) seeded kalamata olives

150g fetta cheese, chopped coarsely

1 tablespoon coarsely chopped fresh oregano

1 tablespoon coarsely chopped fresh

   flat-leaf parsley

1 tablespoon lemon juice

2 tablespoons olive oil

⅓ cup (90g) taramasalata

1 Combine onion, tomato, cucumber, capsicum, lettuce, olives and cheese in large bowl.

2 Sprinkle herbs over salad then drizzle with combined remaining ingredients; serve without tossing.

SERVES 4

per serving 11.4g carbohydrate; 22.9g fat; 1241kJ (297 cal); 11.8g protein
serving suggestion This salad is ideal with barbecued octopus or lamb.

roasted mediterranean vegetables with chilli-and-herb baked ricotta

PREPARATION TIME 20 MINUTES   COOKING TIME 1 HOUR

Ricotta that is sold packaged in paper or tubs is not suitable for this recipe. Buy the ricotta in a wedge, by weight, from a delicatessen where it is kept in a plastic colander.

2 baby eggplants (120g), halved lengthways

2 small zucchini (180g), halved lengthways

1 small red capsicum (150g), quartered

1 small red onion (100g), quartered

1 trimmed celery stalk (100g), quartered

1 large egg tomato (90g), quartered

4 cloves garlic, unpeeled

olive oil spray

1 teaspoon freshly ground black pepper

2 tablespoons extra virgin olive oil

2 tablespoons finely shredded fresh basil

1 tablespoon baby capers, drained

CHILLI-AND-HERB BAKED RICOTTA

400g wedge fresh ricotta cheese

2 teaspoons extra virgin olive oil

½ teaspoon freshly ground black pepper

½ teaspoon dried chilli flakes

1 tablespoon finely chopped fresh oregano

1 Preheat oven to hot. Place eggplant, zucchini, capsicum, onion, celery, tomato and garlic in large shallow baking dish; spray with olive oil spray. Roast, uncovered, in hot oven about 45 minutes or until vegetables are brown and tender.

2 Meanwhile, make chilli-and-herb baked ricotta.

3 Sprinkle vegetables with pepper; drizzle with olive oil. Top with basil and capers; serve with chilli-and-herb baked ricotta.

CHILLI-AND-HERB BAKED RICOTTA Place ricotta on oven tray lined with baking paper. Drizzle with oil; sprinkle with pepper and chilli. Bake, uncovered, in hot oven, about 25 minutes or until warmed through. Sprinkle with oregano.

SERVES 4
per serving 6.6g carbohydrate; 23.9g fat; 1208kJ (289 cal); 12.7g protein

sesame omelette and crisp mixed vegetable salad

PREPARATION TIME 25 MINUTES   COOKING TIME 10 MINUTES

You need about half a medium chinese cabbage for this recipe.

8 eggs

½ cup (125ml) milk

½ cup coarsely chopped fresh garlic chives

2 tablespoons toasted sesame seeds

8 cups (640g) finely shredded chinese cabbage

2 fresh long red chillies, seeded, sliced thinly

1 large red capsicum (350g), sliced thinly

1 large green capsicum (350g), sliced thinly

1 tablespoon coarsely chopped fresh mint

1 tablespoon finely chopped fresh lemon grass

SWEET CHILLI DRESSING

2 teaspoons toasted sesame seeds

¼ cup (60ml) rice vinegar

¼ cup (60ml) peanut oil

1 teaspoon sesame oil

¼ cup (60ml) sweet chilli sauce

1 Whisk eggs in large jug with milk, chives and seeds until well combined. Pour a quarter of the egg mixture into heated lightly oiled wok or large frying pan; cook over medium heat, tilting pan, until omelette is just set. Remove from wok; repeat with remaining egg mixture to make four omelettes. Roll cooled omelettes tightly; cut into 3mm "wheels".

2 Make sweet chilli dressing.

3 Place three-quarters of the omelette in large bowl with cabbage, chilli, capsicums, mint, lemon grass and dressing; toss gently to combine. Divide salad among serving plates; top with remaining omelette.

SWEET CHILLI DRESSING Place ingredients in screw-top jar; shake well.

SERVES 4
per serving 11.1g carbohydrate; 29.9g fat; 1634kJ (391 cal); 19.7g protein
tip Omelettes can be made up to 3 hours ahead and stored, covered, in the refrigerator; roll and slice just before assembling salad.

stir-fried gai larn with grilled tofu

PREPARATION TIME 15 MINUTES (PLUS STANDING TIME)   COOKING TIME 10 MINUTES

500g firm tofu

1kg gai larn, trimmed,
chopped coarsely

⅓ cup (80ml) oyster sauce

1 tablespoon peanut oil

5 green onions, chopped coarsely

2 cloves garlic, crushed

2cm piece fresh ginger (10g), grated

2 tablespoons soy sauce

1 tablespoon fish sauce

2 tablespoons sesame seeds

1 Press tofu between two cutting boards with a weight on top, raise one end to let excess water run out, stand 25 minutes.

2 Boil, steam or microwave gai larn until just tender; drain.

3 Cut tofu into 2cm slices, pat dry with absorbent paper; place under preheated grill about 3 minutes or until browned lightly. Spread half of the oyster sauce onto tofu pieces; place under preheated grill until browned.

4 Meanwhile, heat oil in wok or large frying pan; stir-fry onion, garlic and ginger until fragrant. Add gai larn and sauces; stir until heated through. Toss with sesame seeds; serve with tofu.

SERVES 4
per serving 11g carbohydrate; 16.8g fat; 1221kJ (292 cal); 24g protein

stuffed zucchini flowers and radicchio salad

PREPARATION TIME 20 MINUTES   COOKING TIME 10 MINUTES

Buy zucchini flowers with the tiny young vegetable attached if possible. You need two radicchio for this recipe; use only the inner leaves and hearts, discarding the tough outer leaves. If you can only find a soft goat cheese, crumble rather than grate it.

2 tablespoons finely chopped
fresh sage

2 teaspoons finely grated lemon rind

1 small red onion (100g),
chopped finely

100g firm goat cheese,
grated coarsely

100g ricotta

24 tiny zucchini with
flowers attached

250g yellow teardrop tomatoes

1 tablespoon olive oil

1 teaspoon balsamic vinegar

100g radicchio leaves, torn

1 Preheat oven to very hot.

2 Place sage, rind, onion, goat cheese and ricotta in small bowl; beat with wooden spoon until combined.

3 Remove and discard stamens from centre of flowers; fill flowers with cheese mixture, twist petal tops to enclose filling. Place filled flowers on lightly oiled oven tray. Place tomatoes, in single layer, in small shallow baking dish; drizzle with combined oil and vinegar. Roast flowers and tomatoes, both uncovered, in very hot oven about 10 minutes or until flowers are browned lightly and heated through, and tomatoes are softened.

4 Toss tomatoes and pan juices in medium bowl with radicchio; serve with zucchini flowers.

SERVES 4
per serving 5.6g carbohydrate;11.8g fat; 681kJ (163 cal); 8.6g protein
tip You can use a piping bag fitted with a large plain tube to pipe the filling into the zucchini flowers.

stir-fried eggplant and tofu

PREPARATION TIME 15 MINUTES (PLUS STANDING TIME) COOKING TIME 15 MINUTES

1 large eggplant (400g)

cooking salt

300g fresh firm silken tofu

1 medium brown onion (150g)

2 tablespoons peanut oil

1 clove garlic, crushed

2 fresh small red thai chillies, sliced thinly

1 tablespoon grated palm sugar

850g gai larn, chopped coarsely

2 tablespoons lime juice

⅓ cup (80ml) soy sauce

⅓ cup coarsely chopped fresh thai basil

1 Cut unpeeled eggplant in half lengthways; cut each half into thin slices. Place eggplant in colander, sprinkle with salt; stand 30 minutes.

2 Meanwhile, pat tofu all over with absorbent paper; cut into 2cm squares. Spread tofu, in single layer, on absorbent-paper-lined tray; cover tofu with more absorbent paper, stand at least 10 minutes.

3 Cut onion in half, then cut each half into thin wedges. Rinse eggplant under cold water; pat dry with absorbent paper.

4 Heat oil in wok; stir-fry onion, garlic and chilli until onion softens. Add sugar; stir-fry until dissolved. Add eggplant; stir-fry, 1 minute. Add gai larn; stir-fry until just wilted. Add tofu, juice and sauce; stir-fry, tossing gently until combined. Remove from heat; toss basil through stir-fry.

SERVES 4
per serving 10.3g carbohydrate; 14.7g fat; 995kJ (238 cal); 16g protein

japanese omelette salad (see page 307)

PREPARATION TIME 20 MINUTES COOKING TIME 10 MINUTES

1 medium daikon (600g)

2 medium carrots (240g)

6 large red radishes (210g), sliced thinly

1½ cups (120g) shredded red cabbage

1½ cups (120g) bean sprouts

2 tablespoons thinly sliced pickled ginger

6 green onions, sliced thinly

4 eggs, beaten lightly

1 tablespoon soy sauce

½ sheet toasted seaweed (yaki-nori),
    sliced thinly

WASABI DRESSING

1 tablespoon pickled ginger juice

2 tablespoons soy sauce

1 tablespoon mirin

1 teaspoon wasabi paste

1 Make wasabi dressing.

2 Using vegetable peeler, slice daikon and carrots into thin strips. Place in large bowl with radish, cabbage, sprouts, ginger and three-quarters of the onion.

3 Combine egg, soy and seaweed in small jug. Pour half of the egg mixture into heated lightly oiled large frying pan; cook, uncovered, until just set. Slide omelette onto plate; roll into cigar shape. Repeat with remaining egg mixture. Slice omelette rolls into thin rings.

4 Add dressing to salad; toss gently to combine. Divide salad among serving bowls; top with remaining onion and omelette rings.

WASABI DRESSING Place ingredients in screw-top jar; shake well.

SERVES 4
per serving 10.4g carbohydrate; 6.2g fat; 610kJ (146 cal);
11.7g protein

grilled tuna with red cabbage salad

PREPARATION TIME 15 MINUTES   COOKING TIME 10 MINUTES

1 tablespoon olive oil

1 medium red onion (170g), sliced thinly

2 cups (160g) finely shredded red cabbage

2 cups (160g) finely shredded chinese cabbage

¼ cup (60ml) cider vinegar

1 large apple (200g), sliced thinly

1 cup loosely packed fresh flat-leaf parsley leaves

4 x 200g tuna steaks

1   Heat oil in wok or large frying pan; stir-fry onion and cabbages about 2 minutes or until onion just softens. Add vinegar; bring to a boil. Boil, 1 minute. Remove from heat, add apple and parsley; toss gently to combine.

2   Meanwhile, cook tuna on heated oiled grill plate (or grill or barbecue), uncovered, about 8 minutes or until browned on both sides and cooked as desired. Serve tuna on cabbage salad.

SERVES 4
per serving 8.1g carbohydrate; 16.2g fat; 1635kJ (391 cal); 52.5g protein;

char-grilled tuna salad

PREPARATION TIME 10 MINUTES   COOKING TIME 5 MINUTES

600g tuna steak

¼ cup (60ml) mirin

1 teaspoon sugar

1 tablespoon soy sauce

1 clove garlic, crushed

1 fresh small red thai chilli, seeded,

   chopped finely

1 green onion, chopped finely

2 medium red capsicums (400g), sliced thinly

200g mesclun

1   Cook tuna on heated oiled grill plate (or grill or barbecue) until browned both sides and cooked as desired. Cover, stand 2 minutes; cut into thick slices.

2   Meanwhile, place mirin, sugar, soy, garlic, chilli and onion in screw-top jar; shake well.

3   Place tuna and dressing in large bowl with capsicum and mesclun; toss gently to combine.

SERVES 4
per serving 4.1g carbohydrate; 3.6g fat; 769kJ (184 cal); 32.9g protein
tip Brushing the whole piece of tuna with olive oil 3 hours ahead of cooking will help keep it moist and soft when it's grilled.

crab salad

PREPARATION TIME 15 MINUTES

500g fresh crab meat

250g chinese cabbage, chopped finely

1 lebanese cucumber (130g), seeded,
    chopped coarsely

1 medium red onion (170g), halved,
    sliced thinly

6 green onions, cut into 4cm lengths

1 cup loosely packed fresh thai mint leaves

DRESSING

2 cloves garlic, crushed

2 tablespoons lime juice

2 tablespoons fish sauce

1 tablespoon brown sugar

2 fresh small red thai chillies, chopped finely

1 Drain crab in strainer; remove any shell and if necessary shred the meat to desired texture.

2 Make dressing.

3 Combine crab in large bowl with remaining ingredients and dressing; toss gently to combine.

DRESSING Place all ingredients in screw-top jar; shake well.

SERVES 4
per serving 9.6g carbohydrate; 1.1g fat; 518kJ (124 cal); 18.8g protein

fish cakes with herb salad

PREPARATION TIME 15 MINUTES   COOKING TIME 10 MINUTES

500g redfish fillets, skinned and boned

2 tablespoons red curry paste

2 fresh kaffir lime leaves

2 green onions, chopped coarsely

1 tablespoon fish sauce

3 tablespoons lime juice

2 tablespoons finely chopped fresh coriander

3 snake beans (30g), chopped finely

2 fresh small red thai chillies, chopped finely

peanut oil, for deep-frying

1 cup loosely packed fresh basil leaves

1 cup loosely packed fresh mint leaves

1 cup (80g) bean sprouts

1 Cut fish into small pieces. Blend or process fish with curry paste, lime leaves, onion, sauce and 1 tablespoon juice until mixture forms a smooth paste. Combine fish mixture in medium bowl with coriander, beans and chilli.

2 Roll heaped tablespoons of the fish mixture into balls, then flatten into cake shapes.

3 Heat oil in wok or large saucepan; deep-fry fish cakes, in batches, until browned lightly and cooked through. Drain on absorbent paper.

4 Place basil, mint, sprouts and remaining juice in medium bowl; toss gently to combine. Serve salad on fish cakes.

SERVES 4
per serving 2.7g carbohydrate; 15.1g fat; 1078kJ (258 cal); 28g protein

salmon and asparagus salad with creamy horseradish dressing

PREPARATION TIME 30 MINUTES   COOKING TIME 20 MINUTES

450g turnips

4 x 220g salmon fillets, skin on

1 cup (250ml) milk

1.25 litres (5 cups) water

500g asparagus, trimmed

175g watercress, trimmed

1 small red onion (100g),
    sliced thinly

CREAMY HORSERADISH DRESSING

1 egg

2 tablespoons prepared
    horseradish

1 teaspoon honey

⅔ cup (160ml) olive oil

1   Boil, steam or microwave turnips until tender; drain. When cool enough to handle, slice thickly.

2   Meanwhile, remove any bones from fish. Place fish in large frying pan; cover with milk and the water. Weigh fish down with heavy plate or lid to keep submerged; bring to a boil. Reduce heat; simmer, about 5 minutes or until fish is cooked as desired. Discard cooking liquid; when fish is cool enough to handle, remove skin, cut each fillet in half lengthways.

3   Meanwhile, make creamy horseradish dressing.

4   Boil, steam or microwave asparagus until tender; drain. Rinse under cold water; drain.

5   Divide asparagus, watercress, onion, turnip and fish among serving plates; drizzle with dressing.

CREAMY HORSERADISH DRESSING Blend or process egg, horseradish and honey until combined. With motor operating, add oil in a thin, steady stream until dressing thickens slightly.

serves 4
per serving 11.5g carbohydrate; 48.9g fat; 2884kJ (690 cal); 52g protein

prawn, endive and pink grapefruit with lime aïoli

PREPARATION TIME 30 MINUTES

2 small pink grapefruits (700g)

1kg cooked large prawns

350g curly endive, torn

¼ cup coarsely chopped
  fresh chives

2 trimmed celery stalks (200g),
  sliced thinly

1 small red onion (100g),
  sliced thinly

LIME AIOLI

2 egg yolks

2 teaspoons dijon mustard

½ teaspoon finely grated lime rind

2 tablespoons lime juice

2 cloves garlic, quartered

¾ cup (180ml) olive oil

1 tablespoon hot water

1 Peel grapefruits; separate the segments. Shell and devein prawns, leaving tails intact.

2 Make lime aïoli.

3 Combine grapefruit and prawns in large bowl with remaining ingredients. Serve with lime aïoli.

LIME AÏOLI Blend or process egg yolks, mustard, rind, juice and garlic until combined. With motor operating, gradually add oil in a thin, steady stream until aïoli thickens. With motor operating, add enough of the water (if any) to achieve desired consistency.

SERVES 4
per serving 7.7g carbohydrate; 45.5g fat; 2408kJ (576 cal); 34.3g protein
tip Lime aïoli can be prepared a day ahead; keep, covered, in the refrigerator.

crisp fish salad with chilli lime dressing

PREPARATION TIME 20 MINUTES   COOKING TIME 30 MINUTES

250g firm white fish fillets

vegetable oil, for deep-frying

1 medium red onion (170g), sliced thinly

6 green onions, sliced thinly

**2 lebanese cucumbers (260g), seeded,
    sliced thinly**

1 cup firmly packed fresh thai mint leaves

1 cup firmly packed fresh coriander leaves

**2 tablespoons coarsely chopped toasted
    unsalted peanuts**

2 teaspoons finely grated lime rind

CHILLI LIME DRESSING

**4 small green thai chillies, seeded,
    chopped finely**

2 tablespoons fish sauce

⅓ cup (80ml) lime juice

1 tablespoon brown sugar

1   Preheat oven to moderate. Place fish on wire rack over oven tray; roast, uncovered, 20 minutes. When cool enough to handle, cut fish into pieces, then blend or process, pulsing, until mixture resembles coarse breadcrumbs.

2   Heat oil in wok or deep frying pan; deep-fry processed fish, in batches, until browned lightly and crisp. Drain on absorbent paper.

3   Make chilli lime dressing.

4   Place onions, cucumber, herbs and dressing in large bowl; toss gently to combine. Sprinkle salad with crisp fish, nuts and lime rind; serve immediately.

CHILLI LIME DRESSING Place ingredients in screw-top jar; shake well.

SERVES 4
per serving 9.1g carbohydrate; 5.7g fat; 640kJ (153 cal); 16g protein

smoked salmon and avocado salad

PREPARATION TIME 20 MINUTES

150g mesclun

500g smoked salmon, sliced thinly

2 medium avocados (500g), chopped coarsely

1 medium red onion (170g), sliced thinly

300g baked ricotta, crumbled

2 tablespoons finely chopped fresh dill

⅓ cup (80ml) lemon juice

1 tablespoon dijon mustard

1 tablespoon honey

2 cloves garlic, crushed

1 tablespoon white vinegar

1 tablespoon olive oil

1   Combine mesclun, salmon, avocado, onion and cheese in large bowl.

2   Whisk remaining ingredients in small bowl then pour over salad; toss gently to combine.

SERVES 4
per serving 10.2g carbohydrate; 38.9g fat; 2295kJ (549 cal); 39.9g protein

fish provençale with herbed fresh tomatoes

PREPARATION TIME 10 MINUTES   COOKING TIME 20 MINUTES

We used blue-eye in this recipe, but you can use any firm fish, such as perch or ling.

**2 medium yellow zucchini (240g),
quartered lengthways**

**3 medium green zucchini (360g),
quartered lengthways**

¼ cup (60ml) olive oil

4 x 150g white fish fillets

**2 medium egg tomatoes (150g), seeded,
chopped finely**

2 tablespoons lemon juice

1 tablespoon coarsely chopped fresh dill

**1 tablespoon coarsely chopped fresh
flat-leaf parsley**

**1 tablespoon coarsely chopped
fresh tarragon**

1 Boil, steam or microwave both zucchini until just tender; drain.

2 Meanwhile, heat 2 teaspoons of the oil in medium non-stick frying pan; cook fish, uncovered, until browned both sides and cooked as desired. Remove from pan; cover to keep warm.

3 Heat remaining oil in same cleaned pan; cook tomato and juice, stirring, until just hot. Remove from heat; stir in herbs. Serve vegetables with fish, tomato mixture and lemon wedges, if desired.

SERVES 4
per serving 3.3g carbohydrate; 17.4g fat; 1250kJ (299 cal); 32.2g protein

ocean trout with buttered almonds

PREPARATION TIME 10 MINUTES   COOKING TIME 10 MINUTES

¼ cup (35g) plain flour

½ teaspoon salt

½ teaspoon ground white pepper

8 x 100g ocean trout fillets

2 tablespoons olive oil

90g butter

½ cup (25g) flaked almonds

125g baby spinach leaves

2 tablespoons lemon juice

1 Combine flour, salt and pepper in medium bowl; toss fish in flour mixture, shake off excess.

2 Heat oil with a third of the butter in large frying pan; cook fish, in batches, until browned both sides and cooked as desired. Drain on absorbent paper; cover to keep warm.

3 Heat remaining butter in same cleaned pan; cook almonds, stirring constantly, until browned lightly. Add spinach; stir until spinach just wilts. Stir in juice; serve fish topped with almond mixture.

SERVES 4
per serving 7.3g carbohydrate; 38.8g fat; 2278kJ (545 cal); 42g protein

salade niçoise (see back cover)

PREPARATION TIME 20 MINUTES   COOKING TIME 10 MINUTES

200g green beans, trimmed,
  chopped coarsely
250g cherry tomatoes, halved
½ cup (80g) seeded black olives
2 lebanese cucumbers (260g),
  sliced thinly
1 medium red onion (170g),
  sliced thinly
150g mesclun
6 hard-boiled eggs, quartered
425g can tuna in springwater

LIGHT VINAIGRETTE

1 teaspoon olive oil
¼ cup (60ml) lemon juice
1 clove garlic, crushed
2 teaspoons dijon mustard

1 Boil, steam or microwave beans until just tender; drain. Rinse under cold water; drain.

2 Meanwhile, make light vinaigrette.

3 Place tomato, olives, cucumber, onion, mesclun and eggs in large bowl with vinaigrette; toss gently to combine. Divide salad among serving plates.

4 Carefully turn tuna out of can into colander; cut into wedge-shaped quarters. Place one-quarter piece tuna on each salad.

LIGHT VINAIGRETTE Place ingredients in screw-top jar; shake well.

SERVES 4
per serving 10.9g carbohydrate; 13.8g fat; 1496kJ (358 cal); 46.8g protein

tarragon and lime scallops

PREPARATION TIME 15 MINUTES   COOKING TIME 10 MINUTES

Uncooked scallops and lime wedges can be skewered up to 4 hours ahead. Cover; refrigerate until required. Soak 24 bamboo skewers in water for at least 1 hour before using to prevent them splintering and scorching.

24 scallops, without roe (500g)
2 tablespoons coarsely chopped
  fresh tarragon
¼ cup (60ml) lime juice
⅓ cup (80ml) olive oil
3 limes
2 medium witlof (350g),
  leaves separated
¼ cup firmly packed fresh flat-leaf
  parsley leaves

1 Rinse scallops under cold water; dry with absorbent paper. Combine scallops in medium bowl with tarragon, 1 tablespoon of the juice and 1 tablespoon of the oil; toss to coat scallops all over.

2 Cut each lime into eight wedges. Thread one scallop and one lime wedge on each skewer. Cook, in batches, on heated oiled grill plate (or grill or barbecue) until scallops are cooked through.

3 Meanwhile, place whitlof and parsley in medium bowl with remaining juice and remaining oil; toss gently to combine.

4 Serve skewers on salad.

SERVES 4
per serving 1.8g carbohydrate; 19.4g fat; 1049kJ (251 cal); 16.4g protein

jerusalem artichoke and smoked trout soup

PREPARATION TIME 30 MINUTES   COOKING TIME 1 HOUR 15 MINUTES

Crème fraîche is a commercially soured, mature thick cream; substitute sour cream, if preferred. Pick over the trout and discard even the most minuscule bone fragments.

¼ cup (60ml) olive oil

1kg small fresh jerusalem
    artichokes (approximately 32),
    trimmed, peeled

20g butter

3 shallots, chopped coarsely

1 clove garlic, quartered

2 litres (8 cups) chicken stock

2 tablespoons lemon juice

½ cup (120g) crème fraîche

1 medium smoked trout (375g),
    flaked

1 tablespoon finely grated lemon rind

1 Preheat oven to hot.

2 Combine oil and artichokes in large baking dish; toss artichokes to coat with oil. Roast, uncovered, in hot oven, turning occasionally, about 1 hour or until artichokes are tender.

3 Melt butter in large saucepan; cook shallot and garlic, stirring, until both just soften. Add artichokes, stock and juice; bring to a boil. Reduce heat; simmer, uncovered, 10 minutes; cool 10 minutes.

4 Blend or process soup mixture, in batches, until smooth. Return soup to same cleaned pan; stir over heat until hot. Stir in crème fraîche and trout then divide soup among serving bowls; sprinkle each with rind.

SERVES 6
per serving 7g carbohydrate; 23g fat; 1229kJ (294 cal); 15.1g protein
tip Jerusalem artichokes, available in autumn and winter, can be kept, sealed tightly in a plastic bag in the refrigerator, for about a fortnight.

prawn and green onion skewers

PREPARATION TIME 25 MINUTES (PLUS REFRIGERATION TIME)   COOKING TIME 10 MINUTES

Soak 12 bamboo skewers in water for at least 1 hour before using to prevent them from splintering and scorching.

36 medium uncooked king
    prawns (1.5kg)

2 tablespoons lime juice

1 tablespoon olive oil

2 cloves garlic, crushed

12 green onions

500g cherry tomatoes

2 limes, cut into wedges

1 Shell and devein prawns, leaving tails intact. Combine prawns in medium bowl with juice, oil and garlic. Cover; refrigerate 1 hour.

2 Cut onions into 4cm lengths. Thread prawns, onion and tomatoes onto skewers. Cook on heated oiled grill plate (or grill or barbecue) until prawns change in colour. Serve with lime wedges.

SERVES 4
per serving 4.3g carbohydrate; 6g fat; 1116kJ (267 cal); 40g protein
tip If using metal skewers, oil them first to stop the prawns from sticking.

prawn, scallop and asparagus salad with ginger dressing

PREPARATION TIME 25 MINUTES   COOKING TIME 20 MINUTES

400g medium uncooked
**   king prawns**
400g scallops, roe removed
200g asparagus, trimmed, halved
⅓ cup coarsely chopped
**   fresh chives**
100g baby spinach leaves
1 large red capsicum (350g),
**   chopped coarsely**

GINGER DRESSING

5cm piece fresh ginger (25g),
**   grated**
1 tablespoon olive oil
2 tablespoons lemon juice
1 teaspoon sugar

1 Peel and devein prawns.

2 Cook prawns, scallops and asparagus, in batches, on heated lightly oiled grill plate (or grill or barbecue) until browned lightly and cooked as desired.

3 Meanwhile, make ginger dressing.

4 Place prawns, scallops and asparagus in large bowl with chives, spinach, capsicum and dressing; toss gently to combine.

GINGER DRESSING Press grated ginger between two spoons over large bowl; discard solids. Place oil, juice and sugar in bowl with ginger liquid; whisk to combine.

SERVES 4
per serving 6.0g carbohydrate; 5.9g fat; 749kJ (179 cal); 25g protein

prawn, scallop and asparagus salad with ginger dressing

stir-fried cauliflower, choy sum and snake beans

stir-fried cauliflower, choy sum and snake beans

PREPARATION TIME 20 MINUTES   COOKING TIME 10 MINUTES

1 tablespoon peanut oil

2 cloves garlic, crushed

1 teaspoon ground turmeric

1 teaspoon finely chopped
   coriander root and stem mixture

4 green onions, sliced thinly

500g cauliflower florets

¼ cup (60ml) water

200g snake beans,
   cut into 5cm pieces

200g choy sum, chopped coarsely

1 tablespoon lime juice

1 tablespoon soy sauce

1 tablespoon coarsely chopped
   fresh coriander

1   Heat oil in wok or large saucepan; cook garlic, turmeric, coriander mixture and onion; stir-fry until onion just softens. Remove from wok.

2   Stir-fry cauliflower with the water in same wok until cauliflower is almost tender. Add beans and choy sum; stir-fry until vegetables are just tender.

3   Add juice, sauce, chopped coriander and onion mixture; stir-fry until heated through.

SERVES 4
per serving 4.7g carbohydrate; 5.1g fat; 368kJ (88 cal); 5.5g protein

manhattan clam chowder

PREPARATION TIME 25 MINUTES   COOKING TIME 25 MINUTES

The word "chowder" comes from chaudière, the French name for the huge cauldron used on seaport docks by fishermen to stew their fresh catch.

1.5kg clams

1 cup (250ml) dry white wine

40g butter

1 medium brown onion (150g),
    chopped finely

2 bacon rashers (140g),
    chopped finely

2 trimmed celery stalks (200g),
    chopped finely

¼ cup (35g) plain flour

3 cups (750ml) fish stock

400g can tomatoes

3 cups (750ml) water

1 tablespoon fresh thyme leaves

2 bay leaves

1kg fennel, sliced thinly

¼ cup coarsely chopped fresh
    flat-leaf parsley

1   Rinse clams under cold water; combine with wine in medium saucepan having a tight-fitting lid. Bring to a boil; steam, covered tightly, about 5 minutes or until clams have opened (discard any that do not). Strain clams over large bowl; reserve ¼ cup of the cooking liquid.

2   Melt butter in large saucepan; cook onion, stirring, until soft. Add bacon and celery; cook, stirring, 5 minutes. Add flour; cook, stirring, until mixture thickens and bubbles. Gradually stir in stock, then add undrained crushed tomatoes and the water; cook, stirring, until mixture boils and thickens. Stir in thyme, bay leaves and fennel; cook, covered, stirring occasionally, about 15 minutes or until fennel is tender.

3   Just before serving, stir clams, reserved cooking liquid and parsley into chowder.

SERVES 6
per serving 11.1g carbohydrate; 7.8g fat; 849kJ (203 cal); 14.9g protein
tips Dry red wine can be substituted for the white wine but be certain that whatever wine you use you would also consider drinking..

tom yum goong (see back cover)

PREPARATION TIME 20 MINUTES   COOKING TIME 20 MINUTES

1kg large uncooked king prawns

1 tablespoon peanut oil

7cm stick (15g) fresh lemon grass, coarsely chopped

2 cloves garlic, quartered

3cm piece fresh ginger (15g), coarsely chopped

3 litres (12 cups) water

2 fresh kaffir lime leaves, shredded finely

2 tablespoons fish sauce

¼ cup (60ml) lime juice

2 fresh long red chillies, sliced thinly

3 green onions, sliced thinly

⅓ cup loosely packed fresh coriander leaves

¼ cup coarsely chopped fresh mint

1 Shell and devein prawns, reserve meat and shells separately. Discard heads.

2 Heat oil in large saucepan; cook shells and tails, stirring, about 3 minutes or until deep orange in colour. Add lemon grass, garlic and ginger, stirring until fragrant.

3 Add the water and lime leaves, cover; bring to a boil. Reduce heat; simmer, uncovered, 10 minutes. Strain stock through muslin-lined strainer into large heatproof bowl; discard solids.

4 Return stock to same cleaned pan; bring to a boil. Reduce heat, add prawn meat; cook, until prawn meat changes in colour. Remove from heat; stir in sauce and juice. Serve soup hot, topped with chilli, onions, coriander and mint.

SERVES 4
per serving 7.9g carbohydrate; 8.3g fat; 1057kJ (252 cal); 34.3g protein

salmon teriyaki

PREPARATION TIME 10 MINUTES (PLUS STANDING TIME)   COOKING TIME 10 MINUTES

Daikon is a large white radish with a sweet, fresh taste. In Japan it is often served, grated raw, as an accompaniment.

4 salmon fillets (700g), skinned

½ cup (120g) finely shredded daikon

TERIYAKI MARINADE

⅔ cup (160ml) japanese soy sauce

⅔ cup (160ml) mirin

2 tablespoons sake

1 tablespoon sugar

1 Make teriyaki marinade.

2 Place salmon in teriyaki marinade for 10 minutes, turning occasionally. Drain salmon over medium bowl; reserve marinade.

3 Soak daikon in small bowl of iced water for 15 minutes; drain well.

4 Cook salmon on heated oiled grill plate (or grill or barbecue), brushing occasionally with a little of the reserved marinade, until cooked as desired. Bring reserved marinade to a boil in small saucepan. Reduce heat; simmer, uncovered, about 5 minutes or until sauce thickens slightly.

5 Serve salmon with daikon, drizzle with sauce.

TERIYAKI MARINADE   Combine ingredients in medium bowl; stir until sugar dissolves.

SERVES 4
per serving 11.3g carbohydrate; 12.6g fat; 1404kJ (336 cal); 36.6g protein
tip Bought teriyaki sauce may be used, but it's stronger than homemade. Dilute it with mirin, sake or water.

teriyaki steak

PREPARATION TIME 10 MINUTES (PLUS MARINATING TIME)   COOKING TIME 10 MINUTES

750g piece beef rump steak, sliced thinly

¼ cup (60ml) rice vinegar

2 tablespoons kecap manis

2 teaspoons brown sugar

¼ cup (60ml) lime juice

1 clove garlic, crushed

2 fresh small red thai chillies, seeded, chopped finely

1 teaspoon sesame oil

1 tablespoon peanut oil

1 medium carrot (120g), cut into matchsticks

200g cabbage, shredded finely

¼ cup (50g) japanese pickled cucumber

1 Combine beef, vinegar, kecap manis, sugar, juice, garlic, chilli and sesame oil in large bowl, cover; refrigerate 3 hours or overnight. Drain beef; reserve marinade.

2 Heat peanut oil in wok or large frying pan; stir-fry beef, in batches, until browned all over. Cover to keep warm.

3 Pour reserved marinade into wok; bring to a boil. Boil, uncovered, until sauce reduces by a third. Divide combined carrot and cabbage among serving plates; top with beef, drizzle with sauce. Serve with pickles.

SERVES 4
per serving 11.5g carbohydrate; 18.4g fat; 1622kJ (388 cal); 43g protein
tips Japanese pickled cucumber has a sour taste and is available, packaged in brine, from most Asian food stores.

fajitas and guacamole

PREPARATION TIME 15 MINUTES (PLUS REFRIGERATION TIME)   COOKING TIME 20 MINUTES

600g piece beef scotch fillet

2 cloves garlic, crushed

¼ cup (60ml) lemon juice

1½ teaspoons ground cumin

½ teaspoon cayenne pepper

2 tablespoons olive oil

1 small yellow capsicum (150g)

1 small red capsicum (150g)

12 small flour tortillas

375g jar chunky salsa

GUACAMOLE

2 medium avocados (500g)

2 medium tomatoes (380g), seeded,
  chopped finely

1 small red onion (100g), chopped finely

2 tablespoons lime juice

2 tablespoons coarsely chopped
  fresh coriander

1   Cut beef into thin 2cm-wide slices; place in medium bowl with garlic, juice, spices and oil, toss to coat beef in marinade. Cover; refrigerate for 3 hours.

2   Quarter capsicums; remove seeds and membranes. Roast capsicum under grill or in very hot oven, skin-side up, until skin blisters and blackens. Cover with plastic or paper for 5 minutes. Peel away skin; cut capsicums into thin strips.

3   Cook beef, in batches, on heated oiled grill plate (or grill or barbecue) until browned all over and cooked as desired; cover to keep warm. Reheat capsicum strips on same heated grill.

4   Meanwhile, make guacamole.

5   Serve beef and capsicum immediately, accompanied by guacamole, tortillas and salsa.

GUACAMOLE   Mash avocados roughly in medium bowl; add remaining ingredients, mix to combine.

SERVES 4
per serving   11.9g carbohydrate; 35.9 fat; 2182kJ (522 cal); 37.7g protein

carpaccio with fennel salad

PREPARATION TIME 10 MINUTES (PLUS FREEZING TIME)

400g piece beef eye fillet

2 medium fennel bulbs (600g)

2 trimmed celery stalks (200g)

2 tablespoons finely chopped fresh
  flat-leaf parsley

2 tablespoons lemon juice

1 clove garlic, crushed

¼ teaspoon sugar

½ teaspoon dijon mustard

⅓ cup (80ml) olive oil

1   Remove any excess fat from beef, wrap tightly in plastic wrap; freeze about 1 hour or until partially frozen. Using sharp knife, slice beef as thinly as possible.

2   Meanwhile, slice fennel and celery finely. Toss in medium bowl with remaining ingredients.

3   Arrange carpaccio slices in single layer on serving plates; top with fennel salad.

SERVES 4
per serving   4.5g carbohydrate; 22.1g fat; 1283kJ (307 cal); 22.9g protein

thai char-grilled beef salad

PREPARATION TIME 20 MINUTES (PLUS REFRIGERATION AND STANDING TIME)
COOKING TIME 5 MINUTES

This is a loose interpretation of one of our favourite Thai dishes, yum nuah, and is a good introduction to the flavours of South-East Asian cuisine.

600g piece beef rump steak

2 teaspoons sesame oil

⅓ cup (80ml) kecap manis

1 cup loosely packed fresh
    mint leaves

1 cup loosely packed fresh
    coriander leaves

½ cup loosely packed fresh thai
    basil leaves

6 green onions, sliced thinly

5 shallots (150g), sliced thinly

250g cherry tomatoes, halved

1 telegraph cucumber (400g),
    seeded, sliced thinly

10 fresh kaffir lime leaves,
    shredded finely

100g mesclun

SWEET AND SOUR DRESSING

½ cup (125ml) lime juice

¼ cup (60ml) fish sauce

1 teaspoon sugar

2 fresh small red thai chillies,
    sliced thinly

1   Place beef in shallow dish; brush all over with combined oil and kecap manis. Cover; refrigerate 30 minutes.

2   Meanwhile, place herbs, onion, shallot, tomato and cucumber in large bowl; toss gently to combine.

3   Make sweet and sour dressing.

4   Cook beef on heated oiled grill plate (or grill or barbecue) until charred lightly and cooked as desired. Stand, covered, 10 minutes; slice thinly.

5   Place beef, lime leaves and mesclun in bowl with herb mixture and dressing; toss gently to combine.

SWEET AND SOUR DRESSING Place ingredients in screw-top jar; shake well.

SERVES 4
per serving 11.3g carbohydrate; 13.1g fat; 1354kJ (324 cal); 39g protein
tip Thai basil, also known as horapa, has a sweet licorice flavour; it is one of the basic flavours that typify Thai cuisine.

souvlaki with greek salad

PREPARATION TIME 30 MINUTES (PLUS REFRIGERATION TIME)   COOKING TIME 15 MINUTES

Soak 8 bamboo skewers in water for at least 1 hour before using to prevent them splintering and scorching.

750g beef rump steak, cut into
   2cm cubes
1 large brown onion (200g),
   cut into wedges
¼ cup (60ml) olive oil
¼ cup (60ml) lemon juice
1 tablespoon dried rigani

GREEK SALAD

3 medium egg tomatoes (225g),
   chopped coarsely
2 lebanese cucumbers (260g),
   chopped coarsely
1 small red onion (100g),
   sliced thinly
1 large green capsicum (350g),
   chopped coarsely
½ cup (80g) seeded
   kalamata olives
150g fetta cheese,
   chopped coarsely
1 tablespoon olive oil
1 tablespoon lemon juice
2 teaspoons fresh oregano leaves

1 Thread beef and onion alternately on skewers; place souvlaki, in single layer, in large shallow dish. Combine oil, juice and rigani in jug; pour over souvlaki. Cover; refrigerate 3 hours or overnight.

2 Make greek salad.

3 Cook souvlaki, in batches, on heated oiled grill plate (or grill or barbecue) until browned all over and cooked as desired. Serve souvlaki with greek salad.

GREEK SALAD   Combine tomato, cucumber, onion, capsicum, olives and cheese in large bowl. Place remaining ingredients in screw-top jar; shake well. Pour dressing over salad; toss gently to combine.

SERVES 4
per serving 11.7g carbohydrate; 40.g fat; 2562kJ (613 cal); 51.8g protein

laila's lamb kofta with spiced yogurt

PREPARATION TIME 30 MINUTES (PLUS REFRIGERATION TIME)   COOKING TIME 20 MINUTES

2 tablespoons burghul

250g lamb mince

1 egg

1 small brown onion (80g), chopped finely

2 tablespoons pine nuts, chopped finely

1 tablespoon finely chopped fresh mint

1 tablespoon finely chopped fresh
    flat-leaf parsley

vegetable oil, for shallow-frying

300g iceberg lettuce, shredded finely

1 small red onion (100g), sliced thinly

⅓ cup loosely packed fresh flat-leaf
    parsley leaves

SPICED YOGURT

2 fresh small red thai chillies, seeded,
    chopped finely

1 tablespoon finely chopped fresh mint

1 tablespoon finely chopped fresh
    flat-leaf parsley

1 tablespoon finely chopped fresh coriander

1 clove garlic, crushed

½ teaspoon ground cumin

300g thick yogurt

1   Cover burghul with cold water in small bowl; stand 10 minutes. Drain; pat dry with absorbent paper to remove as much water as possible.

2   Using one hand, combine burghul in large bowl with lamb, egg, onion, nuts and herbs. Roll rounded teaspoons of the lamb mixture into kofta balls. Place on tray, cover; refrigerate 30 minutes.

3   Heat oil in large frying pan; shallow-fry kofta, in batches, until browned all over and cooked through. Drain on absorbent paper.

4   Meanwhile, place remaining ingredients in medium bowl; toss gently to combine.

5   Serve kofta with spiced yogurt and salad.

SPICED YOGURT   Combine ingredients in medium bowl.

SERVES 4
per serving   10.7g carbohydrate; 25.7g fat; 1496kJ (358 cal); 20.6g protein

pork and snow pea stir-fry with sesame seeds

PREPARATION TIME 10 MINUTES   COOKING TIME 10 MINUTES

1 tablespoon sesame oil

600g snow peas, trimmed

2 green onions, sliced thinly

1 tablespoon toasted sesame seeds

400g chinese barbecued pork, sliced thinly

1   Heat oil in wok or large frying pan; stir-fry snow peas and onion about 5 minutes or until snow peas are just tender.

2   Add seeds and pork to wok; stir-fry to combine.

SERVES 4
per serving   10g carbohydrate; 21.6g fat; 1409kJ (337 cal); 26.2g protein

pork larb

PREPARATION TIME 20 MINUTES   COOKING TIME 20 MINUTES

Larb is a classic Thai salad that can be made with beef, chicken or pork mince, or vegetables.

1 tablespoon peanut oil

2 tablespoons finely chopped fresh
   lemon grass

2 fresh small red thai chillies, chopped finely

2 cloves garlic, crushed

8cm piece fresh ginger (40g), grated

1.4kg lean pork mince

2 tablespoons fish sauce

⅔ cup (160ml) lime juice

5 fresh kaffir lime leaves, shredded finely

⅔ cup loosely packed fresh mint leaves

½ cup loosely packed fresh coriander leaves

4 green onions, sliced thinly

4 shallots (100g), sliced thinly

8 large iceberg lettuce leaves

1   Heat oil in large non-stick frying pan; cook lemon grass, chilli, garlic and ginger, stirring, about 2 minutes or until fragrant. Add pork; cook, stirring, about 10 minutes or until pork is browned. Add sauce and half of the juice; cook, stirring, 5 minutes. Transfer mixture to large bowl; stir in lime leaves, herbs, onion, shallot and remaining juice.

2   Place two lettuce leaves together to form a "bowl" on each serving plate; divide larb among leaves.

SERVES 4
per serving 3.5g carbohydrate; 31.3g fat; 2558kJ (612 cal); 77.9g protein

grilled chicken with herbed butter, almonds and gruyère

PREPARATION TIME 15 MINUTES   COOKING TIME 20 MINUTES

80g butter, softened

1 tablespoon finely chopped fresh
   flat-leaf parsley

2 teaspoons lemon juice

4 single chicken breast fillets (680g)

3 medium carrots (360g), cut into thin
   8cm matchsticks

250g baby green beans

¼ cup (35g) toasted slivered almonds

¼ cup (30g) finely grated gruyère cheese

1   Combine butter, parsley and juice in small bowl, cover; refrigerate until required.

2   Cook chicken on heated oiled grill plate (or grill or barbecue) until browned both sides and cooked through. Cover loosely to keep warm.

3   Meanwhile, boil, steam or microwave carrot and beans, separately, until tender; drain.

4   Serve chicken on vegetables; divide parsley butter among chicken pieces, sprinkle with nuts and cheese.

SERVES 4
per serving 6.1g carbohydrate; 27.5g fat; 1868kJ (447 cal); 44.2g protein

asian chicken broth

PREPARATION TIME 30 MINUTES   COOKING TIME 20 MINUTES

1 litre (4 cups) chicken stock

1 litre (4 cups) water

1 stalk lemon grass, finely chopped

4cm piece fresh ginger (20g),
sliced thinly

2 fresh small red thai chillies,
sliced thinly

2 tablespoons soy sauce

1 tablespoon lime juice

1 tablespoon fish sauce

500g choy sum, trimmed,
chopped coarsely

3 green onions, sliced thinly

⅓ cup loosely packed fresh
coriander leaves

CHICKEN DUMPLINGS

400g chicken breast mince

1 tablespoon finely chopped
fresh coriander

2 cloves garlic, crushed

1   Combine stock, the water, lemon grass, ginger, chilli and soy sauce in large saucepan: bring to a boil. Reduce heat; simmer, uncovered, about 5 minutes.

2   Meanwhile, make chicken dumplings.

3   Add chicken dumplings to simmering stock; simmer, covered, about 5 minutes or until dumplings are cooked through.

4   Add juice, fish sauce, choy sum and onion to stock; cook, uncovered, about 2 minutes or until choy sum just wilts. Stir in coriander just before serving.

CHICKEN DUMPLINGS   Combine ingredients in small bowl. Roll level tablespoons of the mixture into balls.

SERVES 4
per serving 4.3g carbohydrate; 9.4g fat; 844kJ (202 cal); 24.6g protein

mixed satay sticks

PREPARATION TIME 20 MINUTES (PLUS REFRIGERATION TIME) COOKING TIME 15 MINUTES

250g chicken breast fillets

250g beef eye fillet

250g pork fillet

2 cloves garlic, crushed

2 teaspoons brown sugar

¼ teaspoon sambal oelek

1 teaspoon ground turmeric

¼ teaspoon curry powder

½ teaspoon ground cumin

½ teaspoon ground coriander

2 tablespoons peanut oil

100g mesclun

SATAY SAUCE

½ cup (80g) toasted
   unsalted peanuts

2 tablespoons red curry paste

¾ cup (180ml) coconut milk

¼ cup (60ml) chicken stock

1 tablespoon kaffir lime juice

1 tablespoon brown sugar

1 Cut chicken, beef and pork into long 1.5cm-thick strips; thread strips onto skewers. Place skewers, in single layer, on tray or in shallow baking dish; brush with combined garlic, sugar, sambal, spices and oil. Cover; refrigerate 3 hours or overnight.

2 Make satay sauce.

3 Cook skewers on heated oiled grill plate (or grill or barbecue) until browned all over and cooked as desired. Serve with satay sauce.

SATAY SAUCE Blend or process nuts until chopped finely; add paste, process until just combined. Bring coconut milk to a boil in small saucepan; add peanut mixture, whisking until smooth. Reduce heat, add stock; cook, stirring, about 3 minutes or until sauce thickens slightly. Add juice and sugar, stirring, until sugar dissolves.

SERVES 4
per serving 9.9g carbohydrate; 36.5g fat; 2345kJ (561 cal); 49.2g protein

smoked chicken and artichoke salad with caper dressing

PREPARATION TIME 30 MINUTES   COOKING TIME 20 MINUTES

2 medium yellow capsicums (400g)

4 baby eggplants (240g), sliced thinly

2 large zucchini (300g), sliced thinly

2 tablespoons olive oil

340g jar marinated quartered
   artichokes, drained

550g smoked chicken breasts, sliced thinly

400g watercress, trimmed

CAPER DRESSING

2 hard-boiled eggs, quartered

1 tablespoon drained capers

2 tablespoons white wine vinegar

2 tablespoons coarsely chopped
   fresh oregano

1 clove garlic, quartered

⅓ cup (80ml) olive oil

1   Quarter capsicums; discard seeds and membranes. Roast under grill or in very hot oven, skin-side up, until skin blisters and blackens. Cover capsicum pieces with plastic or paper for 5 minutes; peel away skin, then slice capsicum thinly.

2   Meanwhile, make caper dressing.

3   Brush eggplant and zucchini with oil; cook, in batches, on heated oiled grill plate (or grill or barbecue) until browned lightly and just tender. Cool 10 minutes.

4   Place capsicum, eggplant and zucchini in large bowl with artichoke, chicken and dressing; toss gently to combine. Serve salad on watercress.

CAPER DRESSING   Blend or process egg, capers, vinegar, oregano and garlic until chopped finely. With motor operating, add oil in thin, steady stream until dressing thickens.

SERVES 4
per serving   5.6g carbohydrate; 40.1g fat; 2312kJ (553 cal); 42.7g protein

chicken and vegetable soup (see page 55)

PREPARATION TIME 25 MINUTES   COOKING TIME 15 MINUTES

2 cups (500ml) water

1.5 litres (6 cups) chicken stock

1 medium carrot (120g), diced into 1cm pieces

2 trimmed celery stalks (200g), sliced thinly

½ small cauliflower (500g), cut into florets

350g chicken breast fillets, sliced thinly

2 large zucchini (300g), cut into 1cm pieces

150g snow peas, trimmed, sliced thinly

3 green onions, sliced thinly

1   Combine the water and stock in large saucepan; bring to a boil. Add carrot, celery and cauliflower; return to a boil. Reduce heat; simmer, covered, about 10 minutes or until cooked through.

2   Add chicken and zucchini; cook, covered, about 5 minutes or until chicken is cooked through.

3   Stir in snow peas and onion.

SERVES 4
per serving   10.2g carbohydrate; 4g fat; 794kJ (190 cal); 28.2g protein

mediterranean chicken salad

PREPARATION TIME 30 MINUTES   COOKING TIME 25 MINUTES

1½ cups (375ml) chicken stock

½ cup (125ml) dry white wine

4 single chicken breast fillets (680g)

2 medium yellow capsicums (400g)

150g baby rocket leaves

250g teardrop tomatoes, halved

⅓ cup (40g) seeded black olives

ANCHOVY DRESSING

½ cup firmly packed fresh basil leaves

½ cup (125ml) extra virgin olive oil

2 tablespoons finely grated parmesan cheese

2 drained anchovy fillets

1 tablespoon lemon juice

1   Bring stock and wine to a boil in large frying pan. Add chicken, reduce heat; simmer, covered, about 8 minutes or until cooked through, turning once halfway through cooking time. Stand chicken in stock mixture for 10 minutes; slice chicken thinly. Discard stock mixture.

2   Meanwhile, quarter capsicums; discard seeds and membranes. Roast under grill or in very hot oven, skin-side up, until skin blisters and blackens. Cover capsicum pieces with plastic or paper for 5 minutes; peel away skin, then slice capsicum thinly.

3   Meanwhile, make anchovy dressing.

4   Place chicken and capsicum in large bowl with rocket, tomato, olives and dressing; toss gently to combine.

ANCHOVY DRESSING Blend or process ingredients until smooth.

SERVES 4
per serving 8.7g carbohydrate; 34.6g fat; 2261kJ (541 cal); 44.1g protein
tip Chicken can be poached a day ahead.

lemony chicken with baby spinach salad

PREPARATION TIME 15 MINUTES   COOKING TIME 15 MINUTES

12 chicken tenderloins (900g)

2 tablespoons lemon juice

1 tablespoon fresh thyme leaves

½ cup (125ml) olive oil

100g baby spinach leaves

1 small red onion (100g), chopped finely

250g cherry tomatoes, halved

80g alfalfa sprouts

⅓ cup (80ml) red wine vinegar

½ teaspoon dijon mustard

1   Place chicken in large bowl with juice, thyme and 2 tablespoons of the oil; toss to coat chicken in lemon mixture. Cook chicken, in batches, on heated oiled grill plate (or grill or barbecue) until browned lightly and cooked through.

2   Meanwhile, combine spinach, onion, tomato and sprouts in large bowl. Place vinegar, mustard and remaining oil in screw-top jar; shake well. Drizzle dressing over salad; toss gently to combine. Serve salad topped with chicken.

SERVES 4
per serving 7.5g carbohydrate; 33.9g fat; 2312kJ (553 cal); 54g protein

mexican tortilla soup

PREPARATION TIME 25 MINUTES (PLUS SOAKING TIME)   COOKING TIME 45 MINUTES

3 guajillo chillies

¾ cup (180ml) boiling water

2 teaspoons vegetable oil

1 large brown onion (200g),
chopped coarsely

3 cloves garlic, crushed

4 medium tomatoes (760g),
chopped coarsely

1.5 litres (6 cups) chicken stock

2 tablespoons lime juice

2 cups (500ml) water, extra

350g chicken breast fillets,
chopped coarsely

4 corn tortillas

vegetable oil, for shallow-frying, extra

1 small red onion (100g),
chopped finely

1 small avocado (200g),
chopped finely

1 medium tomato (190g), seeded,
chopped finely

1 Remove stems from chillies. Place chillies in small heatproof bowl; cover with the water, stand 10 minutes.

2 Meanwhile, heat oil in large saucepan; cook brown onion and garlic, stirring, until onion is soft. Add coarsely chopped tomato and undrained chillies; cook, stirring, about 10 minutes or until tomato is pulpy. Blend or process chilli mixture until pureed.

3 Return chilli mixture to same cleaned pan, stir in stock, juice and the extra water; bring to a boil. Add chicken, reduce heat; simmer, uncovered, about 25 minutes or until chicken is cooked through.

4 Meanwhile, slice tortillas into 1cm strips. Heat extra oil in large frying pan; shallow-fry tortilla strips, in batches, until browned lightly. Drain on absorbent paper.

5 Just before serving, divide soup among serving bowls; sprinkle with tortilla strips and combined red onion, avocado and finely chopped tomato.

SERVES 6
per serving 8.8g carbohydrate; 10.3g fat; 857kJ (205 cal);
18.9g protein

chicken with salsa verde

PREPARATION TIME 10 MINUTES   COOKING TIME 20 MINUTES

1 tablespoon olive oil

4 single chicken breast fillets
   (680g), halved lengthways

2 medium zucchini (240g),
   quartered lengthways

SALSA VERDE

½ cup coarsely chopped fresh
   flat-leaf parsley

¼ cup coarsely chopped fresh basil

1 clove garlic, crushed

2 teaspoons drained baby
   capers, rinsed

1 teaspoon dijon mustard

¼ cup (60ml) olive oil

2 teaspoons red wine vinegar

1 Heat oil in large frying pan; cook chicken, in batches, until browned both sides and cooked through. Cover to keep warm.

2 Meanwhile, boil, steam or microwave zucchini until tender; drain.

3 Make salsa verde.

4 Serve chicken with zucchini topped with salsa verde.

SALSA VERDE Combine herbs, garlic and capers in small bowl; whisk in mustard, oil and vinegar until salsa thickens.

SERVES 4
per serving 2.5g carbohydrate; 23.1g fat; 1597kJ (382 cal); 41.2g protein

leek and smoked chicken salad with orange mustard dressing

PREPARATION TIME 35 MINUTES

1 small leek (200g)

1 large carrot (180g)

1 medium red capsicum (200g),
   sliced thinly

1 medium yellow capsicum (200g),
   sliced thinly

500g smoked chicken breast,
   sliced thinly

200g snow peas, trimmed,
   sliced thinly

1 green mignonette lettuce,
   trimmed, torn

ORANGE MUSTARD DRESSING

2 tablespoons orange juice

2 tablespoons apple cider vinegar

2 teaspoons finely grated
   orange rind

1 tablespoon wholegrain mustard

1 tablespoon sour cream

¼ cup (60ml) olive oil

1 Make orange mustard dressing.

2 Cut leek into 8cm lengths. Cut each in half lengthways; slice into matchstick-sized pieces. Cut carrot into 8cm pieces. Cut each lengthways into thin slices; cut slices into matchstick-sized pieces.

3 Place leek and carrot in large bowl with remaining ingredients and dressing; toss gently to combine.

ORANGE MUSTARD DRESSING Place ingredients in screw-top jar; shake well.

SERVES 4
per serving 10.2g carbohydrate; 4g fat; 794kJ (190 cal); 28.2g protein

chicken and vegetable soup (see page 50)

mixed mushrooms with garlic and chives (see page 59)

vegetable and tofu skewers

PREPARATION TIME 20 MINUTES   COOKING TIME 15 MINUTES

200g swiss brown mushrooms

1 medium green capsicum (200g),
    chopped coarsely

2 medium red capsicums (400g),
    chopped coarsely

3 baby eggplants (180g),
    chopped coarsely

350g piece firm tofu, diced into
    3cm pieces

8 yellow patty pan squash (200g),
    halved

100g baby rocket leaves

BLUE CHEESE DRESSING

50g piece blue cheese

2 tablespoons buttermilk

200g low-fat yogurt

1 small white onion (80g), grated

1 clove garlic, crushed

1 tablespoon chives, chopped finely

1 tablespoon lemon juice

1   Thread mushroom, capsicums, eggplant, tofu and squash alternately onto skewers.

2   Cook skewers on heated lightly oiled grill plate (or grill or barbecue) until tofu is browned all over and vegetables are just tender.

3   Meanwhile, make blue cheese dressing.

4   Serve skewers on rocket; drizzle with dressing.

BLUE CHEESE DRESSING   Crumble blue cheese into a small bowl, add remaining ingredients; stir to combine.

SERVES 4
per serving   11.7g carbohydrate; 12.7g fat; 1047kJ (250 cal); 21.8g protein
tip   You will need to soak twelve 25cm bamboo skewers for at least 1 hour before using to prevent them from splintering and scorching.

curried eggs with wilted spinach

PREPARATION TIME 10 MINUTES   COOKING TIME 20 MINUTES

¼ cup (60ml) peanut oil

8 hard-boiled eggs

1 teaspoon black mustard seeds

1 clove garlic, crushed

1cm piece fresh ginger (5g), grated

1 small brown onion (80g), sliced thinly

1 teaspoon ground cumin

2 tablespoons mild curry powder

½ teaspoon ground cardamom

425g can tomatoes

1 teaspoon sugar

½ cup (125ml) water

1 tablespoon peanut oil, extra

1 clove garlic, crushed, extra

200g baby spinach

1   Heat oil in medium saucepan; cook eggs, stirring occasionally, until eggs are well browned all over. Drain on absorbent paper.

2   Reserve 1 tablespoon of the oil from saucepan; discard remaining oil. Reheat reserved oil in same pan; cook seeds, covered, about 30 seconds or until seeds begin to crack.

3   Stir in garlic, ginger and onion; cook, stirring constantly, until onion softens. Stir in cumin, curry powder, cardamom, undrained tomatoes, sugar and the water; bring to a boil. Add eggs, reduce heat; simmer, covered, about 5 minutes or until mixture thickens slightly.

4   Meanwhile, heat the extra oil in medium frying pan; cook garlic, stirring, until fragrant. Add spinach; cook, stirring, until spinach just wilts.

5   Serve eggs with spinach.

SERVES 4
per serving 7.3g carbohydrate; 25.3g fat; 1325kJ (317 cal); 15.6g protein

mixed vegetable and herb frittata

PREPARATION TIME 25 MINUTES   COOKING TIME 20 MINUTES

2 teaspoons olive oil

2 cloves garlic, crushed

2 medium zucchini (240g), sliced thinly

80g swiss brown mushrooms, sliced thinly

180g baby spinach leaves

3 eggs

8 egg whites

¼ cup coarsely chopped fresh basil

¼ cup (20g) coarsely grated
   parmesan cheese

TOMATO SALAD

250g yellow teardrop tomatoes, halved

250g cherry tomatoes, halved

¼ cup loosely packed fresh baby basil leaves

2 tablespoons balsamic vinegar

1   Make tomato salad.

2   Heat oil in large frying pan; cook garlic and zucchini, stirring, until zucchini is just tender. Add mushrooms and spinach; cook, stirring, until spinach just wilts.

3   Beat eggs and egg whites in medium bowl; stir in basil.

4   Pour egg mixture into pan; cook, uncovered, over medium heat about 10 minutes or until set. Sprinkle with cheese; place under preheated grill until frittata is browned lightly. Serve with salad.

TOMATO SALAD Combine tomatoes and basil in medium bowl. Stir in vinegar just before serving.

SERVES 4
per serving 4.6g carbohydrate; 8.5g fat; 694kJ (166 cal); 17.2g protein

pan-fried tofu with cabbage salad

PREPARATION TIME 20 MINUTES (PLUS STANDING TIME)   COOKING TIME 15 MINUTES

You need half a chinese cabbage for this recipe.

3 x 300g pieces fresh firm silken tofu

1 tablespoon finely chopped fresh lemon grass

2 fresh small red thai chillies, sliced thinly

1 medium red onion (170g), sliced thinly

1 cup (80g) bean sprouts

4 cups (320g) shredded chinese cabbage

¾ cup firmly packed fresh coriander leaves

SWEET AND SOUR DRESSING

⅓ cup (80ml) lime juice

2 teaspoons grated palm sugar

2 tablespoons soy sauce

1 Pat tofu all over with absorbent paper. Slice each tofu block vertically into 4 x 2.5cm slices. Spread tofu, in single layer, on absorbent-paper-lined tray; cover tofu with more absorbent paper, stand at least 10 minutes.

2 Meanwhile, make sweet and sour dressing.

3 Cook tofu, in batches, in heated lightly oiled frying pan until browned both sides.

4 Meanwhile, place lemon grass, chilli, onion, sprouts, cabbage and coriander in large bowl; toss gently to combine.

5 Divide cabbage salad among serving plates; top with tofu, drizzle with dressing.

SWEET AND SOUR DRESSING Whisk ingredients in small jug until sugar dissolves.

SERVES 4
per serving 8.2g carbohydrate; 15.6g fat; 1233kJ (295 cal); 29.9g protein

mixed mushrooms with garlic and chives (see page 56)

PREPARATION TIME 15 MINUTES   COOKING TIME 40 MINUTES

800g medium flat mushrooms

100g shiitake mushrooms

100g swiss brown mushrooms

100g oyster mushrooms

cooking-oil spray

¼ cup (60ml) red wine vinegar

1 tablespoon olive oil

2 cloves garlic, crushed

⅔ cup coarsely chopped fresh chives

2 cups loosely packed fresh flat-leaf parsley leaves

1 medium red onion (170g), sliced thinly

1 Preheat oven to slow.

2 Cut flat mushrooms coarsely into large pieces; combine with shiitake, swiss brown and oyster mushrooms, in single layer, in two large shallow baking dishes. Spray mushrooms lightly with cooking-oil spray; bake, uncovered, in slow oven about 40 minutes or until tender.

3 Stir vinegar and oil in small saucepan over heat for 1 minute; place with mushrooms and remaining ingredients in large bowl; toss gently to combine. Serve warm or cold.

SERVES 4
per serving 6.7g carbohydrate; 6.3g fat; 552kJ (132 cal); 11.6g protein

goat-cheese-stuffed roast capsicum with tapenade

PREPARATION TIME 30 MINUTES   COOKING TIME 20 MINUTES

The name tapenade derives from tapeno, the Provençal word for capers, a vital ingredient in this tangy condiment that perfectly complements goat cheese.

4 medium red capsicums (800g)

300g firm goat cheese

200g ricotta cheese

2 tablespoons sour cream

2 tablespoons extra virgin olive oil

1 tablespoon basil leaves

cracked black pepper

TAPENADE

1 tablespoon drained capers, rinsed

3 drained anchovy fillets

½ cup (60g) seeded black olives

1 tablespoon lemon juice

¼ cup (60ml) extra virgin olive oil

1 Roast whole capsicums under grill or in very hot oven until skin blisters and blackens. Cover capsicum with plastic or paper for 5 minutes; peel away skin. Slice off and discard top and bottom of capsicums; carefully remove and discard seeds and membrane from inside capsicum. Trim capsicum to 8cm in depth; cut each in half to make two 4cm "rings" (you will have eight rings).

2 Blend or process cheeses and sour cream until smooth. Fit one capsicum ring inside a 5.5cm-round cutter, place on serving plate, spoon cheese mixture inside capsicum ring; carefully remove cutter. Repeat with remaining capsicum and cheese mixture.

3 Serve capsicum with tapenade, drizzled with oil and sprinkled with basil leaves and pepper.

TAPENADE Blend or process ingredients until smooth.

SERVES 4
per serving 11.5g carbohydrate; 44.8g fat; 2169kJ (519 cal); 18.9g protein

red snapper parcels
with caper and anchovy salsa

PREPARATION TIME 30 MINUTES   COOKING TIME 15 MINUTES

A modern take on the traditional method of cooking "en papillote" (in sealed packets), this recipe uses aluminium foil rather than parchment paper to enclose the ingredients. Cooking this way reduces the need for any added fat, plus mingles and intensifies the flavours of the contents.

2 cloves garlic, crushed

1 tiny fennel (130g), sliced thinly

4 x 200g red snapper fillets

4 large fresh basil leaves

⅓ cup (80ml) dry white wine

¼ cup coarsely chopped
   fresh chives

⅓ cup loosely packed fresh
   tarragon leaves

⅓ cup loosely packed fresh
   basil leaves

½ cup loosely packed fresh
   chervil leaves

30g watercress

1 tablespoon lemon juice

1 teaspoon olive oil

CAPER AND ANCHOVY SALSA

1 small red capsicum (150g),
   chopped finely

2 tablespoons finely chopped
   seeded kalamata olives

1 tablespoon drained baby
   capers, rinsed

8 drained anchovy fillets,
   chopped finely

¼ cup finely chopped fresh basil

1 tablespoon balsamic vinegar

1 Preheat oven to hot.

2 Combine garlic and fennel in small bowl.

3 Place fillets, skin-side down, on four separate squares of lightly oiled foil large enough to completely enclose fish. Top each fillet with equal amounts of the fennel mixture; top with one basil leaf each, drizzle each with 1 tablespoon of the wine. Gather corners of foil squares together above snapper filling; twist to enclose.

4 Place parcels on oven tray; bake in hot oven about 15 minutes or until fish is cooked as desired.

5 Meanwhile, make caper and anchovy salsa.

6 Place remaining ingredients in medium bowl; toss gently to combine.

7 Discard foil from parcels just before serving; top with salsa. Serve with herb salad.

CAPER AND ANCHOVY SALSA Combine capsicum, olives, capers, anchovies, basil and vinegar in small bowl.

SERVES 4
per serving 3.6g carbohydrate; 5.3g fat; 1066kJ (255 cal); 43.9g protein

lobster tails with avocado and capsicum

PREPARATION TIME 20 MINUTES   COOKING TIME 20 MINUTES

**4 medium uncooked lobster
    tails (1.5kg)**

40g butter, melted

2 cloves garlic, crushed

AVOCADO PUREE

2 medium avocados (500g)

1 tablespoon lime juice

RED CAPSICUM SAUCE

4 medium red capsicums (800g)

1 tablespoon olive oil

**1 medium white onion (150g),
    chopped finely**

1 clove garlic, crushed

½ cup (125ml) chicken stock

1   Make avocado puree and red capsicum sauce.

2   Remove and discard skin from underneath lobster tails to expose flesh.

3   Cut each tail in half lengthways. Combine butter and garlic in small bowl; brush over lobster flesh. Cook lobster on heated oiled grill plate (or grill or barbecue) until browned both sides and changed in colour. Serve lobster with avocado puree and red capsicum sauce.

AVOCADO PUREE   Blend or process avocados and juice until smooth.

RED CAPSICUM SAUCE   Quarter capsicums; remove and discard seeds and membranes. Cook capsicum, skin-side-down, on heated oiled barbecue until skin blisters and blackens. Cover capsicum pieces in plastic or paper 5 minutes; peel away skin. Heat oil in small pan; cook onion and garlic, stirring, until onion softens. Add capsicum and stock; bring to a boil. Remove from heat; blend or process capsicum mixture until almost smooth.

SERVES 4
per serving 9.5g carbohydrate; 35.8g fat; 2713kJ (649 cal); 72.2g protein

tuna steaks with olive and fetta salsa

PREPARATION TIME 10 MINUTES   COOKING TIME 5 MINUTES

1 tablespoon olive oil

1 tablespoon lemon juice

¼ teaspoon cracked black pepper

4 x 200g tuna steaks

OLIVE AND FETTA SALSA

**2 medium tomatoes (380g), seeded,
    chopped coarsely**

**⅔ cup (100g) seeded black
    olives, sliced thinly**

150g fetta cheese, chopped coarsely

**¼ cup coarsely chopped fresh
    oregano leaves**

1 tablespoon toasted pine nuts

1   Combine oil, juice and pepper in small jug; brush over tuna. Cook tuna on heated oiled barbecue, uncovered, brushing occasionally with lemon mixture, until browned both sides and cooked as desired.

2   Meanwhile, make olive and fetta salad.

3   Serve tuna with salad.

OLIVE AND FETTA SALSA   Combine ingredients in small bowl.

SERVES 4
per serving 7.2g carbohydrate; 27.6g fat; 2134kJ (510 cal); 58.2g protein

salmon with peas and green onion

PREPARATION TIME 15 MINUTES   COOKING TIME 15 MINUTES

60g butter

4 salmon fillets (800g)

2 cloves garlic, crushed

2 medium brown onions (300g),
   sliced thinly

¾ cup (180ml) fish stock

2 tablespoons lemon juice

1½ cups (185g) frozen peas

8 green onions, trimmed, cut into
   4cm lengths

1 tablespoon finely grated lemon rind

1 teaspoon sea salt flakes

1 Melt half of the butter in large heated frying pan; cook salmon until browned both sides. Remove from pan; cover to keep warm.

2 Melt remaining butter in same pan; cook garlic and brown onion, stirring, until onion softens. Add stock, juice, peas and green onion; bring to a boil. Reduce heat; simmer, uncovered, 2 minutes.

3 Return salmon to pan; sprinkle with rind and salt. Cook, uncovered, until salmon is cooked as desired.

SERVES 4
per serving 9.2g carbohydrate; 26.9g fat; 1898kJ (454 cal); 43.7g protein

balsamic-flavoured octopus

PREPARATION TIME 20 MINUTES   COOKING TIME 5 MINUTES

1.5kg cleaned baby octopus

2 cloves garlic, crushed

¼ cup (60ml) olive oil

¼ cup (60ml) balsamic vinegar

1 tablespoon brown sugar

2 teaspoons chopped fresh thyme

150g curly endive

2 tablespoons olive oil, extra

2 tablespoons balsamic vinegar, extra

1 Cut each octopus in half; combine in large bowl with garlic, oil, vinegar, sugar and thyme. Cover; refrigerate 3 hours or overnight.

2 Drain octopus over small bowl; reserve marinade. Cook octopus, in batches, on heated oiled grill plate (or grill or barbecue) until browned all over and just cooked through, brushing occasionally with reserved marinade. Serve octopus with curly endive, drizzled with combined extra oil and extra vinegar.

SERVES 4
per serving 8.8g carbohydrate; 26.8g fat; 2094kJ (501 cal); 55.9g protein

roast salmon with mango and lime mayonnaise

PREPARATION TIME 30 MINUTES   COOKING TIME 1 HOUR

1.5kg whole salmon

1 lime, sliced thinly

2 sprigs fresh dill

cooking-oil spray

2 tablespoons olive oil

1 tablespoon drained capers, rinsed

100g rocket

MANGO AND LIME MAYONNAISE

1 egg yolk

¼ teaspoon dry mustard

¼ cup (60ml) light olive oil

2 tablespoons olive oil

1 tablespoon lime juice

½ teaspoon finely grated lime rind

1 small mango (300g),

   peeled, quartered

1 Preheat oven to moderate.

2 Wash fish, pat dry inside and out with absorbent paper; place lime and dill inside cavity. Place two large pieces of foil, overlapping slightly, on oven tray; spray lightly with cooking-oil spray. Place fish on foil, fold foil over to completely enclose fish. Roast in moderate oven about 45 minutes or until cooked as desired.

3 Meanwhile, heat oil in small frying pan; cook capers, stirring, until crisp. Drain on absorbent paper.

4 Make mango and lime mayonnaise.

5 Starting behind gills of salmon, peel away and discard skin; scrape away any dark flesh. Flake salmon coarsely; sprinkle with capers. Serve salmon warm or cold on rocket with mango and lime mayonnaise.

MANGO AND LIME MAYONNAISE Blend or process egg yolk and mustard until smooth. With motor operating, gradually add combined oils in thin, steady stream until mixture thickens. Add remaining ingredients; blend until smooth.

SERVES 4
per serving 7.8g carbohydrate; 39.4g fat; 2286kJ (547 cal); 40.9g protein
tips Salmon is best served rare in the centre so it remains moist. Mayonnaise can be made a day ahead and refrigerated, covered.

prawn salad with gazpacho salsa

PREPARATION TIME 35 MINUTES   COOKING TIME 2 MINUTES

Saffron, the dried stigma from the crocus flower, is one of the world's costliest spices. Buy it in small amounts and keep it, sealed tightly, in the refrigerator to preserve its freshness.

1kg cooked large king prawns

2 medium avocados (500g)

GAZPACHO SALSA

2 lebanese cucumbers (260g),
    seeded, chopped finely

2 medium tomatoes (380g), seeded,
    chopped finely

1 clove garlic, crushed

1 tablespoon olive oil

2 tablespoons tomato juice

1 tablespoon raspberry vinegar

SAFFRON MAYONNAISE

2 tablespoons lemon juice

¼ teaspoon saffron threads

2 egg yolks

1 tablespoon dijon mustard

⅓ cup (80ml) olive oil

1 tablespoon finely chopped
    fresh dill

1 tablespoon warm water

1   Make gazpacho salsa. Make saffron mayonnaise.

2   Shell and devein prawns, leaving tails and heads intact.

3   Halve avocados; discard seeds.

4   Divide three-quarters of the salsa among serving plates. Place avocado halves on top; fill avocado centres with remaining salsa and prawns, spoon mayonnaise over prawns.

GAZPACHO SALSA   Combine ingredients in medium bowl.

SAFFRON MAYONNAISE   Heat juice and saffron in small saucepan, over low heat, about 2 minutes or until juice has changed in colour; cool 10 minutes. Blend or process strained juice, egg yolks and mustard until smooth. With motor operating, gradually add oil in thin, steady stream until mixture thickens. Stir in dill; add the water to thin mayonnaise, if desired.

SERVES 4
per serving 3g carbohydrate; 46.2g fat; 2341kJ (560 cal); 33.6g protein
tip Saffron mayonnaise is even better if made a day ahead; keep, covered, in the refrigerator.

fish and zucchini stacks

PREPARATION TIME 15 MINUTES   COOKING TIME 10 MINUTES

You could use any firm, white-fleshed fish — ling, bream, snapper, blue-eye or silver warehou would all be perfect for this recipe.

4 x 200g firm white fish fillets

2 medium green zucchini (240g)

2 medium yellow zucchini (240g)

4 medium tomatoes (760g),

　sliced thinly

⅓ cup (80ml) dry white wine

coarsely ground black pepper

2 tablespoons balsamic vinegar

2 tablespoons baby basil leaves

1   Preheat oven to very hot.

2   Halve fish pieces lengthways. Using vegetable peeler, peel zucchini lengthways into long thin ribbons.

3   Place four pieces of fish on large individual pieces of lightly oiled foil; top with zucchini ribbons then remaining fish pieces. Cut eight slices of tomato in half; place four half-slices on top of each stack. Drizzle stacks with wine; sprinkle with pepper.

4   Fold foil to enclose fish stacks; place in single layer in baking dish. Bake in very hot oven about 10 minutes or until fish is cooked as desired.

5   Divide remaining tomato slices equally among serving plates; top with unwrapped fish stacks. Drizzle stacks with vinegar; sprinkle with basil.

SERVES 4
per serving 4.6g carbohydrate; 4.9g fat; 1058kJ (253 cal); 43.4g protein
tip Fish stacks can be assembled and wrapped in foil several hours ahead; store in refrigerator.

fish with wasabi mayonnaise

PREPARATION TIME 5 MINUTES   COOKING TIME 10 MINUTES

Wasabi, japanese horseradish, is available as a paste in tubes or powdered in tins from Asian food stores and some supermarkets. Gai larn, also known as chinese broccoli, can be found in Asian food stores and many greengrocers.

⅓ cup (100g) mayonnaise

2 teaspoons wasabi paste

2 green onions, chopped finely

2 tablespoons coarsely chopped

　fresh coriander

2 tablespoons lime juice

1 tablespoon peanut oil

4 x 200g firm white fish fillets

750g gai larn

1   Combine mayonnaise, wasabi, onion, coriander and juice in small bowl; reserve.

2   Heat oil in large frying pan; cook fish, in batches, until browned both sides and cooked as desired.

3   Meanwhile, boil, steam or microwave gai larn until just tender; drain. Divide gai larn among serving plates; top with fish and wasabi mayonnaise.

SERVES 4
per serving 6.8g carbohydrate; 17.1g fat; 1476kJ (353 cal); 42.6g protein
tip For a stronger, more fiery taste, add an extra teaspoon of wasabi to the mayonnaise mixture.

seared scallops with mixed cabbage salad

PREPARATION TIME 15 MINUTES   COOKING TIME 10 MINUTES

You need approximately half a medium red cabbage and a quarter of a medium savoy cabbage for this recipe.

32 scallops (1.3kg), roe removed

2 lebanese cucumbers (260g)

3 cups (240g) finely shredded red cabbage

2 cups (160g) finely shredded savoy cabbage

½ cup coarsely chopped fresh chives

2 tablespoons toasted sesame seeds

HONEY SOY DRESSING

2 tablespoons soy sauce

2 tablespoons lemon juice

2 teaspoons sesame oil

1 tablespoon honey

1 clove garlic, crushed

¼ cup (60ml) peanut oil

1   Make honey soy dressing.

2   Sear scallops in large heated oiled frying pan, in batches, until browned both sides and cooked as desired.

3   Using vegetable peeler, slice cucumbers into ribbons. Combine cucumber in large bowl with cabbages, chives, seeds and three-quarters of the dressing.

4   Divide salad among serving plates; top with scallops, drizzle with remaining dressing.

HONEY SOY DRESSING Place ingredients in screw-top jar; shake well.

SERVES 4
per serving 10.9g carbohydrate; 20.1g fat; 1208kJ (289 cal); 16.3g protein

prawn and mint salad

PREPARATION TIME 30 MINUTES

40 medium cooked large king prawns (1kg)

1 lebanese cucumber (130g)

1 tablespoon fish sauce

¼ cup (60ml) lime juice

½ cup (125ml) coconut milk

2 tablespoons sugar

1 clove garlic, crushed

2cm piece fresh ginger (10g), grated

1 fresh small red thai chilli, sliced thinly

80g curly endive

60g watercress

2 cups (160g) bean sprouts

½ cup thinly sliced fresh mint

1   Shell and devein prawns, leaving tails intact. Halve cucumber lengthways, slice thinly on the diagonal.

2   Whisk sauce, juice, milk, sugar, garlic, ginger and chilli in large bowl. Add prawns, cucumber and remaining ingredients; toss salad gently to combine.

SERVES 4
per serving 10.3g carbohydrate; 7.9g fat; 1024kJ (245 cal); 33g protein

warm balmain bug salad with saffron dressing

PREPARATION TIME 30 MINUTES   COOKING TIME 20 MINUTES

24 uncooked balmain bugs

(approximately 3kg)

500g cherry tomatoes

2 large avocados (640g),

sliced thinly

1 medium red onion (170g),

sliced thinly

80g watercress

½ cup firmly packed fresh purple

basil leaves

SAFFRON DRESSING

8 saffron threads

¼ cup (60ml) boiling water

1 egg yolk

1 clove garlic, crushed

1 teaspoon english mustard

2 tablespoons lemon juice

½ cup (125ml) light olive oil

1   Place each bug, upside down, on chopping board; cut tail from body. Discard body; cut through tail lengthways, remove and discard vein. Remove bug meat from both tail halves.

2   Cook bug meat and tomatoes, in batches, on heated oiled grill plate (or grill or barbecue) until browned all over.

3   Meanwhile, make the saffron dressing.

4   Just before serving, combine tomatoes in large bowl with avocado, onion, watercress, basil and one-third of the saffron dressing. Divide salad among serving plates; top with bug meat, drizzle with remaining dressing.

SAFFRON DRESSING Combine saffron and the water in small heatproof bowl; stand 10 minutes. Strain through fine strainer into small bowl; discard threads. Whisk egg yolk, garlic, mustard and juice in small bowl; gradually add oil, in thin, steady stream, whisking continuously until mixture thickens. Whisk in saffron liquid.

SERVES 4
per serving 6.7g carboydrate; 60.7g fat; 4715kJ (1128 cal); 138.4g protein
tips Slice the avocado just before assembling the salad.
Tomatoes can be browned on an oven tray under a grill or in a hot oven.

cajun blue-eye cutlets with cucumber salad

PREPARATION TIME 5 MINUTES   COOKING TIME 10 MINUTES

2 teaspoons ground cumin

2 teaspoons ground coriander

2 teaspoons sweet paprika

2 teaspoons mustard powder

2 teaspoons onion powder

½ teaspoon garlic powder

¼ teaspoon cayenne pepper

2 teaspoons fennel seeds

4 x 250g blue-eye cutlets

2 limes, sliced thickly

CUCUMBER SALAD

2 lebanese cucumbers (260g)

2 fresh small red thai chillies,
   seeded, chopped finely

¼ cup (60ml) peanut oil

2 tablespoons lime juice

1 clove garlic, crushed

2 teaspoons toasted cumin seeds

1 tablespoon finely shredded
   fresh mint

1 Combine spices, powders, pepper and seeds with fish in large bowl; turn to coat fish in spice mixture. Cook fish, in batches, on heated oiled grill plate (or grill or barbecue) until browned both sides and cooked as desired.

2 Meanwhile, make cucumber salad. Cook lime on heated oiled grill plate until browned both sides.

3 Cook lime on heated oiled grill plate (or grill or barbecue) until browned both sides.

4 Divide fish and salad among serving plates; top fish with lime.

CUCUMBER SALAD Using vegetable peeler, slice cucumber lengthways into thin ribbons. Place cucumber in medium bowl with remaining ingredients; toss gently to combine.

SERVES 4
per serving 1.9g carbohydrate; 19.4g fat; 1639kJ (392 cal); 51.8g protein
tips Any firm white fish, such as ling, can be used instead of the blue-eye. You can use ⅓ cup bottled cajun spice mix, available from supermarkets, instead of making your own, if preferred.

fish fillets pan-fried with pancetta and caper herb butter

PREPARATION TIME 15 MINUTES   COOKING TIME 10 MINUTES

80g butter, softened

2 tablespoons coarsely chopped fresh
   flat-leaf parsley

1 tablespoon drained capers, rinsed

2 cloves garlic, quartered

2 green onions, chopped coarsely

8 slices pancetta (120g)

4 x 200g white fish fillets

1 tablespoon olive oil

250g asparagus, trimmed

1 Blend or process butter, parsley, capers, garlic and onion until mixture forms a smooth paste.

2 Spread 1 heaped tablespoon of the butter mixture and two slices of the pancetta on each fish fillet.

3 Heat oil in large heavy-base frying pan; cook fish, pancetta-butter side down, until pancetta is crisp. Turn fish carefully; cook, uncovered, until fish is cooked as desired.

4 Meanwhile, boil, steam or microwave asparagus until tender; drain.

5 Serve fish and asparagus drizzled with pan juices.

SERVES 4
per serving   1.7g carbohydrate; 28.6g fat; 1898kJ (454 cal); 48.2g protein

swordfish with thai dressing

PREPARATION TIME 5 MINUTES   COOKING TIME 10 MINUTES

4 x 200g swordfish steaks

⅓ cup (80ml) sweet chilli sauce

1 tablespoon fish sauce

½ cup (125ml) lime juice

2 teaspoons finely chopped fresh
   lemon grass

2 tablespoons finely chopped fresh coriander

½ cup finely chopped fresh mint

1cm piece fresh ginger (5g), grated

150g mesclun

1 Cook fish on heated oiled grill plate (or grill or barbecue) until browned both sides and cooked as desired.

2 Place sauces, juice, lemon grass, herbs and ginger in screw-top jar; shake well. Divide mesclun among serving plates; top with fish, drizzle with dressing.

SERVES 4
per serving   5.3g carbohydrate; 5.1g fat; 1012kJ (242 cal); 42.2g protein
tip   You can substitute tuna steaks or cutlets for the swordfish.

swordfish with chermoulla

PREPARATION TIME 10 MINUTES (PLUS REFRIGERATION TIME)   COOKING TIME 10 MINUTES

Chermoulla is a spicy Moroccan marinade which can also be served as a sauce. If hot paprika is unavailable, substitute it with ½ teaspoon of sweet paprika and a hearty pinch of cayenne pepper.

2 cloves garlic, crushed

½ teaspoon ground cumin

¼ teaspoon hot paprika

1 tablespoon coarsely chopped
   fresh coriander

1 tablespoon coarsely chopped fresh
   flat-leaf parsley

2 tablespoons olive oil

2 tablespoons lemon juice

1 teaspoon finely grated lemon rind

4 x 150g swordfish steaks

125g rocket leaves

1   Combine garlic, spices, herbs, oil, juice and rind in large non-metallic bowl; remove and reserve half of the chermoulla mixture. Place fish in bowl; toss to coat all over in remaining chermoulla. Cover fish mixture and reserved chermoulla, separately; refrigerate 3 hours or overnight.

2   Remove fish; discard marinade. Cook fish in large heated non-stick frying pan until browned both sides and cooked as desired. Serve fish topped with rocket leaves and drizzled with reserved chermoulla.

SERVES 4
per serving 1.1g carbohydrate; 12.7g fat; 1028kJ (246 cal); 31.6g protein

ling and snow pea green curry

PREPARATION TIME 30 MINUTES   COOKING TIME 15 MINUTES

2 teaspoons peanut oil

1 medium brown onion (150g),
   chopped finely

3 small green chillies, seeded, sliced thinly

¼ cup (75g) green curry paste

2 baby eggplants (120g), sliced thickly

1⅔ cups (400ml) coconut milk

800g ling fillets, skinned, chopped coarsely

200g snow peas, trimmed, halved

4 green onions, sliced thinly

¼ cup coarsely chopped fresh coriander

1   Heat oil in large saucepan; cook brown onion, chilli and curry paste, stirring, until onion softens. Add eggplant; cook, stirring, until just tender. Stir in coconut milk; bring to a boil.

2   Add fish, reduce heat; simmer, uncovered, 5 minutes. Add snow peas and green onion; stir gently until vegetables are just tender. Remove from heat; stir in half of the coriander. Serve curry sprinkled with remaining coriander.

SERVES 4
per serving 10.5g carbohydrate; 33.2g fat; 2182kJ (522 cal); 46.2g protein

herbed and spiced sashimi with ginger cabbage salad

PREPARATION TIME 45 MINUTES   COOKING TIME 5 MINUTES

Salmon and tuna sold as sashimi have to meet stringent guidelines regarding their handling and treatment after leaving the water; however, it is best to seek local advice from knowledgeable authorities before eating any raw fish. You need half a medium chinese cabbage for this recipe.

2 tablespoons sesame seeds

1 tablespoon black sesame seeds

2 teaspoons coriander seeds

1 teaspoon sea salt

½ teaspoon cracked black pepper

**2 tablespoons finely chopped
    fresh chives**

300g piece sashimi tuna

300g piece sashimi salmon

**200g green beans, trimmed,
    sliced thinly**

6 trimmed red radishes (90g)

**3 cups (240g) finely shredded
    chinese cabbage**

6 green onions, sliced thinly

1½ cups (150g) mung bean sprouts

**1 cup firmly packed fresh
    coriander leaves**

GINGER DRESSING

2cm piece fresh ginger (10g), grated

2 tablespoons rice vinegar

2 tablespoons vegetable oil

2 teaspoons sesame oil

1 tablespoon mirin

1 tablespoon soy sauce

1   Dry-fry seeds in small frying pan, stirring, until fragrant; cool 10 minutes. Using mortar and pestle, crush seeds; combine in large bowl with salt, pepper and chives.

2   Cut each piece of fish into three 5cm-thick pieces. Roll each piece in seed mixture; enclose tightly, individually, in plastic wrap. Refrigerate until required.

3   Make ginger dressing.

4   Boil, steam or microwave green beans until just tender; drain. Rinse green beans under cold water; drain. Slice radishes thinly; cut slices into matchstick-sized pieces.

5   Place green beans and radish in large bowl with cabbage, onion, sprouts, coriander leaves and half of the dressing; toss gently to combine.

6   Unwrap fish; slice thinly. Divide fish and salad among serving plates; drizzle fish with remaining dressing.

GINGER DRESSING   Place ingredients in screw-top jar; shake well.

SERVES 4
per serving 3.8g carbohydrate; 26.1g fat; 1710kJ (409 cal); 39.2g protein

herbed and spiced sashimi with ginger cabbage salad

steamed belgian mussels

steamed belgian mussels

PREPARATION TIME 30 MINUTES   COOKING TIME 10 MINUTES

1.3kg mussels

2 teaspoons olive oil

2 cloves garlic, crushed

3 shallots (75g), sliced thinly

2 trimmed celery stalks (200g),
  sliced thinly

2 large egg tomatoes (180g),
  chopped finely

½ cup (125ml) dry white wine

180g curly endive

½ cup loosely packed fresh
  parsley leaves

¼ cup coarsely chopped
  fresh chives

¼ cup (60ml) lemon juice

1   Scrub mussels under cold water; remove beards.

2   Heat oil in wok or large frying pan; stir-fry garlic, shallots and
    celery until shallots soften. Add tomato; stir-fry 30 seconds.
    Add wine; bring to a boil. Boil, until liquid reduces by half.

3   Add mussels, reduce heat; simmer, covered, about 3 minutes or
    until mussels open (discard any that do not).

4   Add remaining ingredients to wok; toss gently to combine.

SERVES 4
per serving 6.8g carbohydrate; 3.8g fat; 519kJ (124 cal);
9.9g protein

char-grilled swordfish with roasted mediterranean vegetables

PREPARATION TIME 20 MINUTES   COOKING TIME 25 MINUTES

1 medium red capsicum (200g), sliced thickly

1 medium yellow capsicum (200g),
   sliced thickly

1 medium eggplant (300g), sliced thickly

2 large zucchini (300g), sliced thickly

½ cup (125ml) olive oil

250g cherry tomatoes

¼ cup (60ml) balsamic vinegar

1 clove garlic, crushed

2 teaspoons sugar

4 x 250g swordfish steaks

¼ cup coarsely chopped fresh basil

1 Preheat oven to hot.

2 Combine capsicums, eggplant, zucchini and 2 tablespoons of the oil in large baking dish; roast, uncovered, in hot oven 15 minutes. Add tomatoes; roast, uncovered, in hot oven about 5 minutes or until vegetables are just tender.

3 Meanwhile, place vinegar, garlic, sugar and remaining oil in screw-top jar; shake well. Brush a third of the dressing over fish; cook fish, in batches, on heated oiled grill plate (or grill or barbecue) until browned both sides and cooked as desired.

4 Place vegetables in large bowl with basil and remaining dressing; toss gently to combine. Divide vegetables among serving plates; top with fish.

SERVES 4
per serving 8.4g carbohydrate; 33.9g fat; 2211kJ (529 cal); 48g protein

seared tuna with salsa verde

PREPARATION TIME 10 MINUTES   COOKING TIME 5 MINUTES

Tuna is at its best if browned both sides but still fairly rare in the middle; overcooking will make it dry.

4 x 200g tuna steaks

100g baby rocket leaves

SALSA VERDE

½ cup firmly packed fresh flat-leaf
   parsley leaves

¼ cup loosely packed fresh mint leaves

⅔ cup (160ml) extra virgin olive oil

¼ cup (50g) drained capers, rinsed

2 teaspoons dijon mustard

2 tablespoons lemon juice

8 drained anchovy fillets

1 clove garlic, quartered

1 Make salsa verde.

2 Cook fish, in batches, on heated oiled grill plate (or grill or barbecue) until browned both sides and cooked as desired.

3 Divide rocket among serving plates; top with fish, drizzle with salsa verde.

SALSA VERDE Blend or process ingredients until just combined. Transfer to medium jug; whisk before pouring over fish.

SERVES 4
per serving 2.2g carbohydrate; 48.5g fat; 2742kJ (656 cal); 53.4g protein

grilled leatherjacket with sumac-roasted tomatoes

PREPARATION TIME 20 MINUTES   COOKING TIME 30 MINUTES

500g cherry tomatoes, halved

2 teaspoons sumac

4 x 200g leatherjackets

80g butter

2 tablespoons lemon juice

1 clove garlic, crushed

500g broccolini, trimmed

1 Preheat oven to hot.

2 Place tomato, cut-side up, on lightly oiled oven tray; sprinkle with sumac. Roast, uncovered, in hot oven about 10 minutes or until softened.

3 Meanwhile, cook fish on heated oiled grill plate (or grill or barbecue) until browned both sides and cooked as desired.

4 Heat butter, juice and garlic in small saucepan; stir until butter sauce is smooth.

5 Meanwhile, boil, steam or microwave broccolini until just tender; drain.

6 Divide tomato, fish and broccolini among serving plates; drizzle with butter sauce.

SERVES 4
per serving 3.7g carbohydrate; 21.2g fat; 1626kJ (389 cal); 45.6g protein
tip Sumac is a purple-red, astringent spice that adds a lemony flavour to foods; it is available from Middle-Eastern food stores and some supermarkets.

whole roasted snapper in salt crust with gremolata

PREPARATION TIME 10 MINUTES (PLUS STANDING TIME)   COOKING TIME 30 MINUTES

1kg whole snapper, gutted,
  scales left on

1.5kg coarse sea salt, approximately

GREMOLATA

¼ cup finely chopped fresh
  flat-leaf parsley

1 clove garlic, crushed

2 teaspoons finely grated
  lemon rind

1 tablespoon extra virgin olive oil

350g watercress

1 tablespoon lemon juice

1 Preheat oven to very hot. Make gremolata.

2 Wash fish, pat dry inside and out with absorbent paper; stuff cavity with half of the gremolata.

3 Sprinkle half of the salt over large oven tray, place fish on tray. Wet remaining salt with water; drain, press firmly over fish to completely enclose fish.

4 Roast fish, uncovered, in very hot oven about 30 minutes or until fish is cooked as desired. Stand 5 minutes.

5 Break crust with meat mallet; lift away crust with scales and skin. Sprinkle fish with remaining gremolata to serve.

GREMOLATA Combine ingredients in small bowl.

SERVES 4
per serving 1g carbohydrate; 7.1g fat; 786kJ (188 cal); 29.6g protein

mixed seafood with crisp thai basil

PREPARATION TIME 25 MINUTES   COOKING TIME 10 MINUTES

250g squid hoods

250g firm white fish fillets

12 medium uncooked king
prawns (600g)

250g cleaned baby octopus

2 tablespoons peanut oil

1 clove garlic, crushed

2 fresh small red thai chillies,
sliced thinly

1 medium carrot (120g), halved,
sliced thinly

1 medium red capsicum (200g),
sliced thinly

4 green onions, sliced thinly

1 tablespoon fish sauce

1 teaspoon oyster sauce

1 tablespoon lime juice

¼ cup (60ml) peanut oil, extra

⅓ cup loosely packed fresh thai
basil leaves

1   Cut squid down centre to open; score in a diagonal pattern then cut into thick strips. Cut squid and fish into 3cm pieces; shell and devein prawns, leaving tails intact. Cut each octopus in half, rinse under cold water; drain.

2   Heat half of the oil in wok or large saucepan; stir-fry seafood, in batches, until prawns are changed in colour, fish is cooked as desired, and squid and octopus are tender. Cover to keep warm.

3   Heat remaining oil in same wok; stir-fry garlic, chilli and carrot until carrot is just tender. Add capsicum; stir-fry until capsicum is just tender. Return seafood to wok with onion, sauces and juice; stir-fry gently, until hot.

4   Heat extra oil in small frying pan until sizzling; fry basil leaves, in batches, until crisp but still green. Drain on absorbent paper. Top seafood with basil leaves.

SERVES 4
per serving 4.7g carbohydrate; 26.2g fat; 1885kJ (451 cal);
49.4g protein

blue-eye fillet, baby leek and fennel parcels with fried cauliflower

PREPARATION TIME 20 MINUTES   COOKING TIME 15 MINUTES

A modern take on the traditional method of cooking "en papillote" (in sealed packets), this recipe uses aluminium foil rather than parchment paper to enclose the ingredients. Cooking this way allows the flavours to mingle and intensify.

4 x 200g blue-eye fillets, with skin

½ medium fennel bulb (150g), trimmed, sliced thinly

4 baby leeks (320g), quartered lengthways

30g butter, melted

vegetable oil, for deep-frying

1 medium cauliflower (1.5kg), cut into florets

1   Preheat oven to hot.

2   Place each fillet on a square of lightly oiled foil large enough to completely enclose fillet; top each fillet with a quarter of the fennel and a quarter of the leek, drizzle with butter. Gather corners of foil squares together above fish; twist to enclose securely.

3   Place parcels on oven tray; bake in hot oven about 15 minutes or until fish is cooked as desired.

4   Meanwhile, heat oil in wok or large frying pan; deep-fry cauliflower, in batches, until browned and crisp. Drain on absorbent paper.

5   Discard foil from parcels just before serving on cauliflower.

SERVES 4
per serving 9.5g carbohydrate; 29.4g fat; 2082kJ (498 cal); 49.3g protein
tip When deep-frying the cauliflower, make sure the oil is very hot so the vegetable crisps and browns. If not, the cauliflower will absorb excess oil and become limp and soggy.

grilled snapper fillets with fennel and onion salad

PREPARATION TIME 15 MINUTES   COOKING TIME 10 MINUTES

1 medium red onion (170g), sliced thinly

4 green onions, sliced thinly

1 large fennel bulb (550g), trimmed,
   sliced thinly

2 trimmed celery stalks (200g), sliced thinly

½ cup coarsely chopped fresh
   flat-leaf parsley

⅓ cup (80ml) orange juice

¼ cup (60ml) olive oil

2 cloves garlic, crushed

2 teaspoons sambal oelek

4 x 250g snapper fillets, with skin

1   Combine onions, fennel, celery and parsley in medium bowl.

2   Place juice, oil, garlic and sambal in screw-top jar; shake well.

3   Cook fish on heated oiled grill plate (or grill or barbecue) until browned both sides and cooked as desired.

4   Pour half of the dressing over salad in bowl; toss gently to combine. Serve salad topped with fish; drizzle with remaining dressing.

SERVES 4
per serving 8g carbohydrate; 18.4g fat; 1797kJ (430 cal); 57.9g protein

tuna tartare

PREPARATION TIME 45 MINUTES   COOKING TIME 5 MINUTES

You need one small chinese cabbage weighing about 400g for this recipe.

200g green beans, halved

600g piece sashimi tuna

3 cups (240g) finely shredded
   chinese cabbage

4 green onions, sliced thinly

½ cup firmly packed fresh coriander leaves

2 cups (160g) bean sprouts

GINGER DRESSING

7cm piece fresh ginger (35g)

⅓ cup (80ml) lime juice

¼ cup (60ml) olive oil

1 tablespoon soy sauce

2 teaspoons finely chopped coriander root

2 cloves garlic, crushed

2 teaspoons sesame oil

2 teaspoons sugar

1   Boil, steam or microwave beans until just tender; drain. Rinse under cold water; drain.

2   Meanwhile, make ginger dressing.

3   Cut tuna into 5mm pieces. Place in medium bowl with a third of the dressing; toss gently to combine.

4   Place beans in large bowl with cabbage, onion, coriander, sprouts and remaining dressing; toss gently to combine.

5   Divide undrained tuna among serving plates, shaping into mound; serve with cabbage salad.

GINGER DRESSING Cut ginger into thin slices; cut slices into thin strips. Combine ginger with remaining ingredients in small bowl.

SERVES 4
per serving 5.8g carbohydrate; 24.8g fat; 1731kJ (414 cal); 41.5g protein
tip Sashimi salmon can be used in place of the tuna.

fish and spinach with olive and basil sauce

PREPARATION TIME 5 MINUTES   COOKING TIME 10 MINUTES

We used perch in this recipe, but you can use any firm fish, such as ling or blue-eye.

750g spinach, trimmed,

   chopped coarsely

⅓ cup (80ml) extra virgin olive oil

4 x 200g firm white fish fillets

1 tablespoon lemon juice

¼ teaspoon dried chilli flakes

1 clove garlic, crushed

⅓ cup (50g) seeded kalamata olives

¼ cup finely shredded fresh basil

1 Boil, steam or microwave spinach until just wilted; drain. Cover to keep warm.

2 Meanwhile, heat 1 tablespoon of the oil in large non-stick frying pan; cook fish until browned both sides and cooked as desired. Remove from pan; cover to keep warm.

3 Place remaining oil in same cleaned pan with remaining ingredients; cook, stirring, until heated through. Divide spinach among serving plates; top with fish, drizzle with olive and basil sauce.

SERVES 4
per serving 3.1g carbohydrate; 23.4g fat; 1651kJ (395 cal); 43.3g protein

prawns with garlic

PREPARATION TIME 20 MINUTES (PLUS REFRIGERATION TIME)   COOKING TIME 5 MINUTES

1kg medium uncooked king prawns

3 teaspoons coarsely chopped fresh

   coriander root and stem mixture

2 teaspoons dried coriander seeds

1 teaspoon dried green peppercorns

4 cloves garlic, quartered

2 tablespoons peanut oil

1 cup (80g) bean sprouts

1 tablespoon finely chopped

   fresh coriander

1 tablespoon packaged fried shallot

1 tablespoon packaged fried garlic

1 tablespoon fresh coriander leaves

1 Shell and devein prawns, leaving tails intact.

2 Using mortar and pestle, crush coriander mixture, coriander seeds, peppercorns and garlic to a paste. Place paste in large bowl with prawns and half of the oil; toss to coat prawns in marinade. Cover; refrigerate 3 hours or overnight.

3 Heat remaining oil in wok; stir-fry prawn mixture, in batches, until prawns are changed in colour. Remove from heat; toss bean sprouts and chopped coriander through stir-fry; serve sprinkled with fried shallot, fried garlic and coriander leaves.

SERVES 4
per serving 0.9g carbohydrate; 10.2g fat; 844kJ (202 cal); 26.6g protein

ceviche

PREPARATION TIME 20 MINUTES (PLUS REFRIGERATION TIME)

Ceviche, also known as seviche or cebiche, is an everyday fish salad eaten throughout the Caribbean and all over Latin America. While marinating the fish in lime juice appears to "cook" it, it is still raw. You will need about 10 limes for this recipe.

1kg redfish fillets

1½ cups (375ml) lime juice

¼ cup (40g) canned jalapeño chilli slices, drained

¼ cup (60ml) olive oil

1 large (250g) tomato, chopped coarsely

¼ cup coarsely chopped fresh coriander

1 small white onion (80g), chopped finely

1 clove garlic, crushed

30g watercress

⅓ cup loosely packed fresh basil leaves

¼ cup loosely packed fresh coriander leaves

2 tablespoons lime juice, extra

¼ cup (60ml) olive oil, extra

1 Remove any remaining skin or bones from fish; cut fish into 3cm pieces.

2 Combine fish and juice in non-metallic large bowl, cover; refrigerate 4 hours or overnight.

3 Drain fish; discard juice. Return fish to bowl, add chilli, oil, tomato, chopped coriander, onion and garlic; toss gently to combine. Cover; refrigerate 1 hour.

4 Just before serving, place watercress, basil, coriander, extra juice and extra oil in medium bowl; toss gently to combine. Serve ceviche with watercress mixture.

SERVES 4
per serve 4.1g carbohydrate; 32.2g fat; 2203kJ (527 cal); 53.3g protein
tip Fish must be marinated with the lime juice in a non-reactive bowl (one made from glazed porcelain or glass is best), to avoid the metallic taste that can result if marinating takes place in a stainless-steel or an aluminium bowl. Ensure all of the fish is completely covered with juice.

cajun seafood kebabs with avocado salsa

PREPARATION TIME 30 MINUTES (PLUS REFRIGERATION TIME)   COOKING TIME 10 MINUTES

800g medium uncooked
   king prawns
600g firm white fish fillets
2 tablespoons cajun seasoning
2 teaspoons ground cumin
2 tablespoons coarsely chopped
   fresh oregano
2 cloves garlic, crushed
¼ cup (60ml) olive oil

AVOCADO SALSA

1 large avocado (320g),
   chopped finely
3 medium tomatoes (570g),
   seeded, chopped finely
1 small red onion (100g),
   chopped finely
2 tablespoons finely chopped
   fresh coriander
2 tablespoons lemon juice
1 tablespoon olive oil
½ teaspoon sugar

1 Peel and devein prawns, leaving tails intact. Cut fish into 3cm pieces.

2 Combine prawns and fish with remaining ingredients in medium bowl. Cover; refrigerate 1 hour.

3 Thread prawns and fish onto 12 skewers. Cook seafood kebabs on heated oiled grill plate (or grill or barbecue), until browned and cooked as desired.

4 Meanwhile, make avocado salsa.

5 Serve seafood kebabs with salsa.

AVOCADO SALSA Combine ingredients in medium bowl.

SERVES 4
per serving 3.8g carbohydrate; 36.2g fat; 2483kJ (594 cal); 63.6g protein
tip If using bamboo skewers, soak in water for at least 1 hour before using to avoid them splintering and scorching.

mussels with basil and lemon grass

PREPARATION TIME 20 MINUTES   COOKING TIME 10 MINUTES

1kg large mussels (approximately 30)

1 tablespoon peanut oil

1 medium brown onion (150g),

   chopped finely

2 cloves garlic, crushed

2 tablespoons thinly sliced fresh lemon grass

1 fresh small red thai chilli, chopped finely

1 cup (250ml) dry white wine

2 tablespoons lime juice

2 tablespoons fish sauce

½ cup loosely packed fresh thai basil leaves

½ cup (125ml) coconut milk

1 fresh small red thai chilli, seeded,

   sliced thinly

2 green onions, sliced thinly

1 Scrub mussels under cold water; remove beards.

2 Heat oil in wok or large frying pan; stir-fry brown onion, garlic, lemon grass and chopped chilli until onion softens and mixture is fragrant.

3 Add wine, juice and sauce; bring to a boil. Add mussels, reduce heat; simmer, covered, about 5 minutes or until mussels open (discard any that do not).

4 Meanwhile, shred half of the basil finely. Add shredded basil and coconut milk to wok; stir-fry until heated through. Place mussel mixture in large serving bowl; sprinkle with sliced chilli, green onion and remaining basil.

SERVES 4
per serving 6.7g carbohydrate; 12.1g fat; 874kJ (209 cal); 8.2g protein

salmon steaks with fennel salad

PREPARATION TIME 20 MINUTES   COOKING TIME 5 MINUTES

2 tablespoons red wine vinegar

1 tablespoon olive oil

2 teaspoons sugar

2 teaspoons dijon mustard

1 tablespoon finely chopped fresh chives

1 tablespoon finely chopped fresh dill

4 x 200g salmon steaks

200g baby spinach leaves

2 medium apples (300g), sliced thinly

2 baby fennel (260g), trimmed, sliced thinly

1 lebanese cucumber (170g), seeded,

   sliced thinly

½ cup coarsely chopped fresh chives, extra

¼ cup coarsely chopped fresh dill, extra

1 Place vinegar, oil, sugar and mustard in screw-top jar; shake well.

2 Place 1 tablespoon of the dressing with chives, dill and fish in large bowl; toss to coat fish in mixture. Cook fish in heated oiled large frying pan about 5 minutes each side or until fish is cooked as desired.

3 Place spinach, apple, fennel, cucumber, extra chives and extra dill in large bowl with remaining dressing; toss gently to combine. Serve fish with salad.

SERVES 4
per serving 10.7g carbohydrate; 19g fat; 1584kJ (379 cal); 41.1g protein

beef stroganoff with spinach

PREPARATION TIME 15 MINUTES   COOKING TIME 20 MINUTES

2 tablespoons vegetable oil

600g beef rump steak, sliced thinly

1 medium brown onion (150g), sliced thinly

3 cloves garlic, crushed

1 teaspoon sweet paprika

400g swiss brown mushrooms, sliced thickly

300g baby spinach leaves

2 tablespoons dry red wine

1 tablespoon lemon juice

2 tablespoons tomato paste

1¼ cups (300g) sour cream

1 tablespoon coarsely chopped fresh dill

1 tablespoon olive oil

1 teaspoon dried chilli flakes

1   Heat half of the vegetable oil in large frying pan; cook beef, in batches, until browned lightly.

2   Heat remaining vegetable oil in same pan; cook onion and two-thirds of the garlic, stirring, until onion softens. Add paprika and mushrooms; cook, stirring, until mushrooms are just tender.

3   Meanwhile, boil, steam or microwave spinach until just wilted; drain.

4   Return beef to pan with wine and juice; bring to a boil. Reduce heat; simmer, covered, about 5 minutes or until beef is tender. Add paste, sour cream and dill; cook, stirring, until heated through.

5   Meanwhile, heat olive oil in medium frying pan; cook chilli and remaining garlic, stirring, until fragrant. Remove from heat; stir in the spinach.

6   Serve beef stroganoff with spinach.

SERVES 4
per serving 7.6g carbohydrate; 51.9g fat; 2771kJ (663 cal); 40.6g protein

filet mignon with mushroom sauce and baby carrots

PREPARATION TIME 15 MINUTES   COOKING TIME 15 MINUTES

4 bacon rashers (140g)

4 x 200g beef eye fillet steaks

30g butter

2 tablespoons olive oil

200g baby carrots

2 medium white onions (300g),

    chopped finely

250g button mushrooms, sliced thinly

1 tablespoon cornflour

2 cups (500ml) beef stock

1 teaspoon fresh oregano leaves

30g butter, melted

1   Cut rind from bacon using scissors or sharp knife. Wrap one bacon rasher around each piece steak; secure bacon with metal skewer or toothpick.

2   Heat butter and oil in heavy-base frying pan; cook steaks over high heat about 2 minutes or until steaks are browned underneath. Turn steaks; cook over high heat until browned on other side. Reduce heat; cook until steaks are cooked as desired. Remove steaks from pan; cover to keep warm.

3   Meanwhile, boil, steam or microwave carrots until just tender; drain.

4   Add onion to remaining butter mixture in pan; stir over medium heat until onion is soft. Add mushrooms; stir over medium heat about 2 minutes or until mushrooms are just soft. Blend cornflour with a tablespoon of the stock; stir in remaining stock and herbs. Add to pan; stir constantly over high heat until sauce boils and thickens. Place steaks on serving plates; remove skewers. Pour over sauce; serve immediately with carrots.

SERVES 4
per serving 9.6g carbohydrate; 32g fat; 2282kJ (546 cal); 55.6g protein

greek-style beef with tzatziki and rocket salad

PREPARATION TIME 25 MINUTES (PLUS REFRIGERATION TIME)   COOKING TIME 10 MINUTES

¼ cup (60ml) lemon juice

¼ cup (60ml) olive oil

⅓ cup finely chopped
   fresh oregano

2 cloves garlic, crushed

2 tablespoons dry white wine

4 x 350g beef T-bone steaks

TZATZIKI

200g yogurt

1 clove garlic, crushed

2 teaspoons lemon juice

1 medium lebanese cucumber
   (130g), chopped finely

½ teaspoon ground cumin

1 tablespoon finely chopped
   fresh mint

GARLIC ROCKET SALAD

1 tablespoon dry white wine

1 tablespoon lemon juice

2 teaspoons olive oil

2 cloves garlic, crushed

250g rocket leaves, torn

100g baby spinach leaves

1   Combine juice, oil, oregano, garlic, wine and beef in large bowl. Cover; refrigerate 3 hours or overnight.

2   Make tzatziki. Make garlic rocket salad.

3   Drain beef; discard marinade. Cook beef on heated oiled grill plate (or grill or barbecue) until browned both sides and cooked as desired. Serve with tzatziki and salad.

TZATZIKI   Combine ingredients in small bowl.

GARLIC ROCKET SALAD   Place wine, juice, oil and garlic in screw-top jar; shake well. Place rocket, spinach and dressing in large bowl; toss gently to combine.

SERVES 4
per serving 5.7g carbohydrate; 35.4g fat; 2132kJ (510 cal); 54.3g protein

beef, red wine and chilli casserole with mesclun

PREPARATION TIME 15 MINUTES   COOKING TIME 1 HOUR 45 MINUTES

2 teaspoons butter

1.5kg lean beef chuck steak,
    cut into 3cm pieces

2 cloves garlic, crushed

3 fresh small red thai chillies,
    seeded, sliced thinly

2 teaspoons dijon mustard

1 large brown onion (200g),
    sliced thickly

2 medium tomatoes (380g),
    chopped coarsely

410g can tomato puree

¾ cup (180ml) dry red wine

½ cup (125ml) beef stock

½ cup (125ml) water

150g mesclun

2 tablespoons coarsely chopped
    fresh flat-leaf parsley

TARRAGON DRESSING

⅓ cup (80ml) olive oil

2 tablespoons tarragon vinegar

1 teaspoon wholegrain mustard

1 clove garlic, crushed

¼ teaspoon sugar

1   Melt butter in large saucepan; cook beef, in batches, until browned all over. Cook garlic, chilli, mustard and onion in same pan, stirring, until onion softens. Return beef to pan with tomato; cook, stirring, 2 minutes.

2   Add puree, wine, stock and the water to pan; bring to a boil. Reduce heat; simmer, covered, about 1 hour 30 minutes or until beef is tender, stirring occasionally.

3   Make tarragon dressing.

4   Just before serving, combine mesclun and dressing in large bowl. Stir parsley into beef casserole. Serve beef casserole with salad.

TARRAGON DRESSING Place ingredients in screw-top jar; shake well.

SERVES 4
per serving 10.3g carbohydrate; 25.4g fat; 2617kJ (626 cal); 80.7g protein

new-york steaks in herbed mushroom sauce

PREPARATION TIME 20 MINUTES (PLUS REFRIGERATION TIME)   COOKING TIME 30 MINUTES

4 x 250g boneless sirloin steaks
   (new york cut)
⅔ cup (160ml) dry red wine
1 tablespoon horseradish cream
2 teaspoons finely chopped fresh
   lemon thyme
1 tablespoon olive oil
1 tablespoon brown sugar
30g butter
1 large white onion (200g), sliced thinly
1 clove garlic, crushed
500g mushrooms, sliced thickly
¼ cup (60ml) beef stock
1 tablespoon coarsely chopped fresh
   flat-leaf parsley

1 Place beef in large shallow dish with ½ cup of the wine, 2 teaspoons of the horseradish cream, 1 teaspoon of the thyme, and all of the oil and sugar. Cover; refrigerate 3 hours or overnight.

2 Cook beef on heated oiled grill plate (or grill or barbecue) until browned both sides and cooked as desired. Meanwhile, melt butter in large pan on barbecue; cook onion and garlic, stirring, until onion softened. Add mushrooms; cook, stirring, until soft. Add remaining horseradish, remaining thyme and remaining wine with stock; bring to a boil. Reduce heat; simmer, uncovered, about 5 minutes or until most of the liquid has evaporated. Stir in parsley. Serve beef with herbed mushroom sauce.

SERVES 4

per serving 9.2g carbohydrate; 34.5g fat; 2521kJ (603 cal); 57.8g protein

beef and vegetable teppenyaki

PREPARATION TIME 10 MINUTES (PLUS REFRIGERATION TIME)   COOKING TIME 15 MINUTES

4 x 150g beef fillet steaks
¼ cup (60ml) japanese dark soy sauce
2 tablespoons mirin
2 tablespoons sake
1cm piece fresh ginger (5g), grated
2 teaspoons brown sugar
1 clove garlic, crushed
250g snow peas, trimmed
250g asparagus, trimmed

1 Place beef in large bowl with combined soy, mirin, sake, ginger, sugar and garlic. Cover; refrigerate 3 hours or overnight.

2 Boil, steam or microwave snow peas and asparagus, separately, until just tender; drain. Drain beef over medium bowl; place vegetables in bowl with marinade. Cook beef on heated oiled grill plate (or grill or barbecue) until browned both sides and cooked as desired.

3 Meanwhile, drain vegetables; discard marinade. Cook vegetables on same grill plate, until browned all over.

SERVES 4
per serving 6.0g carbohydrate; 9.2g fat; 1091kJ (261 cal); 35.7g protein

beef with spiced sea salt crust and pepper-cream vegetables

PREPARATION TIME 35 MINUTES (PLUS REFRIGERATION TIME)   COOKING TIME 1 HOUR 20 MINUTES

2 tablespoons dried juniper berries, crushed

2 tablespoons finely grated lemon rind

1 tablespoon sea salt flakes

2 teaspoons ground cumin

3 tablespoons cracked black pepper

1.5kg beef sirloin roast

1 tablespoon olive oil

1 medium brown onion (150g), sliced thinly

2 medium carrots (240g), sliced thickly

3 baby eggplants (180g), sliced thickly

250g mushrooms, halved

2 medium zucchini (240g), sliced thickly

1 medium red capsicum (200g), sliced thickly

1 clove garlic, crushed

½ cup (125ml) vegetable stock

½ cup (125ml) cream

1 Combine berries, rind, salt, cumin and 2 tablespoons of the pepper in small bowl; press onto beef. Cover; refrigerate 3 hours or overnight.

2 Place beef on roasting rack or basket, or in disposable baking dish. Cook in covered barbecue, using indirect heat, following manufacturer's instructions, about 1 hour 20 minutes or until browned all over and cooked as desired. Remove from heat, cover; stand 10 minutes before slicing.

3 Meanwhile, heat oil in wok or large saucepan; stir-fry vegetables and garlic, in batches, until just tender. Cover to keep warm.

4 Combine stock, cream and remaining pepper in same wok; stir until sauce thickens slightly.

5 Serve beef with vegetables and sauce.

SERVES 4
per serving 10.6g carbohydrate; 43.2g fat; 3164kJ (757 cal); 81.8g protein

moroccan minted beef

PREPARATION TIME 15 MINUTES   COOKING TIME 20 MINUTES

1 tablespoon vegetable oil

1 large brown onion (200g), sliced thinly

2 teaspoons ground cumin

1 teaspoon finely grated lemon rind

425g can tomatoes

200g green beans, trimmed

750g beef strips

2 tablespoons toasted slivered almonds

2 teaspoons finely shredded fresh mint

1 Heat oil in medium frying pan; cook onion, stirring, until softened. Add cumin and rind; cook, stirring, until fragrant. Stir in undrained tomatoes; bring to a boil. Reduce heat; simmer, stirring occasionally, about 5 minutes or until mixture thickens slightly.

2 Meanwhile, boil, steam or microwave beans until just tender; drain. Cover to keep warm.

3 Cook beef, in batches, in large heated oiled frying pan until browned all over and tender; stir in tomato mixture, nuts and mint. Serve beef mixture with beans.

SERVES 4
per serving 7.5g carbohydrate; 19.1g fat; 1559kJ (373 cal); 43g protein

lamb cutlets and black-eyed bean salad

PREPARATION TIME 20 MINUTES (PLUS REFRIGERATION TIME)   COOKING TIME 35 MINUTES

1½ cups (300g) dried black-eyed beans

12 french-trimmed lamb cutlets (900g)

2 teaspoons ground coriander

½ teaspoon cayenne pepper

2 teaspoons smoked paprika

1 tablespoon vegetable oil

10 baby vine-ripened truss tomatoes (200g), quartered

2 trimmed celery stalks (200g), sliced thinly

1 small red mignonette lettuce, trimmed

2 tablespoons lemon juice

PARSLEY DRESSING

2 tablespoons coarsely chopped fresh flat-leaf parsley

1 tablespoon wholegrain mustard

1 clove garlic, crushed

¼ cup (60ml) extra virgin olive oil

¼ cup (60ml) white wine vinegar

1 Place beans in large bowl, cover with water; soak overnight. Rinse under cold water; drain.

2 Combine lamb, coriander, pepper, paprika and oil in large bowl. Cover; refrigerate 3 hours or overnight.

3 Cook beans in medium saucepan of boiling water, uncovered, about 30 minutes or until just tender.

4 Meanwhile, cook lamb, in batches, on heated oiled grill plate (or grill or barbecue) until browned both sides and cooked as desired.

5 Make parsley dressing. Place drained beans in large bowl with tomato, celery and dressing; toss gently to combine.

6 Divide lettuce leaves among serving plates; top with bean salad and lamb, drizzle with juice.

PARSLEY DRESSING Place ingredients in screw-top jar; shake well.

SERVES 4
per serving 10.9g carbohydrate; 37.9g fat; 2069kJ (495 cal); 28.6g protein

lamb cutlets and black-eyed bean salad

spicy citrus char-grilled beef salad

spicy citrus char-grilled beef salad

PREPARATION TIME 25 MINUTES (PLUS REFRIGERATION TIME)   COOKING TIME 10 MINUTES

You need two oranges and three limes for this recipe.

800g beef rump steak

2 garlic cloves, crushed

⅓ cup (80ml) orange juice

¼ cup (60ml) lime juice

1 tablespoon soy sauce

1 teaspoon dried chilli flakes

1 tablespoon white wine vinegar

250g asparagus, trimmed

1 medium orange (240g)

150g mesclun

250g witlof, chopped coarsely

½ cup coarsely chopped fresh basil

3 shallots (75g), sliced thinly

250g cherry tomatoes, halved

ORANGE DRESSING

⅓ cup (80ml) lime juice

1 tablespoon orange juice

2 teaspoons olive oil

1   Place beef in large bowl with garlic, juices, sauce, chilli and vinegar; toss to coat beef in mixture. Cover; refrigerate 3 hours or overnight.

2   Cook beef on heated oiled grill plate (or grill or barbecue) until browned both sides and cooked as desired. Cover; stand 10 minutes before slicing thinly.

3   Meanwhile, cook asparagus on heated oiled grill plate (or grill or barbecue) until browned lightly and just tender; cut each spear into thirds.

4   Make orange dressing.

5   Segment orange over large bowl. Add beef, asparagus, dressing and remaining ingredients; toss gently to combine.

ORANGE DRESSING   Place ingredients in screw-top jar; shake well.

SERVES 4
per serving 10.3g carbohydrate; 13g fat; 1488kJ (356 cal); 46.8g protein

ginger beef stir-fry

PREPARATION TIME 20 MINUTES   COOKING TIME 10 MINUTES

6cm piece fresh ginger (30g)

2 tablespoons peanut oil

600g beef rump steak, sliced thinly

2 cloves garlic, crushed

120g snake beans, cut into 5cm lengths

8 green onions, sliced thinly

2 teaspoons grated palm sugar

2 teaspoons oyster sauce

1 tablespoon fish sauce

1 tablespoon soy sauce

½ cup loosely packed fresh thai basil leaves

1 Slice peeled ginger thinly; stack slices, then slice again into thin strips.

2 Heat half of the oil in wok; stir-fry beef, in batches, until browned all over.

3 Heat remaining oil in wok; stir-fry ginger and garlic until fragrant. Add beans; stir-fry until just tender.

4 Return beef to wok with onion, sugar and sauces; stir-fry until sugar dissolves and beef is cooked as desired. Remove from heat; toss basil through stir-fry.

SERVES 4
per serving 4.7g carbohydrate; 19.4g fat; 1396kJ (334 cal); 35.4g protein

minted veal with baby squash

PREPARATION TIME 15 MINUTES   COOKING TIME 1 HOUR

2 tablespoons olive oil

12 veal loin chops (1.5kg)

2 medium brown onions (300g), sliced thickly

3 cloves garlic, crushed

2 teaspoons ground turmeric

4 cardamom pods, bruised

1 teaspoon ground nutmeg

1 teaspoon finely grated lemon rind

1 tablespoon tomato paste

2 tablespoons coarsely chopped fresh mint

2 cups (500ml) beef stock

200g baby patty-pan squash, halved

1 tablespoon cornflour

2 tablespoons water

1 Heat oil in large saucepan; cook veal, in batches, until browned all over.

2 Cook onion, garlic and spices in same pan; stirring, until onion softens. Add rind, paste, mint, stock and veal, reduce heat; simmer, covered, about 30 minutes or until veal is tender.

3 Add squash; simmer, uncovered, about 10 minutes or until squash is tender. Add blended cornflour and water; stir over heat until mixture boils and thickens.

SERVES 4
per serving 9.4g carbohydrate; 17g fat; 2082kJ (498 cal); 76g protein

fillet steak, cheese and capsicum stacks

PREPARATION TIME 20 MINUTES   COOKING TIME 15 MINUTES

1 medium red capsicum (200g)

4 beef fillet steaks (500g)

4 thick slices gouda cheese (125g)

50g baby spinach leaves

400g sugar snap peas

1 Quarter capsicum; remove seeds and membranes. Roast capsicum under grill or in very hot oven, skin-side up, until skin blisters and blackens. Cover with plastic or paper for 5 minutes. Peel away skin.

2 Preheat oven to hot.

3 Cut steaks in half horizontally; divide cheese, spinach and capsicum among four steak halves, cover with remaining steak halves. Tie stacks with kitchen string; cook, uncovered, in lightly oiled large non-stick frying pan until browned both sides. Transfer to oven tray; cook, uncovered, in hot oven about 10 minutes or until cooked as desired.

4 Meanwhile, boil, steam or microwave peas until just tender; drain.

5 Serve stacks with peas.

SERVES 4
per serving 6.3g carbohydrate; 17.3g fat; 1396kJ (334 cal); 38.4g protein

T-bones with blue-cheese butter and pear salad

PREPARATION TIME 15 MINUTES   COOKING TIME 10 MINUTES

4 x 400g beef T-bone steaks

2 tablespoons olive oil

50g soft blue cheese

50g butter, softened

2 green onions, chopped finely

1 tablespoon wholegrain mustard

1 teaspoon honey

1 tablespoon red wine vinegar

¼ cup (60ml) olive oil, extra

100g mesclun

1 pear (300g), sliced thinly

½ cup (60g) toasted pecans

1 Brush beef with oil; cook on heated oiled grill plate (or grill or barbecue) until browned both sides and cooked as desired.

2 Meanwhile, combine cheese, butter and onion in small bowl. Place mustard, honey, vinegar and extra oil in screw-top jar; shake well.

3 Place mesclun, pear and dressing in medium bowl; toss gently to combine. Sprinkle with nuts.

4 Spread blue-cheese butter on hot beef; serve with salad.

SERVES 4
per serving 10g carbohydrate; 63.1g fat; 3490kJ (835 cal); 59g protein

braised vinegared beef with chinese greens

PREPARATION TIME 15 MINUTES (PLUS REFRIGERATION TIME)   COOKING TIME 20 MINUTES

800g beef rump steak, sliced thinly

1 tablespoon lime juice

4cm piece fresh ginger (20g), grated

2 cloves garlic, crushed

**1 tablespoon finely shredded
   fresh basil**

1 teaspoon sugar

1 tablespoon vegetable oil

2 teaspoons sesame oil

**1 medium white onion (150g),
   sliced thinly**

**1 small chinese cabbage (400g),
   shredded finely**

400g bok choy, shredded coarsely

350g choy sum, shredded coarsely

2 tablespoons balsamic vinegar

250g baby spinach leaves

150g snow peas, trimmed

1 tablespoon toasted sesame seeds

1 Combine beef in large bowl with juice, ginger, garlic, basil and sugar. Cover; refrigerate 3 hours or overnight.

2 Drain beef; discard marinade. Heat half of the combined oils in wok; stir-fry onion until soft. Add beef, in batches, stir-fry until browned and cooked as desired. Transfer beef mixture to large bowl. Add cabbage, bok choy, choy sum, half of the vinegar and remaining oils to wok; stir-fry until greens just wilt, add to bowl with beef. Add spinach, snow peas and remaining vinegar to wok; stir-fry until spinach just wilts. Return beef and vegetables to wok; stir-fry until heated through, sprinkle with sesame seeds.

SERVES 4
per serving 9.7g carbohydrate; 22.7g fat; 1881kJ (450 cal); 51.4g protein

beef skewers on lettuce cups

PREPARATION TIME 45 MINUTES (PLUS REFRIGERATION TIME)   COOKING TIME 10 MINUTES

500g beef rump steak, sliced thinly

½ telegraph cucumber (200g), peeled,
  halved, then quartered lengthways

6 green onions, cut into 5cm lengths, then
  into thin strips

1 cup (80g) bean sprouts

1 large carrot (180g), cut into 5cm lengths,
  then into thin strips

8 lettuce leaves

MARINADE

2 tablespoons finely chopped fresh
  lemon grass

1 medium white onion (150g), sliced thinly

2 cloves garlic, crushed

2 teaspoons sugar

2 fresh small red thai chillies, seeded,
  chopped finely

2 teaspoons sesame oil

2 teaspoons sesame seeds

SAUCE

2 cloves garlic, chopped finely

1 fresh small red thai chilli, seeded,
  chopped finely

1 tablespoon sugar

2 tablespoons lime juice

¼ cup (60ml) rice vinegar

¼ cup (60ml) fish sauce

¼ cup (60ml) water

1 Make marinade.

2 Combine beef and marinade in large bowl. Cover; refrigerate
3 hours or overnight.

3 Thread beef onto 16 skewers. Cook beef on heated oiled grill
plate (or grill or barbecue) until browned and cooked as desired.

4 Meanwhile, make sauce.

5 Divide cucumber, onion, sprouts and carrot among lettuce leaves.
Top with beef; drizzle with sauce.

MARINADE Combine ingredients in small bowl.

SAUCE Blend or process ingredients until combined.

SERVES 4
per serving 10.9g carbohydrate; 11.8g fat; 1179kJ (282 cal);
32.3g protein
tip If using bamboo skewers, soak in water for at least 1 hour before
using to prevent them splintering and scorching.

veal steaks with lemon and thyme sauce

PREPARATION TIME 10 MINUTES (PLUS REFRIGERATION TIME)   COOKING TIME 20 MINUTES

60g butter

2 tablespoons sweet chilli sauce

2 teaspoons finely grated lemon rind

⅓ cup (80ml) lemon juice

1 tablespoon finely chopped
fresh thyme

8 x 125g veal leg steaks

500g choy sum

1   Melt butter in small pan; cook sauce, rind and juice, stirring, over low heat, without boiling, until sauce thickens slightly. Stir in thyme; cool 15 minutes. Cover; refrigerate until just set.

2   Spread half of the sauce over both sides of steaks; cook steaks on heated oiled grill plate (or grill or barbecue) until browned both sides and cooked as desired.

3   Meanwhile, boil, steam or microwave choy sum until just wilted; drain.

4   Just before serving, spread steaks with remaining sauce; serve with choy sum.

SERVES 4
per serving 2.7g carbohydrate; 20.3g fat; 1781kJ (426 cal); 57.7g protein

standing rib roast provençal with pine nut cauliflower

PREPARATION TIME 15 MINUTES (PLUS REFRIGERATION TIME)   COOKING TIME 1 HOUR 25 MINUTES

1.5kg standing beef rib roast

2 cups (500ml) dry red wine

⅓ cup (80ml) olive oil

3 cloves garlic, sliced thinly

2 teaspoons finely chopped
fresh thyme

2 teaspoons finely chopped
fresh rosemary

3 medium white onions (450g),
quartered

4 bay leaves

1 small cauliflower (1kg)

2 cloves garlic, crushed

2 tablespoons pine nuts

2 teaspoons dried chilli flakes

2 tablespoons coarsely chopped
fresh flat-leaf parsley

1   Place beef in large shallow dish with combined wine, 2 tablespoons of the oil, sliced garlic, thyme, rosemary, onion and bay leaves. Cover; refrigerate 3 hours or overnight.

2   Drain beef and onion over small saucepan; reserve marinade. Bring marinade to a boil. Reduce heat; simmer, uncovered, until it reduces by half.

3   Cook beef on heated oiled barbecue until browned all over. Place beef and onion on roasting rack or basket, or in disposable baking dish. Cook in covered barbecue, using indirect heat, following manufacturer's instructions, and brushing occasionally with marinade, about 1 hour or until cooked as desired.

4   Meanwhile, separate cauliflower into florets. Boil, steam or microwave until almost tender; drain. Pat dry with absorbent paper.

5   Heat remaining oil in medium frying pan; cook crushed garlic, pine nuts and chilli, stirring, over low heat until fragrant. Add cauliflower; cook, stirring, until heated through. Remove from heat; stir in parsley.

6   Serve beef with cauliflower mixture.

SERVES 4
per serving 11.9g carbohydrate; 43.5g fat; 3440kJ (823 cal); 76.2g protein

veal with anchovy butter and mixed beans

PREPARATION TIME 10 MINUTES COOKING TIME 15 MINUTES

80g butter, softened

4 drained anchovy fillets, chopped finely

2 teaspoons lemon juice

1 tablespoon coarsely chopped fresh dill

8 x 150g veal cutlets

300g green beans, trimmed

300g yellow string beans, trimmed

1 Combine butter, anchovies, juice and dill in small bowl.

2 Cook veal, in batches, on heated oiled grill plate (or grill or barbecue) until browned both sides and cooked as desired.

3 Meanwhile, boil, steam or microwave beans until just tender; drain.

4 Serve veal with beans; top with anchovy butter.

SERVES 4
per serving 4.1g carbohydrate; 24.4g fat; 1664kJ (398 cal); 40.8g protein
tip Chicken, fish, beef, lamb and pork are all suitable substitutes for the veal.

stir-fried beef, bok choy and gai larn

PREPARATION TIME 10 MINUTES   COOKING TIME 25 MINUTES

Beef strips can be prepared from blade, fillet, rib-eye, round, rump, sirloin or topside steak.

2 tablespoons peanut oil

500g beef strips

2 cloves garlic, crushed

2cm piece fresh ginger (10g), grated

**1 tablespoon finely chopped fresh
    lemon grass**

**2 fresh small red thai chillies, seeded,
    sliced thinly**

1kg baby bok choy, chopped coarsely

500g gai larn, chopped coarsely

4 green onions, sliced thinly

2 tablespoons kecap manis

1 tablespoon fish sauce

¼ cup (60ml) sweet chilli sauce

¼ cup (60ml) lime juice

¼ cup coarsely chopped fresh mint

¼ cup coarsely chopped fresh coriander

1 Heat half of the oil in wok or large frying pan; stir-fry beef, in batches, until browned all over.

2 Heat remaining oil in same wok; stir-fry garlic, ginger, lemon grass and chilli until fragrant. Add bok choy and gai larn; stir-fry until vegetables just wilt. Return beef to wok with onion, sauces and juice; stir-fry until heated through. Remove from heat; stir in herbs.

SERVES 4
per serving 8.6g carbohydrate; 17.7g fat; 1384kJ (331 cal); 33.9g protein

corned beef with redcurrant glaze and red cabbage

PREPARATION TIME 15 MINUTES   COOKING TIME 2 HOURS

1.5kg piece beef corned silverside

2 bay leaves

¼ cup (60ml) malt vinegar

8 black peppercorns

8 cloves

1 medium brown onion (150g),
    chopped coarsely

1 trimmed celery stalk (150g),
    chopped coarsely

½ cup (120g) redcurrant jelly

2 tablespoons port

1 tablespoon fresh rosemary leaves

1½ cups (375ml) chicken stock

1 tablespoon olive oil

4½ cups (360g) coarsely shredded
    red cabbage

1   Place beef, bay leaves, vinegar, peppercorns, cloves, onion and celery in large saucepan, cover with cold water; bring to a boil. Reduce heat; simmer, uncovered, 1 hour. Remove beef from cooking liquid. Discard cooking liquid.

2   Preheat oven to hot.

3   Combine jelly, port and rosemary in small bowl. Place beef in large flameproof baking dish; brush beef with half of the glaze. Bake, uncovered, in hot oven about 30 minutes or until browned all over and tender, brushing beef occasionally with remaining glaze. Remove beef from dish.

4   Place stock into same dish; bring to a boil. Reduce heat; simmer, uncovered, stirring, until sauce thickens slightly.

5   Meanwhile, heat oil in large frying pan; cook cabbage, stirring, 2 minutes.

6   Serve beef with sauce and cabbage.

SERVES 4
per serving 11.9g carbohydrate; 22.2g fat; 2525kJ (604 cal); 86.1g protein

venetian calves liver and onions

PREPARATION TIME 10 MINUTES COOKING TIME 25 MINUTES

A traditional Venetian dish, the classic fegato alla veneziana is found on the menus of Italian restaurants around the world yet is easy enough to make at home. The secret to its success is that the calves liver should be sliced into paper-thin scallops then quickly seared — overcooking will toughen its delicate texture.

40g butter

2 tablespoons olive oil

3 medium brown onions (450g),
    sliced thinly

2 teaspoons cornflour

¾ cup (180ml) beef stock

2 teaspoons dijon mustard

500g gai larn, chopped coarsely

500g calves liver, sliced thinly

½ teaspoon balsamic vinegar

1   Heat butter and half of the oil in large frying pan; cook onion, stirring, until onion softens. Stir in blended cornflour, stock and mustard; cook, stirring, until sauce boils and thickens.

2   Boil, steam or microwave gai larn until just tender; drain.

3   Heat remaining oil in large frying pan; cook liver quickly over high heat until browned both sides and cooked as desired.

4   Stir vinegar into sauce just before serving with liver and gai larn.

SERVES 4
per serving 12g carbohydrate; 43.3g fat; 2412kJ (577 cal); 35.8g protein

beef and mushrooms in red wine sauce

PREPARATION TIME 20 MINUTES   COOKING TIME 2 HOURS

4 bacon rashers (280g), rind
   removed, sliced thinly
800g gravy beef, diced into
   2cm pieces
1 cup (250ml) dry red wine
2 tablespoons tomato paste
1½ cups (375ml) beef stock
1 cup (250ml) water
2 cloves garlic, crushed
1 teaspoon fresh thyme leaves
1 tablespoon vegetable oil
16 shallots (400g)
400g button mushrooms
500g broccoli, cut into florets
½ cup coarsely chopped fresh
   flat-leaf parsley

1 Cook bacon in large heavy-base saucepan, stirring, until browned; drain on absorbent paper. Cook beef, in batches, in same pan, stirring until browned.

2 Return bacon and beef to pan with wine, paste, stock, the water, garlic and thyme; bring to a boil. Reduce heat, simmer, covered, 1½ hours or until beef is tender.

3 Meanwhile, heat oil in large frying pan; cook shallots, stirring occasionally, until browned lightly. Add mushrooms; cook, stirring, about 10 minutes or until mushrooms softened.

4 Using slotted spoon, remove beef from pan; cover to keep warm. Bring pan mixture sauce to a boil. Reduce heat; simmer, uncovered, until sauce reduces by half.

5 Meanwhile, boil, steam or microwave broccoli until tender; drain.

6 Return beef to pan with shallot mixture; stir gently until heated through. Remove from heat; stir in parsley. Serve beef with broccoli.

SERVES 4
per serving 8.7g carbohydrate; 30.8g fat; 2617kJ (626 cal); 67.7g protein

veal parmigiana

PREPARATION TIME 15 MINUTES   COOKING TIME 25 MINUTES

2 teaspoons olive oil

1 medium white onion (150g),
    chopped finely

2 cloves garlic, crushed

400g can tomatoes

¼ cup (60ml) tomato paste

1 tablespoon balsamic vinegar

1 teaspoon sugar

1 tablespoon finely shredded
    fresh basil

2 small eggplants (460g)

8 x 240g veal leg steaks

1½ cups (150g) grated pizza cheese

1   Heat oil in medium frying pan; cook onion and garlic, stirring, until onion softens. Add undrained crushed tomatoes, paste, vinegar and sugar; bring to a boil. Reduce heat; simmer, uncovered, about 10 minutes or until sauce thickens. Stir in basil.

2   Meanwhile, cut unpeeled eggplants into 1cm slices lengthways; cook on heated oiled grill plate (or grill or barbecue) until browned both sides. Cook veal on same heated oiled grill plate until browned one side. Turn veal, top with sauce, eggplant and cheese; cook until cheese is melted and veal is cooked as desired.

SERVES 4
per serving 10.4g carbohydrate; 11.8g fat; 1710kJ (409 cal); 64.3g protein

asian roast beef

PREPARATION TIME 15 MINUTES   COOKING TIME 55 MINUTES

Gai larn is also commonly known as gai lum or chinese broccoli; it is available in most supermarkets and greengrocers.

800g boneless beef rib roast

2 tablespoons kecap manis

1 tablespoon sesame seeds

2 cloves garlic, crushed

2 teaspoons sesame oil

1cm piece fresh ginger (5g), grated

1 small red capsicum (150g),
    sliced thinly

600g gai larn, chopped coarsely

⅓ cup (80ml) oyster sauce

2 tablespoons water

1 tablespoon lime juice

1   Preheat oven to moderately hot.

2   Cook beef, uncovered, in heated oiled wok or large frying pan about 10 minutes or until browned. Place beef on oiled wire rack in baking dish; brush with combined kecap manis, sesame seeds and half of the garlic. Roast beef, uncovered, in moderately hot oven about 45 minutes or until cooked as desired. Cover; stand 5 minutes, slice thickly.

3   Meanwhile, heat oil in same wok or frying pan; stir-fry ginger and remaining garlic until fragrant. Add remaining ingredients; stir-fry until gai larn is just wilted. Serve beef on gai larn mixture, drizzled with sauce from wok.

SERVES 4
per serving 11.6g carbohydrate; 10.1g fat; 1283kJ (307 cal); 41.5g protein

mustard T-bone with chilli garlic mushrooms

PREPARATION TIME 10 MINUTES   COOKING TIME 20 MINUTES

2 tablespoons olive oil

20g butter

3 cloves garlic, crushed

1 fresh small red thai chilli,
    chopped finely

500g button mushrooms

1 tablespoon lemon juice

½ teaspoon cracked black pepper

4 beef T-bone steaks (1kg)

2 tablespoons dijon mustard

¼ cup coarsely chopped fresh
    flat-leaf parsley

1 tablespoon coarsely chopped
    fresh rosemary

1   Heat oil and butter in large saucepan; cook garlic, chilli and mushrooms, stirring, about 5 minutes or until mushrooms are tender. Stir in lemon juice and pepper.

2   Meanwhile, brush beef all over with mustard; cook on heated oiled grill plate (or grill or barbecue), until browned and cooked as desired.

3   Serve beef and mushrooms sprinkled with combined herbs.

SERVES 4
per serving 2.7g carbohydrate; 24.1g fat; 1714kJ (410 cal); 45.9g protein

veal cutlets with oregano and vegetables

PREPARATION TIME 30 MINUTES   COOKING TIME 1 HOUR 15 MINUTES

12 small veal cutlets (1kg)

2 tablespoons plain flour

2 tablespoons vegetable oil

1½ cups (375ml) chicken stock

⅓ cup (80ml) dry white wine

10 spring onions, trimmed

2 teaspoons finely chopped
    fresh oregano

2 bay leaves

8 baby carrots

80g baby green beans, halved

100g fresh baby corn

1 tablespoon finely chopped fresh
    flat-leaf parsley

1   Toss veal in flour; shake away excess flour. Reserve excess flour mixture.

2   Heat oil in large saucepan; cook veal, in batches, until browned both sides.

3   Stir reserved flour into pan; stir over heat until mixture bubbles. Remove from heat; gradually stir in stock and wine. Stir over heat until sauce boils and thickens.

4   Return veal to pan. Stir in onion, oregano and bay leaves. Reduce heat; simmer, covered, 20 minutes, stirring occasionally.

5   Stir in carrots, beans and corn; simmer, covered, about 15 minutes or until veal and vegetables are tender. Discard bay leaves; stir in parsley.

SERVES 4
per serving 11.9g carbohydrate; 17g fat; 1705kJ (408 cal); 48.2g protein

veal cutlets with black olive anchovy butter

PREPARATION TIME 25 MINUTES (PLUS REFRIGERATION TIME)   COOKING TIME 55 MINUTES

2 cloves garlic, crushed

2 tablespoons olive oil

4 x 180g veal cutlets

2 medium eggplants (600g)

3 cloves garlic, unpeeled

3 green onions, chopped finely

2 tablespoons lemon juice

2 tablespoons yogurt

BLACK OLIVE ANCHOVY BUTTER

¼ cup (30g) seeded black olives

2 drained anchovy fillets

100g butter, softened

1 Place crushed garlic and half of the oil with veal in large bowl; toss to coat all over. Cover; refrigerate 30 minutes.

2 Preheat oven to moderate.

3 Cut eggplant in half lengthways; score flesh, brush with half of the remaining oil. Place eggplant on lightly oiled oven tray with unpeeled garlic cloves; bake, uncovered, in moderate oven about 45 minutes or until eggplant softens. Cover to keep warm; reserve roasted garlic for black olive anchovy butter.

4 Make black olive anchovy butter.

5 Scrape flesh from eggplant; chop coarsely then push through fine strainer into medium bowl. Discard skin.

6 Heat remaining oil in small frying pan; cook onion, stirring, until soft. Remove pan from heat; stir in eggplant, juice and yogurt.

7 Cook veal on heated oiled grill plate (or grill or barbecue) until browned all over and cooked as desired. Divide eggplant mixture among serving plates; top each with veal cutlet then butter.

BLACK OLIVE ANCHOVY BUTTER Remove skin from roasted garlic. Blend or process garlic with remaining ingredients until smooth. Cover; stand at room temperature until ready to use.

SERVES 4
per serving 6.1g carbohydrate; 34.1g fat; 1935kJ (463 cal); 33g protein

vietnamese beef, chicken and tofu soup

PREPARATION TIME 20 MINUTES   COOKING TIME 1 HOUR 5 MINUTES

3 litres (12 cups) water

500g gravy beef

1 star anise

2.5cm piece fresh galangal (15g),
    halved

¼ cup (60ml) soy sauce

2 tablespoons fish sauce

350g chicken breast fillet

1½ cups (120g) bean sprouts

1 cup loosely packed fresh
    coriander leaves

4 green onions, sliced thinly

2 fresh small red thai chillies,
    sliced thinly

⅓ cup (80ml) lime juice

300g firm tofu, cut into 2cm cubes

1   Combine the water, beef, star anise, galangal and sauces in large saucepan; bring to a boil. Reduce heat; simmer, covered, 30 minutes. Uncover; simmer, 20 minutes. Add chicken; simmer, uncovered, 10 minutes.

2   Combine sprouts, coriander, onion, chilli and juice in medium bowl.

3   Remove beef and chicken from pan; reserve broth. Discard fat and sinew from beef; slice thinly. Slice chicken thinly. Return beef and chicken to pan; reheat soup.

4   Divide tofu among serving bowls; ladle hot soup over tofu, sprinkle with sprout mixture. Serve with lime wedges and extra chilli, if desired.

SERVES 4
per serving 3.6g carbohydrate; 18.8g fat; 1409kJ (337 cal); 37.6g protein

steak with redcurrant sauce

PREPARATION TIME 5 MINUTES   COOKING TIME 10 MINUTES

¼ cup (60ml) olive oil

4 x 200g beef scotch fillet steaks

½ cup (125ml) dry red wine

¾ cup (180ml) beef stock

2 tablespoons redcurrant jelly

700g broccoli, cut into florets

½ cup (40g) coarsely grated
   parmesan cheese

1 teaspoon cracked black pepper

1   Heat 1 tablespoon of the oil in large frying pan; cook beef, in batches, until browned both sides and cooked as desired. Cover to keep warm.

2   Combine wine, stock and jelly in same pan; cook, stirring, until mixture boils and thickens slightly.

3   Meanwhile, boil, steam or microwave broccoli until just tender; drain. Place broccoli in large bowl with cheese, pepper and remaining oil; toss gently until cheese melts.

4   Serve beef with redcurrant sauce and cheesy broccoli.

SERVES 4
per serving   9.3g carbohydrate; 29.1g fat; 2211kJ (529 cal); 53g protein
tips   We used scotch fillet steaks for this recipe, however, you could use boneless sirloin or rump, if you prefer. If you don't have redcurrant jelly, cranberry sauce is a good substitute.

veal medallions with olive paste and grilled zucchini salad

PREPARATION TIME 15 MINUTES   COOKING TIME 20 MINUTES (PLUS STANDING TIME)

2 cups firmly packed fresh
   parsley leaves

½ cup (60g) seeded black olives

2 tablespoons drained capers, rinsed

1 tablespoon lemon juice

1 clove garlic, crushed

6 medium zucchini (720g)

⅓ cup (80ml) olive oil

2 tablespoons red wine vinegar

2 tablespoons chopped fresh basil

2 fresh small red thai chillies,
   chopped finely

4 x 200g veal eye fillet medallions

8 slices prosciutto (120g)

1   Blend or process parsley until finely chopped. With motor operating, add olives, capers, juice and garlic; blend until almost smooth.

2   Cut zucchini lengthways into 5mm slices; cook, in batches, on heated oiled grill plate (or grill or barbecue) until tender. Combine hot zucchini with oil, vinegar, basil and chilli in large bowl, cover; stand at room temperature for at least 1 hour before serving.

3   Spread olive mixture around the edge of each medallion; wrap 2 slices prosciutto around each piece to cover olive mixture, secure with toothpicks. Cook veal on same grill plate until browned both sides and cooked as desired. Just before serving, remove toothpicks.

4   Serve veal with zucchini salad.

SERVES 4
per serving   6.1g carbohydrate; 23.5g fat; 1877kJ (449 cal); 52.5g protein
tip   Olive paste can be kept in the refrigerator, covered, for up to 1 week.

steaks with green capsicum salsa

PREPARATION TIME 15 MINUTES   COOKING TIME 10 MINUTES

4 x 200g small beef eye fillet steaks

100g rocket leaves

GREEN CAPSICUM SALSA

2 small green capsicums (300g),
   chopped finely

1 small red onion (100g), chopped finely

1 fresh small red thai chilli, seeded,
   chopped finely

6 green onions, sliced thinly

¼ cup (60ml) lime juice

2 tablespoons finely chopped fresh mint

1   Make green capsicum salsa.

2   Cook beef on heated oiled grill plate (or grill or barbecue) until browned both sides and cooked as desired.

3   Divide rocket among serving plates; top with beef and salsa.

   GREEN CAPSICUM SALSA   Combine ingredients in medium bowl.

   SERVES 4
   per serving 3.9g carbohydrate; 7g fat; 1028kJ (246 cal); 41.3g protein
   tips The salsa can be made several hours ahead and refrigerated, covered. Sirloin, scotch fillet or rump can be substituted for the eye fillet steaks.

lamb with garlic and shiitake mushrooms

PREPARATION TIME 10 MINUTES   COOKING TIME 50 MINUTES

12 cloves garlic, peeled

1 tablespoon sugar

¼ cup (60ml) olive oil

900g lamb eye of loin

400g shiitake mushrooms, halved

40g butter, melted

2 tablespoons coarsely chopped fresh chives

1   Combine garlic, sugar and 2 tablespoons of the oil in disposable baking dish. Cook in covered barbecue, using indirect heat, following manufacturer's instructions, about 15 minutes or until garlic is soft and slightly caramelised. Remove from barbecue; cover to keep warm.

2   Brush lamb with remaining oil; cook, uncovered, on heated oiled barbecue until browned all over and cooked as desired.

3   Meanwhile, combine mushrooms, butter and chives in large bowl. Transfer mushroom mixture to heated oiled barbecue plate; cook until tender. Serve lamb with roasted garlic and mushroom mixture.

   SERVES 4
   per serving 6.1g carbohydrate; 42.1g fat; 2512kJ (601 cal); 50.9g protein

basil and oregano steak with char-grilled vegetables

PREPARATION TIME 20 MINUTES (PLUS REFRIGERATION TIME)   COOKING TIME 30 MINUTES

2 teaspoons finely chopped fresh oregano

¼ cup finely chopped fresh basil

1 tablespoon finely grated lemon rind

2 tablespoons lemon juice

4 drained anchovy fillets, chopped finely

4 x 250g beef sirloin steaks

2 baby fennel bulb (260g), quartered

3 small zucchini (270g), chopped coarsely

1 large red capsicum (350g) sliced thickly

200g portobello mushrooms, sliced thickly

4 baby eggplants (240g), chopped coarsely

2 small red onions (200g), sliced thickly

2 teaspoons olive oil

¼ cup (60ml) lemon juice

2 tablespoons fresh oregano leaves

1   Combine chopped oregano, basil, rind, juice and anchovies in large bowl; add steaks, toss to coat steaks. Cover; refrigerate 15 minutes.

2   Meanwhile, cook combined fennel, zucchini, capsicum, mushrooms, eggplant, onion and oil, in batches, on heated lightly oiled grill plate (or grill or barbecue) until browned all over and just tender. Toss in large bowl with juice and oregano leaves; cover to keep warm.

3   Cook steaks on same grill plate until browned both sides and cooked as desired. Serve steaks with vegetables.

SERVES 4
per serving 10.7g carbohydrate; 37.7g fat; 2362kJ (565 cal); 45.2g protein

tarragon chicken with carrot mash and leek

PREPARATION TIME 20 MINUTES (PLUS REFRIGERATION TIME)   COOKING TIME 25 MINUTES

4 single chicken breast fillets (680g),
    sliced thickly

1 tablespoon finely chopped
    fresh tarragon

1 tablespoon wholegrain mustard

2 tablespoons butter

2 large leeks (500g), trimmed,
    chopped finely

4 medium carrots (480g),
    chopped coarsely

1½ cups (375ml) chicken stock

pinch nutmeg

1   Thread equal amounts of chicken onto 12 skewers. Using fingers, press combined tarragon and mustard all over chicken, cover skewers; refrigerate 30 minutes.

2   Meanwhile, melt butter in large non-stick frying pan; cook leek, stirring, until softened. Cover to keep warm.

3   Preheat oven to moderately hot.

4   Boil or microwave carrot in stock until just tender; drain in strainer over small bowl. Reserve ½ cup of the stock; discard the remainder. Blend or process carrot with nutmeg until pureed. Cover to keep warm.

5   Place chicken and reserved stock in large shallow baking dish; bake, uncovered, in moderately hot oven about 15 minutes or until chicken is cooked through.

6   Divide carrot mash among serving plates; top with chicken and leek.

SERVES 4
per serving 9.4g carbohydrate; 12.6g fat; 1333kJ (319 cal); 40g protein

tarragon chicken with carrot mash and leek

crying tiger

crying tiger

PREPARATION TIME 25 MINUTES (PLUS REFRIGERATION TIME)   COOKING TIME 10 MINUTES

600g piece beef eye fillet

1 teaspoon tamarind concentrate

2 cloves garlic, crushed

2 teaspoons pickled green
   peppercorns, crushed

2 tablespoons fish sauce

2 tablespoons soy sauce

10cm stick fresh lemon grass (20g),
   chopped finely

2 fresh small red thai chillies,
   chopped finely

1 medium red capsicum (200g),
   sliced thickly

1 cup (80g) finely shredded
   chinese cabbage

6 trimmed red radishes (90g),
   sliced thickly

4 green onions, cut into 3cm pieces

CRYING TIGER SAUCE

2 teaspoons tamarind concentrate

¼ cup (60ml) fish sauce

¼ cup (60ml) lime juice

2 teaspoons grated palm sugar

1 fresh small red thai chilli,
   chopped finely

1 green onion, sliced thinly

2 teaspoons finely chopped
   fresh coriander

1   Halve beef lengthways, place in large bowl with combined tamarind, garlic, peppercorns, sauces, lemon grass and chilli; toss to coat beef. Cover; refrigerate 3 hours or overnight.

2   Cook beef on heated oiled grill plate (or grill or barbecue) about 10 minutes or until browned and cooked as desired. Cover beef; stand 10 minutes, slice thinly.

3   Meanwhile, make crying tiger sauce.

4   Place beef on serving platter with capsicum, cabbage, radish and onion; accompany with crying tiger sauce.

CRYING TIGER SAUCE Whisk ingredients in small bowl until sugar dissolves.

SERVES 4
per serving 6.6g carbohydrate; 7.8g fat; 1070kJ (256 cal); 38.7g protein

stir-fried lamb in black bean sauce

PREPARATION TIME 15 MINUTES   COOKING TIME 15 MINUTES

600g lamb strips

1 teaspoon five-spice powder

2 teaspoons sesame oil

2 tablespoons peanut oil

2 cloves garlic, crushed

1cm piece fresh ginger (5g), grated

1 medium brown onion (150g), sliced thinly

1 small red capsicum (150g), sliced thinly

1 small yellow capsicum (150g), sliced thinly

6 green onions, sliced thinly

1 teaspoon cornflour

½ cup (125ml) chicken stock

1 tablespoon soy sauce

2 tablespoons black bean sauce

1   Place lamb in medium bowl with combined five-spice and sesame oil; toss to coat lamb in five-spice mixture.

2   Heat half of the peanut oil in wok or large frying pan; stir-fry lamb, in batches, until browned lightly.

3   Heat remaining peanut oil in same wok; stir-fry garlic, ginger and brown onion until onion just softens. Add capsicums and green onion; stir-fry until capsicum is just tender.

4   Blend cornflour with stock and sauces in small jug. Add cornflour mixture to wok with lamb; stir until sauce boils and thickens slightly and lamb is cooked as desired.

SERVES 4
per serving 7.9g carbohydrate; 17.4g fat; 1388kJ (332 cal); 35.8g protein

lamb and artichoke kebabs

PREPARATION TIME 5 MINUTES   COOKING TIME 15 MINUTES

Soak eight large bamboo skewers in water for about 1 hour before using to prevent them splintering and scorching.

1kg diced lamb

2 x 400g cans artichoke hearts, drained, halved

1 large red capsicum (350g), chopped coarsely

300g mushrooms, halved

GARLIC BASIL DRESSING

½ cup (125ml) red wine vinegar

¼ cup (60ml) olive oil

1 tablespoon finely shredded fresh basil

1 clove garlic, crushed

1 teaspoon sugar

1 teaspoon dijon mustard

1   Thread lamb, artichokes, capsicum and mushrooms on large skewers.

2   Cook kebabs, in batches, on heated oiled grill plate (or grill or barbecue) until browned all over and cooked as desired.

3   Meanwhile, make garlic basil dressing.

4   Serve kebabs with dressing.

GARLIC BASIL DRESSING Place ingredients in screw-top jar; shake well.

SERVES 4
per serving 6.9g carbohydrate; 19.9g fat; 1956kJ (468 cal); 63.6g protein

tomato and bocconcini lamb stacks

PREPARATION TIME 10 MINUTES   COOKING TIME 15 MINUTES

2 teaspoons olive oil

2 tablespoons balsamic vinegar

2 cloves garlic, crushed

24 french-trimmed lamb cutlets (1.8kg)

3 large egg tomatoes (270g), sliced thickly

300g bocconcini cheese, sliced thickly

2 tablespoons coarsely chopped fresh basil

1   Combine oil, vinegar and garlic in small jug; brush over cutlets. Cook cutlets on heated oiled grill plate (or grill or barbecue) until brown on one side; remove, place on oven tray, cooked-side up.

2   Layer tomato, bocconcini and basil on cooked side of 12 cutlets; top with remaining 12 cutlets, cooked-side down. Tie cutlets together with kitchen string; return to grill plate. Cook until browned both sides and cooked as desired.

SERVES 4
per serving   1.4g carbohydrate; 28.4g fat; 2115kJ (506 cal); 59.2g protein

lamb and ratatouille salad with pesto dressing

PREPARATION TIME 35 MINUTES   COOKING TIME 20 MINUTES

5 baby eggplants (300g), sliced thickly

2 medium zucchini (240g), sliced thickly

1 medium red onion (170g), halved,
    cut into wedges

1 large red capsicum (350g), cut into
    2cm pieces

1 medium yellow capsicum (200g), cut into
    2cm pieces

250g grape tomatoes

2 cloves garlic, crushed

2 tablespoons olive oil

900g lamb backstraps

1 cup loosely packed fresh basil leaves

150g firm goat cheese, crumbled

PESTO DRESSING

2 cloves garlic, crushed

2 tablespoons finely grated parmesan cheese

1 tablespoon toasted pine nuts

1 tablespoon lemon juice

½ cup firmly packed fresh basil leaves

½ cup (125ml) olive oil

1   Preheat oven to very hot. Oil two large shallow baking dishes.

2   Divide combined eggplant, zucchini, onion, capsicums, tomatoes, garlic and oil between dishes. Roast, uncovered, in very hot oven about 20 minutes or until tender, stirring occasionally.

3   Meanwhile, make pesto dressing.

4   Cook lamb in heated large non-stick frying pan until browned and cooked as desired. Cover; stand 5 minutes. Slice lamb thickly.

5   Place vegetables in large bowl with basil and cheese; toss gently to combine. Divide vegetables among serving plates; top with lamb, drizzle with dressing.

PESTO DRESSING   Blend or process ingredients until smooth.

SERVES 4
per serving   11.6g carbohydrate; 54.8g fat; 3561kJ (852 cal); 78.7g protein

minted lamb cutlets with mixed fresh beans

PREPARATION TIME 30 MINUTES (PLUS REFRIGERATION TIME)   COOKING TIME 20 MINUTES

12 french-trimmed lamb cutlets (900g)

2 tablespoons olive oil

2 tablespoons lemon juice

2 cloves garlic, crushed

2 tablespoons finely chopped fresh mint

2 tablespoons finely grated lemon rind

150g yellow string beans

150g snow peas, trimmed

150g sugar snap peas

150g watercress

1 cup loosely packed fresh mint leaves

1 cup loosely packed fresh basil leaves

BALSAMIC DRESSING

2 tablespoons balsamic vinegar

1 teaspoon dijon mustard

1 teaspoon sugar

¼ cup (60ml) olive oil

1   Combine lamb, oil, juice, garlic, chopped mint and half of the rind in large bowl; toss to coat lamb. Cover; refrigerate 1 hour.

2   Meanwhile, boil, steam or microwave beans, snow peas and sugar snap peas, separately, until just tender; drain. Rinse under cold water; drain.

3   Make balsamic dressing.

4   Cook lamb, in batches, on heated oiled grill plate (or grill or barbecue) until browned both sides and cooked as desired.

5   Place beans, snow peas and sugar snap peas in large bowl with watercress, herbs, remaining rind and half of the dressing; toss gently to combine. Divide bean salad and lamb among serving plates; drizzle with remaining dressing.

BALSAMIC DRESSING   Place ingredients in screw-top jar; shake well.

SERVES 4
per serving   7.8g carbohydrate; 42.5g fat; 2174kJ (520 cal); 27.1g protein

lamb with white wine and mascarpone sauce

PREPARATION TIME 10 MINUTES   COOKING TIME 15 MINUTES

¼ cup (60ml) olive oil

12 fresh sage leaves

100g sliced prosciutto

8 lamb steaks (640g)

1 clove garlic, crushed

¾ cup (180ml) dry white wine

½ cup (120g) mascarpone

¼ cup (60ml) cream

400g asparagus, trimmed

1   Heat oil in medium frying pan; cook sage until crisp. Drain on absorbent paper. Cook prosciutto in same pan, stirring, until crisp; drain on absorbent paper.

2   Cook lamb in same pan until browned both sides and cooked as desired. Remove from pan.

3   Cook garlic in same pan, stirring, until fragrant. Add wine; bring to a boil. Reduce heat; simmer, uncovered, until liquid reduces by half. Add mascarpone and cream; cook, stirring, over heat until sauce boils and thickens slightly.

4   Meanwhile, boil, steam or microwave asparagus until tender; drain.

5   Divide lamb and asparagus among serving plates; top with prosciutto and sage, drizzle with sauce.

SERVES 4
per serving   2.2g carbohydrate; 51.9g fat; 2767kJ (662 cal); 40.5g protein

herbed lamb steaks with walnut gremolata tomatoes

PREPARATION TIME 15 MINUTES (PLUS REFRIGERATION TIME)   COOKING TIME 30 MINUTES

2 tablespoons finely chopped fresh oregano

2 tablespoons finely chopped fresh

   flat-leaf parsley

1 tablespoon finely chopped fresh rosemary

⅓ cup (80ml) dry red wine

¼ cup (60ml) olive oil

4 x 200g lamb leg steaks

1 tablespoon coarsely chopped fresh

   flat-leaf parsley

WALNUT GREMOLATA TOMATOES

4 medium tomatoes (750g), halved

1 tablespoon balsamic vinegar

2 tablespoons walnuts, chopped finely

1 tablespoon finely grated lemon rind

1 clove garlic, crushed

½ cup finely chopped fresh flat-leaf parsley

1 Combine oregano, finely chopped parsley, rosemary, wine and oil in shallow dish; add lamb, toss to coat lamb. Cover; refrigerate 3 hours or overnight.

2 Make walnut gremolata tomatoes.

3 Cook lamb on same grill plate until browned and cooked as desired.

4 Sprinkle lamb with coarsely chopped parsley; serve lamb with tomatoes.

WALNUT GREMOLATA TOMATOES Cook tomatoes on heated oiled grill plate (or grill or barbecue) until soft. Combine remaining ingredients in small bowl. Sprinkle tomatoes with walnut mixture.

SERVES 4
per serving 3.2g carbohydrate; 27.8g fat; 1931kJ (462 cal); 46.7g protein

lamb steaks with brussels sprouts

PREPARATION TIME 10 MINUTES   COOKING TIME 10 MINUTES

400g brussels sprouts

40g butter

8 x 150g lamb steaks

1 small brown onion (80g), chopped finely

¼ cup (60ml) dry white wine

½ cup (125ml) beef stock

1 teaspoon dijon mustard

1 tablespoon coarsely chopped

   fresh chives

1 Boil, steam or microwave sprouts until just tender; drain.

2 Meanwhile, melt half of the butter in large frying pan; cook lamb, in batches, until browned both sides and cooked as desired. Cover to keep warm.

3 Cook onion in same pan, stirring, until softened. Stir in wine, stock and mustard; bring to a boil. Reduce heat; simmer, uncovered, 1 minute.

4 Toss brussels sprouts and remaining butter in large bowl with chives. Serve lamb with sauce and brussels sprouts.

SERVES 4
per serving 3.7g carbohydrate; 36g fat; 2533kJ (606 cal); 67.3g protein
tip To cook sprouts evenly, cut a shallow cross in the stem end. Brussels sprouts are far more palatable if they're not overcooked.

lemon and garlic lamb cutlets with sprout, tomato and fetta salad

PREPARATION TIME 15 MINUTES   COOKING TIME 15 MINUTES

12 french-trimmed lamb
  cutlets (600g)
1 tablespoon finely grated
  lemon rind
2 tablespoons lemon juice
2 cloves garlic, crushed
90g alfalfa sprouts, trimmed
150g baby roma tomatoes, halved
1 cup coarsely chopped fresh mint
1 cup coarsely chopped fresh basil
180g fetta cheese, crumbled
⅓ cup (55g) seeded kalamata olives

LEMON DRESSING

¼ cup (60ml) lemon juice
2 teaspoons extra virgin olive oil
1 teaspoon dijon mustard

1 Place cutlets in large bowl with combined rind, juice and garlic; toss to coat cutlets in mixture.

2 Meanwhile, make lemon dressing.

3 Cook cutlets, in batches, on heated oiled grill plate (or grill or barbecue) until browned both sides and cooked as desired.

4 Place alfalfa, tomato, herbs, cheese, olives and half of the dressing in medium bowl; toss gently to combine.

5 Serve salad topped with cutlets; drizzle with remaining dressing.

LEMON DRESSING Place ingredients in screw-top jar; shake well.

SERVES 4
per serving 11.5g carbohydrate; 38g fat; 2061kJ (493 cal); 26.4g protein

iskander kebab

PREPARATION TIME 15 MINUTES   COOKING TIME 15 MINUTES

You need eight skewers for this recipe; if using bamboo skewers, soak them in water for an hour before using to prevent them from splintering and scorching.

1kg lamb rump, cut into 2cm cubes

1 cup (280g) yogurt

2 tablespoons lemon juice

2 cloves garlic, crushed

2 teaspoons finely chopped
 fresh thyme

40g mesclun

CHILLI TOMATO SAUCE

1 tablespoon olive oil

1 small brown onion (80g),
 chopped coarsely

1 clove garlic, crushed

2 long green chillies, seeded,
 chopped coarsely

2 medium tomatoes (380g),
 chopped coarsely

1 tablespoon tomato paste

⅓ cup (80ml) dry red wine

1   Thread lamb onto skewers. Combine yogurt, juice, garlic and thyme in small bowl. Place two thirds of the yogurt mixture into separate bowl; reserve. Use remaining yogurt mixture to brush lamb.

2   Cook lamb skewers, in batches, on heated oiled grill plate (or grill or barbecue) until browned all over and cooked as desired.

3   Meanwhile, make chilli tomato sauce.

4   Serve kebabs with reserved yogurt mixture, sauce and mesclun.

CHILLI TOMATO SAUCE   Heat oil in medium frying pan; cook onion and garlic, stirring, until onion softens. Add remaining ingredients; bring to a boil. Reduce heat; simmer, uncovered, about 5 minutes or until sauce thickens slightly. Blend or process sauce until smooth.

SERVES 4
per serving 7.1g carbohydrate; 20.6g fat; 1973kJ (472 cal); 60.3g protein
tip You can also use boned-out leg of lamb, cut into cubes.

lamb with caramelised onions and asparagus and watercress salad

PREPARATION TIME 15 MINUTES   COOKING TIME 25 MINUTES

10g butter

2 medium red onions (340g), sliced thinly

⅓ cup (80ml) red wine vinegar

1 tablespoon brown sugar

¼ cup (60ml) water

600g lamb backstraps

500g asparagus, trimmed

350g watercress

1 tablespoon dijon mustard

2 cloves garlic, crushed

1 tablespoon lemon juice

2 tablespoons olive oil

1 Melt butter in large frying pan; cook onion, stirring, until softened. Add vinegar, sugar and the water; cook, stirring, until sugar dissolves, then bring to a boil. Reduce heat; simmer, uncovered, stirring occasionally, about 10 minutes or until onion caramelises.

2 Meanwhile, cook lamb, in batches, on heated oiled grill plate (or grill or barbecue) until browned all over and cooked as desired. Stand 5 minutes; slice lamb thickly.

3 Boil, steam or microwave asparagus until just tender; drain. Place asparagus in large bowl with watercress. Add combined remaining ingredients; toss gently to combine. Serve salad topped with lamb and caramelised onions.

SERVES 4
per serving 9.8g carbohydrate; 17.2g fat; 1480kJ (354 cal); 39.2g protein

garlic and sage lamb racks with roasted red onion

PREPARATION TIME 10 MINUTES   COOKING TIME 25 MINUTES

3 large red onions (900g)

⅓ cup (80ml) extra virgin olive oil

4 cloves garlic, chopped coarsely

2 tablespoons coarsely chopped fresh sage

4 racks of lamb (4 cutlets each)

1 Preheat oven to hot.

2 Halve onions then slice into thin wedges; place in large baking dish with half of the oil.

3 Combine remaining oil in small bowl with garlic and sage. Using hands, press sage mixture all over lamb; place lamb on onion. Roast, uncovered, in hot oven about 25 minutes or until lamb is browned all over and cooked as desired. Cover with foil; stand 10 minutes before serving.

SERVES 4
per serving 11.5g carbohydrate; 44.2g fat; 2391kJ (572 cal); 33.5g protein
tip Red onions are sweet and have a less aggressive scent than their brown and white counterparts.

herb and garlic barbecued lamb

PREPARATION TIME 15 MINUTES (PLUS REFRIGERATION TIME)   COOKING TIME 35 MINUTES

1kg butterflied leg of lamb

2 tablespoons olive oil

2 cloves garlic, crushed

1 tablespoon wholegrain mustard

½ cup (125ml) dry white wine

1 tablespoon finely chopped fresh rosemary

1 tablespoon mint jelly

200g green beans, trimmed

20g butter

2 cloves garlic, crushed, extra

¼ cup (60ml) dry white wine, extra

¼ cup (60ml) chicken stock

1   Place lamb in large shallow dish; pour combined oil, garlic, mustard, wine and rosemary over lamb. Cover; refrigerate 3 hours or overnight.

2   Remove lamb from marinade; place marinade in small saucepan, reserve. Place lamb, covered with foil, on heated oiled grill plate (or grill or barbecue); cook about 30 minutes or until cooked as desired, turning halfway through cooking time.

3   Brush lamb all over with jelly; cook, uncovered, until jelly melts and forms a glaze. Stand lamb, covered, 10 minutes before slicing.

4   Meanwhile, boil, steam or microwave beans until just tender; drain. Rinse under cold water; drain. Heat butter in medium frying pan; cook extra garlic, stirring until fragrant. Add extra wine; bring to a boil. Reduce heat; simmer, uncovered, until liquid reduces by half. Add beans; stir until heated through.

5   Add stock to reserved marinade; bring to a boil. Reduce heat; simmer, uncovered, 5 minutes. Serve sliced lamb with sauce and beans.

SERVES 4
per serving 3.0g carbohydrate; 34.2g fat; 2378kJ (569 cal); 55g protein
tip The lamb can also be cooked, covered, in a hot oven for about 25 minutes or until cooked as desired.

teriyaki lamb stir-fry

PREPARATION TIME 15 MINUTES   COOKING TIME 15 MINUTES

2 teaspoons olive oil

800g lean lamb strips

1 teaspoon sesame oil

2 cloves garlic, crushed

1 medium brown onion (150g), sliced thickly

1 fresh long red chilli, seeded, sliced thinly

⅓ cup (80ml) bottled teriyaki sauce

¼ cup (60ml) sweet chilli sauce

500g baby bok choy, quartered

175g broccolini, trimmed, chopped coarsely

1   Heat olive oil in wok or large frying pan; stir-fry lamb, in batches, until browned all over.

2   Heat sesame oil in same wok; stir-fry garlic, onion and chilli until fragrant. Add sauces; bring to a boil. Add bok choy and broccolini; stir-fry until bok choy just wilts and broccolini is just tender.

3   Return lamb to wok; stir-fry until heated through.

SERVES 4
per serving 7.3g carbohydrate; 12.6g fat; 1426kJ (341 cal); 48.4g protein

mint and pistachio kebabs with chermoulla-dressed zucchini

PREPARATION TIME 30 MINUTES   COOKING TIME 25 MINUTES

1kg diced lamb

4 medium zucchini (480g),
  halved lengthways

CHERMOULLA DRESSING

1 small red onion (100g), chopped finely

1 clove garlic, crushed

½ teaspoon hot paprika

1 teaspoon ground cumin

⅓ cup (80ml) olive oil

2 tablespoons lemon juice

¾ cup finely chopped fresh
  flat-leaf parsley

MINT AND PISTACHIO PESTO

1 cup firmly packed fresh mint leaves

⅓ cup (50g) pistachios, toasted

⅓ cup (25g) coarsely grated
  parmesan cheese

2 cloves garlic, crushed

1 tablespoon lemon juice

¼ cup (60ml) olive oil

2 tablespoons water, approximately

1 Thread lamb onto 12 skewers. Cook lamb on heated oiled grill plate (or grill or barbecue) until browned and cooked as desired. Cover to keep warm.

2 Meanwhile, cook zucchini on same grill plate until browned lightly both sides and just tender.

3 Make chermoulla dressing. Make mint and pistachio pesto.

4 Serve zucchini topped with chermoulla and lamb with pesto.

CHERMOULLA DRESSING Place ingredients in screw-top jar; shake well.

MINT AND PISTACHIO PESTO Blend or process mint, nuts, cheese, garlic and juice until well combined. With motor operating, gradually pour in oil and just enough of the water to give the desired consistency.

SERVES 4
per serving 6g carbohydrate; 63.4g fat; 3457kJ (827 cal); 59.5g protein
tip If using bamboo skewers, soak in water for at least 1 hour before using to avoid them splintering and scorching.

lamb shanks in five-spice, tamarind and ginger (see page 326)

PREPARATION TIME 20 MINUTES   COOKING TIME 2 HOURS 10 MINUTES

2 teaspoons five-spice powder

1 teaspoon dried chilli flakes

1 cinnamon stick

2 star anise

¼ cup (60ml) soy sauce

½ cup (125ml) chinese rice wine

2 tablespoons tamarind concentrate

2 tablespoons brown sugar

8cm piece fresh ginger (40g), grated

2 cloves garlic, chopped coarsely

1¼ cups (310ml) water

8 french-trimmed lamb shanks (1.6kg)

500g choy sum, chopped into 10cm lengths

350g broccolini, trimmed

1   Preheat oven to moderate.

2   Dry-fry five-spice, chilli, cinnamon and star anise in small frying pan, stirring, until fragrant; combine spices with soy sauce, wine, tamarind, sugar, ginger, garlic and the water in medium jug.

3   Place shanks, in single layer, in large shallow baking dish; drizzle with spice mixture. Bake, covered, in moderate oven, turning occasionally, 2 hours. Remove shanks from dish; cover to keep warm. Skim away excess fat; strain sauce into small saucepan.

4   Meanwhile, boil, steam or microwave choy sum and broccolini, separately, until tender; drain.

5   Bring sauce to a boil in small saucepan. Divide vegetables among serving plates; serve with shanks, drizzle with sauce.

SERVES 4
per serving   10.8g carbohydrate; 20.2g fat; 1906kJ (456 cal); 50.5g protein

lamb shank soup

PREPARATION TIME 30 MINUTES   COOKING TIME 2 HOURS 30 MINUTES (PLUS COOLING AND REFRIGERATION TIME)

8 french-trimmed lamb shanks (1.6kg)

1 medium brown onion (150g),
**   chopped finely**

2 trimmed celery stalks (200g), sliced thinly

2 medium red capsicums (400g),
**   chopped coarsely**

2 cloves garlic, crushed

2 litres (8 cups) water

400g silverbeet, trimmed, chopped finely

⅓ cup (80ml) lemon juice

1   Heat large lightly oiled saucepan; cook shanks, in batches, until browned. Cook onion, celery, capsicum and garlic in same pan, stirring, about 5 minutes or until onion softens. Return shanks to pan with the water; bring to a boil. Reduce heat; simmer, covered, 1 hour 45 minutes.

2   Remove soup mixture from heat; when shanks are cool enough to handle, remove meat, chop coarsely. Refrigerate cooled soup mixture and shank meat, covered separately, overnight.

3   Discard fat from surface of soup mixture. Place soup mixture and shank meat in large saucepan; bring to a boil. Reduce heat; simmer, covered, 30 minutes. Add silverbeet and juice; simmer, uncovered, until silverbeet just wilts.

SERVES 4
per serving   7.5g carbohydrate; 20.8g fat; 1726kJ (413 cal); 48.1g protein

grilled lamb steak with ratatouille

PREPARATION TIME 20 MINUTES   COOKING TIME 25 MINUTES

5 baby eggplants (300g), peeled, chopped coarsely

2 medium red capsicums (400g), chopped coarsely

1 medium yellow capsicum (200g), chopped coarsely

4 medium egg tomatoes (540g), chopped coarsely

1 medium brown onion (150g), chopped coarsely

2 cloves garlic, sliced thickly

cooking-oil spray

4 x 150g lamb steaks

BALSAMIC DRESSING

1 tablespoon olive oil

1 tablespoon lemon juice

1 tablespoon balsamic vinegar

1 clove garlic, crushed

¼ cup loosely packed fresh oregano leaves

1 Preheat oven to hot.

2 Combine vegetables and garlic, in single layers, in two large shallow baking dishes. Spray vegetables lightly with cooking-oil spray; bake, uncovered, in hot oven, stirring occasionally, about 25 minutes or until ratatouille vegetables are just tender.

3 Meanwhile, cook lamb on heated oiled grill plate (or grill or barbecue) uncovered, until browned both sides and cooked as desired.

4 Place half of the dressing in large bowl with ratatouille; toss gently to combine. Divide ratatouille and lamb among serving plates; drizzle with remaining dressing.

BALSAMIC DRESSING Place ingredients in screw-top jar; shake well.

SERVES 4
per serving 11g carbohydrate; 13.3g fat; 1308kJ (313 cal); 36.5g protein

omelette spring rolls

PREPARATION TIME 10 MINUTES   COOKING TIME 30 MINUTES

500g pork mince

2 green onions, chopped

115g fresh baby corn, sliced thinly

50g button mushrooms, sliced thinly

2 tablespoons oyster sauce

1 tablespoon mild chilli sauce

1 tablespoon kecap manis

2 tablespoons dry sherry

6 eggs

2 tablespoons water

1 Cook mince, stirring, in large heated oiled non-stick frying pan until browned and cooked through. Stir in onion, corn, mushrooms and combined sauces and sherry until heated through. Remove from pan; cover to keep warm.

2 Whisk eggs and the water in medium bowl; pour a quarter of the egg mixture into same cleaned pan. Cook, tilting pan, over medium heat until omelette is browned lightly underneath and almost set; turn, cook other side until browned lightly. Remove omelette from pan; cover to keep warm. Repeat process with remaining egg mixture.

3 Place a quarter of the mince mixture along one edge of an omelette; roll omelette over filling, fold in sides, roll to enclose filling. Repeat with remaining mince and omelettes.

SERVES 4
per serving 9g carbohydrate; 16.9g fat; 1450kJ (347 cal); 36.9g protein

chilli pork with oyster sauce

PREPARATION TIME 15 MINUTES   COOKING TIME 20 MINUTES

1 tablespoon peanut oil

450g pork fillets, sliced thinly

1 medium white onion (150g),
    sliced thinly

1 clove garlic, crushed

1 large red capsicum (350g),
    sliced thinly

1 small green zucchini (90g),
    sliced thinly

1 small yellow zucchini (90g),
    sliced thinly

¼ cup (60ml) oyster sauce

1 tablespoon sweet chilli sauce

1 tablespoon coarsely chopped
    fresh coriander

1 Heat oil in large wok or frying pan; stir-fry pork, in batches, until browned.

2 Stir-fry onion and garlic in same wok until onion softens. Add capsicum and zucchini; stir-fry until vegetables are just tender.

3 Return pork to wok. Add sauces; stir-fry until hot. Serve sprinkled with chopped coriander.

SERVES 4
per serving 10g carbohydrate; 7.6 g fat; 920kJ (220 cal); 27.2g protein

pork steaks with caraway cabbage

PREPARATION TIME 10 MINUTES   COOKING TIME 20 MINUTES

4 x 200g pork loin medallion steaks

2 bacon rashers (140g), rind removed,
    sliced thinly

1 medium brown onion (150g),
    chopped finely

1 tablespoon caraway seeds

3 cups (240g) finely shredded cabbage

2 tablespoons brown sugar

¼ cup (60ml) cider vinegar

40g butter

2 teaspoons finely chopped fresh sage

2 tablespoons sour cream

1 Cook pork on heated oiled grill plate (or grill or barbeuce), until browned both sides and cooked through.

2 Meanwhile, cook bacon, onion and seeds in medium frying pan until onion softens. Add cabbage; cook, stirring, 2 minutes. Stir in sugar, vinegar and butter; cook, stirring, about 3 minutes or until cabbage is just soft.

3 Just before serving, stir in sage. Serve pork topped with cabbage and sour cream.

SERVES 4
per serving 10.4g carbohydrate; 25g fat; 2169kJ (519 cal); 62.9g protein

sang choy bow (see back cover)

PREPARATION TIME 15 MINUTES   COOKING TIME 10 MINUTES

1 tablespoon sesame oil

**1 medium brown onion (150g),
    chopped finely**

2 cloves garlic, crushed

300g pork mince

300g veal mince

¼ cup (60ml) soy sauce

¼ cup (60ml) oyster sauce

**1 medium red capsicum (150g),
    chopped finely**

3 cups (200g) bean sprouts

3 green onions, chopped coarsely

1 tablespoon toasted sesame seeds

8 large iceberg lettuce leaves

1 Heat oil in wok or large saucepan; cook brown onion and garlic, stirring, until onion softens. Add pork and veal mince; cook, stirring, until mince is just browned.

2 Add combined sauces and capsicum, reduce heat; simmer, uncovered, stirring occasionally, 3 minutes.

3 Just before serving, stir in sprouts, green onion and sesame seeds. Divide mince mixture among lettuce leaves. Serve immediately.

SERVES 4
per serving 10.1g carbohydrate; 17.2g fat; 1463kJ (350 cal); 37.9g protein

teriyaki pork with wasabi dressing

PREPARATION TIME 10 MINUTES   COOKING TIME 15 MINUTES

750g pork fillets

¼ cup (60ml) teriyaki marinade

50g snow pea sprouts

100g mesclun

**1 medium red capsicum (200g),
    sliced thinly**

250g yellow teardrop tomatoes, halved

WASABI DRESSING

1½ teaspoons wasabi powder

¼ cup (60ml) cider vinegar

⅓ cup (80ml) vegetable oil

1 tablespoon light soy sauce

1 Trim pork; brush with teriyaki marinade. Cook pork, in batches, on heated oiled grill plate (or grill or barbecue), brushing frequently with marinade, until browned both sides and cooked. Cover to keep warm.

2 Meanwhile, combine sprouts, mesclun, watercress, capsicum and tomato in large bowl.

3 Make wasabi dressing.

4 Pour wasabi dressing over salad mixture; toss gently to combine. Slice pork; serve with salad.

WASABI DRESSING Blend wasabi powder with vinegar in small jug; whisk in remaining ingredients.

SERVES 4
per serving 3.9g carbohydrate; 23.3g fat; 1680kJ (402 cal); 44.1g protein

roasted pork fillets with orange salad

PREPARATION TIME 10 MINUTES (PLUS STANDING TIME)   COOKING TIME 35 MINUTES

800g pork fillets

2 cloves garlic, sliced thinly lengthways

8 small fresh sage leaves

1 teaspoon fennel seeds

2 tablespoons olive oil

1 small brown onion (80g), sliced thickly

½ cup (125ml) chicken stock

2 tablespoons orange juice

2 medium oranges (480g)

150g mesclun

ORANGE VINAIGRETTE

2 tablespoons orange juice

1 tablespoon lemon juice

1 clove garlic, crushed

⅓ cup (80ml) olive oil

1   Cut a few small slits along the top of pork; push in garlic and sage. Sprinkle pork with seeds; stand 30 minutes.

2   Preheat oven to hot.

3   Heat half of the oil in large flameproof baking dish; cook pork until browned all over. Remove from dish.

4   Heat remaining oil in same dish; cook onion, stirring, until browned lightly. Return pork to dish; drizzle with stock and juice. Roast, uncovered, in hot oven about 10 minutes or until pork is cooked through. Stand, covered, 10 minutes.

5   Meanwhile, make orange vinaigrette. Place mesclun in medium bowl. Segment oranges over mesclun, add dressing; toss gently to combine.

6   Serve sliced pork with pan juices and salad.

ORANGE VINAIGRETTE   Place ingredients in screw-top jar; shake well.

SERVES 4
per serving 10g carbohydrate; 32.2g fat; 2140kJ (512 cal); 45.9g protein

pork with eggplant

PREPARATION TIME 20 MINUTES   COOKING TIME 25 MINUTES

3 fresh small red thai chillies, halved

6 cloves garlic, quartered

1 medium brown onion (150g),
   chopped coarsely

500g baby eggplants

2 tablespoons peanut oil

500g pork mince

1 tablespoon fish sauce

1 tablespoon soy sauce

1 tablespoon grated palm sugar

4 purple thai shallots, sliced thinly

150g snake beans, cut into 5cm lengths

1 cup loosely packed fresh thai
   basil leaves

1   Blend or process (or crush using mortar and pestle) chilli, garlic and onion until mixture forms a paste.

2   Quarter eggplants lengthways; slice each piece into 5cm lengths. Cook eggplant in large saucepan of boiling water until just tender; drain, pat dry with absorbent paper.

3   Heat oil in wok; stir-fry eggplant, in batches, until browned lightly. Drain on absorbent paper.

4   Stir-fry garlic paste in wok about 5 minutes or until browned lightly. Add pork; stir-fry until pork is changed in colour and cooked through. Add sauces and sugar; stir-fry until sugar dissolves. Add shallot and beans; stir-fry until beans are just tender. Return eggplant to wok; stir-fry, tossing gently until combined. Remove from heat; toss thai basil leaves through stir-fry.

SERVES 4
per serving 9.5g carbohydrate; 18.5g fat; 1342kJ (321 cal); 29.3g protein

pork steaks with beetroot salad

PREPARATION TIME 20 MINUTES   COOKING TIME 45 MINUTES

300g fresh beetroot

1 tablespoon caraway seeds

2 teaspoons olive oil

4 x 150g butterflied pork steaks

150g firm goat cheese, crumbled

5 large radishes (175g), trimmed, sliced thinly

125g baby rocket leaves

DIJON VINAIGRETTE

2 teaspoons dijon mustard

2 teaspoons olive oil

2 tablespoons red wine vinegar

1 Preheat oven to moderately hot.

2 Discard beetroot stems and leaves; place unpeeled beetroots in large shallow baking dish. Roast, uncovered, in moderately hot oven about 45 minutes or until vegetables are tender. Cool 10 minutes; peel, cut into quarters.

3 Meanwhile, make dijon vinaigrette.

4 Blend or process seeds and oil until mixture is smooth; rub into pork. Cook pork on heated oiled grill plate (or grill or barbecue) until browned and cooked as desired.

5 Place beetroot and vinaigrette in large bowl with cheese, radish and rocket; toss gently to combine. Serve salad with pork.

DIJON VINAIGRETTE Place ingredients in screw-top jar; shake well.

SERVES 4
per serving 7.4g carbohydrate; 23.5g fat; 1804kJ (431 cal); 47.4g protein

pork steaks with beetroot salad

pork, lime and peanut salad

pork, lime and peanut salad

PREPARATION TIME 25 MINUTES (PLUS REFRIGERATION TIME)   COOKING TIME 15 MINUTES

800g pork fillets, sliced thinly

¼ cup (60ml) lime juice

4cm piece fresh ginger (20g), grated

500g choy sum, chopped coarsely

2 tablespoons water

2 medium carrots (240g), cut into
matchstick-sized pieces

½ cup firmly packed fresh basil leaves

1 cup firmly packed fresh
coriander leaves

4 green onions, sliced thinly

¼ cup (35g) coarsely chopped toasted
unsalted peanuts

SWEET CHILLI DRESSING

1 tablespoon fish sauce

1 tablespoon sweet chilli sauce

2 tablespoons lime juice

1 fresh small red thai chilli,
chopped finely

1   Place pork in large bowl with juice and ginger; toss to coat pork in mixture. Cover; refrigerate 3 hours or overnight.

2   Make sweet chilli dressing.

3   Stir-fry pork, in batches, in heated lightly oiled wok or large frying pan until cooked through. Cover to keep warm.

4   Stir-fry choy sum with the water in same wok until just wilted.

5   Place pork and choy sum in large bowl with carrot, herbs, onion and dressing; toss gently to combine, sprinkle with nuts.

SWEET CHILLI DRESSING   Place ingredients in screw-top jar; shake well.

SERVES 4
per serving 6.8g carbohydrate; 10.4g fat; 1342kJ (321 cal); 48.8g protein

lemon pepper chicken with zucchini salad

PREPARATION TIME 20 MINUTES   COOKING TIME 40 MINUTES

1 tablespoon finely grated lemon rind

2 teaspoons cracked black pepper

⅓ cup (80ml) lemon juice

2 teaspoons olive oil

4 single chicken breast fillets (680g)

4 medium green zucchini (480g)

4 medium yellow zucchini (480g)

1 clove garlic, crushed

4 green onions, chopped finely

1 cup coarsely chopped fresh

  flat-leaf parsley

¼ cup coarsely chopped

  fresh tarragon

1 Place rind, pepper, 1 tablespoon of the juice and half of the oil in large bowl, add chicken; toss to coat chicken in mixture. Cover; refrigerate until required.

2 Peel zucchini randomly; slice into thin strips lengthways. Cook zucchini strips, in batches, on heated lightly oiled grill plate (or grill or barbecue) until browned lightly and crisp.

3 Cook chicken on same grill plate until browned both sides and cooked through.

4 Meanwhile, whisk remaining juice and remaining oil with garlic in large bowl; add zucchini, onion and herbs; toss gently to combine. Serve chicken with zucchini salad.

SERVES 4
per serving 4.1g carbohydrate; 7.5g fat; 1195kJ (286 cal); 48.9g protein

greek salad with smoked chicken

PREPARATION TIME 20 MINUTES

Smoked chicken breast may be slightly pink, like bacon and ham, but this does not mean it is undercooked.

1 small red onion (100g), sliced thinly

200g fetta cheese, crumbled

250g grape tomatoes

400g smoked chicken breast,

  sliced thinly

200g baby spinach leaves

⅔ cup (110g) seeded kalamata olives

1 medium red capsicum (200g),

  sliced thinly

⅓ cup (80ml) olive oil

¼ cup (60ml) lemon juice

1 clove garlic, crushed

1 Combine onion, cheese, tomatoes, chicken, spinach, olives and capsicum in large bowl.

2 Place remaining ingredients in screw-top jar; shake well. Drizzle dressing over salad; toss gently to combine.

SERVES 4
per serving 10.2g carbohydrate; 38.1g fat; 2207kJ (528 cal); 36.3g protein

clay pot chicken

PREPARATION TIME 10 MINUTES (PLUS REFRIGERATION TIME)   COOKING TIME 1 HOUR

800g chicken thigh fillets

1 large brown onion (200g), quartered

1 fresh long red chilli, sliced thinly

½ cup (125ml) chicken stock

100g shiitake mushrooms, halved

4 green onions, cut into 4cm pieces

500g savoy cabbage,

    cut into 6cm squares

HOISIN AND CITRUS MARINADE

4 cloves garlic, crushed

1 tablespoon fish sauce

1 tablespoon soy sauce

1 tablespoon hoisin sauce

2 tablespoons lime juice

10cm stick fresh lemon grass (20g),

    chopped finely

1 Make hoisin and citrus marinade.

2 Cut each thigh fillet in half, place in large bowl with marinade; toss to coat chicken in marinade. Cover; refrigerate 3 hours or overnight.

3 Preheat oven to moderate.

4 Place chicken mixture in clay pot or 2.5-litre (10-cup) ovenproof dish with brown onion, chilli and stock; mix gently to combine. Cook, covered, in moderate oven 45 minutes. Add mushrooms, green onion and cabbage to dish; cook, covered, stirring occasionally, about 15 minutes or until chicken is cooked through.

HOISIN AND CITRUS MARINADE Combine ingredients in large bowl.

SERVES 4

per serving 9.4g carbohydrate; 9.2g fat; 1296kJ (310 cal); 46.6g protein

roasted whole chicken with caramelised lemon

PREPARATION TIME 10 MINUTES (PLUS COOLING TIME)   COOKING TIME 1 HOUR 30 MINUTES

40g butter

2 medium lemons (280g), sliced thickly

4 small red onions (400g),

   chopped coarsely

1.6kg chicken

¼ cup (60ml) olive oil

¼ cup (60ml) lemon juice

350g broccolini

1   Heat half of the butter in medium pan; cook lemon, stirring, until just softened and caramelised slightly. Remove from pan; cool 10 minutes. Heat remaining butter in same pan; cook onion, stirring, until browned lightly. Remove from pan; cool 10 minutes.

2   Push lemon between flesh and skin of chicken; spoon onion into body cavity. Tuck trimmed neck flap under body, securing with toothpicks; tie legs together with kitchen string. Place chicken on oiled roasting rack or basket, or in disposable baking dish. Brush all over with combined oil and juice. Cook chicken in covered barbecue, using indirect heat, following manufacturer's instructions, about 1 hour 20 minutes or until browned all over and cooked through.

3   Just before serving, boil, steam or microwave broccolini until just tender; drain. Serve chicken with broccolini and lemon wedges, if desired.

SERVES 4
per serving 6.3g carbohydrate; 56.6g fat; 3244kJ (776 cal); 59.9g protein

lemon grass and asparagus chicken

PREPARATION TIME 15 MINUTES   COOKING TIME 15 MINUTES

3 cloves garlic, crushed

2 tablespoons finely chopped fresh

   lemon grass

1 teaspoon sugar

1cm piece fresh ginger (5g), grated

1 tablespoon peanut oil

500g chicken breast fillets, sliced thickly

400g asparagus, trimmed

1 large brown onion (200g), sliced thickly

2 medium tomatoes (380g), seeded,

   chopped coarsely

2 teaspoons finely chopped

   fresh coriander

2 tablespoons toasted sesame seeds

1   Combine garlic, lemon grass, sugar, ginger and half of the oil in medium bowl, add chicken; toss to coat chicken in mixture.

2   Cut asparagus spears into thirds; boil, steam or microwave until just tender; drain. Rinse immediately under cold water; drain.

3   Heat remaining oil in wok or large frying pan; stir-fry onion until softened, remove from wok. Stir-fry chicken mixture, in batches, in same wok until chicken is browned and cooked through.

4   Return chicken mixture and onion to wok with asparagus and tomato; stir-fry until heated through. Serve chicken mixture sprinkled with coriander and sesame seeds.

SERVES 4
per serving 5.5g carbohydrate; 10.8g fat; 1041kJ (249 cal); 32.4g protein
tip Chicken can be marinated for up to 3 hours before using.

chicken tagine with olives and preserved lemon

PREPARATION TIME 15 MINUTES   COOKING TIME 45 MINUTES

In Morocco, the word "tagine" refers both to a slowly cooked stew and the special cone-topped pottery casserole dish in which it is served.

1 tablespoon olive oil

1 tablespoon butter

8 chicken thigh cutlets (1.3kg), skinned

1 large red onion (300g), chopped finely

½ teaspoon saffron threads, toasted, crushed

1 teaspoon ground cinnamon

1 teaspoon ground ginger

1½ cups (375ml) chicken stock

1 cup (120g) seeded large green olives

2 tablespoons finely chopped

   preserved lemon

1 Heat oil and butter in large heavy-base saucepan with tight-fitting lid; cook chicken, in batches, until browned all over.

2 Place onion and spices in same pan; cook, stirring, until onion softens. Return chicken to pan with stock; bring to a boil. Reduce heat; simmer, covered, about 30 minutes or until chicken is cooked through.

3 Remove chicken from pan; cover to keep warm. Skim and discard fat from top of sauce; bring to a boil. Reduce heat; cook, stirring, until sauce reduces by half.

4 Return chicken to pan with olives and lemon; stir until heated through.

SERVES 4
per serving 10g carbohydrate; 25.4g fat; 1856kJ (444 cal); 44.6g protein

chicken cacciatore

PREPARATION TIME 20 MINUTES   COOKING TIME 55 MINUTES

4 chicken marylands (1.4kg)

2 tablespoons plain flour

1 tablespoon olive oil

2 cloves garlic, crushed

4 slices pancetta (60g), chopped coarsely

1 large brown onion (200g), chopped finely

1 medium (200g) yellow capsicum,

   chopped coarsely

3 medium tomatoes (450g), peeled,

   chopped coarsely

½ cup (125ml) dry white wine

½ cup (125ml) tomato puree

2 teaspoons finely chopped fresh sage

1 teaspoon finely chopped fresh rosemary

1 bay leaf

1 Cut chicken through joint into two pieces. Toss chicken in flour; shake away excess flour.

2 Heat oil in large saucepan; cook chicken, in batches, until browned all over. Drain on absorbent paper.

3 Drain all but 1 tablespoon of the juices from pan; cook garlic, pancetta, onion and capsicum, stirring, until onion softens. Add tomato, wine and puree; bring to a boil. Reduce heat; simmer, uncovered, 2 minutes.

4 Return chicken to pan. Add herbs and bay leaf; simmer, covered, about 30 minutes or until chicken is cooked through. Discard bay leaf before serving.

SERVES 4
per serving 11.4g carbohydrate; 39.5g fat; 2562kJ (613 cal); 48.6g protein

chicken, lemon and artichoke skewers (see page 308)

PREPARATION TIME 20 MINUTE (PLUS REFRIGERATION TIME)   COOKING TIME 15 MINUTES

You will need to soak 12 bamboo skewers in water for at least an hour before using to prevent them from splintering or scorching.

3 medium lemons (420g)

3 red onions (270g)

500g chicken breast fillets, diced into 2cm pieces

2 x 400g can marinated quartered artichoke hearts, drained

300g button mushrooms

100g baby rocket leaves

2 tablespoons drained baby capers, rinsed

LEMON DRESSING

1 tablespoon lemon juice

2 cloves garlic, crushed

½ teaspoon mild english mustard

1 tablespoon white wine vinegar

1 tablespoon olive oil

1 Make lemon dressing.

2 Cut each lemon into eight wedges; cut two of the onions into six wedges. Thread lemon wedges, onion wedges, chicken, artichoke and mushroom alternately onto skewers.

3 Place skewers on shallow baking dish; pour half of the dressing over skewers. Cover; refrigerate 3 hours.

4 Cook skewers on heated lightly oiled grill plate (or grill or barbecue) until browned and cooked through.

5 Meanwhile, slice remaining onion thinly, place in large bowl with rocket, capers and remaining dressing; toss gently to combine. Serve chicken skewers with salad.

LEMON DRESSING Place ingredients in screw-top jar; shake well.

SERVES 4
per serving 9.4g carbohydrate; 13.1g fat; 1317kJ (315 cal); 37.4g protein

grilled sumac and paprika-spiced chicken with chunky herb salad

PREPARATION TIME 20 MINUTES   COOKING TIME 15 MINUTES

You need to soak 8 bamboo skewers in water for at least an hour before using to prevent them from splintering or scorching.

800g chicken tenderloins

2 cloves garlic, crushed

2 teaspoons sweet paprika

2 tablespoons sumac

2 teaspoons finely chopped fresh oregano

2 tablespoons water

1 teaspoon vegetable oil

2½ cups coarsely chopped fresh flat-leaf parsley

1 cup coarsely chopped fresh coriander

½ cup coarsely chopped fresh mint

4 medium tomatoes (600g), chopped coarsely

1 medium red onion (170g), chopped coarsely

⅓ cup (80ml) lemon juice

1 tablespoon olive oil

1 Thread chicken onto eight skewers. Using fingers, rub combined garlic, paprika, sumac, oregano, the water and oil all over chicken. Cook chicken on heated lightly oiled grill plate (or grill or barbecue) until browned and cooked through.

2 Meanwhile, place herbs, tomato and onion in medium bowl with combined juice and oil; toss gently to combine.

3 Serve chicken skewers with herb salad.

SERVES 4
per serving 6.6g carbohydrate; 10.7g fat; 1367kJ (327 cal); 48.8g protein

cajun chicken with chunky salsa (see back cover)

PREPARATION TIME 20 MINUTES (PLUS REFRIGERATION TIME)   COOKING TIME 20 MINUTES

1 teaspoon cracked black pepper

2 tablespoons finely chopped fresh oregano

2 teaspoons sweet paprika

1 teaspoon dried chilli flakes

2 cloves garlic, crushed

2 teaspoons olive oil

4 single chicken breasts fillets (680g)

CHUNKY SALSA

2 medium tomatoes (300g), chopped coarsely

1 small red onion (100g), chopped coarsely

1 medium green capsicum (200g), chopped coarsely

2 tablespoons coarsely chopped fresh coriander

2 teaspoons olive oil

2 tablespoons lime juice

1 Combine pepper, oregano, paprika, chilli flakes, garlic and oil in large bowl, add chicken; toss to coat chicken in mixture. Cover, refrigerate 15 minutes.

2 Meanwhile, make chunky salsa.

3 Cook chicken in large lightly oiled non-stick frying pan until browned both sides and cooked through. Serve chicken with salsa.

CHUNKY SALSA Combine ingredients in medium bowl.

SERVES 4
per serving 3.9g carbohydrate; 8.7g fat; 1083kJ (259 cal); 40.3g protein

soy chicken and green-onion omelette salad

PREPARATION TIME 20 MINUTES (PLUS REFRIGERATION TIME)   COOKING TIME 25 MINUTES

750g chicken breast fillets

2 tablespoons soy sauce

1 clove garlic, crushed

1 tablespoon peanut oil

6 eggs

4 green onions, sliced thinly

50g baby spinach leaves

50g watercress

CHILLI DRESSING

1 tablespoon sweet chilli sauce

2 tablespoons lime juice

2 fresh small red thai chillies, chopped finely

¼ cup (60ml) peanut oil

1 tablespoon sugar

1 Combine chicken, soy sauce and garlic in large bowl, cover; refrigerate 3 hours or overnight.

2 Drain chicken; discard marinade. Heat oil in large frying pan; cook chicken, in batches, until browned all over and cooked through. Cover chicken; stand 5 minutes, slice thinly.

3 Meanwhile, whisk eggs in medium bowl with onion. Pour half of the egg mixture into heated large non-stick frying pan; cook, tilting pan, over medium heat until egg mixture is almost set. Turn; cook further 2 minutes. Repeat with remaining egg mixture. Roll omelettes together; cut into thin slices.

4 Meanwhile, make chilli dressing.

5 Gently toss chicken and omelette in large bowl with spinach, watercress and three-quarters of the dressing. Serve salad with remaining dressing.

CHILLI DRESSING   Place ingredients in screw-top jar; shake well.

SERVES 4
per serving 7.4g carbohydrate; 30g fat; 2103kJ (503 cal); 50.8g protein

chicken breasts in spinach and fetta sauce

PREPARATION TIME 10 MINUTES   COOKING TIME 30 MINUTES

2 tablespoons olive oil

4 chicken breast fillets (680g)

1 medium onion (150g), chopped finely

2 cloves garlic, crushed

¼ cup (60ml) dry white wine

300ml cream

125g firm fetta cheese, chopped coarsely

250g spinach, trimmed, chopped coarsely

1 Heat oil in large frying pan; cook chicken, uncovered, until browned both sides and cooked through. Remove from pan; cover to keep warm.

2 Place onion and garlic in same pan; cook, stirring, until onion softens. Stir in wine; bring to a boil. Reduce heat; simmer, uncovered, until liquid is almost evaporated. Add cream and cheese; simmer, uncovered, about 5 minutes or until sauce thickens slightly. Add spinach; stir until spinach just wilts. Serve chicken topped with sauce.

SERVES 4
per serving 3.2g carbohydrate; 27.8g fat; 462 cal; 46.7g protein

pesto-grilled chicken drumsticks

PREPARATION TIME 10 MINUTES   COOKING TIME 30 MINUTES

We use a sun-dried tomato pesto in this recipe but you might prefer to experiment with one of the other different flavours.

12 chicken drumsticks (1.8kg)

1 tablespoon olive oil

2 tablespoons lemon juice

3 cloves garlic, crushed

125g butter, softened

2 tablespoons bottled pesto

300g broccoli, cut into florets

1 Make deep diagonal cuts across each chicken drumstick. Combine oil, juice and garlic in large bowl, add chicken; toss to coat chicken in mixture.

2 Combine butter and pesto in small bowl; press two-thirds of the pesto mixture into cuts and all over chicken.

3 Cook chicken on heated oiled grill plate (or grill or barbecue), brushing with remaining pesto mixture occasionally, until browned all over and cooked through.

4 Meanwhile, boil, steam or microwave broccoli until tender; drain.

5 Brush chicken with pan juices just before serving with broccoli.

SERVES 4
per serving 1.1g carbohydrate; 59.6g fat; 3160kJ (756 cal); 55.1g protein

chicken with almond sauce

PREPARATION TIME 15 MINUTES (PLUS REFRIGERATION TIME)   COOKING TIME 25 MINUTES

2 tablespoons olive oil

⅓ cup (80ml) orange juice

2 cloves garlic, crushed

4 single chicken breast fillets (680g)

1 tablespoon olive oil, extra

2 medium fennel bulbs (600g), sliced thinly

400g spring onions, halved

ALMOND SAUCE

1 tablespoon olive oil

2 tablespoons stale breadcrumbs

½ cup (60g) almond meal

pinch ground cloves

¾ cup (180ml) chicken stock

2 tablespoons dry white wine

¼ cup (60ml) thickened cream

1 Combine oil, juice and garlic in medium bowl, add chicken; toss gently to combine. Cover; refrigerate 3 hours or overnight.

2 Heat extra oil in large saucepan; cook fennel and onion, stirring, until onions are soft and browned lightly. Remove from heat; cover to keep warm.

3 Cook drained chicken on heated oiled grill plate (or grill or barbecue) until browned both sides and cooked through.

4 Meanwhile, make almond sauce.

5 Serve chicken with fennel mixture and almond sauce.

ALMOND SAUCE Heat oil in medium saucepan; cook breadcrumbs, stirring, until browned lightly. Add almond meal and cloves; cook, stirring, until browned lightly. Gradually add combined stock and wine, stir over heat until mixture is smooth; bring to a boil. Remove from heat; stir in cream.

SERVES 4
per serving 12g carbohydrate; 35.1g fat; 2286kJ (547 cal); 44.7g protein

rosemary-smoked chicken

PREPARATION TIME 10 MINUTES (PLUS REFRIGERATION TIME)   COOKING TIME 40 MINUTES

You need 250g smoking chips for this recipe.

1 clove garlic, crushed

1½ cups (375ml) dry white wine

1 tablespoon finely chopped
  fresh rosemary

4 single chicken breast fillets (680g)

2 cups (500ml) water

1 clove garlic, crushed, extra

2 tablespoons coarsely chopped
  fresh rosemary

2 tablespoons olive oil

200g oyster mushrooms

200g enoki mushrooms

400g baby spinach leaves

1 Combine garlic, ½ cup of the wine and finely chopped rosemary in large shallow dish, add chicken; toss to coat chicken in mixture. Cover; refrigerate 3 hours or overnight.

2 Combine the water, remaining wine, extra garlic and coarsely chopped rosemary in large bowl, add smoking chips; mix well. Stand at least 2 hours or overnight.

3 Cook chicken on heated oiled barbecue until browned both sides. Place chicken on oiled roasting rack or basket, or in disposable baking dish. Place drained smoking chips in smoke box; place alongside chicken on barbecue. Cook in covered barbecue, using indirect heat, following manufacturer's instructions, about 35 minutes or until chicken is browned all over and cooked through.

4 Just before serving, heat half of the oil in wok; stir-fry oyster mushrooms until just tender, remove from wok. Heat remaining oil in wok; stir-fry enoki mushrooms and spinach until heated through. Serve chicken with spinach and mushrooms.

SERVES 4
per serving 2.2g carbohydrate; 13.6g fat; 1555kJ (372 cal); 44.5g protein

chicken larb

PREPARATION TIME 20 MINUTES   COOKING TIME 15 MINUTES

2 tablespoons peanut oil

**1 tablespoon finely chopped fresh
   lemon grass**

**2 fresh small red thai chillies,
   seeded, chopped finely**

1 clove garlic, crushed

4cm piece fresh ginger (20g), grated

750g chicken mince

4 kaffir lime leaves

1 tablespoon fish sauce

⅓ cup (80ml) lime juice

**1 medium white onion (150g),
   sliced thinly**

**1 cup loosely packed fresh
   coriander leaves**

1¼ cups (100g) bean sprouts

**½ cup loosely packed fresh thai
   basil leaves**

**½ cup loosely packed fresh
   vietnamese mint leaves**

100g watercress

**1 medium green cucumber (170g),
   sliced thinly**

**1 tablespoon finely chopped fresh
   vietnamese mint**

1   Heat half of the oil in large frying pan; cook lemon grass, chilli, garlic and ginger, stirring, until fragrant. Add chicken; cook, stirring, about 10 minutes or until cooked through. Add torn lime leaves, half of the fish sauce and half of the lime juice; cook, stirring, 5 minutes.

2   Combine onion, coriander, sprouts, basil, mint leaves, watercress and cucumber in large bowl; drizzle with combined remaining fish sauce, remaining juice and remaining oil; toss salad gently to combine.

3   Place salad mixture on serving plate, top with chicken mixture; sprinkle with finely chopped mint.

SERVES 4
per serving 4.3g carbohydrate; 24.7g fat; 1659kJ (397 cal); 39.3g protein

barbecued chicken with tomato salad

PREPARATION TIME 10 MINUTES

6 medium egg tomatoes (450g),
   chopped coarsely

1 tablespoon drained baby capers

1 small red onion (100g), sliced thinly

½ cup coarsely chopped fresh
   flat-leaf parsley

1 tablespoon red wine vinegar

¼ cup (60ml) extra virgin olive oil

1 large barbecued chicken (900g), quartered

1   Combine tomato, capers, onion, parsley, vinegar and oil in medium bowl.

2   Serve chicken with tomato salad.

SERVES 4
per serving 3.9g carbohydrate; 34.7g fat; 1923kJ (460 cal); 34g protein
tip Purchase the barbecued chicken on the same day you serve it.

chicken with herb sauce

PREPARATION TIME 15 MINUTES   COOKING TIME 15 MINUTES

4 single chicken breast fillets (680g)

1 tablespoon olive oil

4 green onions, chopped coarsely

2 teaspoons cornflour

1½ cups (375ml) chicken stock

100g soft garlic and herb cheese, crumbled

1 tablespoon coarsely chopped fresh
   flat-leaf parsley

1 tablespoon coarsely chopped fresh chives

20g butter

200g green beans, halved

1 clove garlic, crushed

1 medium green capsicum (200g),
   sliced thinly

1 medium red capsicum (200g), sliced thinly

1   Split chicken fillets through centre horizontally. Heat oil in large non-stick frying pan; cook chicken, in batches, until browned both sides and cooked through. Cover to keep warm.

2   Place onion in same pan; cook, stirring, 2 minutes. Add blended cornflour and stock; cook, stirring, until mixture boils and thickens. Add cheese; stir until cheese melts. Stir in herbs.

3   Melt butter in medium frying pan; cook beans, stirring, until just tender. Add garlic and capsicums; cook, stirring, until capsicum is just tender.

4   Serve vegetables topped with chicken and sauce.

SERVES 4
per serving 6.7g carbohydrate; 21.5g fat; 1655kJ (396 cal); 44.1g protein

chicken with tomatoes and green olives

PREPARATION TIME 10 MINUTES   COOKING TIME 30 MINUTES

1 tablespoon olive oil

4 chicken thighs (880g)

4 chicken drumsticks (600g)

½ cup (125ml) dry white wine

8 cloves garlic, peeled

**1 tablespoon finely chopped fresh
    lemon thyme**

3 bay leaves

500g semi-dried tomatoes

1½ cups (375ml) chicken stock

250g asparagus, trimmed

2 teaspoons cornflour

1 tablespoon water

⅓ cup (50g) seeded green olives

1 Heat oil in large heavy-base frying pan; cook chicken, in batches, until browned lightly all over.

2 Place wine in same pan; bring to a boil. Add garlic, thyme, bay leaves, tomatoes and stock, reduce heat; simmer, covered, about 15 minutes or until chicken is cooked through. Remove chicken from pan; cover to keep warm.

3 Meanwhile, boil, steam or microwave asparagus until tender; drain.

4 Add blended cornflour and water to sauce in pan; stir until mixture boils and thickens slightly.

5 Return chicken to pan with olives; simmer, uncovered, until heated through. Discard bay leaves before serving. Serve with asparagus.

SERVES 4
per serving 10.2g carbohydrate; 48.6g fat; 3047kJ (729 cal); 58g protein

chicken and thai basil stir-fry

PREPARATION TIME 20 MINUTES   COOKING TIME 15 MINUTES

2 tablespoons peanut oil

600g chicken breast fillets, sliced thinly

2 cloves garlic, crushed

1cm piece fresh ginger (5g), grated

4 fresh small red thai chillies, sliced thinly

4 kaffir lime leaves, shredded

1 medium brown onion (150g), sliced thinly

100g mushrooms, quartered

1 large carrot (180g), sliced thinly

¼ cup (60ml) oyster sauce

1 tablespoon soy sauce

1 tablespoon fish sauce

⅓ cup (80ml) chicken stock

1 cup (80g) bean sprouts

¾ cup loosely packed fresh thai basil leaves

1 Heat half of the oil in wok; stir-fry chicken, in batches, until browned all over and cooked through.

2 Heat remaining oil in wok; stir-fry garlic, ginger, chilli, lime leaves and onion until onion softens and mixture is fragrant. Add mushrooms and carrot; stir-fry until carrot is just tender. Return chicken to wok with sauces and stock; stir-fry until sauce thickens slightly. Remove from heat; toss bean sprouts and basil leaves through stir-fry.

SERVES 4
per serving 9.4g carbohydrate; 17.9g fat; 1438kJ (344 cal); 36g protein

poached chicken
with ruby grapefruit salad

PREPARATION TIME 40 MINUTES   COOKING TIME 10 MINUTES

2½ cups (625ml) water

2½ cups (625ml) chicken stock

4 single chicken breast fillets (680g)

1 small red onion (100g)

4 ruby red grapefruits (2kg)

4 green onions, sliced thinly

2 fresh small red thai chillies,

   sliced thinly

1 cup coarsely chopped

   fresh coriander

¼ cup (35g) toasted

   unsalted peanuts

100g baby spinach leaves

2 cloves garlic, crushed

1 tablespoon grated palm sugar

1 tablespoon lime juice

1 tablespoon soy sauce

1 Bring the water and stock to a boil in large frying pan. Add chicken; return to a boil. Reduce heat; simmer, covered, about 10 minutes or until chicken is cooked through. Cool chicken in poaching liquid 10 minutes. Remove chicken from pan; discard poaching liquid. Slice chicken thinly.

2 Meanwhile, halve red onion; cut each half into thin wedges.

3 Segment peeled grapefruit over large bowl; add chicken and onion, then chilli, coriander, nuts and spinach.

4 Place remaining ingredients in small jug; whisk until sugar dissolves. Pour dressing over salad; toss gently to combine.

SERVES 4
per serving 7g carbohydrate; 8g fat; 1066kJ (255 cal); 37.8g protein

anise and ginger braised duck

PREPARATION TIME 30 MINUTES (PLUS REFRIGERATING TIME)   COOKING TIME 2 HOURS

1.7kg duck

¼ cup (60ml) sweet sherry

1 cup (250ml) water

2 tablespoons soy sauce

4 cloves garlic, sliced thinly

3cm piece fresh ginger (15g), sliced thinly

3 star anise

1 teaspoon sambal oelek

1 teaspoon cornflour

2 teaspoons water, extra

500g baby bok choy

1   Using knife or poultry shears, cut down either side of duck backbone; discard. Cut duck in half through breastbone, then cut each half into two pieces. Trim excess fat from duck, leaving skin intact.

2   Place duck pieces in single layer, skin-side down, in large saucepan; cook over low heat 10 minutes or until skin is crisp. Drain on absorbent paper.

3   Place duck in clean saucepan. Add sherry, the water, soy sauce, garlic, ginger, star anise and sambal oelek, reduce heat; simmer, covered, about 1½ hours or until duck is very tender. Turn duck halfway through cooking. Cover undrained duck mixture; refrigerate overnight.

4   Next day, discard fat layer from surface; place duck mixture in large, saucepan. Cover; cook over low heat until duck is heated through. Remove duck from pan; cover to keep warm.

5   Strain liquid into small saucepan; stir in blended cornflour and extra water. Stir over heat until mixture boils and thickens slightly.

6   Meanwhile, boil, steam or microwave baby bok choy until just tender; drain. Serve sauce over duck with greens.

SERVES 4
per serving 4.3g carbohydrate; 40g fat; 2165kJ (518 cal); 32.2g protein

salt and pepper duck with shallots and cucumber

PREPARATION TIME 10 MINUTES   COOKING TIME 2 HOURS 10 MINUTES

2kg duck

1 tablespoons finely ground

   sichuan peppercorns

2 teaspoons sea salt

1 tablespoon peanut oil

20g butter

16 shallots (200g)

2 lebanese cucumbers (260g), sliced thickly

1 tablespoon oyster sauce

½ cup (125ml) chicken stock

¼ cup coarsely chopped fresh coriander

1 Preheat oven to moderate.

2 Place duck, breast-side up, on wire rack in baking dish; rub combined pepper and salt into duck breast. Bake, uncovered, in moderate oven 1½ hours. Remove duck from oven; increase oven temperature to very hot.

3 Using metal skewer or fork, prick duck skin all over. Turn duck breast-side down; bake, uncovered, in very hot oven 15 minutes. Turn duck breast-side up; bake, uncovered, in very hot oven about 20 minutes or until duck is browned all over and cooked through.

4 Meanwhile, heat oil and butter in large frying pan; cook shallots, stirring, until softened. Add cucumber; cook, stirring, 2 minutes. Stir in combined sauce and stock; bring to a boil. Remove from heat; stir in coriander.

5 Cut duck into four pieces; serve on shallot and cucumber mixture.

SERVES 4
per serving 3.8g carbohydrate; 114.1g fat; 4949kJ (1184 cal); 38.5g protein
tip You may prefer to use zucchini instead of cucumber.

braised spatchcocks with spinach

PREPARATION TIME 30 MINUTES   COOKING TIME 40 MINUTES

3 x 500g spatchcocks, skin removed

1 medium leek (350g), chopped coarsely

2 cloves garlic, crushed

1 medium brown onion (150g),

   chopped coarsely

4 bacon rashers (280g), rind removed,

   chopped finely

½ cup (125ml) dry white wine

1 cup (250ml) chicken stock

2 bay leaves

300g brussels sprouts, halved

500g spinach, trimmed, chopped coarsely

½ cup coarsely chopped fresh mint

1 Cut along both sides of spatchcocks' backbones; discard backbones. Cut each spatchcock into four pieces. Rinse under cold water; pat dry with absorbent paper.

2 Cook spatchcock, in batches, in lightly oiled large saucepan until browned lightly both sides. Cook leek, garlic, onion and bacon in same pan, stirring, about 5 minutes or until leek softens. Add wine, stock and bay leaves; bring to a boil. Return spatchcocks and any pan juices to pan, reduce heat; simmer, uncovered, about 20 minutes or until liquid has almost evaporated. Discard bay leaves. Remove from pan; cover to keep warm.

3 Add sprouts; simmer, uncovered, about 3 minutes or until tender. Stir in spinach and mint; cook, stirring, until spinach just wilts.

4 Serve spatchcock with sprouts and spinach mixture.

SERVES 4
per serving 10.1g carbohydrate; 12.1g fat; 1454kJ (347 cal); 47.6g protein

eggplant, spinach and pumpkin stacks (see page 173)

minted lemon grass and ginger iced tea

minted lemon grass and ginger iced tea

PREPARATION TIME 10 MINUTES (PLUS REFRIGERATION TIME)

6 lemon grass and ginger tea bags

1 litre (4 cups) boiling water

2 tablespoons palm sugar

**10cm stick (20g) finely chopped
   fresh lemon grass**

½ small orange, sliced thinly

½ lemon, sliced thinly

**¼ cup firmly packed fresh mint
   leaves, torn**

1   Place tea bags and the boiling water in large heatproof jug; stand
    5 minutes.

2   Discard tea bags. Add sugar, lemon grass, orange and lemon
    to jug; stir to combine. Refrigerate, covered, until cold.

3   Stir mint into cold tea; serve over ice.

SERVES 4
per serving 8g carbohydrate; 0.1g fat; 146kJ (35 cal); 0.4g protein

chicken yakitori with sesame dipping sauce

PREPARATION TIME 15 MINUTES   COOKING TIME 10 MINUTES

The uncooked chicken can be skewered and sauce made a day ahead. Cover separately; refrigerate until required. You need 16 bamboo skewers for this recipe; remember to soak them in cold water for at least 1 hour before using to prevent them splintering or scorching.

500g chicken breast fillets

2 tablespoons soy sauce

1 tablespoon mirin

1 teaspoon sugar

½ teaspoon sesame oil

1 teaspoon sesame seeds

1   Cut chicken into 16 long thin slices; thread each slice on a skewer. Cook, in batches, on heated oiled grill plate (or grill or barbecue) until chicken is browned all over and cooked through.

2   Meanwhile, combine remaining ingredients in small bowl.

3   Serve chicken hot with dipping sauce.

SERVES 4
per serving 1.7g carbohydrate; 3.8g fat; 673kJ (161 cal); 29g protein

turkish spinach dip

PREPARATION TIME 10 MINUTES (PLUS REFRIGERATION AND COOLING TIME)   COOKING TIME 10 MINUTES

Dip can be made a day ahead. Cover refrigerate until required. You need 1 bunch of spinach weighing 300g for this recipe.

1 tablespoon olive oil

1 small brown onion (80g), chopped finely

1 clove garlic, crushed

1 teaspoon ground cumin

½ teaspoon curry powder

¼ teaspoon ground turmeric

100g trimmed spinach leaves,
    shredded finely

500g thick yogurt

1   Heat oil in medium frying pan; cook onion and garlic, stirring, until onion softens. Add spices; cook, stirring, until fragrant. Add spinach; cook, stirring, until spinach wilts. Transfer mixture to serving bowl; cool 10 minutes.

2   Stir yogurt into spinach mixture, cover; refrigerate 1 hour.

3   Serve cold with assorted crudites.

SERVES 4
per serving 6.8g carbohydrate; 8.9g fat; 581kJ (139 cal); 6.8g protein

peking duck wraps

Buy a whole large barbecued duck from a Chinese food shop the day before serving this recipe. Remove and discard skin and bones; slice the meat thinly. Cover; refrigerate until required.

8 green onions, trimmed

¼ cup (60ml) hoisin sauce

1 tablespoon plum sauce

2 cups (250g) thinly sliced barbecued
 duck meat

16 small butter lettuce leaves

1 Cut white section of onion from green section. Dip green sections in medium bowl of boiling water for 5 seconds, then place in medium bowl of cold water; drain. Thinly slice white sections.

2 Divide combined sauces, duck and slices of white section of onion among lettuce leaves. Roll lettuce to enclose filling; tie each wrap with one piece of green section of onion to secure. Serve peking duck wraps cold or at room temperature.

SERVES 4
per serving 10.6g carbohydrate; 17.3g fat; 1041kJ (249 cal); 13.5g protein
tip You may need extra green onions to ensure you have enough green sections to wrap the lettuce leaves.

bocconcini, olive and cherry tomato with pesto

Pesto can be made up to 2 days ahead. Cover; refrigerate until required.

½ cup (40g) finely grated
 parmesan cheese

½ cup (80g) toasted pine nuts

2 cloves garlic, crushed

1 cup (250ml) extra virgin olive oil

2 cups firmly packed fresh basil leaves

16 cherry tomatoes, halved

32 baby bocconcini (450g)

32 medium seeded green olives (110g)

1 Blend or process cheese, nuts, garlic and half of the oil until combined. Add basil and remaining oil; process until almost smooth. Transfer pesto to serving bowl.

2 Thread one tomato half, one bocconcini and one olive onto each toothpick. Serve cold with pesto.

SERVES 4
per serving 8.5g carbohydrate; 91.7g fat; 3979kJ (952 cal); 26.6g protein

chilli con queso

PREPARATION TIME 10 MINUTES   COOKING TIME 10 MINUTES

2 teaspoons vegetable oil

½ small green capsicum (75g),
   chopped finely

½ small brown onion (40g),
   chopped finely

1 tablespoon drained bottled jalapeño
   chillies, chopped finely

1 clove garlic, crushed

½ x 400g can undrained chopped
   peeled tomatoes

250g packet cream cheese, softened

1   Heat oil in medium saucepan; cook capsicum, onion, chilli and garlic, stirring, until onion softens. Add tomato; cook, stirring, 2 minutes.

2   Add cheese; whisk until cheese melts and dip is smooth. Serve hot.

SERVES 4
per serving 3.8g carbohydrate; 23.1g fat; 1016kJ (243 cal); 5.9g protein

smoked salmon cones

PREPARATION TIME 40 MINUTES (PLUS REFRIGERATION TIME)

Cheese mixture can be made up to a day ahead. Cover; refrigerate until required.

400g smoked salmon slices

⅔ cup (160ml) cream

60g cream cheese, softened

2 tablespoons toasted pistachios,
   chopped finely

2 tablespoons finely chopped
   fresh chives

24 baby spinach leaves (50g)

1   Blend or process 100g of the salmon until chopped finely. Add cream and cheese; process until smooth. Transfer mixture to medium bowl; stir in nuts and chives. Refrigerate until firm.

2   Halve remaining salmon slices widthways; place one spinach leaf on each salmon slice, top with 1 teaspoon of the cheese mixture. Roll each into small cone to enclose filling.

3   Place cones on serving tray, cover; refrigerate 2 hours.

4   Serve cold.

SERVES 4
per serving 3g carbohydrate; 27.3g fat; 1522kJ (364 cal); 27.1g protein

BLT on mini toasts

PREPARATION TIME 20 MINUTES   COOKING TIME 5 MINUTES

1 bacon rasher (70g)

20 mini toasts

2 butter lettuce leaves

2 tablespoons whole egg mayonnaise

10 grape tomatoes, halved

1   Discard rind from bacon; cut bacon into pieces slightly smaller than mini toasts. Heat large frying pan; cook bacon, stirring, until browned and crisp, drain on absorbent paper.

2   Cut lettuce into pieces slightly larger than mini toasts.

3   Divide mayonnaise among mini toasts; top each with lettuce, bacon and tomato. Serve at room temperature.

SERVES 4
per serving 3.7g carbohydrate; 11.6g fat; 539kJ (129 cal); 2.8g protein

fried chorizo with garlic

PREPARATION TIME 5 MINUTES   COOKING TIME 10 MINUTES

2 chorizo sausages (340g)

2 teaspoons olive oil

1 clove garlic, crushed

2 tablespoons finely chopped fresh flat-leaf parsley

1   Cut sausages into 5mm slices. Cook sausage slices in large heated frying pan, stirring, until crisp; drain on absorbent paper. Discard fat from pan.

2   Heat oil in same pan; cook sausage slices, garlic and parsley, stirring, until heated through.

SERVES 4
per serving 2.8g carbohydrate; 21.1g fat; 1003kJ (240 cal); 10.3g protein

denver omelette

PREPARATION TIME 10 MINUTES   COOKING TIME 15 MINUTES

10 eggs

⅓ cup (80g) sour cream

2 fresh small red thai chillies, seeded, chopped finely

2 teaspoons vegetable oil

3 green onions, sliced thinly

1 medium green capsicum (200g), chopped finely

100g leg ham, chopped finely

2 small tomatoes (260g), seeded, chopped finely

½ cup (60g) coarsely grated cheddar cheese

1   Break eggs in large bowl, whisk lightly; whisk in sour cream and chilli.

2   Heat oil in large non-stick frying pan; cook onion and capsicum, stirring, until onion softens. Place onion mixture in medium bowl with ham, tomato and cheese; toss to combine.

3   Pour ½ cup of the egg mixture into same lightly oiled frying pan; cook, tilting pan, over low heat until almost set. Sprinkle about ⅓ cup of the filling over half of the omelette; using spatula, fold omelette over to completely cover the filling.

4   Pour ¼ cup of the egg mixture into empty half of pan; cook over low heat until almost set. Sprinkle about ⅓ cup of the filling over folded omelette, fold omelette over top of first omelette to cover filling. Repeat twice more, using ¼ cup of the egg mixture each time, to form one large layered omelette. Carefully slide omelette onto plate; cover to keep warm.

5   Repeat steps 3 and 4 to make second omelette, using remaining egg and remaining filling. Cut each denver omelette in half.

SERVES 4
per serving 3.4g carbohydrate; 29.5g fat; 1601kJ (383 cal); 26.9g protein

herbed olive, white bean and anchovy dip

PREPARATION TIME 15 MINUTES   COOKING TIME 15 MINUTES

8 drained anchovy fillets

¼ cup (60ml) milk

2 tablespoons olive oil

1 small red onion (100g),

chopped finely

1 clove garlic, crushed

2 tablespoons finely chopped fresh

flat-leaf parsley

2 teaspoons finely chopped

fresh marjoram

1 teaspoon finely chopped

fresh thyme

300g can white beans,

rinsed, drained

¼ cup (30g) seeded black olives,

chopped finely

1½ tablespoons drained

capers, rinsed

2 teaspoons red wine vinegar

1 tablespoon lemon juice

2 tablespoons olive oil, extra

1   Combine anchovies and milk in small bowl, stand 10 minutes; drain well. Heat oil in large frying pan; cook onion, garlic and herbs, stirring, until onion is soft.

2   Blend or process anchovies, onion mixture, beans, olives, capers, vinegar and juice until combined; with motor operating, add extra oil in thin, steady stream, process until almost smooth. Serve with assorted crudites.

SERVES 4
per serving 9.8g carbohydrate; 13.3g fat; 727kJ (174 cal); 4.4g protein

chilli garlic mushrooms

PREPARATION TIME 10 MINUTES   COOKING TIME 5 MINUTES

¼ cup (60ml) olive oil

40g butter

5 cloves garlic, crushed

2 fresh small thai red chillies,
   chopped finely

800g button mushrooms

1 tablespoon lemon juice

½ teaspoon cracked black pepper

2 tablespoons finely chopped fresh
   flat-leaf parsley

1 Heat oil and butter in large saucepan; cook garlic, chillies and mushrooms, stirring, about 5 minutes or until mushrooms are tender.

2 Add remaining ingredients; stir until combined.

SERVES 4
per serving 1.6g carbohydrate; 9.6g fat; 435kJ (104 cal); 3.2g protein
tip Best made just before serving.

prosciutto-wrapped melon with vinaigrette

PREPARATION TIME 10 MINUTES

½ medium rockmelon (850g)

12 slices prosciutto (180g)

1 tablespoon red wine vinegar

¼ cup (60ml) olive oil

½ clove garlic, crushed

¼ teaspoon sugar

1 teaspoon finely chopped fresh
   flat-leaf parsley

1 teaspoon finely chopped
   fresh oregano

1 Peel and seed rockmelon; cut into 12 slices. Wrap a slice of prosciutto around each rockmelon slice.

2 Place remaining ingredients in screw-top jar; shake well. Drizzle vinaigrette over rockmelon.

SERVES 4
per serving 8.4g carbohydrate; 16.4g fat; 903kJ (216 cal); 9g protein

eggplant salad caprese

PREPARATION TIME 20 MINUTES (PLUS STANDING AND REFRIGERATION TIME)   COOKING TIME 15 MINUTES

3 small eggplants (690g), cut into
**   1cm slices**

coarse cooking salt

2 medium tomatoes (380g),
**   sliced thinly**

350g bocconcini cheese, sliced thinly

¼ cup firmly packed fresh
**   basil leaves**

CLASSIC ITALIAN DRESSING

¼ cup (60ml) olive oil

1 clove garlic, crushed

1 teaspoon wholegrain mustard

1 teaspoon sugar

2 tablespoons red wine vinegar

1   Place eggplant slices on wire racks, sprinkle with salt; stand 30 minutes. Rinse eggplant; drain on absorbent paper. Cook eggplant, in batches, on heated oiled grill plate (or grill or barbecue) until browned both sides.

2   Meanwhile, make classic Italian dressing.

3   Layer eggplant with remaining ingredients on serving platter; drizzle with three-quarters of the dressing. Cover; refrigerate at least 15 minutes or up to 3 hours. Just before serving, drizzle with remaining dressing.

CLASSIC ITALIAN DRESSING   Place ingredients in screw-top jar; shake well.

SERVES 4
per serving   5.7g carbohydrate; 27.4g fat; 1409kJ (337 cal); 17.2g protein

tomato, basil and red onion salad

PREPARATION TIME 15 MINUTES

4 large egg tomatoes (360g),
**   sliced thinly**

1 small red onion (100g), sliced thinly

2 tablespoons fresh small
**   basil leaves**

pinch salt

pinch cracked black pepper

pinch sugar

2 teaspoons balsamic vinegar

2 teaspoons extra virgin olive oil

1   Alternate layers of tomato, onion and basil on serving platter; sprinkle with salt, pepper and sugar. Drizzle with vinegar and oil.

SERVES 4
per serving   2.7g carbohydrate; 2.3g fat; 150kJ (36 cal); 1.1g protein

rocket and prosciutto frittata

PREPARATION TIME 15 MINUTES   COOKING TIME 25 MINUTES

4 slices prosciutto (60g)

30g rocket leaves

1 tablespoon finely grated
parmesan cheese

5 eggs, beaten lightly

1 tablespoon cream

1 Preheat oven to moderate.

2 Grease deep 19cm-square cake pan; line base and two opposite sides with baking paper.

3 Cook prosciutto, in batches, in medium non-stick frying pan until browned all over and crisp; drain on absorbent paper.

4 Place half of the prosciutto in prepared pan; cover with half of the rocket then half of the cheese. Repeat with remaining prosciutto, rocket and cheese.

5 Pour combined egg and cream into pan, pressing down on prosciutto mixture to completely cover with egg mixture; bake, uncovered, in moderate oven about 20 minutes or until firm. Stand 5 minutes; turn out of pan, cut into 8 pieces.

SERVES 4
per serving 0.5g carbohydrate; 9.9g fat; 573kJ (137 cal); 11.9g protein
tip Serve frittata hot or cold.

marinated olives

PREPARATION TIME 10 MINUTES (PLUS MARINATING TIME)

1 cup (130g) green olives

¾ cup (120g) kalamata olives

1 lime wedge

1 cup (250ml) olive oil (approx)

1 clove garlic, sliced thinly

¼ cup (60ml) lime juice

3 sprigs fresh thyme, halved

2 sprigs fresh rosemary

1 Combine ingredients in large sterilised jar, ensuring olives are covered in oil; seal jar.

SERVES 4
per serving 8.7g carbohydrate; 58.4g fat; 2332kJ (558 cal); 1.2g protein
tip Olives are best made at least two weeks before you serve them; store, covered, in a cool dark place.

char-grilled radicchio parcels with buffalo-milk mozzarella and semi-dried tomatoes

PREPARATION TIME 15 MINUTES   COOKING TIME 15 MINUTES

While mozzarella is traditionally made from buffalo milk, you could use a variety made from cow milk.

4 large radicchio leaves

2 buffalo-milk mozzarella (140g),

   sliced into 8 pieces

8 semi-dried tomato pieces (30g)

8 fresh basil leaves

1 Boil, steam or microwave radicchio until wilted slightly; drain. Rinse under cold water; drain. Pat dry with absorbent paper.

2 Centre one piece mozzarella on each leaf; top with one piece tomato and one basil leaf. Repeat with one piece each mozzarella, tomato and basil; roll radicchio to enclose filling.

3 Grill radicchio parcels on heated oiled grill plate (or grill or barbecue) until browned all over and heated through.

SERVES 4
per serving 3.5g carbohydrate; 8.4g fat; 552kJ (132 cal); 10.6g protein

citrus crush

PREPARATION TIME 10 MINUTES

2 medium limes, cut into wedges

2 medium lemons, cut into wedges

1 tablespoon brown sugar

½ cup firmly packed fresh

   mint leaves

4 cups crushed ice

500ml diet lemonade

1 Using mortar and pestle, crush lime, lemon, sugar and mint until mixture is pulpy and sugar dissolved.

2 Combine citrus mixture in large jug with crushed ice. Stir lemonade into jug; serve immediately.

SERVES 4
per serving 4.4g carbohydrate; 0.2g fat; 125kJ (30 cal); 0.6g protein

spicy lamb and garlic skewers

PREPARATION TIME 10 MINUTES (PLUS REFRIGERATION TIME)   COOKING TIME 10 MINUTES

You need eight bamboo skewers for this recipe; remember to soak them in water for at least 1 hour before using to avoid them splintering or scorching.

500g lamb fillets

1 small brown onion (80g),
   grated coarsely

1 clove garlic, crushed

1 teaspoon finely grated lemon rind

2 teaspoons finely chopped
   fresh rosemary

¼ teaspoon cayenne pepper

½ teaspoon ground coriander

1 teaspoon ground cumin

2 tablespoons red wine vinegar

¼ cup (60ml) olive oil

1   Cut lamb into 2cm pieces. Thread lamb onto eight skewers. Place skewers in large shallow dish; pour over combined remaining ingredients. Cover; refrigerate 3 hours or overnight. Drain skewers; reserve marinade.

2   Cook skewers, in batches, on heated oiled grill plate (or grill or barbecue), brushing occasionally with reserved marinade, until browned all over and cooked as desired.

SERVES 4
per serving 0.9g carbohydrate; 18.2g fat; 1166kJ (279 cal); 27.7g protein

pesto fish kebabs

PREPARATION TIME 10 MINUTES   COOKING TIME 15 MINUTES

You can use any large fish fillets or steaks — such as ling, gemfish, snapper, kingfish or silver warehou — for this recipe. You need eight bamboo skewers for this recipe; remember to soak them in water for at least 1 hour before using to avoid them splintering or scorching.

600g firm white fish fillets

1 tablespoon bottled pesto

½ cup finely chopped fresh
**   flat-leaf parsley**

½ small savoy cabbage
**   (approximately 600g),**
**   shredded finely**

⅓ cup (65g) drained baby
**   capers, rinsed**

1 teaspoon finely grated lemon rind

½ cup finely chopped fresh mint

1   Cut fish into 2cm cubes; combine with pesto and 1 tablespoon of the parsley in medium bowl. Thread onto eight skewers.

2   Cook kebabs, in batches, in heated large lightly oiled frying pan until browned and cooked as desired. Cover to keep warm.

3   Add cabbage to same heated pan; cook, stirring, until just tender. Stir in remaining parsley with capers, rind and mint.

4   Serve fish kebabs on cabbage mixture.

SERVES 4

per serving 5g carbohydrate; 5.5g fat; 853kJ (204 cal); 33.4g protein
tip Fish can be marinated and threaded onto skewers a day ahead; store, covered, in refrigerator.

Losing Weight Slower (less than 25g carbs per serving)

baked apples with berries and honey yogurt

PREPARATION TIME 10 MINUTES (PLUS REFRIGERATION TIME)   COOKING TIME 45 MINUTES

300g frozen mixed berries

4 large granny smith apples (800g)

4 cardamom pods

½ cup (140g) yogurt

2 teaspoons honey

1   Place berries in fine sieve set over medium bowl, cover; thaw in refrigerator overnight.

2   Preheat oven to moderately slow.

3   Core unpeeled apples about three-quarters of the way in from stem end, making the hole 4cm in diameter. Using small sharp knife, cut shallow ring around circumference of each apple. Pierce small cut in base of each apple; insert one cardamom pod into each cut.

4   Pack berries firmly into cored apples; reserve remaining berries. Place apples in small baking dish; bake, uncovered, in moderately slow oven about 45 minutes or until apples are just tender.

5   Meanwhile, push remaining berries through sieve into small bowl; stir in yogurt and honey. Divide apples among serving plates; top with yogurt mixture.

SERVES 4
per serving 24.2g carbohydrate; 1.2g fat; 506kJ (121 cal); 3.5g protein

citrus compote

PREPARATION TIME 20 MINUTES

2 large limes (160g)

3 large oranges (900g)

2 medium pink grapefruit (850g)

2 teaspoons sugar

½ vanilla bean, split

1 tablespoon small fresh mint leaves

1   Grate the rind of 1 lime and 1 orange finely; reserve grated rind. Peel remaining lime, remaining oranges and grapefruit.

2   Segment all citrus over large bowl to save juice, removing and discarding membrane from each segment. Add segments to bowl with sugar, vanilla bean and reserved rind; stir gently to combine.

3   Stand, covered, 5 minutes; sprinkle with mint leaves.

SERVES 4
per serving 21.6g carbohydrate; 0.5g fat; 460kJ (110 cal); 3.0g protein

banana passionfruit soy smoothie

PREPARATION TIME 10 MINUTES (PLUS REFRIGERATION TIME)

You need about six passionfruit for this recipe.

½ cup (125ml) passionfruit pulp

2 cups (500ml) no-fat soy milk

2 medium ripe bananas (400g),
  chopped coarsely

1 Strain pulp through sieve into small bowl; reserve liquid and seeds.

2 Blend or process passionfruit liquid, soy milk and banana, in batches, until smooth.

3 Pour smoothie into large jug; stir in reserved seeds. Refrigerate, covered, until cold.

MAKES 1 LITRE
per 250ml 19.9g carbohydrate; 0.6g fat; 443kJ (106 cal); 5.3g protein

peach galette

PREPARATION TIME 15 MINUTES   COOKING TIME 20 MINUTES

2 medium peaches (300g)

6 sheets fillo pastry

60g butter, melted

3 teaspoons sugar

1 tablespoon apricot jam,
  warmed, sieved

1 Preheat oven to moderately hot. Line oven tray with baking paper.

2 Halve peaches, discard seeds; slice peach halves thinly.

3 Place two pastry sheets on board; brush lightly with a third of the butter. Top with two more pastry sheets; brush lightly with half of the remaining butter. Repeat layering with remaining pastry and remaining butter.

4 Fold pastry in half to form a square; cut 22cm-diameter circle from pastry square. Arrange peach slices on pastry circle; sprinkle with sugar. Bake, uncovered, in moderately hot oven about 20 minutes or until galette browns.

5 Serve warm galette brushed with jam.

SERVES 4
per serving 23.1g carbohydrate; 12.8g fat; 907kJ (217 cal); 2.7g protein
tips Cover the pastry with greaseproof paper then a damp towel when you're working with it, to prevent it drying out. Nectarines, apricots, apples, plums and pears are all suitable to use in place of the peaches.

mixed berry smoothie

PREPARATION TIME 5 MINUTES

250g frozen low-fat strawberry yogurt, softened slightly

250g frozen mixed berries

3 cups (750ml) low-fat milk

1   Blend or process ingredients, in batches, until smooth. Serve immediately.

MAKES 1 LITRE
per 250ml 23.7g carbohydrate; 3.4g fat; 681kJ(163 cal); 10.3g protein

mixed berry smoothie

crisp prosciutto with mango and avocado salsa

crisp prosciutto with mango and avocado salsa

PREPARATION TIME 15 MINUTES (PLUS REFRIGERATION TIME)   COOKING TIME 5 MINUTES

1 medium mango (400g),
  chopped coarsely

1 large avocado (320g)
  chopped coarsely

1 small red onion (100g),
  chopped finely

1 small red capsicum (150g),
  chopped finely

1 fresh small red thai chilli,
  chopped finely

2 tablespoons lime juice

8 slices prosciutto (120g),
  halved lengthways

1 Place mango, avocado, onion, capsicum, chilli and juice in medium bowl; toss salsa to combine. Refrigerate, covered, 30 minutes.

2 Meanwhile, cook prosciutto, in batches, in medium lightly oiled frying pan until crisp.

3 Serve prosciutto with chilled salsa.

SERVES 4
per serving 12.2g carbohydrate; 14.7g fat; 890kJ (213 cal); 8.2g protein

saffron scrambled eggs on corn cakes

PREPARATION TIME 15 MINUTES   COOKING TIME 20 MINUTES

1 fresh corn cob (250g)

½ cup (75g) plain flour

1 teaspoon sweet paprika

1 tablespoon finely chopped
  fresh coriander

¼ cup (60ml) milk

3 egg whites

3 eggs

3 egg whites, extra

pinch saffron threads

1 Cut corn kernels from cob. Combine corn, flour, paprika and coriander in medium bowl; stir in milk.

2 Beat egg whites in small bowl with electric mixer until soft peaks form; fold egg whites into corn mixture. Cook 2 tablespoon portions of the corn mixture in large heated oiled non-stick frying pan until browned both sides and cooked through.

3 Combine egg, extra egg white and saffron in medium bowl; beat lightly with a fork. Cook egg mixture in lightly oiled non-stick frying pan, stirring gently, until creamy and just set. Serve scrambled eggs with corn cakes.

SERVES 4
per serving 2.9g carbohydrate; 2.6g fat; 631kJ (151 cal); 9.6g protein

pancetta and eggs

PREPARATION TIME 10 MINUTES   COOKING TIME 10 MINUTES

8 slices pancetta (120g)

2 green onions, chopped coarsely

4 eggs

4 thick slices white bread

1 Preheat oven to moderately hot. Oil four holes of 12-hole (⅓ cup/80ml) muffin pan.

2 Line each of the prepared holes with 2 slices of the pancetta, overlapping to form cup shape. Divide onion among pancetta cups; break one egg into each pancetta cup.

3 Bake, uncovered, in moderately hot oven about 10 minutes or until eggs are just cooked and pancetta is crisp around edges. Remove from pan carefully. Serve on toasted bread.

SERVES 4
per serving 18.4g carbohydrate; 10.2g fat; 953kJ (228 cal); 15.6g protein

poached eggs with burned sage butter and asparagus

PREPARATION TIME 10 MINUTES   COOKING TIME 10 MINUTES

80g butter

12 fresh sage leaves

4 eggs

250g asparagus, trimmed

2 multigrain muffins

40g shaved parmesan cheese

1   Melt butter in small saucepan; cook sage, stirring, about 3 minutes or until butter changes colour to deep brown. Remove from heat; cover to keep warm.

2   Half-fill a large shallow frying pan with water; bring to a boil. One at a time, break eggs into cup, then slide into pan. When all eggs are in pan, allow water to return to a boil. Cover pan, turn off heat; stand about 4 minutes or until a light film of egg white sets over yolks. One at a time, remove eggs, using egg slide, and place on absorbent-paper-lined saucer to blot up poaching liquid.

3   Meanwhile, boil, steam or microwave asparagus until tender; drain. Cover to keep warm. Split muffins; toast cut-side.

4   Place muffin halves on serving plates; top each with equal amounts of asparagus, an egg, 1 tablespoon of sage butter and cheese.

SERVES 4
per serving 12.6g carbohydrate; 26.1g fat; 1450Kj (347 cal); 16.2g protein

spiced iced coffee milkshake

PREPARATION TIME 10 MINUTES (PLUS COOLING TIME)

¼ cup (20g) ground espresso coffee

¾ cup (180ml) boiling water

2 cardamom pods, bruised

¼ teaspoon ground cinnamon

1 tablespoon brown sugar

3 scoops (375ml) low-fat
    vanilla ice-cream

2½ cups (625ml) low-fat milk

1   Place coffee and the boiling water in coffee plunger; stand 2 minutes before plunging. Pour coffee into small heatproof bowl with cardamom, cinnamon and sugar; stir to dissolve sugar then cool 10 minutes.

2   Strain coffee mixture through fine sieve into blender or processor; process with ice-cream and milk until mixture is smooth. Serve immediately.

MAKES 1 LITRE
per 250ml 19.9g carbohydrate; 1.6g fat; 510kJ (122 cal); 7.9g protein

soufflé with berry compote

PREPARATION TIME 15 MINUTES   COOKING TIME 10 MINUTES

1 tablespoon caster sugar

2 egg yolks

⅓ cup (55g) icing sugar mixture

4 egg whites

2 teaspoons icing sugar mixture, extra

BERRY COMPOTE

½ cup frozen mixed berries

2 tablespoons fresh orange juice

1 teaspoon sugar

1   Preheat oven to moderate. Lightly oil four 1-cup (250ml) ovenproof dishes.

2   Sprinkle insides of dishes evenly with caster sugar; shake away excess. Place on baking tray.

3   Whisk yolks and 2 tablespoons of the icing sugar in large bowl until mixture is combined.

4   Beat egg whites in small bowl with electric mixer until soft peaks form. Gradually add remaining icing sugar; beat until firm peaks form.

5   Gently fold egg white mixture, in two batches, into egg yolk mixture. Divide mixture among prepared dishes. Bake, uncovered, in moderate oven about 10 minutes or until souffles are puffed and browned lightly. Dust top with extra sifted icing sugar.

6   Meanwhile, make berry compote.

7   Serve soufflés with berry compote.

BERRY COMPOTE   Combine ingredients in small saucepan; bring to a boil. Reduce heat; simmer, uncovered, 2 minutes.

SERVES 4
per serving   15.6g carbohydrate; 2.9g fat; 451kJ (108 cal); 5.4g protein

ham, avocado and roasted tomato toast

PREPARATION TIME 10 MINUTES   COOKING TIME 30 MINUTES

4 large egg tomatoes (360g)

1 tablespoon brown sugar

1 small red onion (100g), sliced thinly

150g shaved ham

4 thick slices vienna loaf

½ small avocado (100g), sliced thinly

1 tablespoon finely shredded
   fresh basil

1   Preheat oven to very hot.

2   Cut tomatoes in half lengthways; place cut-side up on oiled oven tray, sprinkle with sugar. Bake tomato, uncovered, in very hot oven 15 minutes. Add onion; bake further 15 minutes or until tomato is soft.

3   Cook ham in small heated frying pan until browned lightly and almost crisp.

4   Toast bread; top with ham, onion, tomato, avocado and basil.

SERVES 4
per serving   24.8g carbohydrate; 7.5g fat; 907kJ (217 cal); 12.3g protein.

red capsicum and cheese soufflés

PREPARATION TIME 15 MINUTES   COOKING TIME 45 MINUTES

1 medium red capsicum (200g)

60g butter

1 medium leek (350g), sliced thinly

2 tablespoons plain flour

1 cup (250ml) milk

½ cup (125ml) cream

1 tablespoon wholegrain mustard

⅓ cup (25g) finely grated
   parmesan cheese

4 eggs, separated

1   Lightly oil four 1-cup (250ml) ovenproof dishes on oven tray.

2   Quarter capsicum, remove seeds and membrane. Grill capsicum, skin-side up, until skin blisters and blackens. Cover capsicum with plastic or paper for 5 minutes; peel away skin, finely chop capsicum.

3   Preheat oven to moderately hot.

4   Heat butter in large frying pan; cook leek, stirring, until soft. Stir in flour, stir over heat until mixture bubbles. Remove pan from heat; gradually stir in milk, cream, mustard and capsicum. Stir over heat until mixture boils and thickens; cool 5 minutes.

5   Stir cheese and egg yolks into cream mixture. Beat egg whites in small bowl until soft peaks form; gently fold egg whites into capsicum mixture, in two batches. Spoon mixture into prepared dishes. Bake, uncovered, in moderately hot oven about 20 minutes or until soufflés are puffed and browned lightly.

SERVES 4
per serving 12.3g carbohydrate; 33.3g fat; 1676kJ (401 cal); 14.2g protein

grilled haloumi salad (see page 182)

PREPARATION TIME 25 MINUTES   COOKING TIME 30 MINUTES

2 medium red capsicums (400g)

2 medium yellow capsicums (400g)

1 medium eggplant (300g),
  sliced thickly

cooking-oil spray

2 cloves garlic, crushed

360g haloumi, sliced thinly

1 tablespoon lemon juice

1 small red onion (100g),
  sliced thinly

100g baby rocket leaves

¼ cup loosely packed fresh basil

½ cup (80g) drained
  caperberries, rinsed

1 lemon, cut into wedges

LEMON DRESSING

¼ cup (60ml) lemon juice

2 teaspoons olive oil

1 teaspoon sugar

1 Quarter capsicums; discard seeds and membranes. Roast under grill, skin-side up, until skin blisters and blackens. Cover capsicum pieces in plastic or paper for 5 minutes; peel away skin, slice thinly.

2 Place eggplant slices on oiled oven tray; spray with oil, sprinkle with half of the garlic. Roast under grill, turning occasionally, about 15 minutes or until softened. Cool 10 minutes; slice into thick strips.

3 Meanwhile, make lemon dressing.

4 Place cheese in small bowl with juice and remaining garlic; toss gently to combine. Cook cheese in heated oiled large frying pan, turning occasionally, about 5 minutes or until browned both sides.

5 Meanwhile, place capsicum, eggplant and dressing in large bowl with onion, rocket, basil and caperberries; toss gently to combine.

6 Divide salad among serving plates; top with cheese and lemon.

LEMON DRESSING Place ingredients in screw-top jar; shake well.

SERVES 4
per serving 14.5g carbohydrate; 26g fat; 1630kJ (390 cal); 23.9g protein

sesame tofu salad

PREPARATION TIME 25 MINUTES   COOKING TIME 10 MINUTES

2 x 300g blocks firm silken tofu

2 tablespoons toasted
  sesame seeds

2 tablespoons kalonji

2 teaspoons dried chilli flakes

2 tablespoons cornflour

vegetable oil, for deep-frying

5 green onions, sliced thinly

1 large avocado (320g),
  chopped coarsely

100g red oak lettuce leaves, torn

100g mizuna

1 fresh long red chilli, seeded,
  sliced thinly

SESAME DRESSING

2 shallots (50g), chopped finely

2 tablespoons toasted
  sesame seeds

1 tablespoon sesame oil

1 tablespoon kecap manis

1cm piece fresh ginger (5g), grated

¼ cup (60ml) lemon juice

1   Make sesame dressing.

2   Cut each tofu block lengthways into four slices; dry gently with absorbent paper. Combine sesame, kalonji, chilli and cornflour in large shallow bowl; press seed mixture onto both sides of tofu slices.

3   Heat oil in wok or large saucepan; deep-fry tofu, in batches, until browned lightly. Drain on absorbent paper.

4   Place remaining ingredients in large bowl; toss gently to combine. Divide salad among serving plates; top with tofu, drizzle with dressing.

SESAME DRESSING Place ingredients in screw-top jar; shake well.

SERVES 4
per serving 12.5g carbohydrate; 44g fat; 2282kJ (546 cal); 25.7g protein

beetroot soup

PREPARATION TIME 10 MINUTES (PLUS REFRIGERATION TIME)   COOKING TIME 35 MINUTES

1 teaspoon olive oil

1 small brown onion (80g), chopped coarsely

1 clove garlic, crushed

3 medium beetroot (500g), trimmed,
    chopped coarsely

1 medium apple (150g), cored,
    chopped coarsely

1 litre (4 cups) vegetable stock

½ cup (125ml) water

¼ cup (60ml) lemon juice

¼ teaspoon Tabasco sauce

½ lebanese cucumber (65g), seeded,
    chopped finely

½ small red onion (50g), chopped finely

1 tablespoon light sour cream

1   Heat oil in large saucepan; cook onion and garlic, stirring, until onion softens. Add beetroot, apple, stock and the water; bring to a boil. Reduce heat; simmer, covered, about 20 minutes or until beetroot is tender, stirring occasionally.

2   Blend or process soup, in batches, until smooth. Stir in juice and sauce; refrigerate, covered, until cold.

3   Serve chilled soup topped with combined remaining ingredients.

SERVES 4
per serving 17.4g carbohydrate 3.4g fat; 518kJ (124 cal); 5.8g protein

pumpkin, basil and chilli stir-fry

PREPARATION TIME 10 MINUTES   COOKING TIME 15 MINUTES

⅓ cup (80ml) peanut oil

1 large brown onion (200g), sliced thinly

2 cloves garlic, sliced thinly

4 fresh small red thai chillies, sliced thinly

1kg pumpkin, chopped coarsely

200g sugar snap peas

1 teaspoon grated palm sugar

¼ cup (60ml) vegetable stock

2 tablespoons soy sauce

¾ cup loosely packed fresh opal basil leaves

4 green onions, sliced thinly

½ cup (75g) toasted unsalted peanuts

1   Heat oil in wok; cook brown onion, in batches, until browned and crisp. Drain on absorbent paper.

2   Stir-fry garlic and chilli in same wok until fragrant. Add pumpkin; stir-fry until browned all over and just tender. Add peas, sugar, stock and sauce; stir-fry until sauce thickens slightly.

3   Remove from heat; toss basil, green onion and nuts through stir-fry until combined. Serve topped with fried onion.

SERVES 4
per serving 21.1g carbohydrate; 28.2g fat; 1605kJ (384 cal); 12.2g protein

swiss brown mushroom and barley soup

PREPARATION TIME 10 MINUTES   COOKING TIME 55 MINUTES

300g swiss brown mushrooms, quartered

1 clove garlic, crushed

2 teaspoons soy sauce

2 teaspoons water

1 small brown onion (80g), chopped finely

1 litre (4 cups) chicken stock

1 litre (4 cups) water, extra

½ cup (100g) pearl barley

1 untrimmed celery stalk (150g),
   chopped coarsely

2 small carrots (140g), chopped coarsely

½ teaspoon freshly ground black pepper

1 Cook mushrooms, garlic, sauce and the water in heated large non-stick frying pan until mushrooms soften.

2 Cook onion in heated lightly oiled large saucepan, stirring, until softened. Add stock and the extra water; bring to a boil. Add barley, reduce heat; simmer, covered, 30 minutes.

3 Add mushroom mixture to saucepan with remaining ingredients; cook, uncovered, about 20 minutes or until barley and vegetables are tender.

SERVES 4
per serving 21.8g carbohydrate; 1.9g fat; 581kJ (139 cal); 8.5g protein

eggplant, spinach and pumpkin stacks (see page 145)

PREPARATION TIME 15 MINUTES   COOKING TIME 15 MINUTES

1 large eggplant (500g)

coarse cooking salt

200g pumpkin, sliced thinly

700g bottled tomato pasta sauce

100g baby spinach leaves

4 green onions, sliced thinly lengthways

1 cup (100g) coarsely grated
   mozzarella cheese

¼ cup (40g) toasted pine nuts

1 Discard top and bottom of eggplant; cut eggplant lengthways into ten 5mm slices. Discard rounded-skin-side slices; place remaining eight slices in colander, sprinkle all over with salt; stand 10 minutes.

2 Rinse eggplant well under cold water; pat dry with absorbent paper. Cook eggplant and pumpkin, in batches, on heated oiled grill plate (or grill or barbecue) until tender.

3 Meanwhile, place sauce in medium saucepan; bring to a boil. Reduce heat; simmer, uncovered, 2 minutes.

4 Place four slices of the eggplant, in single layer, on large shallow baking dish; top with half of the spinach, half of the pumpkin and half of the onion. Spoon 2 tablespoons of the sauce over each then repeat layering process, using remaining spinach, remaining pumpkin, remaining onion and another 2 tablespoons of the sauce for each stack. Top stacks with remaining eggplant slices; pour over remaining sauce, sprinkle stacks with cheese and nuts. Place under preheated grill until cheese browns lightly.

SERVES 4
per serving 17.4g carbohydrate; 13.2g fat; 1012kJ (242 cal); 13.3g protein

five-coloured salad

PREPARATION TIME 20 MINUTES (PLUS SOAKING TIME)   COOKING TIME 10 MINUTES

6 dried shiitake mushrooms

6cm-long 5cm-diameter piece
   daikon (120g), peeled, sliced
   thinly lengthways

1 medium carrot (120g), sliced
   thinly, lengthways

150g green beans, quartered
   lengthways, cut into 4cm lengths

10 dried apricots, sliced thinly

1 teaspoon finely grated
   lemon rind

DRESSING

200g firm tofu

2 tablespoons tahini

3 teaspoons sugar

2 teaspoons japanese soy sauce

1 tablespoon rice vinegar

1 tablespoon mirin

1 Place mushrooms in small heatproof bowl, cover with boiling water, stand 20 minutes or until just tender; drain. Remove and discard stems, slice caps thinly.

2 Meanwhile, make dressing.

3 Boil, steam or microwave daikon, carrot and beans, separately, until just tender; drain. Rinse under cold water; drain.

4 Place apricot and vegetables in medium bowl; toss gently to combine.

5 Just before serving, pour dressing over salad; toss gently to combine. Divide salad among serving bowls, shape into mounds, sprinkle with rind.

DRESSING Press tofu between two chopping boards with a weight on top, raise one end; stand 25 minutes. Blend or process tofu until smooth, place in small bowl; stir in tahini. Add remaining ingredients; stir until sugar dissolves.

SERVES 4
per serving 12.3g carbohydrate; 10.7g fat; 782kJ (187 cal); 10.4g protein
tip The salad and dressing can be prepared ahead and refrigerated separately. Combine just before serving.

gazpacho

PREPARATION TIME 30 MINUTES (PLUS REFRIGERATION TIME)

A chilled soup originating in the southern province of Andalusia in Spain, gazpacho, like other peasant soups, makes clever use of the garden's overripe vegetables.

1 litre (4 cups) tomato juice

10 medium egg tomatoes (750g),
  chopped coarsely

2 medium red onions (340g),
  chopped coarsely

2 cloves garlic, quartered

1 lebanese cucumber (130g),
  chopped coarsely

2 tablespoons sherry vinegar

1 medium red capsicum (200g),
  chopped coarsely

1 small red onion (100g),
  chopped finely

1 lebanese cucumber (130g),
  chopped finely

1 small red capsicum (150g),
  chopped finely

1 tablespoon finely chopped
  fresh dill

1 Blend or process juice, tomato, coarsely chopped onion, garlic, coarsely chopped cucumber, vinegar and coarsely chopped capsicum, in batches, until pureed. Cover; refrigerate 3 hours.

2 Just before serving, divide soup among serving bowls; stir equal amounts of finely chopped onion, finely chopped cucumber, finely chopped capsicum and dill into each bowl.

SERVES 6
per serving 17.3g carbohydrate; 0.3g fat; 397kJ (95 cal); 4.6g protein
tips A finely chopped red chilli added to the blender or processor makes a spicier gazpacho. Red wine vinegar can be used instead of sherry vinegar.
serving suggestion To make this soup a complete meal, add ½ cup of both finely chopped raw celery and finely chopped green capsicum to the soup, then top each serving with 1 tablespoon of finely diced hard-boiled egg.

deep-fried prawn balls

PREPARATION TIME 25 MINUTES (PLUS STANDING TIME)   COOKING TIME 10 MINUTES

1kg large cooked king prawns

5 green onions, chopped finely

2 cloves garlic, crushed

4 fresh small red thai chillies, seeded,
  chopped finely

1cm piece fresh ginger (5g), grated

1 tablespoon cornflour

2 teaspoons fish sauce

¼ cup coarsely chopped fresh coriander

¼ cup (25g) packaged breadcrumbs

½ cup (35g) stale breadcrumbs

vegetable oil, for deep-frying

⅓ cup (80ml) sweet chilli sauce

1 Shell and devein prawns; cut in half. Blend or process prawns, pulsing, until chopped coarsely. Place in large bowl with onion, garlic, chilli, ginger, cornflour, fish sauce and coriander; mix well.

2 Using hands, roll rounded tablespoons of the prawn mixture into balls. Roll prawn balls in combined breadcrumbs; place, in single layer, on plastic wrap-lined tray. Cover; refrigerate 30 minutes.

3 Heat oil in wok or large saucepan; deep-fry prawn balls, in batches, until browned lightly and cooked through. Serve with sweet chilli sauce.

SERVES 4
per serving 17.2g carbohydrate; 11.3g fat; 1262kJ (302 cal); 32.4g protein

roast baby turnip soup

PREPARATION TIME 25 MINUTES   COOKING TIME 1 HOUR 10 MINUTES

3kg baby turnips

2 tablespoons olive oil

1 large brown onion (200g), chopped coarsely

1 clove garlic, quartered

2 litres (8 cups) chicken stock

½ cup (125ml) cream

¼ cup finely chopped fresh chervil

1 Preheat oven to hot. Trim and discard turnip leaves; leave 3cm-length of stem attached to 24 of the smallest turnips, remove and discard stems on remainder. Scrub turnips thoroughly; peel the 24 small turnips, retaining the 3cm stem. Chop remaining unpeeled turnips coarsely.

2 Combine all turnips with half of the oil in large baking dish; toss to coat thoroughly. Roast, uncovered, in hot oven about 45 minutes or until turnips are tender and browned all over.

3 Heat remaining oil in large saucepan; cook onion and garlic, stirring, until onion softens. Add chopped turnip and stock; bring to a boil. Reduce heat; simmer, uncovered, 10 minutes.

4 Blend or process soup mixture, in batches, until pureed.

5 Return soup to same cleaned pan with whole turnips and cream; stir over heat until hot. Just before serving, stir in chervil.

SERVES 6
per serving 16.6g carbohydrate; 15.1g fat; 995kJ (238 cal); 9.2g protein
tip Choose 24 of the smallest turnips you have, matching them as closely as possible in size. Spoon four of these tiny roasted turnips into each portion of soup when serving.

squid, chorizo and tomato salad

PREPARATION TIME 30 MINUTES   COOKING TIME 15 MINUTES

Chorizo is a sausage made traditionally of coarsely ground pork and seasoned with garlic and chillies.
If you cannot find fresh chorizo, substitute any spicy sausage.

900g squid

2 chorizo sausages (340g),
   sliced thinly

1 tablespoon olive oil

4 medium tomatoes (600g), seeded,
   sliced thickly

3 x 400g cans white beans,
   rinsed, drained

2 cups loosely packed fresh flat-leaf
   parsley leaves

1 teaspoon finely grated lemon rind

¼ cup (60ml) lemon juice

1 Cut squid down centre to open out; score the inside in diagonal pattern then cut into 2cm strips.

2 Cook chorizo in heated large non-stick frying pan, stirring occasionally, until browned.

3 Cook squid, in batches, in same reheated pan until tender.

4 Place chorizo and squid in large bowl with remaining ingredients; toss gently to combine.

SERVES 4
per serving 24.4g carbohydrate; 25.1g fat; 1973kJ (472 cal); 38.2g protein

radicchio with thai crab salad

PREPARATION TIME 20 MINUTES (PLUS REFRIGERATION TIME)   COOKING TIME 5 MINUTES

Dressing can be made a day ahead. Cover; refrigerate until required.
Crab salad can be assembled up to 4 hours ahead. Cover; refrigerate until required.

¼ cup (60ml) water

¼ cup (60ml) lime juice

2 tablespoons sugar

2 fresh small red thai chillies, seeded,
   chopped finely

500g fresh crab meat

1 lebanese cucumber (130g), seeded,
   chopped finely

1 small red capsicum (150g),
   chopped finely

2 green onions, sliced thinly

4 radicchio

1 Combine the water, juice, sugar and chilli in small saucepan; stir over heat, without boiling, until sugar dissolves; bring to a boil. Remove from heat; cool 10 minutes. Cover; refrigerate dressing until cold.

2 Combine crab, cucumber, capsicum, onion and dressing in medium bowl.

3 Trim ends and cores from radicchio; separate leaves. Serve radicchio topped with crab salad.

SERVES 4
per serving 19.1g carbohydrate; 1.5g fat; 731kJ (175 cal); 21g protein
tip We used radicchio, but you can also use red or white witlof if you prefer.

grilled cuttlefish, rocket and parmesan salad

PREPARATION TIME 20 MINUTES   COOKING TIME 10 MINUTES

1kg cuttlefish hoods

2 tablespoons olive oil

1 tablespoon finely grated lemon rind

⅓ cup (80ml) lemon juice

1 clove garlic, crushed

150g rocket

150g sun-dried tomatoes, drained, chopped coarsely

1 small red onion (100g), sliced thinly

1 tablespoon drained baby capers, rinsed

80g parmesan cheese, shaved

2 tablespoons balsamic vinegar

⅓ cup (80ml) olive oil, extra

1   Halve cuttlefish lengthways, score insides in crosshatch pattern then cut into 5cm strips. Combine cuttlefish in medium bowl with oil, rind, juice and garlic, cover; refrigerate 10 minutes.

2   Meanwhile, combine rocket, tomato, onion, capers and cheese in large bowl.

3   Drain cuttlefish; discard marinade. Cook cuttlefish, in batches, on heated oiled grill plate (or grill or barbecue) until browned and cooked through.

4   Add cuttlefish to salad with combined vinegar and extra oil; toss gently to combine.

SERVES 4
per serving 15.6g carbohydrate; 40.1g fat; 2700kJ (646 cal); 55g protein

braised leek and witlof salad with poached eggs

PREPARATION TIME 20 MINUTES   COOKING TIME 35 MINUTES

1 tablespoon olive oil

20 pencil leeks (1.6kg), trimmed to
   15cm in length

6 white witlof (750g),
   halved lengthways

⅔ cup (160ml) dry white wine

1 cup (250ml) vegetable stock

1 teaspoon sugar

8 eggs

CREAMY CHERVIL DRESSING

2 tablespoons lemon juice

1 tablespoon wholegrain mustard

⅔ cup (160ml) cream

¼ cup loosely packed fresh
   chervil leaves

1 Preheat oven to moderately hot. Make creamy chervil dressing.

2 Heat oil in large flameproof baking dish; cook leeks and witlof, cut-side down, in single layer, for 1 minute. Add wine, stock and sugar; bring to a boil. Reduce heat; simmer, uncovered, 2 minutes. Cover tightly; cook in moderately hot oven about 20 minutes or until tender.

3 Meanwhile, half-fill a large shallow frying pan with water; bring to a boil. One at a time, break eggs into cup and slide into pan. When all eggs are in pan, allow water to return to a boil. Cover pan, turn off heat; stand about 4 minutes or until a light film of egg white sets over yolks. One at a time, remove eggs, using slotted spoon, and place on absorbent-paper-lined saucer to blot poaching liquid.

4 Divide witlof among serving plates; top with leeks and 2 eggs each, drizzle with dressing.

CREAMY CHERVIL DRESSING Place ingredients in screw-top jar; shake well.

SERVES 4
per serving 12.3g carbohydrate; 31.2g fat; 1835kJ (439 cal); 21.3g protein

grilled squid and octopus salad

PREPARATION TIME 30 MINUTES (PLUS REFRIGERATION TIME) COOKING TIME 10 MINUTES

500g squid hoods

500g cleaned baby octopus

2 long green chillies,
   chopped finely

6 cloves garlic, crushed

500g asparagus, halved

500g yellow teardrop
   tomatoes, halved

200g cornichons, rinsed, drained

1 large orange (240g), peeled,
   sliced thickly

100g baby rocket leaves

ORANGE VINAIGRETTE

1 tablespoon olive oil

¼ cup (60ml) fresh orange juice

1cm piece fresh ginger (5g), grated

1 teaspoon finely grated
   orange rind

2 tablespoons malt vinegar

1   Cut squid down the centre to open out; score inside in diagonal pattern then cut into thick strips. Quarter octopus lengthways.

2   Combine squid and octopus in large bowl with chilli and garlic; toss to coat seafood in marinade. Cover; refrigerate 3 hours or overnight.

3   Make orange vinaigrette.

4   Boil, steam or microwave asparagus until just tender; drain. Rinse under cold water; drain. Combine in large bowl with remaining ingredients.

5   Cook seafood, in batches, on heated oiled grill plate (or grill or barbecue) until browned lightly and cooked through.

6   Place seafood and vinaigrette in bowl with salad; toss gently to combine.

ORANGE VINAIGRETTE Place ingredients in screw-top jar; shake well.

SERVES 4
per serving 6.8g carbohydrate; 7g fat; 1083kJ (259 cal); 31.3g protein

grilled squid and octopus salad

grilled haloumi salad (see page 170)

crab and apple salad

PREPARATION TIME 20 MINUTES   COOKING TIME 5 MINUTES

250g sugar snap peas, trimmed

1 large apple (200g)

500g cooked blue swimmer
   crab meat

1 medium red onion (170g), halved,
   sliced thinly

2 fresh small red thai chillies, seeded,
   sliced thinly lengthways

2 medium avocados (500g),
   sliced thickly

150g mesclun

⅓ cup (80ml) olive oil

¼ cup (60ml) lemon juice

1 tablespoon dijon mustard

1 clove garlic, crushed

1 Boil, steam or microwave peas until just tender; drain. Rinse under cold water; drain.

2 Slice apple thinly; cut slices into thin strips. Combine peas and apple in large bowl with crab, onion, chilli, avocado and mesclun.

3 Place remaining ingredients in screw-top jar; shake well. Drizzle dressing over salad; toss gently to combine.

SERVES 4
per serving 12.6g carbohydrate; 39.1g fat; 2006kJ (480 cal); 20.4g protein

grilled scallops with pawpaw salsa

PREPARATION TIME 15 MINUTES   COOKING TIME 10 MINUTES

800g firm pawpaw, chopped coarsely

2 medium tomatoes (380g), seeded,
   chopped coarsely

1 medium red onion (170g),
   chopped coarsely

¼ cup (60ml) lime juice

1 fresh small red thai chilli, seeded,
   chopped finely

2 tablespoons coarsely chopped
   fresh coriander

1 tablespoon vegetable oil

36 scallops with roe

1 Combine pawpaw, tomato, onion, juice, chilli, coriander and oil in large bowl.

2 Cook scallops on heated oiled grill plate (or grill or barbecue), in batches, until browned both sides.

3 Serve pawpaw salsa topped with scallops.

SERVES 4
per serving 13.8g carbohydrate; 5.6g fat; 706kJ (169 cal); 15.3g protein

beef and baby corn soup

PREPARATION TIME 10 MINUTES   COOKING TIME 10 MINUTES

1.5 litres (6 cups) water

410g can beef consomme

2cm piece fresh ginger (10g), grated

2 tablespoons soy sauce

1 teaspoon sesame oil

50g bean thread noodles

500g beef rump, trimmed, sliced thinly

1 small red capsicum (150g), sliced thinly

200g fresh baby corn

1 green onion, sliced thinly

500g baby bok choy, chopped coarsely

2 cups (160g) bean sprouts

1 fresh small red thai chilli, sliced thinly

1 Combine the water, consomme, ginger, sauce and oil in large saucepan; bring to a boil. Add noodles; using fork, separate noodles. Reduce heat; simmer, uncovered, until noodles are just tender.

2 Add remaining ingredients; stir until mixture is heated through and beef is cooked as desired.

SERVES 4
per serving 20.4g carbohydrate; 5.7g fat; 1187kJ (284 cal); 36.9g protein

beef salad with blue-cheese dressing

PREPARATION TIME 10 MINUTES   COOKING TIME 20 MINUTES

500g pumpkin, chopped coarsely

2 medium red capsicums (400g),
    chopped coarsely

1 tablespoon olive oil

4 beef fillet steaks (500g)

300g green beans, trimmed,
    halved crossways

250g grape tomatoes, halved

100g baby rocket leaves

BLUE-CHEESE DRESSING

¼ cup (60ml) olive oil

2 cloves garlic, crushed

¼ cup (60ml) orange juice

60g blue cheese, crumbled

1 Preheat oven to very hot.

2 Place pumpkin and capsicum, in single layer, in large shallow baking dish; drizzle with oil. Roast, uncovered, in very hot oven about 20 minutes or until pumpkin is tender.

3 Meanwhile, make blue-cheese dressing.

4 Cook beef on heated oiled grill plate (or grill or barbecue) until browned both sides and cooked as desired. Cover; stand 5 minutes.

5 Meanwhile, boil, steam or microwave beans until just tender; drain.

6 Slice beef thinly. Combine beef, beans, pumpkin and capsicum in large bowl with tomato and rocket, drizzle with dressing; toss gently to combine.

BLUE-CHEESE DRESSING Place ingredients in screw-top jar; shake well.

SERVES 4
per serving 15.3g carbohydrate; 29.3g fat; 1956kJ (468 cal); 36g protein

reuben salad

PREPARATION TIME 15 MINUTES   COOKING TIME 10 MINUTES

2 tablespoons mayonnaise

1 tablespoon mild chilli sauce

1 teaspoon horseradish cream

2 green onions, chopped finely

400g can sauerkraut, drained

1 tablespoon finely chopped fresh chives

4 slices rye bread

8 slices corned beef (240g)

180g swiss cheese, sliced thinly

4 large dill pickles (260g)

1 Combine mayonnaise, sauce, horseradish cream and onion in medium bowl. Combine sauerkraut and chives in small bowl.

2 Divide bread, corned beef, cheese and sliced pickles among serving plates; serve with sauerkraut mixture.

SERVES 4
per serving 22.6g carbohydrate; 18.9g fat; 1710kJ (409 cal); 36g protein

italian fennel and beef-fillet salad
with balsamic vinaigrette (see page 218)

PREPARATION TIME 15 MINUTES   COOKING TIME 15 MINUTES

80g bean thread noodles

4 beef scotch fillet steaks (800g)

2 medium fennel bulbs (600g), sliced thinly

1 medium red onion (170g), sliced thinly

150g baby rocket leaves

1¼ cups (100g) shaved parmesan cheese

BALSAMIC VINAIGRETTE

¼ cup (60ml) lemon juice

2 cloves garlic, crushed

¼ cup (60ml) olive oil

2 tablespoons balsamic vinegar

1 tablespoon coarsely chopped fresh thyme

1 Place noodles in medium heatproof bowl; cover with boiling water, stand until just tender, drain.

2 Make balsamic vinaigrette.

3 Cook beef on heated oiled grill plate (or grill or barbecue) until browned both sides and cooked as desired. Cover; stand 5 minutes.

4 Cut noodles into 5cm lengths; place in large bowl with fennel, onion and rocket. Slice beef thinly, add to noodles with vinaigrette; toss gently to combine. Serve salad topped with cheese.

BALSAMIC VINAIGRETTE Place ingredients in screw-top jar; shake well.

SERVES 4
per serving 19.2g carbohydrate; 32g fat; 2466kJ (590 cal); 55.1g protein

beef and bean tacos

PREPARATION TIME 15 MINUTES   COOKING TIME 20 MINUTES

1 clove garlic, crushed

80g lean beef mince

½ teaspoon chilli powder

¼ teaspoon ground cumin

300g can kidney beans,
**   rinsed, drained**

2 tablespoons tomato paste

½ cup (125ml) water

1 medium tomato (190g),
**   chopped coarsely**

4 taco shells

¼ small iceberg lettuce,
**   shredded finely**

SALSA CRUDA

½ lebanese cucumber (65g),
**   seeded, chopped finely**

½ small red onion (40g),
**   chopped finely**

1 small tomato (130g), seeded,
**   chopped finely**

1 teaspoon mild chilli sauce

1   Preheat oven to moderate.

2   Heat large lightly oiled non-stick frying pan; cook garlic and beef, stirring, until beef is browned all over. Add chilli, cumin, beans, paste, the water and tomato; cook, covered, over low heat about 15 minutes or until mixture thickens slightly.

3   Meanwhile, toast taco shells, upside-down and uncovered, on oven tray in moderate oven for 5 minutes.

4   Make salsa cruda.

5   Just before serving, fill taco shells with beef mixture, lettuce and salsa cruda.

SALSA CRUDA   Combine ingredients in small bowl.

SERVES 4
per serving   17.5g carbohydrate 4.8g fat; 644kJ (154 cal); 9.7g protein

beetroot and pastrami salad with horseradish mayonnaise

PREPARATION TIME 30 MINUTES   COOKING TIME 10 MINUTES

7 trimmed red radishes (100g)

250g red coral lettuce, trimmed

300g pastrami, torn into
   large pieces

12 cornichons (180g), drained,
   halved lengthways

2 tablespoons coarsely chopped
   fresh dill

1 tablespoon olive oil

1 tablespoon red wine vinegar

3 medium fresh beetroot (500g),
   peeled, grated coarsely

HORSERADISH MAYONNAISE

1 egg

1 tablespoon horseradish cream

1 tablespoon lemon juice

½ cup (125ml) olive oil

1   Make horseradish mayonnaise.

2   Slice radishes thinly; cut slices into thin strips. Combine radish in large bowl with lettuce, pastrami, cornichon and dill. Combine oil, vinegar and beetroot in medium bowl.

3   Divide pastrami salad among serving plates; top with beetroot salad, drizzle with mayonnaise.

HORSERADISH MAYONNAISE Blend or process egg, horseradish cream and juice until combined. With motor operating, add oil in thin, steady stream until mayonnaise thickens slightly.

SERVES 4
per serving 16.5g carbohydrate; 38.4g fat; 2115kJ (506 cal); 24.5g protein

harira

PREPARATION TIME 20 MINUTES (PLUS SOAKING TIME)   COOKING TIME 2 HOURS 10 MINUTES

½ cup (100g) dried chickpeas

500g boned shoulder of lamb

2 tablespoons olive oil

1 large brown onion (200g), chopped coarsely

2 teaspoons ground ginger

1 tablespoon ground cumin

1 teaspoon ground cinnamon

2 teaspoons ground coriander

6 saffron threads

3 trimmed celery stalks (300g),
   chopped coarsely

7 medium tomatoes (1.3kg), seeded,
   chopped coarsely

2.5 litres (10 cups) water

½ cup (100g) brown lentils

¼ cup coarsely chopped fresh coriander

1   Place chickpeas in small bowl, cover with water; soak overnight, drain.

2   Trim lamb of excess fat; cut into 2cm cubes.

3   Heat oil in large saucepan; cook onion, stirring, until soft. Add spices; cook, stirring, about 2 minutes or until fragrant. Add lamb and celery; cook, stirring, about 2 minutes or until lamb is coated in spice mixture. Add tomato; cook, stirring, about 10 minutes or until tomato slightly softens. Stir in the water and drained chickpeas; bring to a boil. Reduce heat; simmer, covered, about 1½ hours or until lamb is tender, stirring occasionally.

4   Stir in lentils; cook, covered, about 30 minutes or until lentils are just tender. Just before serving, stir fresh coriander into soup.

SERVES 6
per serving 16.4g carbohydrate; 12.2g fat; 1154kJ (276 cal); 25.1g protein
serving suggestion Serve with lemon wedges.

rosemary lamb open sandwich

PREPARATION TIME 5 MINUTES (PLUS REFRIGERATION TIME)   COOKING TIME 15 MINUTES

2 cloves garlic, crushed

¼ cup (60ml) lemon juice

2 tablespoons fresh rosemary leaves

1 tablespoon wholegrain mustard

1kg lamb fillets

2 small tomatoes (260g)

250g asparagus, halved

4 slices light rye bread

100g butter lettuce, chopped coarsely

1   Combine garlic, juice, rosemary and mustard in medium bowl, add lamb; toss to coat lamb in marinade. Cover; refrigerate 3 hours or overnight.

2   Cut each tomato into six wedges. Cook tomato and asparagus, in batches, on heated oiled grill plate (or grill or barbecue) until browned lightly and just tender. Toast bread both sides.

3   Drain lamb; discard marinade. Cook lamb on same heated grill plate until browned and cooked as desired. Cover; stand 5 minutes. Slice thickly.

4   Place one slice of the toast on each serving plate; top each slice with equal amounts of lettuce, tomato, asparagus and lamb.

SERVES 4
per serving 20.7g carbohydrate; 8.9g fat; 1099kJ (263 cal); 24.3g protein

roasted pumpkin, bacon and fetta frittata

PREPARATION TIME 20 MINUTES   COOKING TIME 1 HOUR 15 MINUTES

600g pumpkin, chopped coarsely

1 tablespoon olive oil

1 medium red capsicum (200g), chopped coarsely

6 green onions, cut into 5cm pieces

4 bacon rashers (280g), rind removed,
  chopped coarsely

1 clove garlic, crushed

½ cup (40g) finely grated parmesan cheese

6 eggs

2 teaspoons cornflour

½ cup (125ml) cream

100g fetta cheese, crumbled

1   Preheat oven to hot.

2   Combine pumpkin and oil in large baking dish; bake, uncovered, in hot oven 15 minutes. Add capsicum, onion, bacon and garlic; bake, uncovered, about 15 minutes or until pumpkin and bacon are browned lightly.

3   Meanwhile, grease deep 19cm-square cake pan; sprinkle base and sides with half of the parmesan.

4   Reduce oven temperature to moderate. Spoon pumpkin mixture into prepared pan. Whisk eggs in medium bowl with remaining parmesan and blended cornflour and cream. Pour egg mixture over pumpkin mixture; sprinkle with fetta. Bake, uncovered, in moderate oven about 45 minutes or until frittata sets. Stand 10 minutes; turn out. Cut into quarters; serve with a fresh green salad, if desired.

SERVES 4
per serving 12.8g carbohydrate; 38.8g fat; 2157kJ (516 cal); 309g protein

pork and peach salad

PREPARATION TIME 20 MINUTES (PLUS STANDING TIME) COOKING TIME 10 MINUTES

1 tablespoon peanut oil

300g pork fillet

500g peaches, chopped coarsely

1 medium red capsicum (200g), sliced thinly

1 stick fresh lemon grass, sliced thinly

2 fresh kaffir lime leaves, shredded finely

100g watercress

2 tablespoons coarsely chopped fresh
  vietnamese mint

2 tablespoons drained thinly sliced pickled ginger

PICKLED GARLIC DRESSING

1 tablespoon drained finely chopped pickled garlic

2 fresh small red thai chillies, seeded, sliced thinly

1 tablespoon rice vinegar

1 tablespoon lime juice

1 tablespoon fish sauce

1 tablespoon palm sugar

1   Heat oil in wok; cook pork, turning, until browned all over and cooked as desired. Cover; stand 10 minutes, slice thinly.

2   Meanwhile, make pickled garlic dressing.

3   Place pork in medium bowl with dressing; toss to coat pork all over. Stand 10 minutes.

4   Meanwhile, place peach, capsicum, lemon grass, lime leaves, watercress and mint in large bowl.

5   Add pork mixture to peach mixture; toss gently to combine. Serve sprinkled with pickled ginger.

PICKLED GARLIC DRESSING Place ingredients in screw-top jar; shake well.

SERVES 4
per serving 12.4g carbohydrate; 6.8g fat; 798kJ (191 cal); 19.3g protein

mixed cabbage coleslaw with chinese barbecued pork

PREPARATION TIME 30 MINUTES

Chinese cabbage, also known as peking or napa cabbage, wong bok or petsai, is elongated in shape with pale-green crinkly leaves. The most common cabbage in South-East Asia, it is the basis of the pickled Korean condiment, kim chi. It can be shredded or chopped and eaten raw or braised, steamed or stir-fried. You need about a quarter of a savoy cabbage, a quarter of a red cabbage, and half a small chinese cabbage for this recipe.

3 cups (240g) finely shredded savoy cabbage

3 cups (240g) finely shredded red cabbage

3 cups (240g) finely shredded chinese cabbage

2 medium carrots (240g), grated coarsely

1 small red capsicum (200g), sliced thinly

⅓ cup coarsely chopped fresh coriander

1 fresh long red chilli, sliced thinly

500g chinese barbecued pork, sliced thinly

SWEET SOY DRESSING

1 tablespoon sesame oil

1 tablespoon fish sauce

2 tablespoons soy sauce

1 tablespoon brown sugar

1 Make sweet soy dressing.

2 Place ingredients and dressing in large bowl; toss gently to combine.

SWEET SOY DRESSING Place ingredients in screw-top jar; shake well.

SERVES 4
per serving 16g carbohydrate; 24.1g fat; 1697kJ (406 cal); 31.7g protein

gypsy ham salad with mustard vinaigrette

PREPARATION TIME 20 MINUTES   COOKING TIME 2 MINUTES

300g snow peas, trimmed

2 medium avocados (500g),
  sliced thickly

1⅓ cups (200g) drained semi-dried
  tomatoes, chopped coarsely

150g baby spinach leaves

350g gypsy ham, torn into
  large pieces

MUSTARD VINAIGRETTE

2 cloves garlic, crushed

2 tablespoons white wine vinegar

2 tablespoons finely chopped fresh
  flat-leaf parsley

1cm piece fresh ginger (5g), grated

1 tablespoon wholegrain mustard

1 tablespoon warm water

¼ cup (60ml) extra light olive oil

1 Boil, steam or microwave snow peas until tender; drain. Rinse under cold water; drain.

2 Meanwhile, make mustard vinaigrette.

3 Place snow peas in large bowl with remaining ingredients; toss gently to combine. Divide salad among serving plates; drizzle with vinaigrette.

MUSTARD VINAIGRETTE Place ingredients in screw-top jar; shake well.

SERVES 4
per serving 21.5g carbohydrate; 40.8g fat; 2332kJ (558 cal); 25.8g protein

grilled pork chops with baby beet salad

PREPARATION TIME 20 MINUTES   COOKING TIME 10 MINUTES

4 x 200g pork chops

750g canned whole baby beets, rinsed,
    drained, quartered

1 cup (80g) bean sprouts

1 small red capsicum (200g), sliced thinly

1 medium carrot (120g), sliced thinly

1 trimmed celery stalk (100g), sliced thinly

1 small red onion (100g), sliced thinly

½ cup loosely packed fresh mint leaves

1 tablespoon finely grated lime rind

¼ cup (60ml) lime juice

2 tablespoons olive oil

1 Cook pork on heated oiled grill plate (or grill or barbecue) until browned both sides and cooked as desired.

2 Meanwhile, place beets, sprouts, capsicum, carrot, celery, onion and mint in large serving bowl.

3 Combine remaining ingredients in screw-top jar; shake well.

4 Drizzle three-quarters of the dressing over salad; toss gently to combine. Serve pork with salad; drizzle remaining dressing over pork.

SERVES 4
per serving 15.5g carbohydrate; 23.9g fat; 1856kJ (444 cal); 41.9g protein

grilled turkey kebabs with witlof and grapefruit salad

PREPARATION TIME 40 MINUTES   COOKING TIME 15 MINUTES

800g turkey breast steaks, diced into
    2cm pieces

2 tablespoons olive oil

1 clove garlic, crushed

3 small pink grapefruits (1kg)

4 white witlof (500g)

2 trimmed celery stalks (200g), sliced thinly

2 cups loosely packed fresh flat-leaf
    parsley leaves

1 medium red onion (170g), sliced thinly

2 tablespoons dried barberries

¼ cup (35g) toasted shelled pistachios,
    chopped coarsely

CITRUS DRESSING

¼ cup (60ml) olive oil

1 tablespoon lime juice

2 teaspoons sugar

1 Thread turkey onto skewers; brush with combined oil and garlic. Cover; refrigerate until required.

2 Segment peeled grapefruits over small bowl to save juice; reserve segments and juice separately.

3 Separate witlof leaves; place in large bowl with grapefruit segments, celery, parsley, onion and barberries.

4 Make citrus dressing.

5 Cook turkey skewers on heated oiled grill plate (or grill or barbecue) until browned and cooked through.

6 Add dressing and nuts to salad; toss gently to combine. Serve salad with turkey skewers.

CITRUS DRESSING Strain reserved grapefruit juice into screw-top jar with oil, juice and sugar; shake well.

SERVES 4
per serving 16.9g carbohydrate; 34.3g fat; 2412kJ (577 cal); 49.7g protein

yakitori seasoned chicken on skewers

PREPARATION TIME 20 MINUTES   COOKING TIME 15 MINUTES (PLUS COOLING TIME)

Chicken wings, chicken liver or vegetables of your choice can be used in this dish, but remember to cut even-sized pieces and use ingredients that take about the same time to cook. You will need to soak eight bamboo skewers in water for an hour before using to prevent them from splintering and scorching.

500g chicken thigh or breast fillets,

cut into 2.5cm pieces

1 medium red capsicum (200g),

chopped coarsely

4 fresh shiitake mushrooms, stems

removed, halved

6 thick green onions, trimmed, cut into

2.5cm lengths

¼ teaspoon japanese pepper (sansho powder)

SAUCE

½ cup (125ml) japanese soy sauce

½ cup (125ml) sake

¼ cup (60ml) mirin

2 tablespoons sugar

1   Thread chicken and vegetables onto eight bamboo skewers, leaving space between pieces to allow even cooking.

2   Make sauce.

3   Cook, in batches, on heated oiled grill plate (or grill or barbecue), turning and brushing with sauce occasionally, until browned all over and cooked through.

4   Serve yakitori sprinkled with japanese pepper.

SAUCE   Combine ingredients in small saucepan; bring to a boil. Reduce heat; simmer, uncovered, over medium heat until sauce reduces by a third, cool.

SERVES 4
per serving   12.7g carbohydrate; 3.1g fat; 1016kJ (243 cal); 32.3g protein
tip   Bottled yakitori sauce is readily available from Asian grocery stores. The sauce can be used as a marinade for the chicken before cooking, but cook chicken on medium heat so marinade does not burn before meat cooks through.

chicken, preserved lemon and green bean salad

PREPARATION TIME 15 MINUTES   COOKING TIME 5 MINUTES

½ cup (80g) sultanas

1 cup (250ml) warm water

¼ cup (60ml) lemon juice

1 barbecued chicken (900g)

175g baby green beans, trimmed

2 tablespoons finely chopped preserved

lemon rind

340g jar marinated quartered

artichokes, drained

2 cups firmly packed fresh flat-leaf

parsley leaves

2 tablespoons olive oil

2 tablespoons white wine vinegar

1   Combine sultanas, the warm water and juice in medium bowl, cover; stand 5 minutes. Drain; discard liquid.

2   Meanwhile, discard skin and bones from chicken; slice meat thickly.

3   Boil, steam or microwave beans until tender; drain. Rinse under cold water; drain.

4   Place sultanas, chicken and beans in large bowl with rind, artichoke, parsley, oil and vinegar; toss gently to combine.

SERVES 4
per serving   16.5g carbohydrate; 20g fat; 1697kJ (406 cal); 39.4g protein

chicken, witlof and cashew salad

PREPARATION TIME 20 MINUTES

Like mushrooms, witlof is grown in the dark to retain its pale colour and bittersweet taste. This versatile vegetable is as good eaten cooked as it is raw. You need to purchase a large barbecued chicken weighing approximately 900g for this recipe.

1 medium witlof (175g)

2 baby cos lettuces

1 medium yellow capsicum (200g),
   sliced thinly

1 small red onion (100g), sliced thinly

1 cup (150g) toasted unsalted cashews

4 cups (400g) coarsely shredded
   cooked chicken

DRESSING

1 cup (280g) yogurt

2 cloves garlic, crushed

2 teaspoons finely grated lemon rind

¼ cup (60ml) lemon juice

¼ cup coarsely chopped fresh coriander

1   Trim and discard 1cm from witlof base; separate leaves. Trim core from lettuce; separate leaves.

2   Make dressing.

3   Place witlof and lettuce in large bowl with capsicum, onion, nuts, chicken and dressing; toss gently to combine.

DRESSING   Place ingredients in screw-top jar; shake well.

SERVES 4
per serving   18.6g carbohydrate; 26g fat; 1986kJ (475 cal); 40.8g protein

grilled piri piri drumettes with coleslaw

PREPARATION TIME 25 MINUTES (PLUS REFRIGERATION TIME)   COOKING TIME 20 MINUTES

Piri piri sauce is a spicy chilli and vinegar mixture sold bottled commercially in most supermarkets. You need about a quarter of both a large red and a large white cabbage for this recipe.

16 chicken drumettes (1.3kg)

½ cup (125ml) piri piri sauce

5 cups (400g) finely shredded red cabbage

5 cups (400g) finely shredded white cabbage

1 cup coarsely chopped fresh mint

PIRI PIRI DRESSING

1 tablespoon piri piri sauce

½ cup (125ml) peanut oil

¼ cup (60ml) lemon juice

1   Combine chicken and sauce in large bowl, cover; refrigerate 3 hours or overnight.

2   Make piri piri dressing.

3   Cook undrained chicken on heated oiled grill plate (or grill or barbecue) until browned and cooked through.

4   Place cabbages and mint in large bowl with dressing; toss gently to combine. Serve coleslaw with chicken.

PIRI PIRI DRESSING   Place ingredients in screw-top jar; shake well.

SERVES 4
per serving   14.3g carbohydrates; 48.3g fat; 2738kJ (655 cal); 41.5g protein

chicken and chorizo gumbo

PREPARATION TIME 30 MINUTES   COOKING TIME 2 HOURS 15 MINUTES

Traditionally made with andouille, a spicy smoked sausage of French descent, gumbo is just as delicious made with the more readily available chorizo.

1.5kg chicken

1 medium brown onion (150g), chopped coarsely

2 medium carrots (240g), chopped coarsely

2 trimmed celery stalks (200g), chopped coarsely

1 bay leaf

12 black peppercorns

3 litres (12 cups) water

60g butter

2 cloves garlic, crushed

1 small brown onion (80g), chopped finely

1 medium green capsicum (200g), chopped finely

1 teaspoon sweet paprika

¼ teaspoon cayenne pepper

¼ teaspoon ground clove

2 teaspoons finely chopped fresh oregano

¼ cup (60g) tomato paste

2 tablespoons worcestershire sauce

400g can crushed tomatoes

200g fresh okra, halved crossways

1 cup (200g) basmati rice

200g chorizo sausage, sliced thinly

1 Rinse chicken under cold water; pat dry with absorbent paper.

2 Combine chicken, coarsely chopped onion, carrot, celery, bay leaf, peppercorns and the water in large saucepan; bring to a boil. Reduce heat; simmer, covered, 1½ hours, skimming occasionally; strain through muslin-lined strainer into large bowl. Reserve stock and chicken; discard vegetables.

3 When chicken is cool enough to handle, remove and discard skin. Remove chicken meat from carcass; shred meat, discard bones.

4 Melt butter in large saucepan; cook garlic and finely chopped onion, stirring, until onion softens. Add capsicum, paprika, cayenne, clove and oregano; cook, stirring, about 2 minutes or until fragrant.

5 Gradually stir in reserved stock, paste, sauce and undrained tomatoes; stir until mixture boils and thickens slightly. Stir in okra and rice; simmer, uncovered, stirring occasionally, about 15 minutes or until both okra and rice are tender.

6 Meanwhile, heat large non-stick frying pan; cook sausage, in batches, until browned, drain on absorbent paper.

7 Add reserved chicken and sausage to gumbo; stir until heated through.

SERVES 6
per serving 22.8g carbohydrate; 19.9g fat; 1756kJ (420 cal); 37.6g protein
tip Fresh rather than canned okra should be used in gumbo (it's used to thicken the soup as well as impart flavour). Choose bright green, small, firm okra pods; large okra are generally tough and stringy. And take great pains not to overcook okra or it will break down to an unpleasantly pulpy state.

honey chilli chicken salad

PREPARATION TIME 15 MINUTES   COOKING TIME 10 MINUTES

500g chicken breast fillets, sliced thinly

¼ cup (90g) honey

4 fresh small red thai chillies, seeded,
   sliced thinly

4cm piece fresh ginger (20g), grated

500g asparagus, trimmed

2 tablespoons peanut oil

4 green onions, sliced thinly

1 medium green capsicum (200g),
   sliced thinly

1 medium yellow capsicum (200g),
   sliced thinly

1 medium carrot (120g), sliced thinly

150g chinese cabbage, shredded finely

⅓ cup (80ml) lime juice

1 Combine chicken, honey, chilli and ginger in medium bowl.

2 Cut aparagus spears in half; boil, steam or microwave until just tender; drain. Rinse immediately under cold water; drain.

3 Meanwhile, heat half of the oil in wok or large frying pan; stir-fry chicken, in batches, until browned all over and cooked through.

4 Place chicken and asparagus in large bowl with onion, capsicums, carrot, cabbage, juice and remaining oil; toss gently to combine.

SERVES 4
per serving 24.1g carbohydrate; 12.3g fat; 1413kJ (338 cal); 32.6g protein
tip A barbecued chicken can also be used; remove and discard bones and skin then shred meat coarsely before tossing with remaining salad ingredients.

curried chicken and zucchini soup

PREPARATION TIME 10 MINUTES   COOKING TIME 25 MINUTES

20g butter

1 small brown onion (80g),
   chopped finely

1 clove garlic, crushed

1 teaspoon curry powder

½ cup (100g) basmati rice

340g chicken breast fillets,
   sliced thinly

2 cups (500ml) water

1 litre (4 cups) chicken stock

4 medium zucchini (480g),
   grated coarsely

1 Melt butter in large saucepan; cook onion and garlic, stirring, until onion softens. Add curry powder; cook, stirring, until mixture is fragrant.

2 Add rice and chicken; cook, stirring, 2 minutes. Add the water and stock; bring to a boil. Reduce heat; simmer, covered, 10 minutes. Add zucchini; cook, stirring, about 5 minutes or until chicken is cooked through.

SERVES 4
per serving 24.7g carbohydrate; 7.4g fat; 1133kJ (271 cal); 25.4g protein

chicken and almonds

PREPARATION TIME 15 MINUTES   COOKING TIME 15 MINUTES

1 cup (160g) blanched almonds

1 tablespoon peanut oil

750g chicken breast fillets,
   sliced thinly

1 medium red onion (170g),
   chopped coarsely

1 small leek (200g), sliced thickly

2 cloves garlic, crushed

2 tablespoons hoisin sauce

200g green beans, trimmed, halved

2 trimmed celery stalks (200g),
   sliced thinly

1 tablespoon soy sauce

1 tablespoon plum sauce

1 Heat wok or large frying pan. Stir-fry almonds until browned lightly; remove from wok. Heat half of the oil in same wok; stir-fry chicken, in batches, until browned all over and cooked through.

2 Heat remaining oil in wok; stir-fry onion, leek and garlic until fragrant. Add hoisin sauce, beans and celery; stir-fry until beans are just tender. Return chicken to wok with remaining sauces; stir-fry until heated through. Toss almonds through chicken mixture.

SERVES 4
per serving 14.6g carbohydrate; 34g fat; 2399kJ (574 cal); 52.9g protein
tip You can use cashews instead of almonds, if preferred.

chicken and haloumi salad

PREPARATION TIME 10 MINUTES   COOKING TIME 15 MINUTES

Assemble this salad just before serving.

300g prepared mixed
   vegetable antipasto

500g chicken tenderloins,
   chopped coarsely

¼ cup (40g) pine nuts

250g haloumi cheese

250g baby rocket leaves

170g marinated artichoke hearts,
   drained, quartered

250g cherry tomatoes

¼ cup (60ml) balsamic vinegar

1 Drain antipasto in strainer over small bowl; reserve ⅓ cup of the oil. Chop antipasto finely.

2 Heat 1 tablespoon of the reserved oil in wok or large frying pan; stir-fry chicken, in batches, until browned all over and cooked through. Cover to keep warm. Stir-fry pine nuts in same wok until browned lightly.

3 Cut haloumi crossways into 16 slices. Heat 1 tablespoon of the reserved oil in same wok; cook haloumi, in batches, until browned both sides.

4 Place antipasto, chicken and haloumi in large bowl with rocket, artichoke and tomatoes; toss gently to combine. Drizzle with combined remaining oil and vinegar; sprinkle with pine nuts.

SERVES 4
per serving 12.2g carbohydrate; 34g fat; 2391kJ (572 cal); 42.6g protein

vegetable curry with yogurt

PREPARATION TIME 25 MINUTES   COOKING TIME 15 MINUTES

2 teaspoons olive oil

4cm piece fresh ginger
  (20g), grated

3 green onions, sliced thinly

2 cloves garlic, crushed

1 long green chilli, seeded,
  chopped finely

¼ teaspoon ground cardamom

1 teaspoon garam masala

1 tablespoon curry powder

1 teaspoon turmeric

2 medium apples (300g),
  grated coarsely

1 tablespoon lemon juice

2 cups (500ml) vegetable stock

300g cauliflower florets

100g yellow patty-pan
  squash, halved

1 large zucchini (150g),
  sliced thickly

150g baby spinach leaves

200g low-fat yogurt

1 Heat oil in large saucepan; cook ginger, onion, garlic, chilli, cardamom, garam masala, curry powder, turmeric and apple, stirring, about 2 minutes or until apple softens and mixture is fragrant. Add juice, stock and cauliflower; cook, uncovered, 5 minutes, stirring occasionally.

2 Add squash and zucchini; cook until vegetables are just tender. Remove from heat; stir spinach and yogurt into curry just before serving.

SERVES 4
per serving 14.5g carbohydrate 3.6g fat; 534kJ (128 cal); 8.5g protein

vegetable curry with yogurt

roasted vegetables with eggplant

roasted vegetables with eggplant

PREPARATION TIME 20 MINUTES   COOKING TIME 50 MINUTES

1 large green capsicum (350g)

2 large red capsicums (700g)

2 large yellow capsicums (700g)

2 medium eggplants (600g)

2 cloves garlic, unpeeled

¼ cup (60ml) lemon juice

2 teaspoons tahini

350g flat mushrooms, sliced thickly

250g cherry tomatoes

360g yellow patty-pan
   squash, halved

400g okra, trimmed

cooking-oil spray

¾ cup loosely packed fresh
   basil leaves

1 teaspoon sumac

1 Preheat oven to hot.

2 Quarter capsicums, discard seeds and membranes. Using fork prick eggplant all over; divide among two lightly oiled baking dishes with garlic and capsicum, skin-side up. Roast vegetables, uncovered, in hot oven about 30 minutes or until skins blisters. Cover capsicum pieces in plastic or paper for 5 minutes; peel away skin, slice thickly.

3 When cool enough to handle, peel eggplant and garlic. Coarsely chop eggplant, finely chop garlic. Combine eggplant and garlic in medium bowl with juice and tahini; cover to keep warm.

4 Meanwhile, cook mushrooms in lightly oiled frying pan, stirring, until browned lightly. Add tomatoes and squash; cook, covered, until vegetables are just tender.

5 Place okra on lightly oiled oven tray; spray with oil. Roast, uncovered, in hot oven about 20 minutes or until tender.

6 Combine capsicum, mushroom, tomato mixture, okra and basil in large bowl; divide among serving plates, top with eggplant mixture. Sprinkle with sumac; serve immediately.

SERVES 4
per serving 21.8g carbohydrate; 3.1g fat; 757kJ (181 cal); 15.8g protein

eggplant bolognese bake

PREPARATION TIME 30 MINUTES   COOKING TIME 1 HOUR 10 MINUTES

2 medium eggplants (600g)

200g baby spinach leaves

150g ricotta

1 egg white

½ cup (50g) coarsely grated
    mozzarella cheese

⅓ cup (25g) coarsely grated
    parmesan cheese

BOLOGNESE SAUCE

2 teaspoons olive oil

1 large brown onion (200g),
    chopped coarsely

1 small red capsicum (150g),
    chopped coarsely

1 small green capsicum (150g),
    chopped coarsely

2 cloves garlic, crushed

250g beef mince

1 large egg tomato (90g),
    chopped coarsely

1 tablespoon tomato paste

½ cup (125ml) dry red wine

400g can whole tomatoes

2 tablespoons coarsely chopped
    fresh basil

1 tablespoon coarsely chopped
    fresh oregano

ROCKET SALAD

100g rocket

½ cup loosely packed fresh
    basil leaves

1 tablespoon balsamic vinegar

1 teaspoon extra virgin olive oil

1   Preheat oven to moderate. Make bolognese sauce.

2   Meanwhile, cut eggplants into 2mm-thick slices; cook eggplant on heated oiled grill plate (or grill or barbecue) until just tender.

3   Boil, steam or microwave spinach until wilted; drain. Press as much liquid as possible from spinach; cool 10 minutes. Combine spinach, ricotta and egg in medium bowl.

4   Spread 1 cup of the sauce over base of shallow 2-litre (8-cup) ovenproof dish. Top with half of the eggplant, then half of the spinach mixture, then another cup of sauce, remaining eggplant and remaining spinach mixture. Spread with remaining sauce.

5   Sprinkle top with cheeses; bake, uncovered, in moderate oven about 20 minutes or until top is browned lightly. Stand 10 minutes.

6   Meanwhile, make rocket salad.

7   Serve bolognese bake with rocket salad.

BOLOGNESE SAUCE Heat oil in medium frying pan; cook onion, capsicums and garlic until onion softens. Add beef to pan; cook, stirring, until beef is browned all over. Add coarsely chopped tomato and paste; cook, stirring, 3 minutes. Add wine; cook, stirring, 2 minutes. Add undrained tomatoes; bring to a boil. Reduce heat; simmer, uncovered, about 25 minutes or until mixture thickens slightly. Stir in herbs.

ROCKET SALAD Place ingredients in medium bowl; toss gently to combine.

SERVES 4
per serving 16.2g carbohydrate; 20.3g fat; 1630kJ (390 cal); 30g protein

cauliflower and broccoli curry

PREPARATION TIME 20 MINUTES   COOKING TIME 15 MINUTES

1 tablespoon peanut oil

2 tablespoons red curry paste

1 large red capsicum (350g),
   sliced thinly

2 teaspoons honey

3⅓ cups (830ml) coconut cream

1 cup (250ml) water

500g broccoli, chopped coarsely

500g cauliflower, chopped coarsely

425g can whole baby corn
   spears, drained

500g choy sum, chopped coarsely

1   Heat oil in large saucepan; cook paste, stirring, until fragrant. Add capsicum; cook, stirring, until almost tender.

2   Stir in honey, coconut cream and the water; bring to a boil. Add broccoli and cauliflower, reduce heat; simmer, uncovered, 2 minutes. Add corn and choy sum; cook, stirring, until choy sum just wilts.

SERVES 4
per serving 20.8g carbohydrate; 52.3g fat; 2562kJ (613 cal); 16.9g protein
tip Different brands of commercially prepared curry pastes vary in strength and flavour, so you may want to adjust the amount of paste to suit your taste.

eggplant with pumpkin and fetta

PREPARATION TIME 20 MINUTES (PLUS STANDING TIME)   COOKING TIME 1 HOUR 25 MINUTES

You will need to cook ⅓ cup (65g) rice for this recipe.

4 medium eggplants (1.2kg), halved

coarse cooking salt

¼ cup (60ml) olive oil

200g pumpkin, chopped finely

1 small onion (80g), chopped finely

2 cloves garlic, crushed

1 teaspoon ground cumin

2 tablespoons brown sugar

1 cup cooked long-grain rice

2 tablespoons finely chopped
   fresh coriander

⅓ cup (50g) hazelnuts, toasted,
   chopped finely

100g fetta cheese, crumbled

1   Preheat oven to moderate.

2   Sprinkle cut surface of eggplants with salt, place on wire rack over dish, stand 30 minutes. Rinse eggplants; pat dry with absorbent paper. Brush cut surface of eggplants with half of the oil, place on wire rack over baking dish. Bake, uncovered, in moderate oven about 40 minutes or until eggplants are tender; cool 10 minutes.

3   Scoop flesh from eggplants, leaving 5mm shells; chop eggplant flesh.

4   Heat remaining oil in pan; cook pumpkin, onion, garlic and cumin, stirring, until pumpkin is just tender. Stir in eggplant flesh with sugar, rice, coriander and nuts.

5   Divide pumpkin mixture between eggplant shells, place on oven tray; top with cheese. Bake, uncovered, in moderate oven about 30 minutes or until cheese is browned lightly.

SERVES 4
per serving 22.7g carbohydrate; 28.3g fat; 1613kJ (386 cal); 11.1g protein

triple mushroom omelette

PREPARATION TIME 15 MINUTES   COOKING TIME 35 MINUTES (PLUS STANDING TIME)

12 dried shiitake mushrooms

3 dried cloud ear mushrooms

2 teaspoons peanut oil

6 green onions, sliced thinly

2cm piece fresh ginger (10g), grated

2 cloves garlic, crushed

½ medium red capsicum (100g),
**   chopped finely**

100g button mushrooms,
**   sliced thinly**

¾ cup (60g) bean sprouts

¼ cup (40g) toasted pine nuts

90g snow peas, sliced thinly

1 tablespoon salt-reduced
**   soy sauce**

1 tablespoon oyster sauce

1 tablespoon water

10 eggs, beaten lightly

⅓ cup (80ml) water, extra

SPICY SAUCE

2 fresh small red thai chillies,
**   sliced thinly**

¼ cup (60ml) chinese
**   barbecue sauce**

⅓ cup (80ml) water

1 Place dried mushrooms in large heatproof bowl; cover with boiling water. Stand 20 minutes; drain. Discard stems; slice caps thinly.

2 Heat oil in wok or large frying pan; stir-fry onion, ginger, garlic, capsicum and button mushrooms until capsicum is just soft. Add sprouts, pine nuts, snow peas, soy sauce, oyster sauce and the water, stir-fry until peas are just tender; cover to keep warm.

3 Meanwhile, whisk eggs with the extra water in large bowl. Heat lightly oiled 24cm heavy-base omelette pan; add ⅓ cup of the egg mixture to pan; swirl pan to form a thin omelette over base. Cook until set; remove. Repeat with remaining egg mixture; cover omelettes with foil to keep warm. You will need eight omelettes.

4 Meanwhile, make spicy sauce.

5 Place ¼ cup of the mushroom mixture on each omelette. Fold omelette over filling; fold over again. Serve omelettes topped with spicy sauce.

SPICY SAUCE Combine ingredients in small saucepan; stir over heat until mixture boils. Reduce heat; simmer, uncovered, about 3 minutes or until sauce thickens slightly.

SERVES 4
per serving 16g carbohydrate; 22.9g fat; 1480kJ (354 cal); 22.2g protein

vegetable and cottage cheese terrine

PREPARATION TIME 40 MINUTES (PLUS REFRIGERATION TIME)   COOKING TIME 5 MINUTES

Buy zucchini just large enough to make 13cm-long strips once trimmed and sliced.

2½ cups low-fat cottage cheese

1 small yellow zucchini (90g),
  grated coarsely

4 green onions, chopped finely

1 tablespoon finely shredded
  fresh basil

1 tablespoon finely chopped
  fresh thyme

1 clove garlic, crushed

1 teaspoon lemon juice

1 large green zucchini (150g)

1 large yellow zucchini (150g)

20g baby spinach leaves,
  shredded coarsely

150g snow peas, trimmed

2 teaspoons olive oil

CAPSICUM AND TOMATO SAUCE

2 medium tomatoes (380g),
  chopped finely

1 small yellow capsicum (150g),
  chopped finely

1 small red capsicum (150g),
  chopped finely

1 tablespoon finely shredded
  fresh basil

1 clove garlic, crushed

2 teaspoons sugar

2 teaspoons olive oil

2 teaspoons lemon juice

1   Drain cheese in muslin-lined strainer or colander set over large bowl. Cover then weight cheese with an upright saucer topped with a heavy can. Drain overnight in refrigerator; discard liquid.

2   Line base and two long sides of 8cm x 25cm bar pan with baking paper or plastic wrap, extending paper 5cm above sides of pan.

3   Combine drained cheese in medium bowl with grated zucchini, onion, herbs, garlic and juice.

4   Discard ends of both large zucchini; using vegetable peeler, slice into thin strips (discard outer strips of both zucchini).

5   Overlap alternate-colored zucchini strips in prepared pan, starting from centre of base and extending over both long sides. Cover both short sides of pan with alternate-colored zucchini strips, ensuring slices overlap to cover corners and extend over both short sides.

6   Spread half of the cheese mixture into zucchini-lined pan; cover with spinach, carefully spread remaining cheese mixture over spinach. Fold zucchini strips at short sides over filling then repeat with strips over long sides to completely enclose filling (mixture will be slightly higher than pan). Cover terrine tightly with foil; refrigerate 1 hour.

7   Meanwhile, make capsicum and tomato sauce.

8   Boil, steam or microwave snow peas; drain.

9   Turn terrine onto serving plate; drizzle with oil. Using fine serrated knife, cut terrine crossways into thick slices; serve with sauce and snow peas.

CAPSICUM AND TOMATO SAUCE Combine ingredients in small bowl.

SERVES 4
per serving 12.1g carbohydrate; 4.4g fat; 828kJ (198 cal); 27g protein
tip Do not add any salt to the cottage-cheese mixture as this will cause the filling to become too wet.

thyme and tofu stir-fry

PREPARATION TIME 25 MINUTES   COOKING TIME 15 MINUTES

350g cauliflower, chopped coarsely

350g broccoli, chopped coarsely

250g asparagus, sliced thickly

350g green beans, sliced thickly

3 medium carrots (360g), sliced thickly

¼ cup (60ml) olive oil

2 cloves garlic, crushed

1 tablespoon finely chopped fresh thyme

1 teaspoon cracked black pepper

375g firm tofu, diced into 3cm pieces

2 medium brown onions (300g), sliced thickly

250g button mushrooms, sliced thickly

½ cup (125ml) dry white wine

3 teaspoons cornflour

1 cup (250ml) vegetable stock

1   Cook cauliflower, broccoli, asparagus, beans and carrot in large saucepan of boiling water, uncovered, 2 minutes; drain. Rinse under cold water; drain.

2   Heat oil in wok or large frying pan; stir-fry garlic, thyme, pepper and tofu until tofu is browned lightly. Remove from wok.

3   Add onion and mushrooms to wok; stir-fry until onion softens. Add cauliflower mixture to wok with wine and blended cornflour and stock; stir-fry until sauce boils and thickens. Return tofu mixture to wok; stir-fry until heated through.

SERVES 4
per serving   15.3g carbohydrate; 21.1g fat; 1513kJ (362 cal); 22.6g protein

turnip ratatouille

PREPRATION TIME 20 MINUTES   COOKING TIME 35 MINUTES

2 medium eggplants (600g)

¼ cup (60ml) olive oil

2 cloves garlic, crushed

1kg turnips, chopped coarsely

2 small red capsicums (300g),
    chopped coarsely

2 medium green zucchini (240g),
    chopped coarsely

2 large yellow zucchini (300g),
    chopped coarsely

2 x 400g cans crushed tomatoes

2 tablespoons tomato paste

1 tablespoon drained capers, rinsed,
    chopped coarsely

2 tablespoons dry red wine

¼ cup finely shredded fresh basil

1   Cut eggplants into 1cm slices; quarter slices.

2   Heat oil in large heavy-based saucepan; cook eggplant and garlic, stirring, about 5 minutes or until eggplant is just tender and browned lightly. Stir in turnips, capsicum, zucchini, undrained tomatoes, paste, capers and wine; bring to a boil. Reduce heat; simmer, covered, about 30 minutes or until vegetables are tender. Stir in half of the basil; sprinkle remaining basil over top of ratatouille just before serving.

SERVES 4
per serving   19.1g carbohydrate; 14.7g fat; 1041kJ (249 cal); 8.2g protein

snapper with roasted turnips

PREPARATION TIME 20 MINUTES COOKING TIME 45 MINUTES

1kg turnips, chopped coarsely

8 cloves garlic, unpeeled

1 tablespoon brown sugar

2 tablespoons olive oil

1 teaspoon cumin seeds

1 tablespoon dijon mustard

1 cup (70g) stale breadcrumbs

⅓ cup (35g) coarsely grated
mozzarella cheese

⅓ cup (40g) coarsely grated
cheddar cheese

⅓ cup (25g) coarsely grated
parmesan cheese

2 tablespoons finely chopped fresh
flat-leaf parsley

2 cloves garlic, crushed

2 teaspoons lemon pepper seasoning

4 x 200g snapper fillets

cooking-oil spray

1 Preheat oven to moderately hot.

2 Toss turnips and garlic cloves with combined sugar, oil and seeds in large bowl. Place in large baking dish; bake, uncovered, in moderately hot oven about 30 minutes or until browned lightly, stirring occasionally. Remove from oven; cover to keep warm. Increase oven temperature to hot.

3 Combine mustard, breadcrumbs, cheeses, parsley, garlic and seasoning in large bowl.

4 Place fish on oiled oven tray; press cheese mixture onto fish, spray with oil. Bake, uncovered, in hot oven about 15 minutes or until cheese browns and fish is cooked as desired.

5 Serve fish with roasted turnips and garlic.

SERVES 4
per serving 22.4g carbohydrate; 21.3g fat; 2077kJ (497 cal); 53.5g protein
tip We used snapper in this recipes but you can use any firm white fish.

swordfish with olive paste and carrot and dill fritters

PREPARATION TIME 20 MINUTES   COOKING TIME 25 MINUTES

1 cup (200g) seeded black olives

¼ cup (50g) drained capers, rinsed

⅓ cup finely chopped fresh dill

⅓ cup finely chopped fresh flat-leaf parsley

2 cloves garlic, quartered

2 tablespoons lemon juice

4 medium carrots (480g), grated coarsely

2 eggs, beaten lightly

1 tablespoon coarsely chopped fresh dill

⅓ cup (50g) plain flour

4 x 200g swordfish steaks

1 Blend or process olives, capers, finely chopped dill, parsley, garlic and juice to a smooth paste.

2 Combine carrot, eggs, coarsely chopped dill and flour in medium bowl. Cook ¼ cup measures of carrot mixture, in batches, on heated oiled grill plate (or grill or barbecue) until browned both sides.

3 Meanwhile, cook fish on same grill plate, until browned both sides and cooked as desired; spread tops with olive paste. Serve with fritters.

SERVES 4
per serving 24.3g carbohydrate 7.9g fat; 1492kJ (357 cal); 46.5g protein

coco-lime fish with pawpaw and raspberry salsa

PREPARATION TIME 10 MINUTES (PLUS REFRIGERATION TIME)   COOKING TIME 20 MINUTES

2 tablespoons finely chopped palm sugar

400ml coconut cream

2 tablespoons finely grated kaffir lime rind

2 fresh small red thai chillies, chopped finely

4 x 200g snapper steaks

PAWPAW AND RASPBERRY SALSA

2 tablespoons raspberry vinegar

250g fresh raspberries

600g pawpaw, chopped coarsely

1 tablespoon finely chopped fresh mint

1   Combine sugar, coconut cream, rind and chilli in small saucepan. Simmer, stirring occasionally, for 10 minutes; cool 10 minutes. Pour coconut mixture over fish in large bowl. Cover; refrigerate 3 hours or overnight.

2   Make pawpaw and raspberry salsa.

3   Drain fish over small pan; reserve marinade. Cook fish, uncovered, on heated oiled grill plate (or grill or barbecue) until browned both sides and cooked as desired.

4   Meanwhile, place reserved marinade in small saucepan; bring to a boil. Reduce heat; simmer, uncovered, until thickened slightly. Drizzle marinade over fish and serve with salsa.

PAWPAW AND RASPBERRY SALSA Combine ingredients in medium bowl, cover; refrigerate 30 minutes.

SERVES 4
per serving 21.1g carbohydrate; 24.3g fat; 1998kJ (478 cal); 43.8g protein
tip We used red snapper in this recipe but you can use any firm white fish.

sweet and spicy mussels with stir-fried asian greens

PREPARATION TIME 20 MINUTES   COOKING TIME 15 MINUTES

1kg large black mussels

1 tablespoon peanut oil

1 clove garlic, crushed

8cm piece fresh ginger (40g), chopped finely

⅓ cup (80ml) pure maple syrup

2 tablespoons soy sauce

1 tablespoon oyster sauce

¼ cup (60ml) fish stock

1 tablespoon lemon juice

4 green onions, sliced thinly

300g baby bok choy, chopped coarsely

400g gai larn, chopped coarsely

2 cups (160g) bean sprouts

1   Scrub mussels; remove beards.

2   Heat oil in wok or large frying pan; stir-fry garlic and ginger until fragrant. Add syrup, sauces, stock and juice; bring to a boil. Add mussels; return to a boil. Reduce heat; simmer, covered, about 5 minutes or until mussels open (discard any that do not). Remove mussels; cover to keep warm.

3   Return stock mixture to a boil. Add remaining ingredients to wok; stir-fry until greens are just wilted. Return mussels to wok; stir-fry until heated through.

SERVES 4
per serving 21.1g carbohydrate; 6 g fat; 769kJ (184 cal); 11.6g protein
tip Use a stiff brush to scrub the mussels under cold water.

moroccan blue-eye fillets with orange and maple baby carrots

PREPARATION TIME 20 MINUTES   COOKING TIME 15 MINUTES

1 clove garlic, crushed

1cm piece fresh ginger (5g), grated

1 teaspoon ground cumin

½ teaspoon ground turmeric

½ teaspoon hot paprika

½ teaspoon ground coriander

4 x 200g blue-eye fillets, skinned

800g baby carrots, halved

20g butter

1 teaspoon finely grated orange rind

1 tablespoon orange juice

1 tablespoon maple syrup

1 tablespoon olive oil

1 Combine garlic, ginger and spices in large bowl. Add fish; toss to coat fish in spice mixture. Refrigerate, covered, 15 minutes.

2 Meanwhile, boil, steam or microwave carrots until just tender; drain.

3 Heat butter in large frying pan; cook rind, juice and syrup; bring to a boil. Reduce heat; simmer, uncovered, until mixture thickens slightly. Add carrots; stir gently to coat carrots in mixture.

4 Heat oil in large frying pan; cook fish, in batches, until browned both sides and cooked as desired. Serve fish with carrots.

SERVES 4
per serving 14.7g carbohydrate; 12.2g fat; 1409kJ (337 cal); 42.1g protein

barbecue sweet and sour blue-eye (see back cover)

PREPARATION TIME 20 MINUTES   COOKING TIME 20 MINUTES

½ small pineapple (450g), chopped coarsely

1 medium red capsicum (200g),
    chopped coarsely

1 medium green capsicum (200g),
    chopped coarsely

1 medium red onion (170g), chopped coarsely

4 x 200g blue-eye fillets, skinned

2 tablespoons caster sugar

½ cup (125ml) white vinegar

2 tablespoons soy sauce

1 fresh long red chilli, seeded, sliced thinly

4cm piece fresh ginger (20g), grated

3 green onions, sliced thinly

1 Cook pineapple, capsicums and red onion on heated oiled grill plate (or grill or barbecue) until browned all over and tender. Cover to keep warm.

2 Cook fish on same heated oiled grill plate until cooked as desired.

3 Place sugar, vinegar, soy, chilli and ginger in large bowl with pineapple, capsicum and red onion; toss gently to combine.

4 Divide sweet and sour mixture among serving plates, top with fish and green onions.

SERVES 4
per serving 16.2g carbohydrate; 1.7g fat; 1016kJ (243 cal); 38.9g protein

salt and pepper salmon cutlets with daikon salad

PREPARATION TIME 25 MINUTES   COOKING TIME 10 MINUTES

2 teaspoons sea salt

1 teaspoon freshly ground black pepper

4 x 265g salmon cutlets

1 tablespoon peanut oil

½ small daikon (200g)

150g snow pea sprouts

200g snow peas, sliced thinly

1 fresh long red chilli, seeded, sliced thinly

½ cup loosely packed fresh thai basil leaves

½ cup loosely packed fresh vietnamese
    mint leaves

2 small pink grapefruit (460g)

CHILLI LIME VINAIGRETTE

2 tablespoons sweet chilli sauce

2 tablespoons lime juice

1 tablespoon rice vinegar

1 tablespoon finely chopped fresh lemon grass

1 clove garlic, crushed

2 teaspoons brown sugar

1   Make chilli lime vinaigrette.

2   Combine salt and pepper in large bowl, add fish; toss gently to coat in mixture. Heat oil in large frying pan; cook fish, in batches, until browned both sides and cooked as desired.

3   Meanwhile, slice daikon thinly lengthways; cut slices into thin sticks. Combine daikon in large bowl with sprouts, snow peas, chilli and herbs.

4   Segment grapefruit over salad to save juice; discard membranes from segments. Add segments and half of the vinaigrette to salad; toss gently to combine. Divide salad among serving plates; top with fish, drizzle with remaining vinaigrette.

CHILLI LIME VINAIGRETTE Place ingredients in screw-top jar; shake well.

SERVES 4
per serving 13.2g carbohydrate; 24.2g fat; 2077kJ (497 cal); 56g protein

baby octopus and eggplant in tomato and caper sauce

PREPARATION TIME 10 MINUTES   COOKING TIME 25 MINUTES

1 tablespoon olive oil

1.2kg cleaned baby octopus

1 clove garlic, sliced thinly

3 shallots (75g), sliced thinly

4 baby eggplants (240g), sliced thinly

1 medium red capsicum (200g), sliced thinly

½ cup (125ml) dry red wine

700g bottled tomato pasta sauce

⅓ cup (80ml) water

¼ cup (40g) drained baby capers, rinsed

2 tablespoons coarsely chopped fresh oregano

1   Heat half of the oil in large deep frying pan; cook octopus, in batches, until just changed in colour and tender. Cover to keep warm.

2   Heat remaining oil in same pan; cook garlic and shallot, stirring, until shallot softens. Add eggplant and capsicum; cook, stirring, about 5 minutes or until vegetables are just tender.

3   Add wine, sauce, the water and octopus to pan; bring to a boil. Reduce heat; simmer, covered, about 10 minutes or until sauce thickens slightly. Stir in capers and oregano.

SERVES 4
per serving 18.4g carbohydrate; 10.5g fat; 2161kJ (517 cal); 80.7g protein

chilli plum crabs with herb salad

PREPARATION TIME 20 MINUTES (PLUS MARINATING TIME)   COOKING TIME 15 MINUTES

4 uncooked blue swimmer crabs

⅓ cup (80ml) plum sauce

⅓ cup (80ml) sweet chilli sauce

2 tablespoons oyster sauce

2 tablespoons peanut oil

1 tablespoon soy sauce

1 clove garlic, crushed

4cm piece fresh ginger (20g), grated

½ teaspoon sesame oil

HERB SALAD

½ cup firmly packed fresh flat-leaf
    parsley leaves

½ cup firmly packed fresh basil leaves

¼ cup firmly packed fresh mint leaves

1 cup (80g) bean sprouts

2 tablespoons lime juice

2 teaspoons sesame oil

1 Remove triangular flap from underside of each crab. Remove top shell and grey fibrous tissue; wash crabs. Crack nippers slightly; cut crabs in half.

2 Combine remaining ingredients in large bowl, add crab; toss to coat crab in mixture. Cover; refrigerate 3 hours or overnight.

3 Cook crab on heated oiled grill plate (or grill or barbecue) until cooked through.

4 Meanwhile, make herb salad.

5 Serve crab with salad.

HERB SALAD Combine ingredients in medium bowl.

SERVES 4
per serving 23.9g carbohydrate; 13.5g fat; 1108kJ (265 cal); 12.3g protein

stir-fried octopus with basil

PREPARATION TIME 20 MINUTES   COOKING TIME 10 MINUTES

2 teaspoons peanut oil

1kg cleaned baby octopus

2 teaspoons sesame oil

2 cloves garlic, crushed

2 fresh small red thai chillies, sliced thinly

2 large red capsicums (500g), sliced thinly

6 green onions, cut into 2cm lengths

¼ cup firmly packed fresh basil leaves

400g tat soi, trimmed, chopped coarsely

¼ cup (60ml) fish sauce

2 tablespoons grated palm sugar

1 tablespoon kecap manis

¾ cup loosely packed fresh coriander leaves

1 Heat peanut oil in wok or large frying pan; stir-fry octopus, in batches, until browned all over and tender. Cover to keep warm.

2 Heat sesame oil in same wok; stir-fry garlic, chilli and capsicum until capsicum is just tender. Return octopus to wok with onion, basil, tat soi, sauce, sugar and kecap manis; stir-fry until greens wilt and sugar dissolves. Remove from heat; stir in coriander.

SERVES 4
per serving 14.5g carbohydrate; 7.7g fat; 1229kJ (294 cal); 41.3g protein

cioppino (see page 1)

PREPARATION TIME 30 MINUTES   COOKING TIME 40 MINUTES

2 teaspoons olive oil

1 medium brown onion (150g), chopped coarsely

1 baby fennel bulb (130g), chopped coarsely

3 cloves garlic, crushed

6 medium tomatoes (1kg), chopped coarsely

425g can crushed tomatoes

½ cup (125ml) dry white wine

1½ cups (375ml) fish stock

2 cooked blue swimmer crabs (700g)

500g uncooked large prawns

450g swordfish steaks

400g clams, rinsed

150g scallops

¼ cup coarsely chopped fresh basil

½ cup coarsely chopped fresh flat-leaf parsley

1   Heat oil in large saucepan; cook onion, fennel and garlic, stirring, until onion softens. Add fresh tomato; cook, stirring, about 5 minutes or until tomato softens. Stir in undrained crushed tomatoes, wine and stock; bring to a boil. Reduce heat; simmer, covered, 20 minutes.

2   Meanwhile, remove back shells from crabs; discard grey gills, wash crabs. Chop each crab into four pieces with cleaver. Shell and devein prawns, leaving tails intact. Chop fish into 2cm pieces.

3   Add clams to pan; simmer, covered, about 5 minutes or until clams open (discard any that do not open). Add remaining seafood; cook, stirring occasionally, about 5 minutes or until seafood has changed in colour and is cooked through. Stir in herbs.

SERVES 4
per serving 13.1g carbohydrate; 6.4g fat; 1471kJ (352 cal); 54.2g protein

vine leaf-wrapped ocean trout with braised fennel

PREPARATION TIME 20 MINUTES   COOKING TIME 50 MINUTES

2 medium fennel bulbs (600g)

1 large brown onion (200g), sliced thinly

2 cloves garlic, sliced thinly

1 tablespoon olive oil

¼ cup (60ml) orange juice

½ cup (125ml) chicken stock

¼ cup (60ml) dry white wine

8 fresh grapevine leaves

4 x 200g ocean trout fillets

1 tablespoon finely grated orange rind

1 cup (175g) seedless white grapes

1   Preheat oven to moderate.

2   Trim fennel, reserving ¼ cup of the fennel tips. Slice fennel thinly; place in large shallow baking dish with onion, garlic, oil, juice, stock and wine. Bake, covered, in moderate oven 30 minutes. Remove cover; bake in moderate oven 20 minutes or until vegetables soften, stirring occasionally.

3   Meanwhile, dip vine leaves in boiling water for 10 seconds. Transfer immediately to bowl of iced water. Drain on absorbent paper.

4   Slightly overlap two vine leaves, vein-side up; centre one fish fillet on leaves, top with quarter of the rind and 1 teaspoon of the reserved fennel tips. Fold leaves over to enclose fish. Repeat with remaining fish fillets, rind and 1 teaspoon of the fennel tips. Place vine leaf parcels on oiled oven tray; cook, uncovered, in moderate oven about 15 minutes or until fish is cooked as desired.

5   Stir grapes and remaining fennel tips through hot fennel mixture. Serve with fish.

SERVES 4
per serving 13.6g carbohydrate; 12.5g fat; 1430kJ (342 cal); 41g protein

grilled kingfish with tamarind vegetable stir-fry

PREPARATION TIME 20 MINUTES   COOKING TIME 10 MINUTES

2 teaspoons peanut oil

5cm piece fresh ginger (25g), cut into matchsticks

2 cloves garlic, crushed

2 fresh long red chillies, chopped finely

1 medium red capsicum (200g), sliced thinly

¼ cup (60ml) chicken stock

2 tablespoons oyster sauce

1 tablespoon fish sauce

2 tablespoons grated palm sugar

1 tablespoon tamarind concentrate

250g baby bok choy, chopped coarsely

250g gai larn, chopped coarsely

8 green onions, cut into 3cm lengths

½ cup firmly packed fresh coriander leaves

4 x 200g kingfish steaks

1 Heat oil in wok or large frying pan; stir-fry ginger, garlic and chilli until fragrant. Add capsicum; stir-fry until capsicum is just tender.

2 Add stock, sauces, sugar and tamarind; bring to a boil. Boil 1 minute. Add bok choy, gai larn and onion; stir-fry until just wilted. Remove from heat; toss coriander leaves through stir-fry.

3 Meanwhile, cook fish on heated oiled grill plate (or grill or barbecue) until browned both sides and cooked as desired.

4 Serve fish with vegetables.

SERVES 4
per serving 17.2g carbohydrate; 16g fat; 1760kJ (421 cal); 52.1g protein

singapore chilli crab

PREPARATION TIME 45 MINUTES (PLUS STANDING TIME)   COOKING TIME 35 MINUTES

2 uncooked mud crabs (1.5kg)

2 tablespoons peanut oil

1 fresh long red chilli, chopped finely

2 cloves garlic, crushed

2cm piece fresh ginger (10g), grated

⅓ cup (80ml) sweet sherry

400g can crushed tomatoes

1 cup (250ml) water

1 tablespoon brown sugar

3 lebanese cucumbers (390g), halved lengthways, sliced thinly

10cm piece fresh ginger (50g), cut into matchsticks

3 green onions, sliced thinly

¼ cup loosely packed fresh coriander leaves

2 fresh long red chillies, seeded, sliced thinly

1 Place crabs in large container filled with ice and water; stand about 1 hour. Slide sharp knife under top of shell at back, lever off shell. Discard whitish gills; rinse crabs under cold water. Chop each body into sixths.

2 Heat oil in wok or large frying pan; stir-fry chopped chilli, garlic and grated ginger until fragrant. Add sherry; cook until liquid has reduced by half. Add undrained tomatoes, the water and sugar; bring to a boil. Reserve half of the sauce in small bowl.

3 Add half of the crab to wok, reduce heat; simmer, covered, about 15 minutes or until crab has changed in colour. Stir in half of the cucumber. Transfer to large serving bowl; cover to keep warm. Repeat with reserved sauce, remaining crab and cucumber.

4 Combine ginger, onion, coriander and sliced chilli; sprinkle over crab.

SERVES 4
per serving 12.3g carbohydrate; 10.5g fat; 1066kJ (255 cal); 23.6g protein

salt-baked whole ocean trout in saffron cream sauce with lemon-roasted onions and carrots

PREPARATION TIME 30 MINUTES   COOKING TIME 1 HOUR 10 MINUTES

2 large brown onions (400g)

2 lemons

7 small carrots (490g)

4 cloves garlic, unpeeled

6 sprigs fresh rosemary

2 tablespoons olive oil

2kg cooking salt

3 egg whites

1.5kg whole ocean trout

350g watercress, trimmed

SAFFRON CREAM SAUCE

⅓ cup (80ml) dry white wine

2 tablespoons white wine vinegar

1 tablespoon lemon juice

pinch saffron threads

⅓ cup (80ml) cream

90g butter, chilled, chopped finely

1   Preheat oven to moderately hot.

2   Cut onions and lemons into eight wedges. Combine onion, lemon, carrot, garlic and rosemary in baking dish. Drizzle with oil; stir gently. Bake, uncovered, in moderately hot oven about 1 hour or until tender.

3   Meanwhile, mix salt with egg whites in medium bowl (mixture will have the consistency of wet sand). Spread about half of the salt mixture evenly over the base of a large baking dish; place fish on salt mixture then cover completely (except for tail) with remaining salt mixture. Bake fish in moderately hot oven 50 minutes.

4   Make saffron cream sauce.

5   Remove fish from oven; break salt crust with heavy knife, taking care not to cut into fish. Discard salt crust; transfer fish to large serving plate. Carefully remove skin from fish; flake meat into large pieces.

6   Divide watercress among serving plates; top with fish, drizzle sauce over fish. Serve with onion mixture.

SAFFRON CREAM SAUCE   Combine wine, vinegar, juice and saffron in medium saucepan; bring to a boil. Boil until mixture is reduced to about a third. Add cream; return to a boil, then whisk in butter, one piece at a time, until mixture thickens slightly. Pour into medium jug; cover to keep warm.

SERVES 4
per serving 12.2g carbohydrate; 43.2g fat; 2700kJ (646 cal); 47.1g protein

cold seafood platter with dipping sauces

PREPARATION TIME 1 HOUR

2 cooked large lobsters (2.4kg)

2 cooked blue swimmer crabs (650g)

4 cooked balmain bugs (800g)

16 cooked large king prawns (1.1kg)

12 oysters, on the half shell

3 lemons, cut into wedges

1 Prepare lobster on cutting board; cut in half lengthways. Remove any green matter, liver and back vein from lobsters. Lightly crack claws. Pat dry with absorbent paper.

2 Rinse crabs well under cold water; pat dry with absorbent paper. Remove and lightly crack claws. Place crab bodies upside-down on cutting board. Remove triangular shell flap; cut crab bodies in half. Discard gills, liver and brain matter from crabs. Rinse under cold water; cut crab bodies into halves.

3 Place bugs upside-down on chopping board; cut in half lengthways. Remove any green matter, liver and back vein from tails. rinse under cold water.

4 Shell and devein prawns, leaving tails intact.

5 Make dipping sauces. Arrange seafood on large serving platter with lemon. Serve with sauces.

SERVES 4
per serving 24.7g carbohydrate; 25.3g fat; 2851kJ (682 cal); 86.3g protein

dipping sauces

chilli mayonnaise

PREPARATION TIME 5 MINUTES

½ cup (150g) mayonnaise

1 tablespoon water

2 tablespoons tomato sauce

1 teaspoon worcestershire sauce

1 teaspoon sambal oelek

Combine ingredients in small bowl.

MAKES ¾ CUP

soy and mirin

PREPARATION TIME 5 MINUTES

2 tablespoons water

1 tablespoon soy sauce

2 tablespoons mirin

2 teaspoons rice vinegar

½ teaspoon sambal oelek

Combine ingredients in small bowl.

MAKES ½ CUP

mustard and dill

PREPARATION TIME 5 MINUTES

½ cup (150g) mayonnaise

1 tablespoon water

1 tablespoon drained baby capers, rinsed

1 teaspoon wholegrain mustard

1 tablespoon coarsely chopped fresh dill

Combine ingredients in small bowl.

MAKES ⅔ CUP

chilli and lime

PREPARATION TIME 5 MINUTES

¼ cup (60ml) sweet chilli sauce

2 tablespoons lime juice

1 tablespoon water

1 teaspoon fish sauce

2 teaspoons finely chopped fresh vietnamese mint

Combine ingredients in small bowl.

MAKES ½ CUP

grilled prawns with tropical fruit salad (see front cover)

PREPARATION TIME 15 MINUTES   COOKING TIME 15 MINUTES

24 large uncooked king prawns (1.6kg)

¼ medium pineapple (300g),
    chopped coarsely

1 large mango (600g),
    chopped coarsely

1 large banana (230g),
    chopped coarsely

¼ cup loosely packed fresh
    mint leaves

2 tablespoons lime juice

MINT AND PARSLEY SAUCE

½ cup loosely packed fresh
    mint leaves

½ cup loosely packed fresh
    flat-leaf parsley

1 clove garlic, crushed

2 tablespoons lime juice

1 tablespoon olive oil

1 Shell and devein prawns, leaving tails intact. Cook prawns on heated oiled grill plate (or grill or barbecue) until prawns change in colour. Cover to keep warm.

2 Grill pineapple, mango and banana on same grill plate until browned lightly.

3 Meanwhile, make mint and parsley sauce.

4 Combine prawns and fruit with mint and juice in large bowl. Divide mixture among serving plates; serve with mint and parsley sauce.

MINT AND PARSLEY SAUCE Blend or process ingredients until combined.

SERVES 4
per serving 25g carbohydrate; 6.2g fat; 1402kJ (335 cal); 43.7g protein

grilled prawns with tropical fruit salad

italian fennel and beef-fillet salad with balsamic vinaigrette (see page 185)

salmon in sesame crust

PREPARATION TIME 10 MINUTES   COOKING TIME 10 MINUTES

2 tablespoons sesame seeds

1 teaspoon coriander seeds

1 teaspoon black peppercorns

4 x 220g skinless salmon fillets

1 tablespoon vegetable oil

1 tablespoon sesame oil

1 clove garlic, crushed

1cm piece fresh ginger (5g), grated

1 fresh small red thai chilli, seeded, sliced
   thinly lengthways

800g baby bok choy, quartered lengthways

¼ cup (60ml) salt-reduced soy sauce

2 tablespoons mirin

2 tablespoons honey

2 tablespoons lime juice

1 Place seeds and peppercorns in strong plastic bag; crush with rolling pin or meat mallet. Coat one side of each fish fillet with seed mixture.

2 Heat vegetable oil in large frying pan; cook fish, seeded-side down, uncovered, 1 minute. Turn; cook, uncovered, until fish is cooked as desired.

3 Meanwhile, heat sesame oil in wok or large frying pan; stir-fry garlic, ginger and chilli until fragrant. Add remaining ingredients; stir-fry until bok choy just wilts.

4 Serve fish with bok choy.

SERVES 4
per serving 15.5g carbohydrate; 28.4g fat; 2119kJ (507 cal); 47.4g protein

salt cod with chilli and tomatoes

PREPARATION TIME 15 MINUTES (PLUS REFRIGERATION TIME)   COOKING TIME 15 MINUTES

450g salt cod

1 large red onion (300g)

1 tablespoon olive oil

2 cloves garlic, sliced thinly

1 fresh small red thai chilli, sliced thinly

4 medium tomatoes (760g), peeled,
   chopped coarsely

½ cup (60g) seeded black olives

¼ cup (60g) tomato paste

¼ cup (60ml) dry white wine

1 tablespoon lemon juice

1 tablespoon drained capers, rinsed,
   chopped coarsely

3 teaspoons sugar

¾ cup coarsely chopped fresh flat-leaf parsley

1 Place cod in large bowl; cover with cold water. Cover bowl with plastic wrap, refrigerate 24 hours, changing water several times. Drain cod, add to large saucepan of boiling water; simmer, uncovered, 1 minute. Drain, rinse under cold water; drain well.

2 Using fork, flake cod; discard skin and bones.

3 Cut onion into wedges. Heat oil in large saucepan; cook onion, garlic and chilli, stirring, until onion is almost soft. Add tomato, olives, paste, wine, juice, capers and sugar; bring to a boil. Reduce heat; simmer, covered, 5 minutes, then simmer, uncovered, another 5 minutes or until mixture slightly thickens. Stir in cod and parsley.

SERVES 4
per serving 14.8g carbohydrate; 5.8g fat; 903kJ (216 cal); 23.2g protein

seafood casserole

PREPARATION TIME 30 MINUTES   COOKING TIME 45 MINUTES

1 tablespoon olive oil

1 medium leek (350g), sliced thinly

4 cloves garlic, crushed

425g can crushed tomatoes

¾ cup (180ml) dry white wine

¼ cup (60ml) sweet sherry

2 cups (500ml) fish stock

pinch saffron threads

2 medium carrots (240g), chopped finely

⅓ cup finely chopped fresh flat-leaf parsley

1 tablespoon finely chopped fresh thyme

1kg small black mussels

1kg uncooked large king prawns

500g squid hoods

500g uncooked lobster tail

350g scallops

1   Heat oil in large saucepan; cook leek and garlic, stirring, until leek softens. Add undrained tomatoes, wine, sherry, stock, saffron, carrot and herbs; bring to a boil. Reduce heat; simmer, covered, 30 minutes.

2   Meanwhile, scrub mussels; remove beards. Shell and devein prawns, leaving tails intact; cut squid open. Score inside surface in diagonal pattern; cut into 6cm pieces. Shell lobster tail; cut lobster meat into 5cm pieces.

3   Add mussels to tomato mixture; simmer, covered, 2 minutes. Add prawns, squid and lobster; simmer, covered, about 2 minutes. Add scallops; simmer, uncovered, about 2 minutes or until seafood is just cooked. Discard any unopened mussels.

SERVES 4
per serving 12.2g carbohydrate; 9.9g fat; 2257kJ (540 cal); 88.5g protein

char-grilled lobster tail salad

PREPARATION TIME 15 MINUTES   COOKING TIME 20 MINUTES

4 uncooked small lobster tails in shell (800g)

2 radicchio (400g), trimmed, leaves separated

1 medium avocado (250g), chopped coarsely

4 red radishes (140g), trimmed, sliced thinly

⅓ cup (50g) toasted pine nuts

4 green onions, sliced thinly

150g drained semi-dried tomatoes,
    chopped coarsely

ROSEMARY VINAIGRETTE

⅓ cup (80ml) vegetable oil

¼ cup (60ml) red wine vinegar

1 tablespoon coarsely chopped
    fresh rosemary

1 tablespoon dijon mustard

1   Make rosemary vinaigrette.

2   Using kitchen scissors, discard soft shell from underneath lobster tails to expose meat; cook, in batches, on heated oiled grill plate (or grill or barbecue) until browned and cooked through, brushing with a third of the vinaigrette. Cut lobster tails in half lengthways.

3   Meanwhile, place remaining ingredients in large bowl with remaining vinaigrette; toss gently to combine. Serve lobster on salad.

ROSEMARY VINAIGRETTE Place ingredients in screw-top jar; shake well.

SERVES 4
per serving 15.8g carbohydrate; 41.7g fat; 2562kJ (613 cal); 43.5g protein

poached flathead
with nam jim and herb salad

PREPARATION TIME 30 MINUTES   COOKING TIME 10 MINUTES

8 flathead fillets (1kg)

1 litre (4 cups) water

1 tablespoon fish sauce

1 tablespoon lime juice

NAM JIM

2 cloves garlic

3 long green chillies, seeded,
**   chopped coarsely**

2 coriander roots

2 tablespoons fish sauce

2 tablespoons grated palm sugar

3 shallots (75g), chopped coarsely

⅓ cup (80ml) lime juice

1 tablespoon peanut oil

HERB SALAD

1½ cups loosely packed fresh
**   mint leaves**

1 cup loosely packed fresh
**   coriander leaves**

1 cup loosely packed fresh basil
**   leaves, torn**

1 medium red onion (170g),
**   sliced thinly**

2 lebanese cucumbers (260g),
**   seeded, sliced thinly**

1 Make nam jim.

2 Cut each fillet in half. Combine the water, sauce and juice in large frying pan; bring to a boil. Reduce heat, add fish; simmer, uncovered, about 5 minutes or until cooked as desired. Remove fish from pan with slotted spoon; cover to keep warm.

3 Meanwhile, make herb salad.

4 Serve fish on salad; top with remaining nam jim.

NAM JIM Blend or process ingredients until smooth.

HERB SALAD Combine ingredients in medium bowl with a third of the nam jim.

SERVES 4
per serving 12.2g carbohydrate; 7.6g fat; 1458kJ (348 cal); 56.7g protein

hot and sour steamed fish with thai salad (see back cover)

PREPARATION TIME 35 MINUTES (PLUS REFRIGERATION TIME)   COOKING TIME 10 MINUTES

4 x 200g trevally fillets

3 fresh small red thai chillies, seeded, sliced thinly

3 fresh kaffir lime leaves, shredded finely

10cm stick (20g) fresh lemon grass, chopped finely

½ cup loosely packed fresh coriander leaves

½ cup loosely packed fresh mint leaves

½ cup loosely packed fresh basil leaves

150g snow peas, trimmed, sliced thinly

2 fresh long red chillies, seeded, sliced thinly

2 green onions, sliced thinly

35g snow pea sprouts

1 large mango (600g), sliced thinly

LIME AND SWEET CHILLI DRESSING

2 teaspoons sweet chilli sauce

⅓ cup (80ml) fish sauce

⅓ cup (80ml) lime juice

2 teaspoons peanut oil

1 clove garlic, crushed

1cm piece fresh ginger (5g), grated

1 teaspoon grated palm sugar

1   Make lime and sweet chilli dressing.

2   Combine fish, thai chilli, lime leaf and lemon grass in large bowl with half of the dressing, cover; refrigerate 30 minutes.

3   Place fish, in single layer, in baking-paper-lined large bamboo steamer; steam, covered, over wok or large frying pan of simmering water about 10 minutes or until fish is cooked as desired.

4   Place remaining ingredients in large bowl with remaining dressing; toss gently to combine. Serve fish with salad.

LIME AND SWEET CHILLI DRESSING   Place ingredients in screw-top jar; shake well.

SERVES 4
per serving 19.8g carbohydrate; 8.7g fat; 1450kJ (347 cal); 46.5g protein

seafood skewers with radicchio and fennel salad

PREPARATION TIME 25 MINUTES (PLUS REFRIGERATION TIME)   COOKING TIME 10 MINUTES

You need to soak eight bamboo skewers in water for at least 1 hour before using to prevent them splintering and scorching. Any firm white fish fillet, such as ling or blue-eye, can be used in this recipe.

8 uncooked large king

prawns (560g)

8 cleaned baby octopus (720g)

400g firm white fish fillets

8 scallops (200g), roe removed

2 teaspoons fennel seeds

2 teaspoons dried

green peppercorns

2 tablespoons white wine vinegar

2 cloves garlic, crushed

1 tablespoon olive oil

2 medium radicchio (400g)

150g sugar snap peas, trimmed

2 small fennel bulbs (400g),

trimmed, sliced thinly

1 cup firmly packed fresh flat-leaf

parsley leaves

MUSTARD DRESSING

⅓ cup (80ml) white wine vinegar

1 teaspoon dijon mustard

2 tablespoons olive oil

1 tablespoon honey

4 green onions, chopped coarsely

1   Shell and devein prawns, leaving tails intact. Remove heads and beaks from octopus; cut fish into 2.5cm pieces. Combine seafood in large bowl.

2   Using mortar and pestle, crush seeds and peppercorns coarsely, add to seafood with vinegar, garlic and oil; toss gently to combine. Cover; refrigerate 3 hours or overnight.

3   Make mustard dressing.

4   Thread seafood, alternating varieties, on skewers; cook on heated oiled grill plate (or grill or barbecue) until seafood is just changed in colour and cooked as desired.

5   Meanwhile, discard dark outer leaves of radicchio, tear inner leaves roughly. Boil, steam or microwave peas until just tender; drain. Place radicchio and peas in medium bowl with fennel, parsley and dressing; toss gently to combine. Serve seafood skewers on salad.

MUSTARD DRESSING Place ingredients in screw-top jar; shake well.

SERVES 4
per serving 12.5g carbohydrate; 20.1g fat; 2441kJ (584 cal); 86.9g protein

beef and haloumi kebabs with caper butter

PREPARATION TIME 10 MINUTES (PLUS REFRIGERATION TIME)   COOKING TIME 15 MINUTES

Soak bamboo skewers in water for about 1 hour before using to prevent them splintering and scorching.

1kg beef rump steak, diced into
   2cm pieces

2 tablespoons olive oil

1 tablespoon finely grated lemon rind

2 tablespoons lemon juice

1 tablespoon finely grated
   fresh horseradish

400g haloumi cheese, cubed

8 medium corn tortillas

CAPER BUTTER

2 tablespoons drained capers, rinsed,
   chopped finely

100g butter, melted

1   Place beef in large shallow dish with combined oil, rind, juice and horseradish. Cover; refrigerate 3 hours or overnight.

2   Thread beef and cheese onto eight skewers; cook on heated oiled grill plate (or grill or barbecue) until browned all over and cooked as desired.

3   Meanwhile, heat tortillas according to manufacturer's instructions. Wrap each skewer in one tortilla; remove skewers. Make caper butter.

4   Serve kebabs with caper butter.

CAPER BUTTER   Combine ingredients in small bowl.

SERVES 4
per serving   19.2g carbohydrate; 64.4g fat; 4063kJ (972 cal); 79.9g protein

balsamic and ginger beef with red cabbage coleslaw

PREPARATION TIME 15 MINUTES (PLUS REFRIGERATION TIME)   COOKING TIME 15 MINUTES

½ cup (125ml) olive oil

¼ cup (60ml) balsamic vinegar

4cm piece fresh ginger (20g), grated

1 teaspoon brown sugar

1 teaspoon soy sauce

4 x 500g beef T-bone steaks

2 medium green apples (300g)

½ medium red cabbage (800g),
   shredded finely

2 tablespoons caraway seeds, toasted

2 teaspoons dijon mustard

⅓ cup (80ml) olive oil, extra

2 tablespoons raspberry vinegar

1   Place oil, balsamic vinegar, ginger, sugar and sauce in jar; shake well. Reserve ¼ cup (60ml) of the oil mixture; brush beef all over using about half of the remaining mixture. Cover; refrigerate for 3 hours or overnight.

2   Cook beef on heated oiled grill plate (or grill or barbecue) until browned both sides and cooked as desired, brushing beef occasionally with remaining oil mixture. Cover beef; stand 10 minutes.

3   Meanwhile, core unpeeled apples; cut into matchstick-size pieces. Place apple in large bowl with cabbage and seeds; drizzle with combined remaining ingredients, toss gently to combine.

4   Pour reserved oil mixture over beef; serve with coleslaw.

SERVES 4
per serving   13.9g carbohydrate; 73.6g fat; 4138kJ (990 cal); 69.4g protein
tip   If your supermarket doesn't stock raspberry vinegar, use any fruit-flavoured vinegar in this recipe.

saltimbocca with brussels sprouts and sun-dried tomatoes

PREPARATION TIME 10 MINUTES   COOKING TIME 25 MINUTES

Saltimbocca is a classic Italian veal dish that literally means "jump in the mouth" — just the sensation the wonderful flavours produce with your first bite.

8 veal steaks (680g)

4 slices prosciutto (60g), halved crossways

8 fresh sage leaves

½ cup (50g) finely grated pecorino cheese

40g butter

1 cup (250ml) dry white wine

1 tablespoon coarsely chopped fresh sage

2 tablespoons olive oil

1kg brussels sprouts, sliced thickly

1 clove garlic, crushed

½ cup (70g) drained sun-dried tomatoes, sliced thinly

¼ cup (40g) toasted pine nuts

2 tablespoons lemon juice

1 Place steaks on board. Place one piece prosciutto, one sage leaf and ⅛ of the cheese on each steak; fold in half to secure filling, secure with a toothpick or small skewer.

2 Melt half of the butter in medium frying pan; cook saltimbocca, in batches, about 5 minutes or until browned both sides and cooked as desired. Cover to keep warm.

3 Pour wine into same frying pan; bring to a boil. Boil, uncovered, until wine reduces by half. Stir in remaining butter then chopped sage.

4 Meanwhile, heat half of the oil in large frying pan; cook sprouts and garlic until sprouts are just tender. Add tomato, nuts, juice and remaining oil; cook, stirring, until heated through.

5 Serve saltimbocca with sprout mixture; drizzle saltimbocca with sauce.

SERVES 4
per serving 12.9g carbohydrate; 34.8g fat; 2638kJ (631 cal); 55.8g protein

red beef curry

PREPARATION TIME 10 MINUTES   COOKING TIME 20 MINUTES

2 tablespoons peanut oil

500g beef rump steak, cut into 2cm pieces

1 large brown onion (200g), sliced thinly

¼ cup (75g) red curry paste

1 large red capsicum (350g), sliced thinly

150g snake beans, chopped

1⅔ cups (400ml) coconut milk

425g can crushed tomatoes

¼ cup coarsely chopped fresh coriander

1 Heat half of the oil in wok or large frying pan; stir-fry beef, in batches, until browned all over.

2 Heat remaining oil in same wok; stir-fry onion until soft. Add paste; stir-fry until fragrant. Add capsicum and snake beans; stir-fry until vegetables just soften.

3 Return beef to wok with remaining ingredients; stir-fry until sauce boils and thickens slightly.

SERVES 4
per serving 12.4g carbohydrate; 44.5g fat; 2437kJ (583 cal); 34.6g protein

corned beef with cheesy cauliflower and mustard sauce

PREPARATION TIME 15 MINUTES   COOKING TIME 2 HOURS 35 MINUTES

1.5kg piece uncooked corned silverside

2 bay leaves

1 teaspoon black peppercorns

2 whole cloves

2 tablespoons brown sugar

2 tablespoons malt vinegar

1 medium cauliflower (1.5kg),
   cut into florets

¾ cup (90g) coarsely grated
   cheddar cheese

½ cup (125ml) water

½ cup (125ml) dry white wine

½ cup (125ml) chicken stock

2 teaspoons cornflour

1 tablespoon wholegrain mustard

½ cup (125ml) cream

1   Place beef in large saucepan with bay leaves, peppercorns, cloves, sugar and vinegar. Cover with cold water; bring to a boil. Reduce heat; simmer, covered, about 2 hours or until beef is tender. Remove from heat; cool 10 minutes in liquid.

2   Meanwhile, preheat oven to hot. Boil, steam or microwave cauliflower until just tender; drain. Place cauliflower in medium shallow baking dish; sprinkle with cheese. Bake, uncovered, in hot oven about 5 minutes or until cheese melts. Cover to keep warm.

3   Bring the water, wine and stock to a boil in small saucepan. Reduce heat; simmer, uncovered, about 5 minutes or until mixture reduces by a third. Stir in blended cornflour, mustard and cream; cook, stirring, until sauce boils and thickens.

4   Remove beef from liquid; slice thinly. Serve beef with cauliflower and mustard sauce.

SERVES 4
per serving 16.8g carbohydrate; 42g fat; 2997kJ (717 cal); 63.2g protein

cajun steaks with mango salsa

PREPARATION TIME 15 MINUTES   COOKING TIME 5 MINUTES

1½ teaspoons cajun seasoning

4 beef minute steaks (700g)

100g mesclun

MANGO SALSA

1 large mango (600g), chopped coarsely

2 medium tomatoes (380g), seeded,
   chopped coarsely

1 small red onion (100g), chopped finely

1 clove garlic, crushed

2 tablespoons finely shredded fresh basil

1 tablespoon balsamic vinegar

1   Make mango salsa.

2   Sprinkle seasoning over beef; cook on heated oiled grill plate (or grill or barbecue) until browned both sides and cooked as desired.

3   Serve beef with mesclun and salsa.

MANGO SALSA Combine ingredients in medium bowl.

SERVES 4
per serving 16.2g carbohydrate; 8.8g fat; 1271kJ (304 cal); 39.1g protein
tip We used thinly sliced boneless beef sirloin for this recipe, however rump steak or scotch fillet are also suitable.

beef and vegetable rolls

PREPARATION TIME 15 MINUTES   COOKING TIME 15 MINUTES

To make larger rolls, use two or three slices of meat, slightly overlapping. You could use rib eye steak (scotch fillet) instead of the beef eye fillet, if you prefer.

2 medium carrots (240g)

6 asparagus spears,
   halved lengthways

3 green onions

12 thin slices beef eye fillet (300g)

1 tablespoon cornflour

1 tablespoon vegetable oil

2 teaspoons sugar

¼ cup (60ml) mirin

2 tablespoons sake

¼ cup (60ml) japanese soy sauce

1 Using vegetable peeler, slice carrot lengthways into thin strips. Cut carrot strips to width of beef. Place asparagus in medium heatproof bowl, cover with boiling water, stand 2 minutes; drain. Rinse under cold water, drain. Cut asparagus and onions to width of beef.

2 Lay beef slices flat and sift 2 teaspoons of the cornflour lightly over top. Lay two pieces each of carrot and onion and one piece of asparagus across the dusted side of each slice of beef and roll up. Tie rolls with kitchen string or secure ends with toothpicks. Dust rolls lightly with remaining cornflour.

3 Heat oil in medium frying pan; cook rolls until browned lightly all over. Remove rolls from pan, wipe oil from pan with absorbent paper; return rolls to pan. Add combined sugar, mirin, sake and sauce; bring to a boil. Reduce heat; simmer, uncovered, turning occasionally, until rolls are cooked through.

4 Remove rolls from pan; cool 2 minutes. Discard toothpicks; cut rolls in half. Serve rolls with remaining sauce in pan.

SERVES 4
per serving 12.9g carbohydrate; 7.9g fat; 953kJ (228 cal); 18.3g protein
tips Very thinly sliced beef, sold as yakiniku or sukiyaki beef, is available from Asian butchers.

indian spiced beef with dhal

PREPARATION TIME 15 MINUTES (PLUS REFRIGERATION TIME)   COOKING TIME 1 HOUR 20 MINUTES

2 tablespoons cumin seeds

1 tablespoon coriander seeds

2 teaspoons sweet paprika

2 teaspoons ground cinnamon

1 teaspoon ground cardamom

1 teaspoon chilli powder

5 cloves garlic, crushed

2cm piece fresh ginger (10g), grated

¼ cup (60ml) peanut oil

1.25kg beef rump roast

DHAL

1 cups (200g) red lentils

¼ cup shredded fresh mint leaves

3 cups (750ml) vegetable stock

1   Cook seeds, paprika, cinnamon, cardamom and chilli powder in dry medium frying pan, stirring, until fragrant. Place seed mixture in small bowl with garlic, ginger and oil; mix to a paste. Trim as much fat from beef as possible; spread paste all over beef. Cover; refrigerate 3 hours or overnight.

2   Place beef on roasting rack or basket, or in disposable baking dish. Cook in covered barbecue, using indirect heat, following manufacturer's instructions, about 1 hour 20 minutes or until browned all over and cooked as desired. Remove from heat, cover; stand 10 minutes before slicing thickly.

3   Meanwhile, make dhal.

4   Serve beef with dhal.

DHAL Combine ingredients in medium saucepan; bring to a boil. Reduce heat; simmer, uncovered, stirring occasionally, about 15 minutes or until lentils are tender.

SERVES 4
per serving 20.9g carbohydrate; 36.5g fat; 3114kJ (745 cal); 84.5g protein

satay beef and stir-fried vegetables

PREPARATION TIME 20 MINUTES   COOKING TIME 20 MINUTES

1 teaspoon peanut oil

600g lean beef topside, sliced thinly

1 large brown onion (200g), sliced thinly

1 clove garlic, crushed

2cm piece fresh ginger (10g), grated

2 fresh small red thai chillies, seeded, chopped finely

2 medium red capsicums (400g), chopped coarsely

100g mushrooms, halved

1 teaspoon curry powder

2 teaspoons cornflour

½ cup (125ml) chicken stock

¼ cup (65g) light smooth peanut butter

2 tablespoons oyster sauce

1 tablespoon toasted peanuts, chopped coarsely

1   Heat oil in wok or large frying pan; stir-fry beef, in batches, until browned all over.

2   Stir-fry onion and garlic in same wok until onion softens. Add ginger, chilli, capsicum, mushrooms and curry powder; stir-fry until vegetables are just tender.

3   Blend cornflour with stock in small jug; pour into wok, stir to combine with vegetable mixture. Return beef to wok with peanut butter and sauce; stir-fry. Boil until sauce boils and thickens slightly. Stir in nuts.

SERVES 4
per serving 16g carbohydrate; 14g fat; 1463kJ (350 cal); 39.8g protein

veal steaks with italian white bean salad

PREPARATION TIME 15 MINUTES   COOKING TIME 10 MINUTES

1 tablespoon olive oil

8 veal steaks (680g)

½ cup (125ml) beef stock

60g butter

ITALIAN WHITE BEAN SALAD

100g baby rocket leaves

1 large tomato (250g), chopped coarsely

½ cup firmly packed fresh basil leaves, torn

2 x 400g cans white beans, rinsed, drained

1 tablespoon finely chopped fresh chives

¼ cup (60ml) lemon juice

2 cloves garlic, crushed

¼ cup (60ml) olive oil

1   Make italian white bean salad.

2   Heat oil in large non-stick frying pan; cook steaks, in batches, until browned both sides and cooked as desired. Cover to keep warm.

3   Pour stock into same pan; bring to a boil, stirring. Add butter; stir until butter melts. Reduce heat; simmer, stirring, 2 minutes.

4   Serve steak, drizzled with sauce, with italian white bean salad.

ITALIAN WHITE BEAN SALAD Place rocket, tomato, basil and beans in large bowl. Place chives, juice, garlic and oil in screw-top jar; shake well. Pour dressing over salad; toss gently to combine.

SERVES 4
per serving 20.1g carbohydrate; 35.1g fat; 2437kJ (583 cal); 44.3g protein

sweet chilli ribs with pamela's coleslaw

PREPARATION TIME 20 MINUTES   COOKING TIME 30 MINUTES

1.5kg pork spareribs

⅓ cup (80ml) sweet chilli sauce

1 tablespoon soy sauce

¼ cup (60ml) rice wine

2 cloves garlic, crushed

1cm piece fresh ginger (5g), grated

2 tablespoons finely chopped fresh coriander

½ medium savoy cabbage (850g), shredded finely

6 green onions, chopped finely

1 fresh small red thai chilli, chopped finely

½ cup coarsely chopped fresh mint

½ cup coarsely chopped fresh flat-leaf parsley

¼ cup coarsely chopped fresh coriander

LEMON DRESSING

2 tablespoons lemon juice

2 teaspoons dijon mustard

⅓ cup (80ml) peanut oil

1   Place ribs in large shallow casserole with combined sauces, wine, garlic, ginger and finely chopped coriander. Cover; refrigerate 3 hours or overnight.

2   Cook ribs in covered barbecue, using indirect heat, following manufacturer's instructions, about 30 minutes or until browned all over and cooked as desired.

3   Meanwhile, make lemon dressing.

4   Place cabbage, onion, chilli and herbs in large bowl with dressing; toss gently to combine.

5   Serve ribs with coleslaw.

LEMON DRESSING Place ingredients in screw-top jar; shake well.

SERVES 4
per serving 15.1g carbohydrate; 35.4g fat; 2646kJ (633 cal); 62.1g protein

herb and mustard-seasoned beef fillet with broad bean and corn salad

PREPARATION TIME 40 MINUTES   COOKING TIME 30 MINUTES

50g butter, softened

2 cloves garlic, crushed

2 teaspoons finely chopped fresh rosemary

1 tablespoon finely chopped fresh flat-leaf parsley

1 tablespoon finely chopped seeded black olives

1 tablespoon coarsely chopped toasted pine nuts

¼ cup (70g) wholegrain mustard

700g piece beef eye fillet, trimmed

1 tablespoon extra virgin olive oil

2 tablespoons horseradish cream

BROAD BEAN AND CORN SALAD

4 trimmed corn cobs (1kg)

200g frozen broad beans, thawed, peeled

1 medium red capsicum (200g), chopped finely

20g butter

1   Combine butter, garlic, herbs, olives, nuts and 2 tablespoons of the mustard in small bowl. Transfer to small piping bag fitted with medium plain tube.

2   Preheat oven to moderately hot.

3   Tie beef firmly with kitchen string at 2cm intervals. Using knife-sharpening steel or thick butcher's skewer, pierce beef through centre lengthways. Pipe butter mixture into cavity.

4   Heat oil in medium flameproof baking dish; cook beef over high heat about 5 minutes or until browned all over. Transfer dish to oven; roast, uncovered, in moderately hot oven about 20 minutes or until cooked as desired. Cover with foil; stand 5 minutes.

5   Meanwhile, make broad bean and corn salad.

6   Serve beef sliced with combined remaining mustard and horseradish cream and salad.

BROAD BEAN AND CORN SALAD Cook corn on heated oiled grill plate (or grill or barbecue) until just tender; cool 10 minutes. Using sharp knife, remove kernels from cob. Meanwhile, boil, steam or microwave broad beans until tender; drain. Place corn and beans in large bowl with capsicum and butter; toss gently to combine.

SERVES 4
per serving 24.2g carbohydrate; 31.4g fat; 2404kJ (575 cal); 49.3g protein

mustard-crusted rack of veal with pumpkin mash

PREPARATION TIME 25 MINUTES   COOKING TIME 35 MINUTES

2 tablespoons wholegrain mustard

3 green onions, chopped finely

1 tablespoon finely chopped
fresh rosemary

2 cloves garlic, crushed

2 tablespoons olive oil

1kg veal rack (8 cutlets), trimmed

750g pumpkin, chopped coarsely

20g butter

⅓ cup (80ml) cream

1 large brown onion (200g),
sliced thinly

400g mushrooms, sliced thinly

1 tablespoon plain flour

¼ cup (60ml) dry white wine

¾ cup (180ml) chicken stock

¼ cup coarsely chopped fresh
flat-leaf parsley

1 Preheat oven to moderately hot.

2 Combine mustard, green onion, rosemary, half of the garlic and half of the oil in small jug. Place veal on wire rack over large shallow flameproof baking dish; coat veal all over with mustard mixture. Roast, uncovered, in moderately hot oven, about 30 minutes or until browned all over and cooked as desired. Cover to keep warm.

3 Meanwhile, boil, steam or microwave pumpkin until tender; drain. Mash pumpkin in large bowl with butter and half of the cream until smooth.

4 Heat remaining oil in same flameproof dish; cook brown onion and remaining garlic, stirring, until onion softens. Add mushrooms; cook, stirring, about 5 minutes or until mushrooms are just tender. Add flour; cook, stirring, until mixture thickens and bubbles. Gradually stir in wine and stock; stir until sauce boils and thickens. Add remaining cream and parsley; stir until heated through.

5 Serve veal with pumpkin mash and mushroom sauce.

SERVES 4
per serving 16.9g carbohydrate; 26.8g fat; 2199kJ (526 cal); 52.3g protein

hearty beef stew with red wine and mushrooms

PREPARATION TIME 10 MINUTES   COOKING TIME 2 HOURS 50 MINUTES

2 tablespoons olive oil

1.5kg beef blade steak, cut into 2cm cubes

1 large brown onion (200g), sliced thickly

2 cloves garlic, crushed

250g mushrooms, quartered

2 trimmed celery stalks (200g), sliced thickly

2 x 425g cans crushed tomatoes

½ cup (125ml) dry red wine

1½ cups (375ml) beef stock

2 teaspoons coarsely chopped fresh thyme

350g green beans, trimmed

350g yellow beans, trimmed

20g butter

¼ cup (35g) toasted slivered almonds

¼ cup loosely packed fresh flat-leaf
   parsley leaves

1 Heat half of the oil in large heavy-base saucepan; cook beef, in batches, until browned all over.

2 Heat remaining oil in same pan; cook onion and garlic, stirring, until onion softens. Add mushrooms and celery; cook, stirring, 3 minutes. Return beef to pan with undrained tomatoes, wine and stock; bring to a boil. Reduce heat; simmer, covered, 2½ hours. Stir in thyme.

3 Meanwhile, boil, steam or microwave beans until just tender; drain. Place beans in medium bowl with butter, nuts and parsley; toss gently to combine.

4 Serve stew with beans.

SERVES 4
per serving 12.4g carbohydrate; 43.6g fat; 3440kJ (823 cal); 89.8g protein

chilli con carne

PREPARATION TIME 25 MINUTES   COOKING TIME 1 HOUR 30 MINUTES

1kg beef chuck steak

2 tablespoons olive oil

2 medium brown onions (300g),
   chopped finely

3 cloves garlic, crushed

3 teaspoons ground cumin

1 teaspoon ground coriander

1 teaspoon chilli powder

1 tablespoon finely chopped fresh oregano

2 x 425g cans crushed tomatoes

1 cup (250ml) beef stock

2 teaspoons brown sugar

430g canned red kidney beans,
   rinsed, drained

1 Cut beef into 2cm pieces. Heat half of the oil in large saucepan; cook beef, in batches, until browned.

2 Heat remaining oil in same pan; cook onion, garlic, spices and oregano, stirring, until onion softens.

3 Add undrained tomatoes, stock, sugar and beef; bring to a boil. Reduce heat; simmer, covered, about 1 hour or until beef is tender.

4 Stir beans into beef mixture; simmer, uncovered, about 5 minutes or until heated through.

SERVES 4
per serving 18.5g carbohydrate; 21.2g fat; 2082kJ (498 cal); 58g protein

barbecue glazed meatloaf

PREPARATION TIME 20 MINUTES   COOKING TIME 50 MINUTES

1 small red capsicum (150g)

400g beef mince

150g sausage mince

1 medium brown onion (150g),
    chopped finely

2 cloves garlic, crushed

¼ cup (25g) packaged breadcrumbs

1 egg, beaten lightly

½ cup (80g) coarsely chopped seeded
    green olives

¼ cup coarsely chopped fresh basil

1 tablespoon coarsely chopped
    fresh oregano

8 bacon rashers (560g), rind removed,
    sliced lengthways

200g green beans, trimmed

BARBECUE GLAZE

¼ cup (60ml) water

1 tablespoon tomato paste

1 tablespoon red wine vinegar

2 tablespoons brown sugar

1   Quarter capsicum; remove and discard seeds and membrane. Roast under grill or in very hot oven, skin-side up, until skin blisters and blackens. Cover capsicum pieces with plastic or paper for 5 minutes. Peel away skin; cut capsicum into thin strips.

2   Preheat oven to moderate (or reduce oven temperature to moderate). Line 8cm x 25cm bar cake pan with plastic wrap. Oil 25cm x 30cm swiss roll pan.

3   Combine minces, onion, garlic, breadcrumbs, egg, olives, basil and oregano in large bowl. Press half of the meatloaf mixture into prepared bar pan. Lay capsicum strips over top, leaving 1cm border; press remaining meatloaf mixture over capsicum.

4   Turn bar pan onto prepared swiss roll pan; remove plastic wrap from meatloaf. Cover top and sides of meatloaf with bacon, overlapping bacon. Bake, uncovered, in moderate oven 15 minutes.

5   Meanwhile, make barbecue glaze.

6   Pour off any excess fat from meatloaf, brush with glaze; bake, uncovered, about 25 minutes or until meatloaf is cooked through. Stand 10 minutes before slicing.

7   Meanwhile, boil, steam or microwave beans until tender; drain.

8   Serve beans with meatloaf.

BARBECUE GLAZE Combine ingredients in small saucepan; bring to a boil. Reduce heat; simmer, uncovered, 5 minutes.

SERVES 4
per serving 20.8g carbohydrate; 27.2g fat; 1998kJ (478 cal); 38.2g protein

italian-style stuffed mushrooms

PREPARATION TIME 15 MINUTES   COOKING TIME 15 MINUTES

Marsala is a sweet fortified wine originally from Sicily; it can be found in liquor stores.

8 medium flat mushrooms (800g)

90g butter

½ medium red capsicum (100g),
    chopped finely

1 clove garlic, crushed

¼ cup (60ml) marsala

1 tablespoon lemon juice

1¼ cups (85g) stale breadcrumbs

2 tablespoons coarsely chopped
    fresh flat-leaf parsley

1 cup (80g) coarsely grated
    pecorino cheese

1   Preheat oven to moderately hot.

2   Carefully remove stems from mushrooms; chop stems finely.

3   Melt butter in small frying pan. Brush mushroom caps with about half of the butter; place on oiled oven trays.

4   Cook capsicum and garlic, stirring, in remaining butter until capsicum is just tender. Add chopped stems, marsala, juice and breadcrumbs; cook, stirring, 3 minutes. Remove from heat; stir in parsley and cheese. Spoon filling into mushroom caps; bake, uncovered, in moderately hot oven about 10 minutes or until browned lightly.

SERVES 4
per serving 21.5g carbohydrate; 27.8g fat; 1739kJ (416 cal); 16.7g protein
tip Vegetable stock can be substituted for marsala, if desired.

tofu and sugar snap pea stir-fry

PREPARATION TIME 25 MINUTES (PLUS STANDING TIME)   COOKING TIME 15 MINUTES

Mirin is a sweetened rice wine used in Japanese cooking; it is sometimes referred to in cookbooks simply as rice wine. You can substitute sweet white wine, or even sherry, if mirin is unavailable.

600g firm tofu

1 tablespoon sesame oil

1 large red onion (300g),
    sliced thickly

2 cloves garlic, crushed

2cm piece fresh ginger (10g), grated

1 teaspoon cornflour

⅓ cup (80ml) soy sauce

400g sugar snap peas, trimmed

1 tablespoon brown sugar

⅓ cup (80ml) oyster sauce

2 tablespoons mirin

¼ cup coarsely chopped
    fresh coriander

1   Preheat oven to moderately hot.

2   Weight tofu between two boards; stand, tilted, 10 minutes. Cut tofu into 2cm cubes; pat tofu dry between layers of absorbent paper. Place tofu on baking-paper-lined oven trays. Bake, uncovered, in moderately hot oven about 10 minutes or until browned lightly.

3   Heat oil in wok or large frying pan; stir-fry onion, garlic and ginger until onion softens. Add blended cornflour and soy sauce to wok with tofu, peas, sugar, oyster sauce and mirin; stir-fry until sauce boils and thickens slightly. Remove from heat; stir in coriander.

SERVES 4
per serving 24.7g carbohydrate; 15.6g fat; 1476kJ (353 cal); 26.7g protein

italian-style stuffed mushrooms

osso buco

osso buco

PREPARATION TIME 30 MINUTES   COOKING TIME 2 HOURS 30 MINUTES

Ask your butcher to cut the veal shin into fairly thick (about 3cm to 4cm) pieces for you.

1 tablespoon olive oil

8 pieces veal osso buco (2kg)

1 medium brown onion (150g),
   chopped coarsely

2 cloves garlic, crushed

1 trimmed celery stalk (100g),
   chopped coarsely

1 large carrot (180g),
   chopped coarsely

2 tablespoons tomato paste

½ cup (125ml) dry white wine

1 cup (250ml) beef stock

1 cup (250ml) water

400g can crushed tomatoes

1 teaspoon fresh rosemary leaves

1 medium eggplant (300g),
   chopped coarsely

1 medium green capsicum (200g),
   chopped coarsely

1 medium yellow capsicum (200g),
   chopped coarsely

GREMOLATA

2 teaspoons finely grated
   lemon rind

¼ cup finely chopped fresh
   flat-leaf parsley

1 tablespoon finely chopped
   fresh rosemary

1 clove garlic, chopped finely

1 Heat half of the oil in large saucepan; cook veal, in batches, until browned all over.

2 Heat remaining oil in same saucepan; cook onion, garlic, celery and carrot, stirring, until vegetables soften. Add paste, wine, stock, the water, undrained tomatoes and rosemary; bring to a boil.

3 Return veal to saucepan, fitting pieces upright and tightly together in single layer; return to a boil. Reduce heat; simmer, covered, 1½ hours. Add eggplant; simmer, uncovered, 15 minutes. Add capsicum; cook about 15 minutes or until vegetables are tender.

4 Meanwhile, make gremolata.

5 Remove veal and vegetables from dish; cover to keep warm. Bring sauce to a boil; boil, uncovered, about 10 minutes or until sauce thickens slightly.

6 Divide veal and vegetables among serving plates; top with sauce, sprinkle with gremolata.

GREMOLATA Combine ingredients in small bowl.

SERVES 4
per serving 13.4g carbohydrate; 20.3g fat; 1563kJ (373 cal); 29.1g protein

tuscan beef stew

PREPARATION TIME 15 MINUTES COOKING TIME 2 HOURS 40 MINUTES

Round steak and skirt steak are also suitable for this recipe.

1 tablespoon olive oil

400g spring onions, trimmed

1kg beef chuck steak, cut into 3cm cubes

30g butter

2 tablespoons plain flour

2 cups (500ml) dry red wine

1 cup (250ml) beef stock

1 cup (250ml) water

2 cloves garlic, crushed

6 sprigs fresh thyme

2 bay leaves

1 trimmed celery stalk (100g),
    chopped coarsely

400g baby carrots, trimmed, halved

2 cups (250g) frozen peas

⅓ cup coarsely chopped fresh
    flat-leaf parsley

1 Heat oil in large heavy-base saucepan; cook onions, stirring occasionally, about 10 minutes or until browned lightly, remove from pan. Cook beef, in batches, in same pan, until browned all over.

2 Melt butter in same pan, add flour; cook, stirring, until mixture bubbles and thickens. Gradually stir in wine, stock and the water; stir until mixture boils and thickens. Return beef to pan with garlic, thyme and bay leaves; bring to a boil. Reduce heat; simmer, covered, 1½ hours.

3 Add onions to pan with celery and carrot; simmer, covered, 30 minutes. Add peas; simmer, uncovered, until peas are just tender. Stir in parsley just before serving.

SERVES 4
per serving 19g carbohydrate; 22.7g fat; 2495kJ (597 cal); 58.2g protein

tandoori beef with grilled limes

PREPARATION TIME 10 MINUTES (PLUS REFRIGERATION TIME)   COOKING TIME 10 MINUTES

4 x 150g beef rib-eye steaks

1 clove garlic, crushed

¼ cup (75g) tandoori paste

4 limes, halved

400g green beans, trimmed

½ cup (160g) mango chutney

¾ cup (210g) yogurt

1 Combine beef, garlic and paste in large bowl. Cover; refrigerate 3 hours or overnight.

2 Cook beef on heated oiled grill plate (or grill or barbecue) until browned and cooked as desired.

3 Meanwhile, cook lime on same grill plate about 2 minutes or until browned.

4 Boil, steam or microwave beans until tender; drain.

5 Serve beef with lime, chutney, yogurt and beans.

SERVES 4
per serving 24.6g carbohydrate; 16.8g fat; 1609kJ (385 cal); 31.4g protein

veal and mushroom casserole

PREPARATION TIME 15 MINUTES COOKING TIME 1 HOUR 10 MINUTES

750g diced veal

2 medium brown onions (300g),

chopped coarsely

1 clove garlic, crushed

½ teaspoon hot paprika

4 medium tomatoes (760g), chopped coarsely

¼ cup (60g) tomato paste

1½ cups (375ml) beef stock

2 cups (500ml) water

200g button mushrooms, halved

1 tablespoon fresh oregano leaves

300g baby carrots, trimmed

30g butter

1 Heat large oiled non-stick saucepan; cook veal, in batches, until browned all over. Cook onion and garlic in same pan, stirring, until onion softens. Add paprika; cook, stirring, until fragrant.

2 Return veal to pan with tomato, paste, stock and the water; bring to a boil. Reduce heat; simmer, uncovered, about 45 minutes or until veal is tender. Add mushrooms; bring to a boil. Reduce heat; simmer, uncovered, until mushrooms are tender. Stir in oregano.

3 Meanwhile, boil, steam or microwave carrots until tender; drain. Place carrots in medium bowl with butter; toss to coat carrots in butter.

4 Serve casserole with carrots.

SERVES 4
per serving 13.3g carbohydrate; 13.4g fat; 1547kJ (370 cal); 48.3g protein
tips This recipe becomes more flavoursome if made a day or two ahead and refrigerated, covered; reheat slowly to serve.

thai-style steaks with pickled cucumber salad

PREPARATION TIME 25 MINUTES (PLUS REFRIGERATION TIME) COOKING TIME 10 MINUTES

4 x 200g beef rib-eye steaks

2 tablespoons sweet chilli sauce

1 clove garlic, crushed

1 teaspoon fish sauce

2 tablespoons lime juice

1 tablespoon coarsely chopped

fresh coriander

PICKLED CUCUMBER SALAD

2 lebanese cucumbers (260g)

2 tablespoons caster sugar

½ cup (125ml) white vinegar

1 fresh small red thai chilli, seeded,

sliced thinly

¼ cup (35g) coarsely chopped unsalted,

toasted peanuts

1 tablespoon coarsely chopped

fresh coriander

1 Make pickled cucumber salad.

2 Combine beef with remaining ingredients in large bowl. Cover; refrigerate 3 hours or overnight.

3 Drain beef; discard marinade. Cook beef on heated oiled grill plate (or grill or barbecue) until browned and cooked as desired.

4 Serve beef with drained cucumber salad.

PICKLED CUCUMBER SALAD Halve cucumbers lengthways. Scoop out and discard seeds; slice cucumber thinly. Combine sugar and vinegar in medium saucepan; stir over heat, without boiling, until sugar dissolves. Reduce heat; simmer, uncovered, about 5 minutes or until reduced to ½ cup. Combine hot vinegar mixture with cucumber and remaining ingredients in medium heatproof bowl. Cover; refrigerate 3 hours or overnight.

SERVES 4
per serving 14.6g carbohydrate; 18g fat; 1743kJ (417 cal); 48.1g protein

hoisin beef stir-fry (see page 325)

PREPARATION TIME 20 MINUTES (PLUS REFRIGERATION TIME)   COOKING TIME 15 MINUTES

1 teaspoon sesame oil

2 green onions, chopped finely

1 fresh small red chilli, chopped finely

2 cloves garlic, crushed

3cm piece fresh ginger (15g), grated

⅓ cup (80ml) chinese rice wine

⅓ cup (80ml) soy sauce

800g beef strips

1 tablespoon peanut oil

1 medium brown onion (150g), sliced thinly

1 medium red capsicum (200g), sliced thinly

100g shiitake mushrooms, trimmed,
   sliced thinly

500g choy sum, halved

¼ cup (60ml) water

¼ cup (60ml) hoisin sauce

4 green onions, sliced thinly

1 Combine sesame oil, chopped green onion, chilli, garlic, ginger, half of the wine and half of the soy sauce in large bowl, add beef; toss to coat beef in marinade. Cover; refrigerate 3 hours or overnight.

2 Heat half of the peanut oil in wok or large frying pan; cook undrained beef, in batches, until beef is browned all over and just cooked through.

3 Heat remaining peanut oil in same wok; stir-fry brown onion until almost tender. Add capsicum, mushroom, choy sum stalks and the water; cook, covered, about 5 minutes or until vegetables are tender.

4 Return beef to wok with hoisin, choy sum leaves, remaining wine and remaining soy sauce; stir-fry until choy sum leaves just wilt.

5 Divide stir-fry between serving bowls, top with sliced green onion.

SERVES 4
per serving 13.7g carbohydrate 16.6g fat; 1726kJ (413 cal); 46.8g protein

grilled sausages and ratatouille

PREPARATION TIME 20 MINUTES   COOKING TIME 20 MINUTES

2 tablespoons olive oil

1 medium red onion (170g), chopped coarsely

2 medium red capsicums (400g),
   chopped coarsely

3 medium green zucchini (360g),
   chopped coarsely

3 baby eggplant (180g), chopped coarsely

3 medium tomatoes (570g), chopped coarsely

3 teaspoons sambal oelek

¼ cup (60g) tomato paste

¾ cup (180ml) beef stock

2 tablespoons coarsely chopped fresh chives

12 veal and mushroom sausages (960g)

1 Heat oil in medium saucepan; cook onion and capsicum, stirring, until onion softens. Add zucchini and eggplant; cook, stirring, 3 minutes. Stir in tomato, sambal, paste and stock; bring to a boil. Reduce heat; simmer, uncovered, about 8 minutes or until mixture thickens. Stir in chives.

2 Meanwhile, cook sausages on heated oiled grill plate (or grill or barbecue) until cooked through. Serve sausages on ratatouille.

SERVES 4
per serving 15.6g carbohydrate; 50.7g fat; 2546kJ (609 cal); 23.9g protein

green chilli stew

PREPARATION TIME 15 MINUTES   COOKING TIME 1 HOUR 40 MINUTES

2 tablespoons olive oil

1kg beef chuck steak, cut into 3cm cubes

1 large brown onion (200g), sliced thinly

2 cloves garlic, sliced thinly

2 teaspoons ground cumin

2 long green chillies, seeded, sliced thinly

2 cups (500ml) beef stock

1 tablespoon tomato paste

3 large egg tomatoes (270g),
  chopped coarsely

2 small turnips (300g), chopped coarsely

2 medium carrots (240g), chopped coarsely

2 trimmed fresh corn cobs (500g), halved

¼ cup coarsely chopped fresh coriander

1 Heat half of the oil in large flameproof baking dish; cook beef, in batches, stirring, until browned all over.

2 Preheat oven to moderate.

3 Heat remaining oil in same dish; cook onion, garlic, cumin and chilli, stirring, until onion softens. Add stock and paste; bring to a boil, stirring. Return beef to dish; cook, covered, in moderate oven 45 minutes.

4 Add tomato and turnips; cook, covered, in moderate oven 35 minutes. Uncover, add carrots; cook 20 minutes.

5 Meanwhile, cook corn on heated oiled grill plate (or grill or barbecue) until cooked through.

6 Stir coriander into stew just before serving with corn.

SERVES 4
per serving 18.6g carbohydrate; 21.5g fat; 2082kJ (498 cal); 57.2g protein

roast beef and rocket salad

PREPARATION TIME 10 MINUTES   COOKING TIME 20 MINUTES

1 tablespoon olive oil

600g piece beef eye fillet

1 lebanese cucumber (130g),
  chopped coarsely

1 medium tomato (150g), chopped coarsely

120g drained semi-dried tomatoes

100g baby rocket leaves

1 small red onion (100g), sliced thinly

4 green onions, sliced thinly

½ cup (125ml) buttermilk

⅓ cup (100g) mayonnaise

1 tablespoon dijon mustard

1 clove garlic, crushed

1 teaspoon freshly ground black pepper

1 Preheat oven to moderately hot.

2 Heat oil in medium flameproof baking dish; cook beef, turning, until browned. Roast, uncovered, in moderately hot oven about 15 minutes or until cooked as desired. Remove from oven. Cover; stand 5 minutes, slice beef thinly.

3 Place beef in large bowl with cucumber, chopped tomato, semi-dried tomato, rocket and onion. Place remaining ingredients in screw-top jar; shake well. Drizzle dressing over salad; toss gently to combine.

SERVES 4
per serving 21.1g carbohydrate; 21.6g fat; 1873kJ (448 cal); 41.4g protein
tip Beef can be cooked up to 2 hours ahead; cover, refrigerate until required.

marjoram and lemon grilled veal chops with greek salad

PREPARATION TIME 25 MINUTES (PLUS REFRIGERATION TIME)   COOKING TIME 10 MINUTES

4 x 200g veal chops

1 teaspoon finely grated lemon rind

¼ cup (60ml) lemon juice

1 tablespoon finely chopped
fresh marjoram

2 teaspoons olive oil

GREEK SALAD

¾ cup (120g) seeded
kalamata olives

200g fetta cheese,
chopped coarsely

6 large egg tomatoes (540g),
seeded, chopped coarsely

1 medium red capsicum (200g),
chopped coarsely

2 lebanese cucumbers (340g),
seeded, sliced thinly

2 trimmed celery stalks (200g),
sliced thinly

1 tablespoon fresh marjoram leaves

LEMON DRESSING

1 clove garlic, crushed

⅓ cup (80ml) lemon juice

2 teaspoons olive oil

1   Place veal in large bowl with combined rind, juice, marjoram and oil; toss to coat veal in mixture. Cover; refrigerate 1 hour.

2   Meanwhile, make greek salad. Make lemon dressing.

3   Cook veal on heated oiled grill plate (or grill or barbecue) until browned both sides and cooked as desired.

4   Pour dressing over salad; toss gently to combine. Serve veal with greek salad.

GREEK SALAD   Combine ingredients in large bowl.

LEMON DRESSING   Place ingredients in screw-top jar, shake well.

SERVES 4
per serving 12.9g carbohydrate; 20.7g fat; 1693kJ (405 cal); 40.6g protein

raan with baby bean salad and spiced yogurt (see page 253)

PREPARATION TIME 25 MINUTES (PLUS REFRIGERATION TIME)   COOKING TIME 20 MINUTES

2 teaspoons coriander seeds

1 teaspoon cumin seeds

5 cardamom pods, bruised

1 teaspoon chilli powder

1 teaspoon ground turmeric

1 cinnamon stick

2 cloves

2 star anise

1 medium brown onion (150g),
    chopped coarsely

4 cloves garlic, quartered

2cm piece fresh ginger (10g),
    chopped coarsely

¼ cup (40g) blanched almonds

½ cup (140g) low-fat yogurt

2 tablespoons lemon juice

1.2kg butterflied leg lamb, trimmed

BABY BEAN SALAD

500g baby green beans

3 shallots (75g), sliced thinly

⅓ cup (45g) toasted slivered almonds

¼ cup (40g) sultanas

⅓ cup loosely packed fresh
    mint leaves

1 teaspoon extra virgin olive oil

⅓ cup (80ml) lemon juice

SPICED YOGURT

1 cup (280g) low-fat yogurt

¼ cup finely chopped fresh mint

1 clove garlic, crushed

¼ teaspoon ground cumin

¼ teaspoon ground coriander

1 Dry-fry seeds, cardamom, chilli, turmeric, cinnamon, cloves and star anise in small heated frying pan, stirring, about 2 minutes or until fragrant. Blend or process spices with onion, garlic, ginger, nuts, yogurt and juice until mixture forms a paste.

2 Pierce lamb all over with sharp knife; place on metal rack in large shallow baking dish. Spread paste over lamb, pressing firmly into cuts. Cover; refrigerate overnight.

3 Cook lamb on heated oiled grill plate (or grill or barbecue), covered, about 20 minutes or until browned both sides and cooked as desired. Cover; stand 10 minutes then slice thickly.

4 Meanwhile, make baby bean salad. Make spiced yogurt.

5 Serve lamb with salad and yogurt.

BABY BEAN SALAD Boil, steam or microwave beans until just tender; drain. Place warm beans with remaining ingredients in medium bowl; toss gently to combine.

SPICED YOGURT Combine ingredients in small bowl.

SERVES 4
per serving 21.5g carbohydrate; 18.8g fat; 2211kJ (529 cal); 66.2g protein

minted lamb with baby beetroot and rocket salad

PREPARATION TIME 10 MINUTES (PLUS REFRIGERATION TIME)   COOKING 35 MINUTES

¼ cup (60ml) olive oil

2 cloves garlic, crushed

½ cup coarsely chopped fresh mint

2 racks of lamb with 8 cutlets each

1 tablespoon olive oil, extra

¼ cup coarsely chopped fresh mint, extra

BABY BEETROOT AND ROCKET SALAD

1kg baby beetroot

1 medium lemon

250g rocket leaves

2 tablespoons olive oil

2 tablespoons raspberry vinegar

¼ cup (20g) parmesan cheese flakes

1 Combine oil, garlic and mint in large shallow dish, add lamb; toss to coat lamb in marinade. Cover; refrigerate 3 hours or overnight.

2 Drain lamb; discard marinade. Place lamb on roasting rack or basket, or in disposable baking dish. Cook in covered barbecue, using indirect heat, following manufacturer's instructions, 25 minutes.

3 Meanwhile, make baby beetroot and rocket salad.

4 Brush top of lamb with extra oil, sprinkle with extra mint; cook, covered, about 10 minutes or until cooked as desired. Remove from heat, cover; stand 10 minutes before serving with salad.

BABY BEETROOT AND ROCKET SALAD Cut beetroot stems 3cm from top of beetroot; discard roots. Wrap beetroot in foil, cook next to lamb on heated barbecue about 10 minutes or until tender; remove from foil. Remove skin from beetroot. Peel rind thinly from lemon, avoiding any white pith; cut rind into thin strips. Place rocket leaves and beetroot in medium bowl; drizzle with combined oil and vinegar, sprinkle with lemon rind. Scatter cheese over salad.

SERVES 4

per serving 21.1g carbohydrate; 41g fat; 2236kJ (535 cal); 21.5g protein

herb-crusted lamb racks with pumpkin and leek

PREPARATION TIME 25 MINUTES   COOKING TIME 55 MINUTES

4 x 3-cutlet racks of lamb (900g)

¼ cup (20g) fresh white breadcrumbs

1 tablespoon finely chopped fresh rosemary

1 tablespoon finely chopped fresh
   flat-leaf parsley

2 teaspoons finely chopped fresh thyme

3 cloves garlic, crushed

3 teaspoons bottled coriander pesto

800g pumpkin, chopped coarsely

vegetable-oil spray

1 teaspoon sea salt

2 medium leeks (700g), trimmed

2 teaspoons low-fat dairy-free spread

¼ cup (60ml) chicken stock

¼ cup (60ml) dry white wine

1 Preheat oven to moderately hot.

2 Remove any excess fat from lamb. Combine breadcrumbs, herbs, garlic and pesto in small bowl. Using hands, press breadcrumb mixture onto lamb racks, cover; refrigerate until required.

3 Place pumpkin in large shallow baking dish; spray with oil, sprinkle with salt. Roast, uncovered, in moderately hot oven 20 minutes.

4 Place lamb on top of the pumpkin; roast, uncovered, in moderately hot oven 10 minutes. Reduce heat to slow; roast about 20 minutes or until pumpkin is tender and lamb is cooked as desired.

5 Meanwhile, cut leeks into 10cm lengths; slice thinly lengthways. Melt spread in large frying pan; cook leek, stirring, until leek softens. Stir in stock and wine; bring to a boil. Reduce heat; simmer, uncovered, until liquid reduces by half.

6 Stand lamb 5 minutes before cutting racks into cutlets; serve cutlets with pumpkin and leek.

SERVES 4

per serving 17.9g carbohydrate; 14.9g fat; 1438kJ (344 cal); 32g protein

olive citrus lamb shanks

PREPARATION TIME 20 MINUTES   COOKING TIME 2 HOURS 15 MINUTES

8 lamb shanks (1.5kg)

1½ tablespoons plain flour

2 tablespoons olive oil

1 large red onion (300g)

4 cloves garlic, crushed

2 teaspoons sweet paprika

6 medium tomatoes (1kg), peeled, seeded, quartered

3 large carrots (540g), chopped coarsely

2 tablespoons tomato paste

1 cup (250ml) dry red wine

½ cup (125ml) water

1 tablespoon beef stock powder

2 sprigs fresh rosemary

3 strips lemon rind

1 cinnamon stick

¾ cup (90g) seeded black olives

2 tablespoons lemon juice

2 tablespoons chopped fresh mint

1 Toss lamb in flour in large bowl. Heat oil in large saucepan; cook lamb, in batches, until browned all over. Drain on absorbent paper.

2 Cut onion in half lengthways, slice into thick wedges. Add onion, garlic and paprika to same pan; cook, stirring, until onion just softens.

3 Return lamb to pan with tomato, carrot, paste, wine, the water, stock powder, rosemary, rind and cinnamon; bring to a boil. Reduce heat; simmer, covered, 1½ hours, stirring occasionally. Stir in olives; simmer, uncovered, about 30 minutes or until lamb shanks are tender. Stir in juice and mint.

SERVES 4
per serving 30.3g carbohydrate; 34.6g fat; 3047kJ (729 cal); 62.9g protein

lamb cutlets with olive salsa, polenta and fennel

PREPARATION TIME 10 MINUTES   COOKING TIME 10 MINUTES

12 lamb cutlets (780g), trimmed

¾ cup (180ml) water

1 cup (250ml) chicken stock

½ cup (85g) instant polenta

⅓ cup (30g) finely grated parmesan cheese

½ cup (125ml) cream

2 tablespoons olive oil

600g baby fennel bulbs, sliced thinly

¾ cup (90g) seeded black olives, chopped coarsely

2 tablespoons lemon juice

1 clove garlic, crushed

1 tablespoon coarsely chopped fresh flat-leaf parsley

1 Cook lamb on heated oiled grill plate (or grill or barbecue) until browned both sides and cooked as desired.

2 Meanwhile, combine the water and stock in medium saucepan; bring to a boil. Stir in polenta gradually; cook, stirring, over low heat until mixture thickens. Stir in cheese and cream.

3 Heat half of the oil in medium frying pan; cook fennel, stirring, until tender.

4 Combine remaining oil with olives, juice, garlic and parsley in small bowl. Serve cutlets with polenta, fennel and olive salsa.

SERVES 4
per serving 24.7g carbohydrate; 30.8g fat; 2048kJ (490 cal); 28.8g protein

greek lamb salad

PREPARATION TIME 40 MINUTES (PLUS REFRIGERATION TIME)   COOKING TIME 10 MINUTES

Skordalia is a pungent Greek sauce or dip made with bread (or sometimes potato), garlic, lemon juice and olive oil. It can be served with almost any kind of dish — from grilled meats and poultry to fish and raw vegetables.

600g lamb fillets, trimmed

2 tablespoons olive oil

2 teaspoons finely grated lemon rind

1 teaspoon finely chopped
   fresh marjoram

1 clove garlic, crushed

1 large green capsicum (350g),
   sliced thinly

1 telegraph cucumber (400g),
   diced into 2cm pieces

400g grape tomatoes, halved

2 trimmed celery stalks (200g),
   sliced thinly

4 green onions, sliced thinly

2 baby cos lettuce, chopped coarsely

1 cup (150g) seeded kalamata olives

200g goat fetta, crumbled

SKORDALIA

2 slices stale white bread

2 cloves garlic, crushed

2 tablespoons olive oil

2 teaspoons white wine vinegar

1 tablespoon lemon juice

⅓ cup (80ml) water

MARJORAM DRESSING

2 tablespoons olive oil

2 tablespoons white wine vinegar

1 tablespoon finely chopped
   fresh marjoram

pinch cayenne pepper

1 Place lamb, oil, rind, marjoram and garlic in large bowl; toss to coat lamb in marinade. Cover; refrigerate 1 hour.

2 Meanwhile, make skordalia. Make marjoram dressing.

3 Heat large non-stick frying pan; cook lamb, in batches, until browned and cooked as desired. Cover; stand 5 minutes. Slice lamb thickly.

4 Place lamb in large bowl with remaining ingredients and dressing; toss gently to combine. Divide salad among serving plates; drizzle with skordalia.

SKORDALIA Discard crusts from bread, soak in small bowl of cold water; drain. Squeeze out excess water; blend or process bread and remaining ingredients until mixture is smooth.

MARJORAM DRESSING Place ingredients in screw-top jar; shake well.

SERVES 4
per serving 23.9g carbohydrate; 45.9g fat; 1672kJ (700 cal); 47.6g protein

roasted lamb with green onions and garlic and baby onions

PREPARATION TIME 40 MINUTES (PLUS REFRIGERATION TIME)
COOKING TIME 1 HOUR 40 MINUTES (PLUS STANDING TIME)

12 green onions

1 clove garlic, crushed

8 sprigs fresh thyme,
   chopped coarsely

1 bay leaf

3 black peppercorns, crushed

1 boned leg of lamb (800g)

⅓ cup (80ml) extra virgin olive oil

20 whole garlic cloves, peeled

2 tablespoons balsamic vinegar

¾ cup (90g) seeded black olives

BABY ONIONS

1 tablespoon balsamic vinegar

2 tablespoons honey

1 tablespoon wholegrain mustard

2 tablespoons vegetable oil

400g baby onions, halved

1 Trim onions to 10cm lengths. Slice one end of onions, lengthways, to halfway. Stand onions, cut-end down, in small jug of cold water; refrigerate 1 hour or until onions separate and curl slightly.

2 Preheat oven to slow.

3 Meanwhile, combine crushed garlic, thyme, bay leaf and peppercorns in small bowl. Place lamb on chopping board, cut-side up; cover with plastic wrap, pound with meat mallet then rub cut-side of lamb with garlic mixture.

4 Roll lamb tightly; tie with kitchen string at 2cm intervals. Place lamb in large deep baking dish; brush with 1 tablespoon of the oil. Roast, uncovered, in slow oven about 1 hour 40 minutes or until lamb is cooked as desired.

5 Meanwhile, place whole garlic cloves in small baking dish, sprinkle with 1 tablespoon of the oil; bake, uncovered, alongside lamb in slow oven, about 20 minutes or until tender.

6 Meanwhile, make baby onions.

7 Dry green onions with absorbent paper. Combine remaining oil and vinegar in small jug. Place onions, cut-end down, in vinegar mixture; reserve.

8 Remove lamb and garlic from oven. Cover lamb with foil to keep warm. Increase oven temperature to moderately hot.

9 Add olives to garlic in baking dish; heat, uncovered, in moderately hot oven 5 minutes.

10 Cut lamb into eight rounds. Divide baby onions among serving plates; top with lamb rounds and green onions. Drizzle with remaining vinegar mixture.

BABY ONIONS Combine vinegar, honey and mustard in small saucepan; bring to a boil. Reduce heat; simmer, uncovered, about 5 minutes or until glaze thickens slightly. Heat oil in large frying pan; cook onions, stirring, until soft, brushing frequently with glaze while cooking.

SERVES 4
per serving 24.8g carbohydrate; 44.9g fat; 2859kJ (684 cal); 46.3g protein

garlic and rosemary lamb with parsnip and carrot chips

PREPARATION TIME 15 MINUTES (PLUS REFRIGERATION TIME)   COOKING TIME 50 MINUTES

1kg boned, rolled lamb loin

4 cloves garlic, halved

8 fresh rosemary sprigs

1 teaspoon dried chilli flakes

1 tablespoon olive oil

2 large parsnips (360g)

2 large carrots (360g)

vegetable oil, for deep-frying

1 Place lamb in large bowl. Pierce lamb in 8 places with sharp knife; push garlic halves and rosemary sprigs into cuts. Sprinkle lamb with chilli; rub with oil. Cover; refrigerate 3 hours or overnight.

2 Cook lamb, uncovered, on heated oiled barbecue until browned all over. Cover; cook lamb on barbecue, using indirect heat, following manufacturer's instructions, about 40 minutes or until cooked as desired.

3 Meanwhile, using vegetable peeler, peel thin strips from parsnips and carrots. Heat oil in large saucepan; deep-fry parsnip and carrot strips, separately, in batches, until browned and crisp. Drain on absorbent paper; serve immediately.

SERVES 4
per serving 12.6g carbohydrate; 51.1g fat; 2959kJ (708 cal); 50.8g protein

lamb, burghul and grilled zucchini salad

PREPARATION TIME 45 MINUTES (PLUS REFRIGERATION AND STANDING TIME)   COOKING TIME 20 MINUTES

800g lamb fillets, trimmed

2 tablespoons olive oil

1 clove garlic, crushed

1 tablespoon coarsely chopped fresh sage

2 tablespoons coarsely chopped fresh oregano

¾ cup (120g) burghul

2 teaspoons finely grated lemon rind

¼ cup loosely packed fresh oregano leaves

2 medium yellow zucchini (240g)

2 medium green zucchini (240g)

250g yellow teardrop tomatoes, halved

250g cherry tomatoes, halved

1 cup firmly packed fresh flat-leaf parsley leaves

LEMON GARLIC DRESSING

2 tablespoons lemon juice

1 clove garlic, crushed

¼ cup (60ml) olive oil

1 Combine lamb in large bowl with combined oil, garlic, sage and chopped oregano, cover; refrigerate 3 hours or overnight.

2 Place burghul in medium bowl; cover with cold water. Stand 10 minutes; drain. Using hands, squeeze out as much excess water as possible. Spread burghul in a thin, even layer on tray; stand 15 minutes. Return dry burghul to same bowl with rind and oregano leaves; toss gently to combine.

3 Meanwhile, make lemon garlic dressing.

4 Cook lamb on heated oiled grill plate (or grill or barbecue) until browned and cooked as desired. Cover; stand 10 minutes. Slice lamb thickly.

5 Meanwhile, using sharp knife, V-slicer or mandoline, cut zucchini into ribbons; cook zucchini, in batches, on same cleaned heated oiled grill plate until just tender. Combine zucchini in medium bowl with tomatoes, parsley and half of the dressing.

6 Add remaining dressing to burghul mixture; toss gently to combine. Divide burghul mixture among serving plates; top with zucchini mixture then lamb.

LEMON GARLIC DRESSING Place ingredients in screw-top jar; shake well.

SERVES 4
per serving 14g carbohydrate; 30.8g fat; 2207kJ (528 cal); 48.2g protein

spicy pork with caramelised onions

PREPARATION TIME 20 MINUTES   COOKING TIME 20 MINUTES

1 tablespoon olive oil

2 large brown onions (400g), chopped finely

1 small red capsicum (150g), chopped finely

4 slices prosciutto (60g), chopped coarsely

4 x 250g pork fillets

2 tablespoons olive oil, extra

1 teaspoon dried chilli flakes

1 tablespoon sweet paprika

2 teaspoons ground cumin

150g mesclun

CARMELISED ONIONS

2 tablespoons olive oil

3 large brown onions (600g), sliced thickly

¼ cup (60ml) red wine vinegar

120g guava paste, chopped coarsely

**1 tablespoon coarsely chopped
   fresh coriander**

1 tablespoon brown sugar

1 Heat oil in large frying pan; cook onion, capsicum and prosciutto, stirring, until onions soften. Remove from pan.

2 Slice pork fillets lengthways down the centre, almost all the way through. Open each fillet flat, pound gently with a meat mallet to an even thickness. Spoon onion mixture along centre of pork, roll up from long side; secure with toothpicks. Heat extra oil in same cleaned pan; cook chilli and spices, stirring, until fragrant. Add pork; cook, uncovered, turning occasionally, about 20 minutes or until just tender.

3 Meanwhile, make caramelised onions.

4 Serve pork with onions.

CARAMELISED ONIONS Heat oil in large frying pan; cook onions, stirring, about 15 minutes or until onion softens and browned lightly. Add remaining ingredients; cook, stirring until guava paste and sugar are dissolved.

SERVES 4
per serving 17.8g carbohydrate; 29.8g fat; 2449kJ (586 cal); 61.6g protein

pork fillet with wilted cabbage

PREPARATION TIME 10 MINUTES   COOKING TIME 30 MINUTES

1 tablespoon olive oil

750g pork fillets, sliced thickly

1 cup (250ml) chicken stock

¾ cup (180ml) port

¼ cup (80g) cranberry sauce

50g butter

700g cabbage, sliced thickly

1 teaspoon caraway seeds

1 Heat oil in large frying pan; cook pork, in batches, until browned both sides. Cover to keep warm.

2 Place stock and port in same pan; bring to a boil. Reduce heat; simmer, uncovered, until mixture reduces by half. Stir in cranberry sauce. Return pork to pan; cook, uncovered, until cooked through.

3 Meanwhile, heat butter in separate large frying pan; cook cabbage, stirring, until just wilted. Stir in caraway seeds.

4 Serve pork and sauce with cabbage.

SERVES 4
per serving 18.7g carbohydrate; 9.3g fat; 1584kJ (379 cal); 44.5g protein

pork, coconut, lime and tofu salad

PREPARATION TIME 40 MINUTES   COOKING TIME 10 MINUTES

1kg pork fillets, trimmed

1 tablespoon vegetable oil

2 tablespoons lime juice

600g baby bok choy, quartered

1 large carrot (180g)

250g fried tofu pieces

½ cup coarsely chopped fresh thai basil

½ cup coarsely chopped fresh coriander

1¼ cups (100g) bean sprouts

4 green onions, sliced thinly

¼ cup (15g) shredded coconut

COCONUT DRESSING

2 tablespoons lime juice

1 tablespoon fish sauce

1 tablespoon sweet chilli sauce

¾ cup (180ml) coconut milk

1 Make coconut dressing.

2 Place pork, oil and juice in medium bowl; toss to coat pork in mixture. Cook pork on heated oiled grill plate (or grill or barbecue) until browned and cooked as desired. Cover; stand 5 minutes. Slice pork thinly.

3 Meanwhile, boil, steam or microwave bok choy until just wilted; drain.

4 Cut carrot into 8cm pieces. Using sharp knife, mandoline or V-slicer, cut pieces lengthways into thin slices; cut slices into matchstick-sized pieces.

5 Place pork, bok choy and carrot in large bowl with dressing and remaining ingredients; toss gently to combine.

COCONUT DRESSING Place ingredients in screw-top jar; shake well.

SERVES 4
per serving 13.2g carbohydrate; 29.7g fat; 2433kJ (582 cal); 65.3 g protein

pork with beans and beer

PREPARATION TIME 20 MINUTES (PLUS SOAKING TIME) COOKING TIME 2 HOURS 20 MINUTES

½ cup (100g) dried haricot beans

2 cloves garlic, crushed

½ teaspoon freshly ground black pepper

900g pork neck

1 tablespoon olive oil

2 bacon rashers (140g), chopped finely

1 medium brown onion (150g), sliced thinly

1 teaspoon caraway seeds

200ml can beer

¾ cup (180ml) chicken stock

150g white cabbage, shredded finely

1 Place beans in large bowl; cover with cold water. Cover; let stand overnight.

2 Rub combined garlic and pepper all over pork. Secure pork with string at 2cm intervals.

3 Heat oil in 5-litre (20-cup) large flameproof casserole dish; cook pork, turning, until browned all over. Remove from dish.

4 Cook bacon, onion and seeds in dish, stirring, until onion softens and bacon browns lightly.

5 Drain beans. Return pork to dish, add beer, stock and beans; bring to a boil. Reduce heat; simmer, covered, 2 hours or until beans and pork are tender.

6 Remove pork from dish. Add cabbage; cook, stirring, until just wilted. Serve pork with cabbage mixture.

SERVES 4
per serving 13.6g carbohydrate; 25.9g fat; 2220kJ (531 cal); 58.5g protein

pork fillet with apple and leek (see page 343)

PREPARATION TIME 20 MINUTES   COOKING TIME 40 MINUTES

800g pork fillets

¾ cup (180ml) chicken stock

2 medium leeks (700g), sliced thickly

1 clove garlic, crushed

2 tablespoons brown sugar

2 tablespoons red wine vinegar

2 medium apples (300g)

10g butter

3 teaspoons brown sugar, extra

300g baby carrots, trimmed, halved

8 medium patty-pan squash (100g), quartered

250g asparagus, trimmed, chopped coarsely

1 Preheat oven to very hot. Place pork, in single layer, in large baking dish; bake, uncovered, in very hot oven about 25 minutes or until pork is browned and cooked as desired. Cover; stand 5 minutes. Slice pork thickly.

2 Meanwhile, heat half of the stock in medium frying pan; cook leek and garlic, stirring, until leek softens and browns lightly. Add sugar and vinegar; cook, stirring, about 5 minutes or until leek caramelises. Add remaining stock; bring to a boil. Reduce heat; simmer, uncovered, about 5 minutes or until liquid reduces by half. Place leek mixture in medium bowl; cover to keep warm.

3 Peel, core and halve apples; cut into thick slices. Melt butter in same pan; cook apple and extra sugar, stirring, until apple is browned and tender.

4 Boil, steam or microwave carrot, squash and asparagus, separately, until just tender; drain. Serve pork with apple, leek and vegetables.

SERVES 4
per serving 24.9g carbohydrate; 7.4g fat; 1505kJ (360 cal); 48.6g protein

pork vindaloo

PREPARATION TIME 15 MINUTES (PLUS REFRIGERATION TIME)   COOKING TIME 50 MINUTES

2 medium brown onions (300g), chopped coarsely

5 cloves garlic, quartered

1 teaspoon ground cardamom

½ teaspoon ground clove

1 teaspoon ground cinnamon

2 teaspoons ground cumin

2 teaspoons cracked black pepper

3 fresh small red thai chillies, quartered

2 teaspoons black mustard seeds

4cm piece fresh ginger (20g), quartered

⅓ cup (80ml) white vinegar

1kg pork fillet, trimmed

1 tablespoon vegetable oil

1 medium brown onion (150g), sliced thinly

1 tablespoon tamarind paste

2 medium tomatoes (300g), chopped coarsely

1½ cups cooked basmati rice

1 Blend or process chopped onion, garlic, spices, chilli, seeds, ginger and vinegar to a smooth paste.

2 Cut pork into 3cm pieces. Combine pork with a quarter of the curry paste in medium bowl; stir to coat pork in paste. Cover; refrigerate 3 hours or overnight. Reserve remaining curry paste.

3 Heat oil in large saucepan; cook sliced onion, stirring, until just soft. Add reserved curry paste; cook, stirring, over low heat 5 minutes. Add pork; cook, stirring, about 5 minutes or until pork changes colour. Stir in tamarind paste and tomato; bring to a boil. Reduce heat; simmer, covered, about 40 minutes or until pork is tender and cooked through.

4 Serve curry with rice.

SERVES 4
per serving 24.6g carbohydrate 11.8g fat; 1877kJ (449 cal); 59.5g protein
tip You will need to cook ½ cup rice for this recipe.

pork and broccolini stir-fry

PREPARATION TIME 15 MINUTES   COOKING TIME 20 MINUTES

2 tablespoons peanut oil

450g pork steaks, sliced thinly

2 medium red onions (340g), sliced thinly

2 medium red capsicums (400g), sliced thinly

1 clove garlic, crushed

1cm piece fresh ginger (5g), grated

300g broccolini

1 teaspoon cornflour

2 tablespoons lemon juice

¼ cup (60ml) water

¼ cup (60ml) sweet chilli sauce

1 teaspoon fish sauce

1 tablespoon soy sauce

1 teaspoon sesame oil

1 tablespoon coarsely chopped fresh coriander

1   Heat half of the peanut oil in wok or large frying pan; stir-fry pork, in batches, until browned.

2   Heat remaining peanut oil in wok; stir-fry onion, capsicum, garlic and ginger until vegetables are just tender.

3   Meanwhile, trim and halve broccolini. Blend cornflour with juice in small bowl; add the water, sauces and sesame oil. Stir to combine.

4   Return pork to wok with broccolini and cornflour mixture; stir-fry about 2 minutes or until mixture boils and thickens slightly. Remove from heat; stir in coriander just before serving.

SERVES 4
per serving 12.9g carbohydrate; 14.3g fat; 1300kJ (311 cal); 31.9g protein

warm pork and mandarin salad

PREPARATION TIME 20 MINUTES (PLUS REFRIGERATION TIME)   COOKING TIME 15 MINUTES

500g pork fillet, sliced thinly

2 cloves garlic, crushed

1cm piece fresh ginger (5g), grated

1 tablespoon sweet chilli sauce

2 teaspoons soy sauce

3 small mandarins (300g), segmented

150g sugar snap peas

2 tablespoons peanut oil

300g curly endive, trimmed

¼ cup firmly packed fresh coriander leaves

1 small red onion (100g), sliced thinly

CHILLI DRESSING

1 tablespoon white wine vinegar

1 tablespoon peanut oil

1 tablespoon sweet chilli sauce

2 teaspoons soy sauce

1   Combine pork, garlic, ginger and sauces in small bowl, cover; refrigerate 3 hours or overnight.

2   Halve mandarin segments lengthways; discard seeds.

3   Boil, steam or microwave peas until just tender; drain.

4   Heat oil in wok or large frying pan; stir-fry pork, in batches, until browned and cooked as desired.

5   Meanwhile, make chilli dressing.

6   Gently toss pork, mandarin and peas in large bowl with endive, coriander, onion and dressing.

CHILLI DRESSING Place ingredients in screw-top jar; shake well.

SERVES 4
per serving 12.4g carbohydrate; 17.4g fat; 1400kJ (335 cal); 31.9g protein

raan with baby bean salad and spiced yogurt (see page 243)

chicken tikka with raita

wilted chinese greens, pork and tofu with macadamia dressing

PREPARATION TIME 30 MINUTES   COOKING TIME 10 MINUTES

2 tablespoons peanut oil

4 green onions, cut into 5cm lengths

200g fresh shiitake mushrooms, quartered

500g chinese barbecued pork, sliced thinly

500g choy sum, chopped coarsely

350g gai larn, chopped coarsely

500g baby bok choy, chopped coarsely

300g fresh tofu, diced into 1cm pieces

1 cup (100g) mung bean sprouts

MACADAMIA DRESSING

½ cup (75g) toasted macadamias, chopped finely

½ cup (125ml) peanut oil

¼ cup (60ml) mirin

1 tablespoon soy sauce

⅓ cup (80ml) rice vinegar

1 Heat half of the oil in wok or large frying pan; stir-fry onion and mushroom until mushrooms are just tender. Add pork; stir-fry 1 minute. Remove mixture from wok.

2 Heat remaining oil in same wok; stir-fry choy sum, gai larn and bok choy until just wilted.

3 Meanwhile, make macadamia dressing.

4 Gently toss pork mixture, vegetable mixture, tofu and sprouts in large bowl with dressing.

MACADAMIA DRESSING Place ingredients in screw-top jar; shake well.

SERVES 4
per serving 19.2g carbohydrate; 75.9g fat; 3921kJ (938 cal); 44.6g protein
tip Ready-to-eat barbecued pork can be purchased from specialty Asian food stores or Asian restaurants. You will need one bunch each of choy sum, gai larn (also known as chinese broccoli) and bok choy.

chicken tikka with raita

PREPARATION TIME 20 MINUTES   COOKING TIME 15 MINUTES

800g chicken thigh fillets, sliced thickly

1 medium brown onion (150g), cut into wedges

1 large red capsicum (350g), chopped coarsely

2 long green chillies, sliced thinly

⅓ cup (100g) tikka curry paste

300ml light cream

250g cherry tomatoes, halved

¾ cup loosely packed fresh coriander leaves

3 cups (240g) bean sprouts

RAITA

200g low-fat yogurt

1 lebanese cucumber (130g), seeded, chopped finely

1 tablespoon finely chopped fresh mint

1 Cook chicken, in batches, in large deep lightly oiled frying pan until browned all over.

2 Cook onion and capsicum in same pan, stirring until onion softens. Add chilli and paste; cook, stirring, until fragrant. Return chicken to pan with cream; bring to a boil. Reduce heat; simmer, uncovered, about 5 minutes or until chicken is cooked through. Remove from heat; stir in tomato and coriander.

3 Meanwhile, make raita.

4 Serve chicken on sprouts topped with raita.

RAITA Combine ingredients in small bowl.

SERVES 4
per serving 16.0g carbohydrate; 38.8g fat; 2532kJ (605 cal); 48.3g protein

barbecue-flavoured chicken and onions with creamed spinach

PREPARATION TIME 15 MINUTES   COOKING TIME 20 MINUTES

We use crème fraîche in our creamed spinach, but light sour cream can be substituted.

2 tablespoons lemon juice

2 tablespoons brown sugar

1 tablespoon honey

1 clove garlic, crushed

¼ cup (60ml) soy sauce

2 medium (300g) onions

1 large cooked chicken, quartered

20g butter

800g spinach

1 tablespoon olive oil

1 medium brown onion (150g),
   chopped finely

4 slices prosciutto (60g), chopped finely

2 cloves garlic, crushed

200ml crème fraîche

¼ cup coarsely chopped fresh chives

¼ teaspoon ground nutmeg

1   Preheat oven to moderately hot.

2   Combine juice, sugar, honey, garlic and sauce in small jug. Chop onions into wedges. Place chicken and onion in shallow baking dish; pour over half of the glaze mixture.

3   Bake, uncovered, in moderately hot oven about 20 minutes or until chicken is crisp and heated through, brushing frequently with remaining glaze mixture.

4   Meanwhile, heat butter in large saucepan; cook spinach, covered, stirring occasionally, until just wilted. Drain; cool 10 minutes. Gently squeeze spinach to remove excess liquid. Heat oil in same pan; cook onion, prosciutto and garlic, stirring, until the prosciutto is browned and crisp. Add spinach and remaining ingredients; cook, stirring, until heated through.

5   Serve chicken and onion with creamed spinach.

SERVES 4
per serving 19.2g carbohydrate; 53.4g fat; 3093kJ (740 cal); 47.4g protein

mexi-wings with cherry tomato salsa

PREPARATION TIME 5 MINUTES   COOKING TIME 25 MINUTES

8 large chicken wings (1kg)

2 x 35g packets taco seasoning mix

2 tablespoons tomato sauce

1 tablespoon vegetable oil

⅓ cup (80ml) lime juice

500g cherry tomatoes

2 medium avocados (500g), chopped coarsely

310g can corn kernels, drained

1 medium red onion (170g), chopped finely

¼ cup firmly packed fresh coriander leaves

1   Preheat oven to moderately hot.

2   Place chicken, seasoning, sauce, oil and 1 tablespoon of the juice in large bowl; toss to coat chicken all over.

3   Place chicken, in single layer, in large shallow oiled baking dish; roast, uncovered, in moderately hot oven about 25 minutes or until chicken is browned all over and cooked through.

4   Meanwhile, quarter tomatoes; combine in medium bowl with avocado, corn, onion, coriander and remaining juice.

5   Serve salsa topped with chicken.

SERVES 4
per serving 18.8g carbohydrate; 34.7g fat; 2312kJ (553 cal); 41.1g protein

chicken with bok choy and flat mushrooms

PREPARATION TIME 10 MINUTES   COOKING TIME 25 MINUTES

2 tablespoons honey

⅓ cup (80ml) soy sauce

2 tablespoons dry sherry

1 teaspoon five-spice powder

4cm piece fresh ginger (20g), grated

1 tablespoon peanut oil

4 x 170g single chicken breast fillets

4 flat mushrooms (360g)

500g baby bok choy, quartered lengthways

1 cup (250ml) chicken stock

2 teaspoons cornflour

2 tablespoons water

1 Combine honey, soy sauce, sherry, five-spice, ginger and oil in small jug. Place chicken in medium bowl with half of the honey mixture; toss to coat chicken in marinade. Cover; refrigerate 10 minutes.

2 Meanwhile, cook mushrooms and bok choy, in batches, on heated lightly oiled grill plate (or grill or barbecue) until just tender; cover to keep warm.

3 Cook drained chicken on same grill plate until browned both sides and cooked through. Cover; stand 5 minutes then slice thickly.

4 Meanwhile, combine remaining honey mixture in small saucepan with stock; bring to a boil. Stir in blended cornflour and water; cook, stirring, until sauce boils and thickens slightly.

5 Divide mushrooms and bok choy among serving plates; top with chicken, drizzle with sauce.

SERVES 4
per serving 16.8g carbohydrate; 9.5g fat; 1471kJ (352 cal); 47.2g protein

good old-fashioned chicken salad

PREPARATION TIME 40 MINUTES   COOKING TIME 15 MINUTES

1 litre (4 cups) boiling water

1 litre (4 cups) chicken stock

800g chicken breast fillets

¾ cup (90g) frozen peas

½ cup (150g) mayonnaise

½ cup (120g) sour cream

2 tablespoons lemon juice

4 trimmed celery stalks (400g), sliced thinly

1 medium white onion (150g), chopped finely

3 large dill pickles (150g), sliced thinly

2 tablespoons finely chopped fresh
** flat-leaf parsley**

1 tablespoon finely chopped fresh tarragon

1 large butter lettuce, leaves separated

1 Bring the water and stock to a boil in large frying pan; poach chicken, covered, about 10 minutes or until cooked through. Cool chicken in liquid 10 minutes; slice thinly. Discard liquid.

2 Meanwhile, boil, steam or microwave peas until tender; drain.

3 Whisk mayonnaise, sour cream and juice in small bowl. Place chicken with celery, onion, pickle and herbs in large bowl; toss gently to combine. Place lettuce leaves on serving platter; top with salad, drizzle with mayonnaise mixture.

SERVES 4
per serving 16.6g carbohydrate; 29.9g fat; 2286kJ (547 cal); 52.3g protein
tip We used whole-egg mayonnaise in this recipe.

mixed pea, broad bean and turkey salad with lemon mustard dressing

PREPARATION TIME 1 HOUR 15 MINUTES   COOKING TIME 50 MINUTES

You need approximately 750g unshelled fresh peas for this recipe.

1.5kg single turkey breasts

1 tablespoon olive oil

1 tablespoon sea salt

½ teaspoon freshly ground
   black pepper

2 teaspoons finely grated
   lemon rind

750g fresh broad beans

1¾ cups (280g) shelled fresh peas

300g sugar snap peas, trimmed

200g snow peas, trimmed

¼ cup coarsely chopped fresh mint

100g snow pea tendrils

150g baby rocket

LEMON MUSTARD DRESSING

2 tablespoons lemon juice

2 teaspoons wholegrain mustard

2 tablespoons white wine vinegar

1 teaspoon sugar

⅓ cup (80ml) olive oil

1 Preheat oven to moderately hot.

2 Tie turkey breasts at 6cm intervals with kitchen string. Place on oiled oven tray; rub with combined oil, salt, pepper and rind. Cover with foil; bake in moderately hot oven 40 minutes. Remove foil; bake in moderately hot oven about 10 minutes or until cooked through.

3 Meanwhile, make lemon mustard dressing.

4 Shell broad beans; discard pods. Boil, steam or microwave beans until just tender; drain. Rinse under cold water; drain. Peel away grey-coloured outer shells.

5 Meanwhile, boil, steam or microwave all peas, together, until just tender; drain. Rinse under cold water; drain.

6 Place beans and pea mixture in large bowl with mint, tendrils, rocket and dressing; toss gently to combine. Slice turkey thinly; top salad with turkey.

LEMON MUSTARD DRESSING Place ingredients in screw-top jar; shake well.

SERVES 4
per serving 24.7g carbohydrate; 33g fat; 2980kJ (713 cal); 78.2g protein
tip You can use a 500g packet of frozen broad beans for this recipe; after thawing, peel away the grey outer shell then boil, steam or microwave the inner bean until just tender.

chicken chermoulla

PREPARATION TIME 10 MINUTES   COOKING TIME 20 MINUTES

Chermoulla is a Moroccan blend of herbs and spices traditionally used for preserving or seasoning meat and fish. We use our chermoulla blend here as a quick baste for chicken, but you can also make it for use as a sauce or marinade.

700g chicken thigh fillets,
sliced thinly

½ cup coarsely chopped fresh
flat-leaf parsley

1 tablespoon finely grated
lemon rind

1 tablespoon lemon juice

2 teaspoons ground turmeric

1 teaspoon cayenne pepper

1 tablespoon ground coriander

1 medium red onion (170g),
chopped finely

2 tablespoons olive oil

1 cup (200g) red lentils

2½ cups (625ml) chicken stock

200g baby spinach leaves

½ cup coarsely chopped
fresh coriander

½ cup coarsely chopped fresh mint

1 tablespoon red wine vinegar

⅓ cup (95g) yogurt

1   Combine chicken, parsley, rind, juice, spices, onion and half of the oil in large bowl. Heat wok or large frying pan; stir-fry chicken mixture, in batches, until chicken is browned and cooked through.

2   Meanwhile, combine lentils and stock in large saucepan; bring to a boil. Reduce heat; simmer, uncovered, about 8 minutes or until just tender, drain. Place lentils in large bowl with spinach, coriander, mint and combined vinegar and remaining oil; toss gently to combine.

3   Serve chicken mixture on lentil mixture; drizzle with yogurt.

SERVES 4
per serving 24g carbohydrate; 24.5g fat; 2140kJ (512 cal); 49.9g protein

chicken marengo

PREPARATION TIME 20 MINUTES   COOKING TIME 1 HOUR 30 MINUTES

6 chicken thigh cutlets (1kg)

6 chicken drumsticks (900g)

2 tablespoons olive oil

250g button mushrooms

250g flat mushrooms, sliced thickly

2 large brown onions (400g), sliced thickly

2 cloves garlic, crushed

2 tablespoons plain flour

½ cup (125ml) chicken stock

½ cup (125ml) dry white wine

1 tablespoon tomato paste

425g can crushed tomatoes

1 tablespoon coarsely chopped fresh flat-leaf parsley

1 Remove skin from chicken.

2 Heat oil in 3.5-litre (14-cup) flameproof dish; cook chicken, in batches, until browned. Drain on absorbent paper.

3 Drain all but 1 tablespoon of the liquid from dish; cook mushrooms, onion and garlic in dish, stirring, until onion softens.

4 Add blended flour and stock, then wine, paste and undrained tomatoes; stir over heat until mixture boils and thickens. Return chicken to dish; cook, covered, in moderate oven about 1 hour or until chicken is tender.

5 Serve chicken sprinkled with parsley.

SERVES 6
per serving 12.5g carbohydrate; 31.5g fat; 2592kJ (620 cal); 66.8g protein

chicken cassoulet

PREPARATION TIME 25 MINUTES (PLUS STANDING TIME)   COOKING TIME 2 HOURS 30 MINUTES

½ cup (100g) dried haricot beans

250g spicy italian sausages

125g pork sausages

2 chicken thighs (450g), halved

2 single chicken breasts on the bone (500g)

2 teaspoons vegetable oil

2 bacon rashers (140g), sliced thinly

1 clove garlic, crushed

1 bay leaf

2 cloves

6 black peppercorns

1 trimmed celery stalk (100g), cut into 5cm lengths

2 medium carrots (240g), sliced thinly

3 baby onions (75g), halved

½ cup (125ml) dry white wine

3 cups (750ml) water

1 tablespoon tomato paste

1 Place beans in large bowl; cover well with cold water. Cover; stand overnight.

2 Drain beans. Place sausages in large saucepan of boiling water. Boil, uncovered, 2 minutes; drain.

3 Discard skin from chicken; cut breasts in half.

4 Reheat oven to moderate.

5 Heat oil in 5-litre (20-cup) flameproof casserole dish; cook chicken and sausages, in batches, until browned. Drain on absorbent paper; slice sausages thickly.

6 Add bacon to dish; cook, stirring, until crisp. Drain on absorbent paper.

7 Return chicken to dish with beans, garlic, bay leaf, cloves, peppercorns, celery, carrot, onion, wine, the water and paste. Cook, covered, in moderate oven 1¾ hours.

8 Add sausages; cook, covered, about 15 minutes or until sausages are cooked through. Serve cassoulet sprinkled with bacon.

SERVES 4
per serving 17.2g carbohydrate; 37.4g fat; 27756kJ (664 cal); 63.7g protein

african-style peanut, okra and tomato gumbo

PREPARATION TIME 30 MINUTES   COOKING TIME 50 MINUTES

300g okra

2 tablespoons peanut oil

800g chicken thigh fillets, chopped coarsely

2 large brown onions (400g), sliced thickly

3 cloves garlic, crushed

1 teaspoon sambal oelek

5 medium tomatoes (650g), peeled, seeded,
  chopped finely

¼ cup (70g) tomato paste

⅓ cup (85g) crunchy peanut butter

1 large potato (300g), chopped coarsely

2 cups (500ml) water

1 Trim stems from okra. Heat half of the oil in large saucepan; cook chicken, in batches, stirring, until browned. Drain on absorbent paper.

2 Heat remaining oil in same pan; cook onion, garlic and sambal oelek, stirring, until onion softens.

3 Return chicken to pan. Add remaining ingredients; bring to a boil. Reduce heat; simmer, covered, about 30 minutes or until potato is tender and chicken is cooked through.

SERVES 4
per serving 20.4g carbohydrate; 34.6g fat; 2479kJ (593 cal); 50.2g protein

green chicken curry

PREPARATION TIME 20 MINUTES   COOKING TIME 20 MINUTES

¼ cup (75g) green curry paste

2 x 400ml cans coconut milk

2 fresh kaffir lime leaves, torn

1kg chicken thigh fillets

2 tablespoons peanut oil

2 tablespoons fish sauce

2 tablespoons lime juice

1 tablespoon grated palm sugar

150g pea eggplants, quartered

1 small zucchini (150g), diced into
  5cm pieces

⅓ cup loosely packed fresh thai basil leaves

¼ cup coarsely chopped fresh coriander

1 tablespoon fresh coriander leaves

1 long green thai chilli, sliced thinly

2 green onions, sliced thinly

1 Place curry paste in large saucepan; stir over heat until fragrant. Add coconut milk and lime leaves; bring to a boil. Reduce heat; simmer, stirring, 5 minutes.

2 Meanwhile, quarter chicken pieces. Heat oil in large frying pan; cook chicken, in batches, until just browned. Drain on absorbent paper.

3 Add chicken to curry mixture with sauce, juice, sugar and eggplants; simmer, covered, about 5 minutes or until eggplants are tender and chicken is cooked through. Add zucchini, basil and chopped coriander; cook, stirring, until zucchini is just tender.

4 Place curry in serving bowl; sprinkle with coriander leaves, sliced chilli and onion.

SERVES 4
per serving 14.5g carbohydrate; 74.7g fat; 3896kJ (932 cal); 53.2g protein

roasted duck and stir-fried greens salad with hoisin dressing

PREPARATION TIME 25 MINUTES   COOKING TIME 20 MINUTES

For this recipe, we deboned a whole chinese barbecued duck, available from Asian barbecue takeaway stores.

1kg chinese barbecued duck

1 tablespoon sesame oil

6 green onions, sliced thinly

500g choy sum, chopped coarsely

500g tat soi, trimmed

200g fresh shiitake
mushrooms, quartered

¼ cup (60ml) water

200g snow peas

2 cups (160g) bean sprouts

2 tablespoons toasted
sesame seeds

HOISIN DRESSING

2cm piece fresh ginger (10g), grated

2 tablespoons soy sauce

1 tablespoon sesame oil

1 clove garlic, crushed

1 fresh small red thai chilli,
chopped finely

¼ cup (60ml) hoisin sauce

1 Preheat oven to hot.

2 Quarter duck; discard all bones. Slice duck meat thickly, keeping skin intact; place on oven tray. Roast, uncovered, in hot oven about 10 minutes or until skin crisps; discard duck fat.

3 Meanwhile, make hoisin dressing.

4 Heat oil in wok or large frying pan; stir-fry onion, choy sum and tat soi, in batches, until greens just wilt. Place mushrooms in same wok; stir-fry 2 minutes. Add the water; bring to a boil. Reduce heat; simmer, uncovered, about 2 minutes or until mushrooms soften.

5 Place duck, vegetable mixture and mushrooms in large bowl with snow peas and dressing; toss gently to combine. Divide sprouts among serving plates; top with salad, sprinkle with sesame seeds.

HOISIN DRESSING Combine ingredients in small saucepan; bring to a boil. Reduce heat; simmer, uncovered, 2 minutes. Cool 10 minutes.

SERVES 4
per serving 18.5g carbohydrate; 46.4g fat; 2570kJ (615 cal); 32.8g protein

spatchcocks with prosciutto, herb butter and rosemary vegetables

PREPARATION TIME 35 MINUTES   COOKING TIME 1 HOUR

750g butternut pumpkin, chopped coarsely

400g medium potatoes, chopped coarsely

1 tablespoon olive oil

2 cloves garlic, sliced thinly

50g butter, softened

2 cloves garlic, crushed

2 tablespoons finely chopped fresh flat-leaf parsley

2 tablespoons finely chopped fresh basil

4 x 500g spatchcocks

12 sprigs fresh thyme

4 slices prosciutto (60g)

2 tablespoons olive oil, extra

2 tablespoons lemon juice

2 tablespoons fresh rosemary leaves

2 teaspoons sea salt

1 Preheat oven to hot.

2 Combine pumpkin, potato, oil and sliced garlic in large baking dish. Roast, uncovered, in hot oven about 1 hour or until vegetables are tender.

3 Combine butter, garlic and herbs in small bowl.

4 Wash spatchcocks under cold water; pat dry with absorbent paper. Loosen skin of spatchcock by sliding fingers between skin and meat at neck joint; push an eighth of the herb butter under skin on spatchcock breast and spread evenly. Place one thyme sprig inside cavity; tie legs together with kitchen string. Wrap prosciutto around spatchcock; secure with toothpick. Repeat with remaining spatchcocks.

5 Place spatchcocks in large deep baking dish; drizzle with combined extra oil and juice. Roast, uncovered, in hot oven 30 minutes. Brush spatchcocks with pan juices; top spatchcocks with remaining thyme sprigs. Roast, uncovered, in hot oven about 20 minutes or until spatchcocks are browned and cooked through.

6 Sprinkle vegetables with rosemary and salt. Serve spatchcocks with remaining herb butter and vegetables.

SERVES 4
per serving 24.6g carbohydrate; 63.5g fat; 3804kJ (910 cal); 61.2g protein

portuguese-style chicken thighs

PREPARATION TIME 15 MINUTES   COOKING TIME 15 MINUTES

2 teaspoons cracked black pepper

2 fresh small red thai chillies, seeded, chopped finely

½ teaspoon hot paprika

1 clove garlic, crushed

1 teaspoon finely grated orange rind

¼ cup (60ml) orange juice

2 tablespoons red wine vinegar

¼ cup (60ml) olive oil

6 chicken thigh fillets (660g), halved

3 medium oranges (720g), peeled, segmented

300g baby spinach leaves

1 medium red onion (170g), sliced thinly

1 Combine pepper, chilli, paprika, garlic, rind, juice, vinegar and oil in medium bowl. Reserve about a quarter of the spicy dressing in small jug; use hands to rub remaining spicy dressing into chicken pieces.

2 Cook chicken, in batches, on heated oiled grill plate (or grill or barbecue) until browned both sides and cooked through.

3 Toss orange segments, spinach and onion in large bowl. Divide among serving plates; top with chicken. Drizzle with reserved spicy dressing.

SERVES 4
per serving 13.8g carbohydrate; 26g fat; 1781kJ (426 cal); 34.6g protein

stir-fried chicken and gai larn

PREPARATION TIME 10 MINUTES   COOKING TIME 15 MINUTES

Gai larn, also known as gai lum or chinese broccoli, can be found in Asian food stores and many greengrocers.

2 tablespoons sesame oil

500g chicken thigh fillets, sliced thinly

2 teaspoons sambal oelek

190g can sliced water chestnuts, drained

227g can bamboo shoot strips, drained

1 large red capsicum (350g), sliced thinly

⅓ cup (80ml) kecap manis

500g gai larn, chopped coarsely

2 cups (160g) bean sprouts

1 Heat half of the oil in wok or large frying pan; stir-fry chicken, in batches, until browned lightly.

2 Heat remaining oil in same wok; stir-fry sambal oelek, water chestnuts, bamboo shoots and capsicum, 2 minutes.

3 Return chicken to wok with kecap manis and gai larn; stir-fry until gai larn is just wilted and chicken is cooked through. Remove from heat; stir in sprouts.

SERVES 4
per serving 21.7g carbohydrate; 18.9g fat; 1563kJ (374 cal); 29.6g protein

quail with pancetta and sun-dried tomatoes

PREPARATION TIME 10 MINUTES (PLUS REFRIGERATION TIME)   COOKING TIME 30 MINUTES

⅔ cup (160ml) peanut oil

2 tablespoons balsamic vinegar

2 tablespoons lemon juice

2 tablespoons soy sauce

1 tablespoon brown sugar

6 quail

12 slices pancetta (180g)

1 cup (200g) drained sun-dried

   tomatoes in oil

150g mesclun

1   Combine oil, vinegar, juice, sauce and sugar in large bowl, add quail; toss to coat quail in marinade. Cover, refrigerate 3 hours or overnight.

2   Drain quail over small saucepan; reserve marinade. Tie legs together with kitchen string; place quail in oiled roasting basket or disposable baking dish. Cook in covered barbecue, using indirect heat, following manufacturer's instructions, about 30 minutes or until browned and cooked through.

3   Meanwhile, cook pancetta on heated oiled barbecue until browned and crisp. Bring reserved marinade to a boil. Reduce heat; simmer, whisking, 2 minutes. Serve quail with tomatoes, mesclun, pancetta and hot marinade.

SERVES 4
per serving 21g carbohydrate; 58g fat; 3340kJ (799 cal); 48.2g protein

spatchcock with fennel and okra

PREPARATION TIME 15 MINUTES   COOKING TIME 1 HOUR

¼ cup (60ml) olive oil

12 baby onions (300g), halved

700g okra

2 cloves garlic, crushed

2 teaspoons ground cumin

1 teaspoon ground cinnamon

½ teaspoon ground allspice

425g can crushed tomatoes

2 cups (500ml) chicken stock

4 x 500g spatchcocks

80g butter

2 medium fennel bulbs (1kg),

   sliced thinly

¼ cup (60ml) Pernod

1   Heat half of the oil in large saucepan; cook onions, stirring occasionally, about 15 minutes or until onions are browned. Remove from pan.

2   Heat remaining oil in same pan; cook okra, garlic and spices, stirring, about 5 minutes or until okra is browned lightly. Remove from pan.

3   Return onions to pan with undrained tomatoes and stock; bring to a boil. Reduce heat; simmer, uncovered, 30 minutes. Return okra to pan; cook, stirring occasionally, about 10 minutes or until okra is tender.

4   Meanwhile, wash spatchcocks under cold water; pat dry with absorbent paper. Cut along both sides of each spatchcock backbone; discard backbones. Place spatchcock, breast-side up, on board; press breastbone to flatten spatchcock.

5   Heat butter in large frying pan; cook fennel, stirring, until soft and browned lightly. Stir in Pernod. Transfer fennel mixture to disposable baking dish. Cook spatchcock on heated oiled barbecue until browned both sides; place spatchcock on top of fennel mixture in dish. Cook spatchcock in covered barbecue, using indirect heat, following manufacturer's instructions, about 30 minutes or until browned all over and cooked through.

6   Serve spatchcocks with okra and baby onions.

SERVES 4
per serving 21.8g carbohydrate; 66.3g fat; 3942kJ (943 cal); 57.9g protein

crisp-skinned soy chicken with spiced salt

PREPARATION TIME 20 MINUTES (PLUS STANDING AND REFRIGERATION TIME)   COOKING TIME 30 MINUTES

4 litres (16 cups) water

1 cup (250ml) soy sauce

5cm piece fresh ginger (25g),
    peeled, sliced thickly

2 cloves garlic, crushed

2 teaspoons five-spice powder

1.5kg chicken

500g yellow patty-pan squash

400g sugar snap peas, trimmed

2 teaspoons sesame oil

1 tablespoon soy sauce, extra

1 tablespoon sesame seeds

vegetable oil, for deep-frying

SOY MARINADE

1 tablespoon honey

1 tablespoon soy sauce

1 tablespoon dry sherry

½ teaspoon five-spice powder

½ teaspoon sesame oil

SPICED SALT

¼ cup sea salt

½ teaspoon cracked black pepper

1 teaspoon five-spice powder

1   Combine the water, sauce, ginger, garlic and five-spice in large saucepan; bring to a boil. Boil, uncovered, 2 minutes. Add chicken; return to a boil. Reduce heat; simmer, uncovered, about 10 minutes, turning once during cooking. Remove from heat, cover; stand 30 minutes. Remove chicken from stock; pat dry with absorbent paper. Discard stock.

2   Make soy marinade. Make spiced salt.

3   Using kitchen scissors, cut chicken in half through breastbone and along side of backbone; cut legs and wings from chicken halves. Place chicken pieces on tray; coat skin in soy marinade. Cover; refrigerate 2 hours.

4   Meanwhile, boil, steam or microwave squash and peas, separately, until tender; drain. Combine vegetables in large bowl with sesame oil and extra soy. Sprinkle with seeds; cover to keep warm.

5   Heat vegetable oil in wok or large saucepan; deep-fry chicken, in batches, until browned all over. Drain on absorbent paper.

6   Cut chicken into serving-sized pieces; serve chicken with spiced salt and vegetables.

SOY MARINADE   Combine ingredients in small bowl.

SPICED SALT   Heat small non-stick frying pan; cook salt and pepper, stirring, 2 minutes. Add five-spice; cook, stirring, about 1 minute or until fragrant.

SERVES 4
per serving   15.8g carbohydrate; 51.6g fat; 3294kJ (788 cal); 64.9g protein
tip   When deep-frying the chicken, have the pan no more than ⅓ filled with oil.

portuguese-style seared spatchcock with olive, tomato and chilli salad

PREPARATION TIME 20 MINUTES   COOKING TIME 40 MINUTES

4 x 500g spatchcocks

1 tablespoon cracked black pepper

1 tablespoon ground cumin

1 tablespoon lemon juice

1 tablespoon olive oil

½ teaspoon chilli powder

½ teaspoon hot paprika

¼ teaspoon cayenne pepper

1 clove garlic, crushed

4 medium egg tomatoes (300g),
    cut into wedges

1 small red onion (100g),
    sliced thickly

2½ cups (400g) seeded black olives

150g watercress sprigs

120g rocket leaves

1 fresh small red thai chilli,
    sliced thinly

1 tablespoon coarsely chopped
    fresh coriander

LEMON DRESSING

2 tablespoons olive oil

1 tablespoon lemon juice

½ teaspoon coarsely chopped
    fresh rosemary

1 teaspoon cumin seeds

2 cloves garlic, crushed

1 Wash spatchcocks under cold water; pat dry with absorbent paper. Cut along both sides of each spatchcock backbone; discard backbones.

2 Insert metal skewer through thigh and opposite wing. Repeat with other thigh and wing.

3 Combine pepper, cumin, juice, oil, chilli powder, paprika, cayenne and garlic to a smooth paste. Using hands, rub chilli paste all over spatchcock pieces. Cook in covered barbecue, using indirect heat, following manufacturer's instructions, 20 minutes. Turn spatchcock; cook about 20 minutes or until browned all over and tender.

4 Meanwhile, make lemon dressing.

5 Place tomato, onion, olives, watercress, rocket leaves, sliced chilli and dressing in medium bowl; toss gently to combine. Top with coriander.

6 Serve spatchcocks with salad.

LEMON DRESSING Place ingredients in screw-top jar; shake well.

SERVES 4
per serving 15.7g carbohydrate; 50.9g fat; 3089kJ (738 cal); 54.5g protein

chicken with lentil salsa

PREPARATION TIME 10 MINUTES   COOKING TIME 15 MINUTES

The spices of North Africa give the chicken a flavour-packed jolt in this dish. And, as it can be served hot or cold, this recipe is a good prepare-ahead dish.

2 teaspoons ground cumin

2 teaspoons ground coriander

1 teaspoon ground turmeric

12 chicken tenderloins (900g)

1 cup (200g) red lentils

1 clove garlic, crushed

1 fresh small red thai chilli, seeded,
   chopped finely

1 lebanese cucumber (130g),
   seeded, chopped finely

1 medium red capsicum (200g),
   chopped finely

¼ cup (60ml) lemon juice

2 teaspoons peanut oil

2 tablespoons coarsely chopped
   fresh coriander

2 limes, cut into wedges

1   Combine spices in medium bowl with chicken; toss to coat chicken with spices.

2   Cook lentils in large saucepan of boiling water, uncovered, until just tender; drain. Rinse under cold water; drain. Combine lentils in large bowl with garlic, chilli, cucumber, capsicum, juice, oil and fresh coriander.

3   Meanwhile, cook chicken on heated oiled grill plate (or grill or barbecue) until browned both sides and cooked through. Add limes to pan; cook until browned both sides. Serve chicken with lentil salsa and lime wedges.

SERVES 4
per serving 21.9g carbohydrate; 8.7g fat; 1772kJ (424 cal); 64.1g protein

mexican chicken with capsicum and barley salad

PREPARATION TIME 10 MINUTES   COOKING TIME 45 MINUTES

⅔ cup (130g) pearl barley

1 cup (250ml) chicken stock

2 cups (500ml) water

35g packet taco seasoning mix

⅓ cup (80ml) chicken stock, extra

4 x 170g single chicken
   breast fillets

1 medium red capsicum (200g),
   chopped finely

1 medium green capsicum (200g),
   chopped finely

1 medium tomato (150g),
   chopped finely

1 clove garlic, crushed

¼ cup (60ml) lime juice

2 teaspoons olive oil

½ cup loosely packed fresh
   coriander leaves

1 Preheat oven to moderately hot.

2 Combine barley with stock and the water in medium saucepan; bring to a boil. Reduce heat; simmer, uncovered, about 45 minutes or until tender, drain. Rinse under cold water; drain.

3 Blend seasoning with extra stock in medium bowl, add chicken; toss to coat chicken in mixture. Drain chicken; reserve marinade. Place chicken, in single layer, on metal rack in large shallow baking dish; bake, uncovered, in moderately hot oven about 30 minutes or until cooked through, brushing with reserved marinade halfway through cooking time. Cover; stand 5 minutes. Slice thickly.

4 Place barley in large bowl with remaining ingredients; toss gently to combine. Divide salad among serving plates; top with chicken.

SERVES 4

per serving 24.7g carbohydrate; 14.6g fat; 1756kJ (420 cal); 46.7g protein

pepper-roasted garlic and lemon chicken

PREPARATION TIME 35 MINUTES   COOKING TIME 1 HOUR 50 MINUTES

2 bulbs garlic

2kg chicken

cooking-oil spray

2 teaspoons salt

2 tabelspoons cracked
    black pepper

1 medium lemon (140g), cut into
    8 wedges

1 cup (250ml) water

3 medium globe artichokes (660g)

2 tablespoons lemon juice

2 medium red onions (340g),
    quartered

3 baby fennel bulbs (390g), halved

2 medium leeks (700g), halved,
    cut into 4 pieces

250g cherry tomatoes

⅓ cup (80ml) dry white wine

¼ cup (60ml) lemon juice, extra

1   Preheat oven to moderately hot.

2   Separate cloves from garlic bulb, leaving skin intact. Wash chicken under cold water; pat dry with absorbent paper. Coat chicken with cooking-oil spray; press combined salt and pepper onto skin and inside cavity. Place garlic and lemon inside cavity; tie legs together with kitchen string. Place chicken, on small wire rack in large baking dish, pour the water in baking dish; bake in moderately hot oven 50 minutes.

3   Meanwhile, discard outer leaves from artichokes; cut tips from remaining leaves. Trim then peel stalks. Quarter artichokes lengthways; using teaspoon, remove chokes. Cover artichokes with cold water in medium bowl; stir in juice.

4   Add drained artichokes, onion, fennel and leeks to dish with chicken, coat with cooking-oil spray, bake, uncovered, in moderately hot oven, about 40 minutes or until vegetables are just tender.

5   Add tomato to dish; roast, uncovered, in moderately hot oven about 20 minutes or until tomatoes soften and chicken is cooked through. Place chicken on serving dish and vegetables in large bowl, cover to keep warm.

6   Heat wine and extra juice in same flameproof baking dish with pan juices; bring to a boil. Boil 2 minutes, then strain over bowl containing vegetables; toss gently to combine.

7   Discard garlic and lemon from cavity; serve chicken with vegetables.

SERVES 4
per serving 19.3g carbohydrate; 42.3g fat; 3060kJ (732 cal); 60.4g protein

pepper-roasted garlic and lemon chicken

neapolitan chicken parcels with rocket and red onion salad

neapolitan chicken parcels with rocket and red onion salad

PREPARATION TIME 20 MINUTES   COOKING TIME 30 MINUTES

4 single chicken breast fillets (680g)

8 large fresh basil leaves

8 drained marinated artichoke heart
quarters (100g)

⅔ cup (100g) drained
semi-dried tomatoes

150g bocconcini cheese,
sliced thinly

ROCKET AND RED ONION SALAD

1 tablespoon olive oil

2 tablespoons lemon juice

1 teaspoon dijon mustard

100g baby rocket leaves

½ cup loosely packed fresh
basil leaves

1 medium red onion (170g),
sliced thinly

1 tablespoon drained baby
capers, rinsed

1 Using meat mallet, gently pound one chicken fillet between sheets of plastic wrap until 1cm in thickness. Place two of the large basil leaves on one side of chicken fillet; top with two artichoke heart quarters, a quarter of the tomato and a quarter of the cheese. Fold chicken fillet over filling; tie with kitchen string to enclose securely. Repeat process with remaining chicken fillets, basil, artichokes, tomato and cheese.

2 Cook chicken parcels, uncovered, on heated oiled grill plate (or grill or barbecue) until browned both sides. Cover parcels with flameproof lid or foil; cook about 15 minutes or until chicken is cooked through.

3 Meanwhile, make rocket and red onion salad.

4 Serve chicken parcels with salad.

ROCKET AND RED ONION SALAD Whisk oil, juice and mustard in large bowl. Add remaining ingredients; toss gently to combine.

SERVES 4
per serving 12.4g carbohydrate; 16.3g fat; 1785kJ (427 cal); 56.3g protein

red fruit salad with lemon mascarpone

PREPARATION TIME 20 MINUTES

800g seedless watermelon

250g strawberries, hulled, quartered

150g raspberries

2 medium plums (225g), sliced thinly

2 teaspoons caster sugar

¼ cup (60ml) kirsch

LEMON MASCARPONE

250g mascarpone

2 teaspoons finely grated lemon rind

2 teaspoons caster sugar

1 tablespoon lemon juice

1 Using melon baller, scoop watermelon into balls. Place watermelon in large serving bowl with strawberries, raspberries, plums, sugar and liqueur; toss gently to combine. Cover; refrigerate until ready to serve.

2 Meanwhile, make lemon mascarpone.

3 Serve fruit salad accompanied by lemon mascarpone.

LEMON MASCARPONE Combine ingredients in small bowl.

SERVES 4
per serving 25g carbohydrate; 21.2g fat; 1430kJ (342 cal); 7.5g protein

guacamole

PREPARATION TIME 20 MINUTES

2 medium avocados (500g)

1 medium white onion (150g),
chopped finely

2 small tomatoes (260g),
chopped finely

1 tablespoon lime juice

2 tablespoons coarsely chopped
fresh coriander

200g corn chips

1 Using fork, mash avocados in medium bowl until almost smooth. Add onion, tomato, juice and coriander; stir to combine.

2 Serve with corn chips.

SERVES 6
per serving 19.3g carbohydrate; 22.9g fat; 1254kJ (300 cal); 4.2g protein

tahini dip with pitta

PREPARATION TIME 10 MINUTES   COOKING TIME 5 MINUTES

Tahini, a paste made from sesame seeds, is available from selected supermarkets and delicatessens.

¾ cup (180ml) tahini

2 cloves garlic, crushed

¼ cup (60ml) lemon juice

¼ cup (60ml) water

¼ teaspoon ground cumin

1 tablespoon finely chopped fresh
   flat-leaf parsley

3 large pitta, cut into wedges

1 Combine tahini and garlic in small bowl.

2 Gradually beat in juice, the water, cumin and parsley; beat until mixture thickens.

3 Toast pitta under preheated grill until crisp.

4 Serve dip with pitta.

SERVES 6
per serving 20.9g carbohydrate; 19.2g fat; 1233kJ (295 cal); 9.9g protein

eggplant dip

PREPARATION TIME 10 MINUTES   COOKING TIME 1 HOUR (PLUS STANDING AND REFRIGERATION TIME)

1 large eggplant (500g)

2 tablespoons toasted pine nuts

1 medium brown onion (150g),
   chopped finely

1 cup (100g) packaged breadcrumbs

2 tablespoons yogurt

3 cloves garlic, crushed

½ cup finely chopped fresh
   flat-leaf parsley

1 tablespoon cider vinegar

2 tablespoons lemon juice

½ cup (125ml) olive oil

1 Preheat oven to hot. Pierce eggplant all over with fork or skewer; place whole eggplant on oiled oven tray. Bake, uncovered, in hot oven about 1 hour or until soft. Stand 15 minutes. Peel eggplant; discard skin. Chop flesh coarsely.

2 Blend or process eggplant with remaining ingredients until smooth. Cover; refrigerate 3 hours or overnight.

3 Serve with assorted crudites.

SERVES 6
per serving 14.4g carbohydrate; 23.4g fat; 1191kJ (285 cal); 4.5g protein

kumara and celeriac chips

PREPARATION TIME 15 MINUTES   COOKING TIME 15 MINUTES

vegetable oil, for deep-frying

1 large kumara (500g), sliced thinly

1kg celeriac, trimmed, sliced thinly

1   Heat oil in wok or large saucepan.

2   Deep-fry kumara and celeriac, in batches, until browned and crisp; drain on absorbent paper.

SERVES 4
per serving 12.5g carbohydrate; 8.6g fat; 577kJ (137 cal); 2.6g protein

pineapple orange frappe

PREPARATION TIME 10 MINUTES

1 medium pineapple (1.25kg),
   chopped coarsely

½ cup (125ml) orange juice

3 cups crushed ice

1 tablespoon finely grated orange rind

1   Blend or process pineapple and orange juice until smooth.

2   Pour into large jug with crushed ice and rind; stir to combine then serve immediately.

SERVES 4
per serving 13.1 carbohydrate ; 0.2g fat; 259kJ (62 cals), 1.6g protein

tuna and tomato pizzas

PREPARATION TIME 10 MINUTES   COOKING TIME 5 MINUTES

1 tablespoon drained capers, rinsed,
   chopped finely

1 teaspoon finely chopped fresh dill

1 teaspoon olive oil

1 tablespoon lemon juice

4 multigrain english muffins

1 medium tomato (190g), seeded,
   sliced thinly

4 green onions, sliced thinly

125g can smoked tuna slices in
   springwater, drained

1   Combine capers, dill, oil and juice in small bowl.

2   Split muffins in half horizontally; toast both sides.

3   Divide tomato and onion among muffin halves; top with tuna. Drizzle with caper mixture.

SERVES 4
per serving 12.8g carbohydrate; 2.1g fat; 435kJ (104 cal); 8.1g protein

zucchini and eggplant little shoes

PREPARATION TIME 15 MINUTES   COOKING TIME 1 HOUR

3 medium green zucchini (360g)

3 baby eggplants (180g)

1 tablespoon olive oil

1 small brown onion (80g),
   chopped finely

2 cloves garlic, crushed

200g beef mince

200g canned crushed tomatoes

2 tablespoons tomato paste

½ cup (125ml) beef stock

¼ cup (50g) short-grain rice

2 tablespoons finely chopped fresh
   flat-leaf parsley

¼ cup (20g) finely grated
   parmesan cheese

SAUCE

30g butter

1½ tablespoons plain flour

1 cup (250ml) milk

1 egg, beaten lightly

pinch ground nutmeg

1 Halve zucchini and eggplants lengthways, scoop out pulp with spoon, leaving thin shells; chop pulp finely.

2 Heat oil in large frying pan; cook onion and garlic, stirring, until onion softens. Add beef; cook, stirring, until browned. Add chopped pulp, undrained crushed tomatoes, paste and stock; bring to a boil. Add rice, reduce heat; simmer, uncovered, about 15 minutes or until rice is tender and mixture is thick. Stir in parsley.

3 Meanwhile, make sauce.

4 Preheat oven to moderate. Place zucchini and eggplant shells on oven trays; fill with beef mixture. Spoon sauce over beef mixture; sprinkle with cheese. Bake, uncovered, in moderate oven about 35 minutes or until vegetables are tender and tops are browned lightly.

SAUCE Melt butter in small saucepan, add flour; cook, stirring, until mixture thickens and bubbles. Gradually stir in milk; stir until it boils and thickens. Cool 15 minutes; stir in egg and nutmeg.

SERVES 4
per serving 21.7g carbohydrate; 19.8g fat; 1379kJ (330 cal); 16.9g protein

salmon sashimi rolls
with lemon dipping sauce

PREPARATION TIME 25 MINUTES   COOKING TIME 5 MINUTES

Lemon dipping sauce can be made a day ahead. Cover; refrigerate until required.

200g sashimi salmon

¼ medium red capsicum (50g)

½ lebanese cucumber (65g)

1 green onion

LEMON DIPPING SAUCE

½ cup (125ml) rice vinegar

¼ cup (55g) caster sugar

2 teaspoons soy sauce

**½ teaspoon finely grated
   lemon rind**

1   Using sharp knife, cut salmon into paper-thin slices (you need 16 slices).

2   Remove and discard seeds and membranes from capsicum; halve cucumber lengthways, scoop out seeds. Halve onion lengthways. Slice capsicum, cucumber and onion into 8cm-long pieces.

3   Lay salmon slices on board in single layer; divide capsicum, cucumber and onion among salmon slices, mounding at one of the narrow edges. Roll slices around filling; place rolls, seam-side down, on serving platter.

4   Meanwhile, make lemon dipping sauce.

5   Serve sashimi rolls with dipping sauce.

LEMON DIPPING SAUCE Heat vinegar, sugar and sauce in small saucepan, stirring, until sugar dissolves. Remove from heat, stir in rind; stand 10 minutes. Strain sauce into serving bowl; discard rind.

SERVES 4
per serving 14.6g carbohydrate; 1.9g fat; 497kJ (119 cal); 10.1g protein

chorizo cheese puffs

PREPARATION TIME 15 MINUTES   COOKING TIME 10 MINUTES

Chorizo is a sausage made traditionally of coarsely ground pork and seasoned with garlic and chillies.
If you cannot find fresh chorizo, substitute with any spicy sausage.

½ cup (75g) self-raising flour

¼ cup (60ml) water

1 egg, beaten lightly

1 chorizo sausage (170g),
    chopped finely

½ small red capsicum (75g),
    chopped finely

¼ cup (20g) finely grated
    parmesan cheese

2 cloves garlic, crushed

2 tablespoons finely chopped
    fresh chives

1 teaspoon ground cumin

vegetable oil, for deep-frying

1   Sift flour into medium bowl; stir in the water, egg, sausage, capsicum, cheese, garlic, chives and cumin.

2   Heat oil in wok or large saucepan; deep-fry tablespoons of the mixture until browned. Drain on absorbent paper.

SERVES 4
per serving 15.4g carbohydrate; 18.9g fat; 1145kJ (274 cal); 10.9g protein

ham and tomato melts

PREPARATION TIME 10 MINUTES   COOKING TIME 10 MINUTES

2 multigrain english muffins

1 teaspoon wholegrain mustard

1 medium tomato (190g), sliced thinly

100g low-fat shaved ham

1 tablespoon coarsely chopped
   fresh basil

¼ small red onion (25g), sliced thinly

½ cup (50g) coarsely grated low-fat
   mozzarella cheese

1   Split muffins in half horizontally; toast both sides.

2   Spread mustard on muffin halves; top with remaining ingredients. Place under preheated grill until cheese melts.

SERVES 4
per serving   12.6g carbohydrate; 4.7g fat; 589kJ (141 cal); 11.9g protein

chicken tikka drumettes

PREPARATION TIME 10 MINUTES   COOKING TIME 20 MINUTES

⅓ cup (100g) tikka curry paste

½ cup (140g) yogurt

12 chicken drumettes (960g)

16 small pappadums

¼ cup coarsely chopped fresh coriander

1   Preheat oven to moderately hot.

2   Combine paste and 2 tablespoons of the yogurt in large bowl, add chicken; toss to coat chicken in paste mixture. Place chicken, in single layer, on wire rack in large baking dish. Roast, uncovered, in moderately hot oven about 20 minutes or until chicken is browned and cooked through.

3   Meanwhile, place 3 pappadums around edge of microwave oven turntable. Cook on HIGH (100%) about 30 seconds or until puffed. Repeat with remaining pappadums.

4   Combine coriander and remaining yogurt in small bowl. Serve chicken drizzled with yogurt mixture; accompany with pappadums.

SERVES 4
per serving   20.3g carbohydrate; 26.5g fat; 1977kJ (473 cal); 38g protein

lime and soy wings

PREPARATION TIME 15 MINUTES (PLUS REFRIGERATION TIME)   COOKING TIME 25 MINUTES

8 small chicken wings (650 kg)

¼ cup (80g) lime marmalade, warmed

¼ cup (60ml) soy sauce

2 tablespoons dry white wine

1 clove garlic, crushed

¼ cup (60ml) barbecue sauce

1 tablespoon lime juice

1   Cut wings into three pieces at joints; discard tips.

2   Combine marmalade, soy sauce, wine and garlic in large bowl, add chicken; toss to coat chicken in marinade. Cover; refrigerate 3 hours or overnight.

3   Cook drained chicken, in batches, on heated oiled grill plate (or grill or barbecue), brushing both sides occasionally with barbecue sauce, about 25 minutes or until chicken is cooked through.

4   Serve chicken drizzled with lime juice.

SERVES 4
per serving 20.7g carbohydrate; 5.5g fat; 982kJ (235 cal); 24.5g protein

Maintaining Weight (no more than 43g carbs per serving)

stewed rhubarb and yogurt cups

PREPARATION TIME 15 MINUTES   COOKING TIME 10 MINUTES

20g butter

7 cups (770g) coarsely chopped rhubarb

⅓ cup (75g) firmly packed brown sugar

2 tablespoons orange juice

2 cups (560g) vanilla yogurt

½ cup (65g) toasted muesli

1 Melt butter in large saucepan; cook rhubarb, sugar and juice, stirring, until sugar dissolves and rhubarb is tender.

2 Divide half of the rhubarb mixture among four 1-cup (250ml) serving glasses; top each with ¼ cup yogurt. Repeat layering with remaining rhubarb and yogurt. Top each with muesli.

SERVES 4
per serving 40.9g carbohydrate; 10.8g fat; 1338kJ (320 cal); 12.2g protein

wholemeal date loaf

PREPARATION TIME 20 MINUTES   COOKING TIME 1 HOUR (PLUS COOLING TIME)

1 cup (170g) seeded dates, halved

2 tablespoons boiling water

½ teaspoon bicarbonate of soda

60g low-fat dairy-free spread

2 teaspoons finely grated lemon rind

¾ cup (150g) firmly packed brown sugar

200g low-fat cottage cheese

2 eggs

2 cups (320g) wholemeal self-raising flour

2 tablespoons wheat germ

1 Preheat oven to moderately slow. Grease 14cm x 21cm loaf pan; line base and two long sides with baking paper, extending paper 5cm above edges of pan.

2 Combine dates, the water and bicarbonate of soda in small bowl, cover; stand 5 minutes.

3 Using electric mixer, beat spread, rind and sugar in small bowl until light and fluffy. Add cheese; beat until smooth. Add eggs, one at a time; beat until combined.

4 Stir in flour, wheat germ and date mixture; pour into prepared pan.

5 Bake, uncovered, in moderately slow oven about 1 hour. Stand 10 minutes; turn onto wire rack to cool.

SERVES 14
per serving 30.6g carbohydrate; 3.9g fat; 761kJ (182 cal); 6.7g protein

grilled mango and ricotta

PREPARATION TIME 10 MINUTES   COOKING TIME 5 MINUTES

200g low-fat ricotta cheese

¾ cup (210g) low-fat tropical yogurt

3 small mangoes (900g)

1 Whisk cheese and yogurt in medium bowl until smooth.

2 Slice cheeks from mangoes; remove skin, cut each cheek in half. Cook mango on heated oiled grill plate (or grill or barbecue) until browned both sides.

3 Top mango with cheese mixture.

SERVES 4
per serving 27.9g carbohydrate; 4.7g fat; 811kJ (194 cal); 9.5g protein
tip If mangoes are unavailable, you could substitute pineapple.

pineapple, honeydew and lychee fruit salad

PREPARATION TIME 25 MINUTES   COOKING TIME 15 MINUTES (PLUS COOLING AND REFRIGERATION TIME)

1½ cups (375ml) water

2 tablespoons grated palm sugar

2 star anise

2 tablespoons lime juice

1 small pineapple (800g), chopped coarsely

1 small honeydew melon (900g),
chopped coarsely

20 fresh lychees (500g), seeded

500g seedless red grapes

½ cup loosely packed fresh mint leaves, torn

1 Combine the water and sugar in medium saucepan, stir over low heat until sugar dissolves. Add star anise; bring to a boil. Reduce heat; simmer, uncovered, without stirring, 10 minutes. Remove from heat; stir in juice. Cover; refrigerate 3 hours or overnight. Strain syrup into medium jug; discard star anise.

2 Just before serving, place fruit and mint in large bowl with syrup; toss gently to combine.

SERVES 4
per serving 39.7g carbohydrate; 0.8g fat; 752kJ (180 cal); 3.7g protein

corned beef hash with poached eggs

PREPARATION TIME 10 MINUTES   COOKING TIME 10 MINUTES

1 medium brown onion (150g),
 chopped finely

1 large kumara (500g),
 shredded coarsely

500g cooked corned beef, shredded

2 tablespoons finely chopped fresh
 flat-leaf parsley

2 tablespoons plain flour

2 eggs, beaten lightly

1 tablespoon vegetable oil

8 eggs, extra

1   Combine onion, kumara, beef, parsley, flour and egg in large bowl.

2   Divide hash mixture into four portions; flatten to form patties.

3   Heat oil in large heavy-base frying pan; cook patties, uncovered, until browned both sides and potato is tender.

4   Half-fill a large shallow frying pan with water; bring to a boil. One at a time, break eggs into cup or saucer, then slide into pan. When all eggs are in pan, allow water to return to a boil. Cover pan, turn off heat; stand about 4 minutes or until a light film of egg white sets over yolks. One at a time, remove eggs, using slotted spoon, place on paper-towel-lined saucer to blot up poaching liquid.

5   Serve hash patties topped with poached eggs.

SERVES 4
per serving 20.6g carbohydrate; 23.4g fat; 1864kJ (446 cal); 38.6g protein

baked beans with fried eggs

PREPARATION TIME 10 MINUTES (PLUS SOAKING TIME)   COOKING TIME 2 HOURS 10 MINUTES

1 cup (200g) dried borlotti beans

3 bacon rashers (210g), rind
   removed, chopped coarsely

1 medium brown onion (150g),
   chopped finely

1 clove garlic, crushed

1 tablespoon tomato paste

400g can crushed tomatoes

1½ cups (375ml) water

1 tablespoon worcestershire sauce

2 teaspoons dijon mustard

1 tablespoon maple syrup

4 eggs

1 Place beans in medium bowl, cover with cold water; soak overnight, drain.

2 Cook bacon, onion and garlic in large saucepan, stirring, until onion softens. Add drained beans with paste, undrained tomato, the water, sauce and mustard; bring to a boil. Reduce heat; simmer, covered, about 1½ hours. Uncover; simmer about 15 minutes or until beans soften. Stir in syrup.

3 Cook eggs, uncovered, in heated oiled medium frying pan until cooked as desired. Serve beans with eggs.

SERVES 4
per serving 30.7g carbohydrate; 10.9g fat; 1283kJ (307 cal); 23.4g protein

french fruit toast with maple yogurt

PREPARATION TIME 5 MINUTES   COOKING TIME 10 MINUTES

1 egg white

⅓ cup (80ml) milk

6 slices fruit loaf

200g low-fat vanilla yogurt

1 tablespoon maple syrup

1 Whisk egg white and milk in large bowl until combined.

2 Cut bread in half diagonally. Heat large oiled frying pan; dip each piece of bread into milk mixture. Cook, in batches, until browned lightly both sides.

3 Place three pieces of toast on each plate; top with combined yogurt and syrup.

SERVES 4
per serving 42.5g carbohydrate; 4.1g fat; 1003kJ (240 cal); 9g protein.

peach smoothie

PREPARATION TIME 10 MINUTES

2 cups (500ml) no-fat soy milk

2 medium bananas (400g), chopped coarsely

4 medium peaches (600g), chopped coarsely

½ teaspoon ground cinnamon

1 Blend or process ingredients, in batches, until smooth.

SERVES 4
per serving 29g carbohydrate; 0.8g fat; 627kJ (150 cal); 6.8g protein

bircher muesli

PREPARATION TIME 10 MINUTES (PLUS REFRIGERATION TIME)

1 cup (90g) rolled oats

500g low-fat yogurt

2 small apples (260g), grated coarsely

1 tablespoon honey

¼ teaspoon ground cinnamon

**1 tablespoon coarsely chopped
    toasted pecans**

250g strawberries, quartered

1   Combine oats, yogurt, apple, honey, cinnamon and nuts in medium bowl. Cover; refrigerate overnight.

2   Just before serving, stir strawberries into muesli.

SERVES 4
per serving 34.9g carbohydrate; 4.6g fat; 966kJ (231 cal); 11.2g protein
tip Any berries can be substituted for strawberries.

strawberry smoothie

PREPARATION TIME 10 MINUTES

250g low-fat frozen strawberry yogurt

250g strawberries, halved

1 litre (4 cups) no-fat milk

1   Soften yogurt slightly; cut into pieces.

2   Blend or process ingredients, in batches, until smooth.

SERVES 4
per serving 28.3g carbohydrate; 1.4g fat; 740kJ (177 cal); 13.7g protein

spiced plums with yogurt

PREPARATION TIME 10 MINUTES   COOKING TIME 10 MINUTES (PLUS COOLING TIME)

1 litre (4 cups) water

½ cup (125ml) orange juice

⅓ cup (75g) caster sugar

5cm strip orange rind

2 star anise

4 cloves

1 teaspoon mixed spice

1 cinnamon stick

1 vanilla bean, split lengthways

8 blood plums (900g)

1⅓ cups (375g) yogurt

1   Place water, juice, sugar, rind and spices into medium frying pan. Scrape seeds from vanilla bean into pan, then add pod; cook mixture, stirring, until sugar dissolves.

2   Add plums to pan; poach, uncovered, over low heat for 10 minutes or until just tender. Using slotted spoon, place two plums in each of four serving dishes (reserve 2 tablespoons of the poaching liquid). Cool plums 20 minutes.

3   Combine yogurt and reserved poaching liquid in small bowl. Serve plums with spiced yogurt.

SERVES 4
per serving 39.1g carbohydrate; 3.4g fat; 907kJ (217 cal); 57g protein

spiced plums with yogurt

tropical fruit salad

tropical fruit salad

PREPARATION TIME 10 MINUTES   COOKING TIME 20 MINUTES (PLUS REFRIGERATION TIME)

2 cups (500ml) water

3 cardamom pods, bruised

4cm piece fresh ginger (20g),
**   quartered**

1 teaspoon finely grated lemon rind

1 tablespoon lemon juice

1 tablespoon lime juice

1 vanilla bean, split lengthways

½ medium (850g) rockmelon,
**   chopped coarsely**

1 small papaya (600g),
**   chopped coarsely**

3 medium kiwi fruit (255g),
**   chopped coarsely**

1 medium mango (430g),
**   chopped coarsely**

⅓ cup (80ml) passionfruit pulp

1 Place the water, cardamom, ginger, rind and juices into medium frying pan. Split vanilla bean in half lengthways; scrape seeds into pan, then add pod; bring to a boil. Reduce heat; simmer, uncovered, without stirring 20 minutes. Strain into medium jug; cool 10 minutes. Refrigerate, covered, until cold.

2 Just before serving, place syrup and remaining ingredients in large bowl; toss gently to combine.

SERVES 4
per serving 30.6g carbohydrate; 0.6g fat; 606kJ (145 cal); 3.4g protein

fresh corn and zucchini chunky salsa

PREPARATION TIME 10 MINUTES   COOKING TIME 10 MINUTES

2 fresh corn cobs (800g), trimmed

100g baby zucchini,
  halved lengthways

2 large avocados (640g),
  chopped coarsely

200g grape tomatoes, halved

1 medium red onion (170g), halved,
  sliced thickly

¼ cup coarsely chopped
  fresh coriander

1 tablespoon sweet chilli sauce

⅓ cup (80ml) lime juice

2 fresh small red thai chillies, seeded,
  sliced thinly

1   Cook corn and zucchini on heated oiled grill plate (or grill or barbecue) until browned lightly and tender. Using sharp knife, remove corn kernels from cobs.

2   Combine corn and zucchini in large serving bowl with avocado, tomato, onion and coriander.

3   Place remaining ingredients in screw-top jar; shake well. Drizzle dressing over salsa; toss gently to combine.

SERVES 4
per serving 29.8g carbohydrate; 35.3g fat; 2015kJ (482 cal); 11.1g protein

roasted ratatouille with rye toast

PREPARATION TIME 15 MINUTES   COOKING TIME 20 MINUTES

5 baby eggplants (300g),
  chopped coarsely

4 small green zucchini (360g),
  chopped coarsely

100g mushrooms, chopped coarsely

250g cherry tomatoes, halved

1 small leek (200g), chopped coarsely

2 cloves garlic, crushed

1 tablespoon olive oil

½ cup coarsely chopped fresh basil

1 tablespoon finely chopped
  fresh oregano

2 tablespoons balsamic vinegar

4 thick slices dark rye bread, toasted

1   Preheat oven to hot.

2   Combine eggplant, zucchini, mushrooms, tomato, leek, garlic and oil in large shallow baking dish; roast, uncovered, in hot oven, stirring occasionally, about 20 minutes or until vegetables are tender.

3   Stir basil, oregano and vinegar into ratatouille. Serve warm on rye toast.

SERVES 4
per serving 25.2g carbohydrate; 6.3g fat; 790kJ (189 cal); 7.2g protein

tofu burgers with barbecue sauce

PREPARATION TIME 15 MINUTES (PLUS REFRIGERATION TIME)   COOKING TIME 15 MINUTES

500g firm tofu

1 clove garlic, crushed

¼ cup (60ml) barbecue sauce

2 tablespoons olive oil

1 medium red onion (170g),
   sliced thinly

4 wholegrain bread rolls

1 baby cos lettuce

1 large tomato (220g), sliced thinly

2 tablespoons barbecue sauce, extra

1   Drain tofu; cut into eight slices. Combine tofu in medium bowl with garlic and sauce; refrigerate, covered, 3 hours or overnight.

2   Heat half of the oil in large frying pan; cook onion, stirring, until onion softens.

3   Drain tofu; discard marinade. Heat remaining oil in same pan; cook tofu, uncovered, until browned both sides. Drain on absorbent paper.

4   Meanwhile, split rolls in half; toast cut sides. Sandwich lettuce leaves, two slices of tofu, tomato, onion and extra sauce between toasted roll halves.

SERVES 4
per serving 40.4g carbohydrate; 19.9g fat; 1781kJ (426 cal); 21.7g protein

grapefruit salad

PREPARATION TIME 30 MINUTES

1 small red onion (100g)

6 large grapefruits (3kg)

2 green onions, sliced thinly

2 fresh small red thai chillies,
   sliced thinly

¼ cup coarsely chopped
   fresh coriander

½ cup (70g) coarsely chopped
   toasted unsalted peanuts

2 cloves garlic, crushed

1 tablespoon grated palm sugar

¼ cup (60ml) lime juice

1 tablespoon soy sauce

1   Halve red onion; cut each half into paper-thin wedges.

2   Peel and carefully segment grapefruit; discard membranes. Place segments in large bowl with onions, chilli, coriander and nuts.

3   Combine remaining ingredients in small jug; stir until sugar dissolves. Pour dressing over grapefruit salad; toss gently to combine.

SERVES 4
per serving 28.3g carbohydrate; 1.1g fat; 652kJ (156 cal); 5.4g protein

pumpkin soup

PREPARATION TIME 10 MINUTES   COOKING TIME 50 MINUTES

30g butter

1 large leek (500g), chopped coarsely

2 cloves garlic, crushed

2kg butternut pumpkin,
    chopped coarsely

1.5 litres (6 cups) chicken stock

½ cup (125ml) cream

1   Melt butter in large saucepan; cook leek and garlic, stirring, until leek softens. Add pumpkin and stock; bring to a boil. Reduce heat; simmer, covered, about 25 minutes or until pumpkin softens.

2   Blend or process pumpkin mixture, in batches, until pureed. Stir in cream.

SERVES 4
per serving 25.6g carbohydrate; 20.4g fat; 1384kJ (331 cal); 12g protein

smoked seafood and mixed vegetable antipasti

PREPARATION TIME 35 MINUTES

⅓ cup (80g) sour cream

2 teaspoons raspberry vinegar

1 tablespoon coarsely chopped
    fresh chives

1 clove garlic, crushed

1 large yellow zucchini (150g)

1 tablespoon raspberry vinegar, extra

¼ cup (60ml) extra virgin olive oil

⅓ cup (45g) toasted slivered almonds

¾ cup (110g) drained
    semi-dried tomatoes

1 large avocado (320g)

1 tablespoon lemon juice

300g hot-smoked ocean trout portions

200g sliced smoked salmon

16 drained caperberries (80g)

1 lemon, cut into wedges

180g wholemeal crackers

1   Combine sour cream, vinegar, chives and garlic in small bowl, cover; refrigerate until required.

2   Meanwhile, using vegetable peeler, slice zucchini lengthways into ribbons; combine zucchini in small bowl with extra vinegar and 2 tablespoons of the oil.

3   Combine nuts, tomatoes and remaining oil in small bowl. Slice avocado thickly into small bowl; sprinkle with juice. Flake trout into bite-sized pieces.

4   Arrange zucchini mixture, tomato mixture, avocado, trout, salmon and caperberries on large platter; serve with sour cream mixture, lemon and crackers.

SERVES 4
per serving 40.1g carbohydrate; 56.6g fat; 3520kJ (842 cal); 42.5g protein
tip You can substitute cherry tomatoes if you cannot obtain the grape variety.

chilli tuna pasta salad

PREPARATION TIME 15 MINUTES   COOKING TIME 15 MINUTES

200g large shell pasta

250g green beans, trimmed, halved

2 x 185g cans tuna in chilli oil

⅓ cup coarsely chopped fresh
    flat-leaf parsley

⅓ cup firmly packed fresh basil leaves, torn

2 tablespoons drained baby capers

150g baby rocket leaves

150g fetta cheese, crumbled

¼ cup (60ml) olive oil

¼ cup (60ml) lemon juice

2 cloves garlic, crushed

2 teaspoons sugar

1   Cook pasta in large saucepan of boiling water, uncovered, until just tender; drain. Rinse under cold water; drain.

2   Meanwhile, boil, steam or microwave beans until just tender; drain. Rinse under cold water; drain.

3   Drain tuna; reserve oil. Place tuna in large bowl; flake with fork. Add pasta and beans with herbs, capers, rocket and cheese.

4   Place remaining ingredients and reserved oil in screw-top jar; shake well. Drizzle dressing over salad; toss gently to combine.

SERVES 4
per serving 39g carbohydrate; 40.8g fat; 2692kJ (644 cal); 30.3g protein
tip The salad, without the dressing, can be made several hours ahead and refrigerated, covered. Toss the dressing through the salad just before serving.

fresh salmon and pasta salad

PREPARATION TIME 10 MINUTES   COOKING TIME 20 MINUTES

You need approximately 500g fresh peas for this recipe.

500g salmon fillets

200g farfalle

1 cup (160g) shelled fresh peas

⅔ cup (160g) sour cream

1 tablespoon lemon juice

2 teaspoons water

2 tablespoons green peppercorns,
    rinsed, drained

1 tablespoon coarsely chopped fresh dill

2 trimmed celery stalks (200g), sliced thinly

⅓ cup coarsely chopped fresh chives

1   Cook salmon, uncovered, in large heated oiled frying pan until browned lightly both sides and cooked as desired. Drain on absorbent paper.

2   Meanwhile, cook pasta in large saucepan of boiling water, uncovered, adding peas about halfway through cooking time; drain when pasta is just tender.

3   Combine sour cream, juice, the water, peppercorns and dill in small bowl.

4   Place salmon in large bowl; using fork, flake salmon. Add celery, chives, sour cream mixture, pasta and peas; toss gently to combine.

SERVES 4
per serving 41.2g carbohydrate; 21.6g fat; 2069kJ (495 cal); 33.4g protein
tip Frozen peas can be thawed and substituted for fresh peas; add them to the pasta just before draining it.

tuna, corn and bean salad with lemon mayonnaise

PREPARATION TIME 15 MINUTES

425g can tuna in brine, drained

420g can red kidney beans,
rinsed, drained

310g can corn kernels,
rinsed, drained

3 trimmed celery stalks (300g),
sliced thinly

½ cup coarsely chopped fresh
flat-leaf parsley

100g baby rocket leaves

⅓ cup (100g) mayonnaise

1 tablespoon lemon juice

1 clove garlic, crushed

1 Place tuna, beans, corn, celery, parsley and rocket in large bowl.

2 Place remaining ingredients in small jug; whisk to combine. Serve salad drizzled with dressing.

SERVES 4
per serving 27.4g carbohydrate; 11.5g fat; 1384kJ (331 cal); 29g protein

veal and eggplant parmigiana

PREPARATION TIME 10 MINUTES   COOKING TIME 20 MINUTES

½ medium eggplant (150g)

⅓ cup (80ml) olive oil

4 veal scaloppine (400g)

500g bottled tomato pasta sauce

1 tablespoon fresh sage leaves

200g bocconcini, sliced thinly

1 Cut eggplant into four 1cm slices. Heat ¼ cup of the oil in large frying pan; cook eggplant, uncovered, until browned both sides and tender. Drain on absorbent paper.

2 Heat remaining oil in same pan; cook veal, uncovered, until browned both sides. Remove pan from heat.

3 Top veal with eggplant, 1 tablespoon of the pasta sauce, sage and bocconcini. Spoon remaining sauce around veal.

4 Return pan to heat; simmer, covered, about 5 minutes or until sauce bubbles. Place pan briefly under hot grill until cheese melts and browns lightly.

SERVES 4
per serving 34.3g carbohydrate; 28.5g fat; 2161kJ (517 cal); 31.9g protein

hamburger with a twist

PREPARATION TIME 15 MINUTES   COOKING TIME 10 MINUTES

80g gorgonzola cheese, crumbled

¼ cup (60g) sour cream

400g beef mince

120g sausage mince

1 small brown onion (80g),
    chopped finely

1 tablespoon barbecue sauce

2 teaspoons worcestershire sauce

½ cup (75g) drained sun-dried
    tomatoes, chopped finely

4 wholemeal bread rolls

50g baby rocket leaves

170g marinated artichoke hearts,
    drained, quartered

1   Blend or process half of the cheese with sour cream until smooth.
    Stir in remaining cheese.

2   Using hand, combine minces, onion, sauces and tomato in medium
    bowl; shape mixture into four patties.

3   Cook patties in large oiled heated frying pan until browned both sides
    and cooked through.

4   Meanwhile, halve buns; toast, cut-side up.

5   Sandwich rocket, patties, gorgonzola cream and artichoke hearts in
    toasted buns.

SERVES 4
per serving 37.7g carbohydrate; 30.5g fat; 2387kJ (571 cal); 36.1g protein

pumpkin wedges with sloppy joe topping

PREPARATION TIME 10 MINUTES   COOKING TIME 30 MINUTES

800g pumpkin, cut into wedges

2 tablespoons olive oil

1 clove garlic, crushed

1 large brown onion (200g),
    chopped finely

1 small green capsicum (150g),
    chopped finely

1 trimmed celery stalk (100g),
    chopped finely

750g beef mince

2 tablespoons mild american mustard

2 tablespoons cider vinegar

1 cup (250ml) tomato sauce

½ cup (60g) coarsely grated
    cheddar cheese

2 green onions, sliced thinly

1   Preheat oven to hot.

2   Place pumpkin in large shallow baking dish; drizzle with half of the
    oil. Roast, uncovered, in hot oven about 30 minutes or until wedges
    are tender.

3   Meanwhile, heat remaining oil in large frying pan; cook garlic, brown
    onion, capsicum and celery, stirring, until vegetables soften. Add mince;
    cook, stirring, until changed in colour. Stir in mustard, vinegar and sauce;
    bring to a boil. Reduce heat; cook, stirring, until sloppy joe is cooked
    through and slightly thickened.

4   Serve wedges topped with sloppy joe mixture; sprinkle with cheese and
    green onion.

SERVES 4
per serving 35.4g carbohydrate; 28.7g fat; 2483kJ (594 cal); 48.7g protein

bread-less steak sandwich

PREPARATION TIME 20 MINUTES   COOKING TIME 1 HOUR 20 MINUTES

4 beef scotch fillet steaks (800g)

60g rocket, trimmed

CHILLI TOMATO JAM

1 tablespoon olive oil

2 cloves garlic, crushed

4 medium tomatoes (760g), chopped coarsely

1 tablespoon worcestershire sauce

½ cup (125ml) sweet chilli sauce

⅓ cup (75g) firmly packed brown sugar

1 tablespoon coarsely chopped
   fresh coriander

CARAMELISED LEEK

30g butter

1 medium leek (350g), sliced thinly

2 tablespoons brown sugar

2 tablespoons dry white wine

1 Make chilli tomato jam and caramelised leek.

2 Cook steaks on heated oiled grill plate (or grill or barbecue) until browned both sides and cooked as desired.

3 Top steaks with rocket, chilli tomato jam and caramelised leek.

   CHILLI TOMATO JAM Heat oil in medium saucepan; cook garlic, stirring, until browned lightly. Add tomato, sauces and sugar; bring to a boil. Reduce heat; simmer, uncovered, about 45 minutes or until mixture thickens. Stand 10 minutes; stir in coriander.

   CARAMELISED LEEK Melt butter in medium frying pan; cook leek, stirring, until softened. Add sugar and wine; cook, stirring occasionally, about 20 minutes or until leek caramelises.

   SERVES 4
   per serving 31.6g carbohydrate; 29.2g fat; 2479kJ (593 cal); 49.9g protein

lamb and parsley salad kebabs

PREPARATION TIME 25 MINUTES   COOKING TIME 10 MINUTES

500g lamb fillets

1 tablespoon olive oil

1 teaspoon sesame seeds

1 clove garlic, crushed

1 teaspoon finely grated lemon rind

1½ cups coarsely chopped fresh flat-leaf parsley

1 large tomato (250g), seeded, sliced thinly

1 small red onion (100g), sliced thinly

2 tablespoons lemon juice

1 tablespoon olive oil

250g prepared hummus

4 large pitta

½ cup (60g) coarsely grated cheddar cheese

1 Place lamb, oil, seeds, garlic and rind in medium bowl; toss to coat lamb in mixture. Cook lamb on heated oiled grill plate (or grill or barbecue) until browned and cooked as desired. Cover; stand 5 minutes, slice lamb thickly.

2 Meanwhile, combine parsley, tomato, onion, juice and oil in medium bowl.

3 Spread hummus evenly over one side of each pitta. Divide cheese, parsley salad and lamb among pitta; roll to enclose filling, cut kebabs in half to serve.

   SERVES 4
   per serving 42.59g carbohydrate; 34.81g fat; 2730kJ (653 cal); 42.31g protein

pea and ham soup

PREPARATION TIME 15 MINUTES (PLUS SOAKING TIME)   COOKING TIME 1 HOUR 10 MINUTES

2 cups (400g) dried split peas

1 medium brown onion (150g),
    chopped coarsely

2 trimmed celery stalks (200g),
    chopped coarsely

2 bay leaves

1.5kg ham bone

2.5 litres (10 cups) water

1 teaspoon cracked black pepper

1 Place peas in large bowl, cover with water; soak overnight, drain.

2 Combine peas in large saucepan with remaining ingredients; bring to a boil. Reduce heat; simmer, covered, about 1 hour or until peas are tender.

3 Remove ham bone; when cool enough to handle, remove ham from bone. Discard bone and fat; shred ham finely.

4 Blend or process half of the pea mixture, in batches, until pureed; return to pan with remaining unprocessed pea mixture and ham. Reheat soup, stirring over heat until hot.

SERVES 6
per serving 31.7g carbohydrate; 4.9g fat; 1124kJ (269 cal); 23.5g protein
tip If you haven't soaked the peas overnight, simply double the cooking time in step 2 to 2 hours.

warm chicken tabbouleh (see page 344)

PREPARATION TIME 15 MINUTES   COOKING TIME 15 MINUTES

Tabbouleh is a traditional Lebanese salad made with a great deal of chopped flat-leaf parsley and varying amounts of burghul, green onion, mint, olive oil and lemon juice.

1 cup (160g) burghul

500g chicken tenderloins,
    sliced thinly

2 cloves garlic, crushed

⅔ cup (160ml) lemon juice

¼ cup (60ml) olive oil

250g cherry tomatoes, halved

3 green onions, chopped coarsely

1 cup coarsely chopped fresh
    flat-leaf parsley

1 cup coarsely chopped fresh mint

1 Place burghul in small bowl; cover with boiling water. Stand 15 minutes; drain. Using hands, squeeze out as much excess water as possible.

2 Meanwhile, combine chicken, garlic, 2 tablespoons of the juice and 1 tablespoon of the oil in medium bowl; stand 5 minutes. Drain; discard marinade.

3 Heat 1 tablespoon of the remaining oil in wok or large frying pan; stir-fry chicken mixture, in batches, until chicken is browned all over and cooked through. Cover to keep warm.

4 Place burghul with tomato and onion in same wok. Stir-fry until onion softens; remove from heat. Add chicken mixture, parsley, mint, remaining juice and oil; toss gently to combine.

SERVES 4
per serving 27.3g carbohydrate; 17.5g fat; 1710kJ (409 cal); 33.9g protein

mexican burgers

PREPARATION TIME 10 MINUTES   COOKING TIME 10 MINUTES

450g chicken mince

35g packet taco seasoning mix

⅓ cup (80g) sour cream

1 tablespoon finely chopped
fresh coriander

4 wholemeal rolls, halved

1 medium avocado (250g),
sliced thinly

⅓ cup (85g) medium chunky salsa

1 Using hand, combine chicken and seasoning in large bowl; shape mixture into four patties. Cook patties on heated oiled grill plate (or grill or barbecue) until browned both sides and cooked through.

2 Meanwhile, combine sour cream and coriander in small bowl.

3 Toast rolls, cut-side up. Spread half of each roll with sour cream mixture; top each with patty, avocado, salsa and remaining half of roll.

SERVES 4
per serving 25.9g carbohydrate; 24.3g fat; 1831kJ (438 cal); 28.7g protein

sweet and sour chicken

PREPARATION TIME 10 MINUTES   COOKING TIME 10 MINUTES

4 chicken breast fillets (680g)

440g can pineapple pieces in
natural juice

1 tablespoon peanut oil

1 small brown onion (80g),
sliced thinly

1 medium red capsicum (200g),
chopped coarsely

1 large green capsicum (350g),
chopped coarsely

1 trimmed celery stalk (100g),
sliced thickly

¼ cup (60ml) tomato sauce

¼ cup (60ml) plum sauce

2 tablespoons soy sauce

¼ cup (60ml) white vinegar

1 tablespoon cornflour

½ cup (125ml) chicken stock

1 Cook chicken on heated oiled grill plate (or grill or barbecue) until browned all over and cooked through. Stand 5 minutes; slice thickly. Cover to keep warm.

2 Meanwhile, drain pineapple; reserve juice. Heat oil in large saucepan; cook pineapple, onion, capsicums and celery, stirring, 4 minutes. Add reserved juice, sauces, vinegar and blended cornflour and stock; stir until mixture boils and thickens.

3 Serve chicken topped with sweet and sour sauce.

SERVES 4
per serving 29.9g carbohydrate; 8.9g fat; 1551kJ (371 cal); 42.1g protein

chicken tenderloins in green peppercorn and tarragon dressing

PREPARATION TIME 10 MINUTES   COOKING TIME 15 MINUTES

2 tablespoons water

2 teaspoons drained green
  peppercorns, crushed

2 teaspoons wholegrain mustard

2 green onions, sliced thinly

1 tablespoon coarsely chopped
  fresh tarragon

1 tablespoon olive oil

1 tablespoon sugar

⅓ cup (80ml) white wine vinegar

2 medium kumara (500g)

8 chicken tenderloins (600g)

1 tablespoon cracked black pepper

4 large tomatoes (1kg), sliced thinly

1 medium red onion (170g), sliced thinly

1   Place the water, peppercorn, mustard, green onion, tarragon, oil, sugar and vinegar in small bowl. Whisk to combine dressing; reserve.

2   Boil, steam or microwave kumara until just tender; drain.

3   Meanwhile, coat chicken all over in pepper; cook chicken, in batches, on heated oiled grill plate (or grill or barbecue) until browned both sides and cooked through. Stand 5 minutes; slice thickly.

4   When kumara are cool enough to handle, slice thickly. Cook kumara, in batches, on same heated oiled grill plate until browned both sides.

5   Arrange chicken, kumara, tomato and red onion on serving plates; drizzle with reserved dressing.

SERVES 4
per serving 25.7g carbohydrate; 8.4g fat; 1421kJ (340 cal); 38.8g protein

chicken pitta pockets

PREPARATION TIME 10 MINUTES   COOKING TIME 15 MINUTES

400g chicken mince

1 clove garlic, crushed

2 teaspoons ground coriander

2 teaspoons ground cumin

1 tablespoon mild chilli sauce

1 tablespoon olive oil

1 large brown onion (200g), sliced thinly

½ cup (80g) pine nuts

300g spinach, trimmed, chopped coarsely

¼ cup coarsely chopped fresh mint

4 pocket pittas

1 cup (280g) yogurt

1 tablespoon lemon juice

1   Using hand, combine chicken, garlic, spices and sauce in large bowl.

2   Heat half of the oil in wok or large frying pan; cook chicken mixture until chicken is browned and cooked through. Remove from wok; cover to keep warm.

3   Heat remaining oil in same wok; stir-fry onion, pine nuts and spinach until spinach just wilts. Remove from heat. Return chicken mixture to wok with mint; toss gently to combine.

4   Cut pitta pockets in half. Open out each half; spoon in chicken mixture. Drizzle combined yogurt and juice into pitta pockets.

SERVES 4
per serving 41.7g carbohydrate; 30.9g fat; 2424kJ (580 cal); 33.1g protein
tip Chilli sauces can vary in degrees of heat—add more or less to suit your taste.

dhal with egg and eggplant

PREPARATION TIME 10 MINUTES   COOKING TIME 1 HOUR 10 MINUTES

2 cups (400g) red lentils

2 teaspoons vegetable oil

1 medium brown onion (150g), chopped finely

1 clove garlic, crushed

2 teaspoons ground cumin

½ teaspoon cumin seeds

1 tablespoon tomato paste

1 litre (4 cups) water

2 cups (500ml) vegetable stock

1 large tomato (250g), chopped coarsely

3 baby eggplants (180g), chopped coarsely

4 hard-boiled eggs

1 Rinse lentils in large colander under cold water until water runs clear.

2 Heat oil in large heavy-base saucepan; cook onion, garlic, ground cumin, seeds and paste, stirring, 5 minutes. Add lentils with the water and stock; bring to a boil. Reduce heat; simmer, uncovered, about 40 minutes or until dhal mixture thickens slightly, stirring occasionally.

3 Add tomato and eggplant; simmer, uncovered, about 20 minutes or until dhal is thickened and eggplant is tender, stirring occasionally. Add whole eggs; stir gently until eggs are heated through.

SERVES 4
per serving 43.5g carbohydrate 10.5g fat; 1651kJ (395 cal); 33.8g protein

spicy okra, corn and capsicum gumbo

PREPARATION TIME 30 MINUTES   COOKING TIME 1 HOUR

1½ tablespoons olive oil

2 small brown onions (160g), chopped coarsely

4 cloves garlic, crushed

1½ teaspoons cajun seasoning

1 teaspoon ground cumin

¼ teaspoon cayenne pepper

3 trimmed celery stalks (300g), chopped coarsely

1 medium green capsicum (200g), chopped coarsely

2 medium red capsicums (400g), chopped coarsely

2 fresh trimmed corn cobs, (500g) chopped coarsely

8 baby carrots, chopped coarsely

2 cups (500ml) vegetable stock

2 x 425g cans crushed tomatoes

2 tablespoons worcestershire sauce

600g okra

⅓ cup (65g) basmati rice

¼ cup finely chopped fresh parsley

1 Heat oil in large heavy-base saucepan; cook onion, garlic and spices, stirring, until onion softens. Add celery, capsicums, corn, carrot, stock, undrained tomatoes and sauce; simmer, covered, 30 minutes.

2 Meanwhile, trim stems from okra; discard stems.

3 Add rice and okra; simmer, covered, about 25 minutes or until rice is tender.

4 Serve sprinkled with parsley.

SERVES 4
per serving 43g carbohydrate; 9.7g fat; 1542kJ (369 cal); 16.6g protein

mixed vegetable salad with roasted eggplant puree

PREPARATION TIME 40 MINUTES   COOKING TIME 1 HOUR 15 MINUTES

1 large green capsicum (350g)

1 large red capsicum (350g)

1 large yellow capsicum (350g)

1 large eggplant (500g)

2 cloves garlic, unpeeled

1 tablespoon lemon juice

½ cup (125ml) olive oil

350g mushrooms, sliced thickly

1 sprig fresh thyme

250g cherry tomatoes

20 baby zucchini (200g), halved

8 yellow patty-pan
    squash (250g), halved

2 small fennel bulbs (400g)
    trimmed, quartered

12 shallots (300g), peeled

⅓ cup (80ml) dry white wine

4 slices pumpernickel bread

½ cup loosely packed fresh
    flat-leaf parsley leaves

1 Preheat oven to hot.

2 Quarter capsicums, discard seeds and membranes. Using fork, prick eggplant all over; place on oiled oven tray with garlic and capsicum, skin-side up. Roast vegetables, uncovered, in hot oven about 30 minutes or until skins blister. Cover capsicum pieces with plastic or paper for 5 minutes; peel away skin then slice thickly.

3 When cool enough to handle, peel eggplant and garlic. Blend or process eggplant, garlic and juice until mixture forms a paste. With motor operating, pour in half of the oil in a thin, steady stream until eggplant mixture is pureed. Reserve.

4 Meanwhile, toss mushrooms and thyme with 1 tablespoon of the remaining oil in large shallow baking dish. Toss tomatoes, zucchini, squash and 1 tablespoon of the remaining oil in another large shallow baking dish. Roast, uncovered, in hot oven about 20 minutes or until mushrooms and vegetables are just tender.

5 Heat remaining oil in medium saucepan; cook fennel and shallots, stirring occasionally, about 5 minutes or until vegetables are browned lightly. Add wine; cook, covered, stirring occasionally, about 20 minutes or until vegetables are tender. Drain vegetables; add cooking liquid to processor with eggplant puree, process until smooth.

6 Place bread on heated oiled grill plate (or grill or barbecue) until browned lightly both sides. Divide bread among serving plates; top with combined mushrooms, vegetables and parsley. Serve with eggplant puree.

SERVES 4
per serving 39.3g carbohydrate; 30.5g fat; 2098kJ (502 cal); 14.8g protein

vegetable moussaka

PREPARATION TIME 10 MINUTES   COOKING TIME 1 HOUR 15 MINUTES (PLUS COOLING TIME)

2 large eggplants (1kg), sliced thickly

1 large red capsicum (350g),
    chopped coarsely

4 large tomatoes (1kg), chopped finely

1 tablespoon sugar

30g butter

2 tablespoons plain flour

2 cups (500ml) skim milk

⅓ cup (35g) finely grated parmesan cheese

⅓ cup finely chopped fresh basil

1 Place eggplant and capsicum, in single layer, on oven tray. Bake, uncovered, in moderately hot oven 15 minutes; turn. Bake further 15 minutes or until eggplant is browned lightly; cool 10 minutes.

2 Meanwhile, combine tomato and sugar in small saucepan; cook, stirring occasionally, about 30 minutes or until tomato is soft and liquid almost evaporates.

3 Melt butter in small saucepan; add flour. Cook, stirring, 1 minute. Gradually add milk; stir over medium heat until sauce boils and thickens. Stir in half of the cheese and half of the basil. Stir remaining basil through tomato mixture.

4 Spread a third of the tomato mixture, eggplant, capsicum and cheese sauce in four 2-cup (500ml) ovenproof dishes; repeat with two more layers. Sprinkle with remaining cheese.

5 Bake, uncovered, in moderate oven, about 15 minutes or until moussaka is browned lightly.

SERVES 4
per serving 26.3g carbohydrate; 7.3g fat; 932kJ (223 cal); 13.2g protein

char-grilled bream and vegetables with chilli basil butter sauce

PREPARATION TIME 20 MINUTES   COOKING TIME 30 MINUTES

4 baby cauliflowers (500g), halved

3 trimmed corn cobs (750g), cut into
    2cm rounds

400g baby carrots, trimmed

2 tablespoons olive oil

4 x 240g whole bream

CHILLI BASIL BUTTER SAUCE

80g butter

2 fresh small red thai chillies, seeded,
    chopped finely

⅓ cup finely shredded fresh basil

1 tablespoon lemon juice

1 Place vegetables and half of the oil in large bowl; toss to combine. Cook vegetables on heated oiled grill plate (or grill or barbecue) about 20 minutes or until browned all over and cooked through.

2 Meanwhile, make chilli basil butter sauce.

3 Score each fish three times both sides; brush all over with remaining oil. Cook fish on heated oiled grill plate (or grill or barbecue) about 5 minutes each side or until cooked as desired. Serve fish and vegetables drizzled with sauce.

CHILLI BASIL BUTTER SAUCE Melt butter in small saucepan; add chilli, basil and juice, stir until combined.

SERVES 4
per serving 29.8g carbohydrate; 34g fat; 237kJ (559 cal); 34g protein

vegetable tagine

PREPARATION TIME 20 MINUTES   COOKING TIME 25 MINUTES

Harissa, a paste originating from North Africa, is made from dried red chillies, garlic, olive oil and caraway seeds. It can be used as a rub for meat, as an ingredient in sauces and dressings or eaten on its own, as a condiment. It is available ready-made from all Middle-Eastern food shops and some supermarkets.

2 teaspoons olive oil

1 large red onion (300g),

   chopped coarsely

2 cloves garlic, crushed

2 teaspoons ground ginger

½ teaspoon ground cinnamon

2 teaspoons ground cumin

2 teaspoons ground coriander

1 medium eggplant (300g),

   chopped coarsely

1 large red capsicum (350g),

   chopped coarsely

400g can crushed tomatoes

2 cups (500ml) vegetable stock

1 large pear (330g), peeled,

   chopped coarsely

2 cups (500ml) water

250g green beans, cut into

   5cm lengths

½ cup (85g) dried seeded dates

½ cup finely chopped fresh

   flat-leaf parsley

½ cup finely chopped fresh mint

1 tablespoon harissa

1 Heat oil in large saucepan; cook onion and garlic, stirring, 5 minutes. Add spices, eggplant and capsicum; cook, stirring, about 1 minute or until spices are fragrant. Add undrained tomatoes and stock; bring to a boil. Reduce heat; simmer, covered, until vegetables are just tender.

2 Meanwhile, place pear and the water in medium saucepan; bring to a boil. Reduce heat; simmer, covered, about 15 minutes or until pear is just tender. Discard cooking liquid; add pear to tagine mixture with beans and dates; cook, stirring, 5 minutes. Stir chopped herbs and harissa into tagine off the heat.

SERVES 4
per serving 37.2g carbohydrate; 3.7g fat; 878kJ (210 cal); 7.4g protein

vegetable and tofu stir-fry

PREPARATION TIME 10 MINUTES   COOKING TIME 15 MINUTES

250g firm tofu

300g fresh rice noodles

1 tablespoon peanut oil

1 large brown onion (200g), sliced thickly

2 cloves garlic, crushed

1 teaspoon five-spice powder

300g button mushrooms, halved

200g swiss brown mushrooms, halved

¼ cup (60ml) soy sauce

1 cup (250ml) vegetable stock

¼ cup (60ml) water

300g baby bok choy, chopped coarsely

300g choy sum, chopped coarsely

4 green onions, chopped coarsely

200g bean sprouts

1   Cut tofu into 2cm cubes. Place noodles in large heatproof bowl; cover with boiling water, separate noodles with fork; drain.

2   Heat oil in wok or large frying pan; stir-fry brown onion and garlic until onion softens. Add five-spice; stir-fry until fragrant. Add mushrooms; stir-fry until almost tender.

3   Add combined sauce, stock and the water; bring to a boil. Add bok choy, choy sum and green onion; stir-fry until bok choy just wilts. Add tofu, noodles and sprouts; stir-fry until heated through.

SERVES 4
per serving 28g carbohydrate; 10.2g fat; 1191kJ (285 cal); 19.4g protein
tip You can use rice stick noodles if fresh noodles are not available. Place rice stick noodles in a large heatproof bowl; cover with boiling water. Stand until just tender then drain.

double pea and tofu stir-fry with pistachios

PREPARATION TIME 10 MINUTES   COOKING TIME 20 MINUTES

2 tablespoons peanut oil

600g firm tofu, drained, chopped coarsely

1 cup (150g) pistachios, shelled

30g butter

2 cloves garlic, crushed

2 fresh small red thai chillies, seeded, chopped finely

2cm piece fresh ginger (10g), grated

400g sugar snap peas, trimmed

400g snow peas, trimmed

¼ cup (60ml) sweet chilli sauce

1   Heat half of the oil in wok or large frying pan; stir-fry tofu and nuts, in batches, until tofu is browned lightly.

2   Heat remaining oil with butter in wok; stir-fry garlic, chilli and ginger until mixture is fragrant. Add peas to wok; stir-fry until just tender.

3   Return tofu and nuts to wok with sauce; stir-fry until heated through.

SERVES 4
per serving 28.4g carbohydrate; 45.6g fat; 2734kJ (654 cal); 34.2g protein

japanese omelette salad (see page 27)

chicken, lemon and artichoke skewers (see page 134)

quartet of beans in chilli lime sauce

PREPARATION TIME 10 MINUTES   COOKING TIME 20 MINUTES

300g rice stick noodles

250g frozen broad beans, thawed, peeled

150g green beans, halved

150g snake beans, chopped coarsely

150g butter beans, halved

vegetable oil, for deep-frying

¼ cup (40g) drained capers

1 tablespoon olive oil

6 cloves garlic, crushed

1 small red onion (100g), cut into wedges

4 fresh small red thai chillies, seeded,
   chopped coarsely

2 tablespoons finely grated lime rind

1 cup (250ml) vegetable stock

1   Place noodles in medium heatproof bowl; cover with boiling water. Stand until just tender; drain. Rinse under cold water; drain.

2   Meanwhile, boil, steam or microwave beans, separately, until just tender; drain. Heat vegetable oil in small frying pan; deep-fry capers until crisp. Drain on absorbent paper.

3   Heat olive oil in wok or large frying pan; stir-fry garlic, onion, chilli and rind until onion softens. Add stock, beans and noodles; cook, stirring gently, until sauce thickens and mixture is hot.

4   Serve topped with capers.

SERVES 4
per serving 29.6g carbohydrate; 6.5g fat; 903kJ (216 cal); 9.1g protein

grilled mahi mahi with roasted corn and chilli salad

PREPARATION TIME 30 MINUTES   COOKING TIME 25 MINUTES

4 trimmed corn cobs (1kg)

1 egg yolk

1 clove garlic, crushed

2 tablespoons lime juice

1 teaspoon dijon mustard

¾ cup (180ml) olive oil

1 medium red onion (170g), chopped finely

2 fresh small red thai chillies, chopped finely

1 small avocado (200g), chopped finely

1 medium green capsicum (200g),
   chopped finely

⅓ cup coarsely chopped fresh coriander

4 x 200g mahi mahi steaks

1   Cook corn on heated oiled grill plate (or grill or barbecue) until browned lightly and just tender.

2   Meanwhile, blend or process yolk, garlic, juice and mustard until smooth. With motor operating, gradually add oil in a thin, steady stream; process until mayonnaise thickens slightly.

3   Using sharp knife, remove kernels from cobs. Place kernels in large bowl with onion, chilli, avocado, capsicum, coriander and half of the mayonnaise; toss gently to combine.

4   Cook fish on same heated oiled grill plate until browned both sides and cooked as desired. Divide corn salad among serving plates; top with fish, drizzle with remaining mayonnaise.

SERVES 4
per serving 33.4g carbohydrate; 56.8g fat; 3532kJ (845 cal); 50.7g protein

salmon parcels with fresh mango sauce

PREPARATION TIME 30 MINUTES   COOKING TIME 15 MINUTES

½ small leek (100g)

⅓ cup loosely packed fresh
   coriander leaves

1 large red capsicum (350g),
   sliced thinly

1 teaspoon five-spice powder

½ teaspoon ground coriander

1 tablespoon grated palm sugar

1 tablespoon lime juice

4 x 220g salmon fillets, skinned

4 x 21.5cm-square spring
   roll wrappers

1 tablespoon cornflour

2 teaspoons water

⅓ cup (80ml) peanut oil

1 medium mango (430g),
   chopped coarsely

100g red coral lettuce

1   Cut leek into 8cm lengths; halve each piece lengthways then slice halves into thin strips. Combine leek in small bowl with fresh coriander and half of the capsicum.

2   Preheat oven to moderately hot.

3   Heat small lightly oiled frying pan; cook five-spice and ground coriander, stirring, until fragrant. Stir in sugar and juice; remove from heat. When cool enough to handle, use fingers to rub half of the spice mixture into both sides of salmon fillets.

4   Place a salmon fillet on bottom half of one spring roll wrapper; top with a quarter of the leek mixture. Lightly brush edges of wrapper with blended cornflour and water; roll to enclose salmon, folding in ends. Repeat with remaining salmon, wrappers, leek mixture and cornflour mixture.

5   Heat oil in large frying pan; cook parcels, in batches, until browned lightly. Place on oiled oven tray; bake parcels in moderately hot oven about 8 minutes or until fish is cooked as desired.

6   Meanwhile, blend or process half of the mango and remaining spice mixture until smooth. Combine remaining mango, remaining capsicum and lettuce in large bowl. Serve salmon parcels with salad topped with mango sauce.

SERVES 4
per serving 32.4g carbohydrate; 35g fat; 2684kJ (642 cal); 49.7g protein

blackened blue-eye with sweet tomato relish

PREPARATION TIME 20 MINUTES (PLUS REFRIGERATION TIME)   COOKING TIME 40 MINUTES

4 x 200g blue-eye fillets

2 tablespoons olive oil

8cm piece fresh ginger (40g), grated

1 tablespoon ground turmeric

1 tablespoon garlic powder

1 tablespoon mustard powder

1 tablespoon sweet paprika

1 tablespoon dried basil leaves

1 tablespoon ground fennel

¼ teaspoon cayenne pepper

¼ teaspoon hot chilli powder

2 teaspoons salt

150g mesclun

SWEET TOMATO RELISH

10 medium egg tomatoes
   (750g), halved

2 cups (500ml) water

½ cup (125ml) dry white wine

1 tablespoon lime juice

½ cup (110g) firmly packed
   brown sugar

1 tablespoon finely grated lime rind

1 tablespoon ground turmeric

1 tablespoon yellow mustard seeds

2 bay leaves

2 stalks fresh lemon grass

1 Place fish in large shallow dish; pour over combined oil and ginger. Cover; refrigerate 3 hours or overnight.

2 Make sweet tomato relish.

3 Drain fish; discard marinade. Coat fish in combined turmeric, garlic, mustard, paprika, basil, fennel, cayenne, chilli and salt; cook on heated oiled grill plate (or grill or barbecue) until browned both sides and just cooked through.

4 Serve fish with relish and mesclun.

SWEET TOMATO RELISH Combine ingredients in medium saucepan; bring to a boil. Reduce heat; simmer, uncovered, about 30 minutes or until most of the liquid has evaporated. Cool, remove and discard bay leaves and lemon grass.

SERVES 4
per serving 28.8g carbohydrate; 13.7g fat; 1789kJ (428 cal); 42.8g protein

salmon cutlets with green apple salad

PREPARATION TIME 20 MINUTES   COOKING TIME 10 MINUTES (PLUS COOLING TIME)

½ teaspoon sea salt

4 x 170g salmon cutlets

2 medium apples (300g), sliced thinly

2 green onions, sliced thinly

1 medium red onion (170g), sliced thinly

1½ cups loosely packed fresh mint leaves

¾ cup loosely packed fresh coriander leaves

½ cup (125ml) lemon juice

¾ cup (110g) toasted unsalted cashews

PALM SUGAR DRESSING

⅓ cup (65g) grated palm sugar

2 tablespoons fish sauce

2cm piece fresh ginger (10g), grated

1   Sprinkle salt evenly over fish. Cook fish on heated oiled grill plate (or grill or barbecue) until browned both sides and cooked as desired.

2   Meanwhile, make palm sugar dressing.

3   Place apple, onions, mint, coriander and juice in large bowl; pour over half of the palm sugar dressing, toss to combine.

4   Divide fish among serving plates; top with salad, then nuts. Drizzle remaining dressing over fish.

PALM SUGAR DRESSING   Combine ingredients in small saucepan; bring to a boil. Remove from heat; strain. Cool 15 minutes.

SERVES 4
per serving   32.6g carbohydrate; 23.6g fat; 1990kJ (476 cal); 33.9g protein

salmon with grilled corn salsa

PREPARATION TIME 20 MINUTES   COOKING TIME 25 MINUTES

2 corn cobs (800g), trimmed

2 medium red capsicums (400g)

1 small red onion (100g), chopped finely

1 fresh small red thai chilli, seeded,
    chopped finely

1 tablespoon olive oil

¼ cup coarsely chopped fresh coriander

4 x 200g salmon fillets, skin on

1   Cook corn on heated oiled grill plate (or grill or barbecue); until browned lightly and tender. When cool enough to handle, cut kernels from cobs.

2   Meanwhile, quarter capsicums; remove and discard seeds and membranes. Roast capsicum under grill or in very hot oven, skin-side up, until skin blisters and blackens. Cover capsicum pieces with plastic or paper for 5 minutes. Peel away skin; chop capsicum finely.

3   Combine corn and capsicum in medium bowl with onion, chilli, oil and coriander.

4   Cook fish on same heated oiled grill plate until browned both sides and cooked as desired. Serve fish with corn salsa.

SERVES 4
per serving   28.6g carbohydrate; 27.8g fat; 2638kJ (631 cal); 66.4g protein

tahitian fish salad

PREPARATION TIME 40 MINUTES (PLUS REFRIGERATION TIME)   COOKING TIME 10 MINUTES

This delicious fish salad captures the tropical flavour of Tahitian cooking with every bite. Unlike that other popular "raw" fish dish, ceviche, where the seafood marinates in citrus juice for such a long time that it is virtually "cooked", here it is assembled quickly and submerged in lime juice only long enough to become slightly opaque on the surface, while remaining raw inside.

600g piece kingfish, skinned

⅔ cup (160ml) lime juice

1 large kumara (500g), sliced thinly

1 large potato (300g), sliced thinly

1 telegraph cucumber (400g)

1 tablespoon finely grated lime rind

3 fresh small red thai chillies, sliced thinly

4 green onions, sliced thinly

1½ cups finely chopped coriander leaf, root and stem mixture

1⅔ cups (400ml) coconut milk

2 medium avocados (500g), sliced thinly

1 Slice fish in half lengthways, remove bones and blood line; slice halves crossways into 5mm strips. Combine fish with juice in large bowl, cover; refrigerate 20 minutes.

2 Meanwhile, cook kumara and potato on heated oiled grill plate (or grill or barbecue) until browned lightly both sides and just tender.

3 Using vegetable peeler, slice cucumber into ribbons. Add cucumber, rind, chilli, onion, coriander and coconut milk to undrained fish; toss gently to combine.

4 Divide kumara and potato among serving plates, top with avocado and fish salad.

SERVES 4
per serving 31.9g carbohydrate; 44.4g fat; 2888kJ (691 cal); 40.4g protein

hot and sour prawn vermicelli salad

PREPARATION TIME 30 MINUTES (PLUS REFRIGERATION TIME)   COOKING TIME 5 MINUTES

1kg cooked medium king prawns

250g rice vermicelli

1 lime

1 lemon

1 medium red capsicum (200g), sliced thinly

1 medium yellow capsicum (200g), sliced thinly

1 medium red onion (170g), sliced thinly

¼ cup (60ml) olive oil

¼ cup (60ml) rice vinegar

1 tablespoon sambal oelek

1 tablespoon fish sauce

2 tablespoons grated palm sugar

1 cup firmly packed fresh coriander leaves

1 Shell and devein prawns, leaving tails intact. Place vermicelli in large heatproof bowl of boiling water, stand until just tender; drain. Rinse under cold water; drain.

2 Meanwhile, halve lime and lemon lengthways; slice one unpeeled half of each thinly, place in large bowl. Squeeze remaining halves over bowl; add prawns, vermicelli and remaining ingredients, toss gently to combine. Cover; refrigerate 1 hour before serving.

SERVES 4
per serving 26.4g carbohydrate; 15.4g fat; 1601kJ (383 cal); 33.7g protein

chilli-seared tuna with avocado cream and tortillas

PREPARATION TIME 30 MINUTES (PLUS REFRIGERATION TIME)   COOKING TIME 10 MINUTES

4 chipotle chillies

1 tablespoon olive oil

1 small brown onion (80g), chopped finely

2 cloves garlic, crushed

⅓ cup loosely packed fresh oregano leaves

2 tablespoons tomato paste

2 tablespoons water

4 x 200g tuna steaks

8 large flour tortillas

2 limes, cut into wedges

AVOCADO CREAM

2 small avocados (400g)

½ cup (120g) sour cream

¼ cup coarsely chopped fresh coriander

1 tablespoon lime juice

2 green onions, sliced thinly

1   Place chillies in small heatproof bowl of boiling water; stand 15 minutes. Drain; chop chillies coarsely.

2   Heat oil in small frying pan; cook onion and garlic, stirring, until onion softens. Stir in chilli, oregano, paste and the water; bring to a boil. Remove from heat; blend or process, pulsing, until mixture forms a thick paste.

3   Place fish, in single layer, in large shallow dish; using fingers, pat chilli paste into both sides of fish. Cover; refrigerate 15 minutes.

4   Make avocado cream.

5   Cook undrained fish on heated oiled grill plate (or grill or barbecue) until browned both sides and cooked as desired. Cover; stand 5 minutes. Slice fish thickly.

6   Meanwhile, heat tortillas according to directions on packet. Divide fish, avocado cream and tortillas among serving plates. Serve with lime wedges.

AVOCADO CREAM Blend or process avocados and sour cream until smooth; stir in coriander, juice and onion.

SERVES 4
per serving 32.2g carbohydrate; 45.6g fat; 3214kJ (769 cal); 57.3g protein

cheese-crumbed fish fillets with stir-fried vegetables

PREPARATION TIME 15 MINUTES   COOKING TIME 15 MINUTES

You could use any firm-fleshed white fish fillets for this recipe — we used blue-eye. Make the breadcrumbs from bread that is at least a day old; grate or process stale bread to make crumbs.

1 cup (70g) stale wholemeal breadcrumbs

½ cup (45g) rolled oats

1 tablespoon drained capers, chopped finely

2 teaspoons finely grated lemon rind

¼ cup (20g) finely grated romano cheese

¼ cup finely chopped fresh flat-leaf parsley

1 tablespoon sesame oil

4 x 150g firm white fish fillets

½ cup (75g) plain flour

2 egg whites, beaten lightly

1 large carrot (180g), sliced thinly

2 trimmed celery stalks (200g), sliced thinly

1 medium green capsicum (200g), sliced thinly

6 green onions, chopped finely

1 fresh small red thai chilli, seeded, chopped finely

1 tablespoon sesame seeds

1 Preheat oven to hot.

2 Combine breadcrumbs, oats, capers, rind, cheese, parsley and oil in medium bowl. Coat fish in flour; shake off excess. Dip in egg, then in breadcrumb mixture.

3 Place fish, in single layer, in baking dish; bake, uncovered, in hot oven about 15 minutes or until cooked through.

4 Meanwhile, stir-fry carrot in heated non-stick wok or large frying pan. Add celery, capsicum, onion, chilli and sesame seeds; stir-fry until vegetables are just tender.

5 Serve sliced fish on stir-fried vegetables.

SERVES 4
per serving 36.6g carbohydrate; 12.8g fat; 1797kJ (430 cal); 41.6g protein

crumbed fish with caper mayonnaise

PREPARATION TIME 25 MINUTES (PLUS REFRIGERATION TIME)   COOKING TIME 10 MINUTES

2 eggs, beaten lightly

2 tablespoons water

1 cup (70g) stale breadcrumbs

¾ cup (60g) finely grated parmesan cheese

½ cup (40g) toasted flaked almonds

750g whiting fillets

½ cup (75g) plain flour

vegetable oil, for shallow-frying

1 cup loosely packed fresh basil leaves

1 cup loosely packed flat-leaf parsley leaves

100g baby rocket leaves

1 lemon, cut into wedges

CAPER MAYONNAISE

¾ cup (225g) mayonnaise

1 tablespoon capers, drained, chopped finely

1 tablespoon coarsely chopped fresh basil

1 clove garlic, crushed

1 tablespoon lemon juice

1 Combine egg and the water in small bowl. Combine breadcrumbs, cheese and almonds in medium bowl.

2 Coat fish in flour; shake off excess. Coat fish in egg mixture, then in breadcrumb mixture. Place fish on oven tray; refrigerate, covered, 30 minutes.

3 Meanwhile, make caper mayonnaise.

4 Heat oil in large frying pan; shallow-fry fish, in batches, until browned lightly both sides and cooked through. Serve with caper mayonnaise.

5 Combine remaining ingredients in medium bowl.

6 Serve fish with salad and caper mayonnaise.

CAPER MAYONNAISE Combine ingredients in small bowl.

SERVES 4
per serving 36.6g carbohydrate; 72.9g fat; 4243kJ (1015 cal); 54.5g protein
tips Mayonnaise can be prepared a day ahead and refrigerated, covered. Fish can be coated and refrigerated up to 2 hours ahead of cooking time.

steaks with parsnip mash

PREPARATION TIME 10 MINUTES (PLUS REFRIGERATION TIME)   COOKING TIME 20 MINUTES

4 beef new york-cut steaks (880g)

⅓ cup (80ml) plum sauce

⅓ cup (80ml) tomato sauce

⅓ cup (80ml) worcestershire sauce

2 cloves garlic, crushed

2 green onions, chopped finely

5 medium parsnips (750g), chopped coarsely

20g butter, chopped

¼ cup (60ml) cream

500g baby spinach leaves

1 Combine beef in large bowl with sauces, garlic and onion; toss to coat beef all over in marinade. Cover; refrigerate 30 minutes.

2 Meanwhile, boil, steam or microwave parsnip until just tender; drain. Mash with butter and cream in large bowl until smooth. Cover to keep warm.

3 Drain beef; discard marinade. Cook beef on heated oiled grill plate (or grill or barbecue) until browned both sides and cooked as desired.

4 Boil, steam or microwave spinach until just wilted; drain. Serve steaks with parsnip mash and spinach.

SERVES 4
per serving 37.4g carbohydrate; 26g fat; 2449kJ (586 cal); 51.3g protein

beef roulade

PREPARATION TIME 20 MINUTES (PLUS REFRIGERATION TIME)   COOKING TIME 55 MINUTES

500g lean beef mince

1 small brown onion (80g), chopped finely

2 cloves garlic, crushed

1 egg

1 tablespoon tomato paste

1 tablespoon coarsely chopped fresh basil

2 cups (140g) stale breadcrumbs

40g baby spinach leaves

6 slices prosciutto (90g)

9 cherry tomatoes (150g)

150g radicchio

2 tablespoons lemon juice

TOMATO AND MUSTARD SAUCE

½ cup (125ml) tomato sauce

2 tablespoons barbecue sauce

2 tablespoons dijon mustard

¼ cup (60ml) water

1 Grease 25cm x 30cm swiss roll pan; line with baking paper, extending paper 5cm over the edge of both long sides.

2 Using hand, combine mince, onion, garlic, egg, paste, basil and breadcrumbs in large bowl; press mixture into prepared pan, top with spinach leaves then prosciutto.

3 Place cherry tomatoes along one long side. Starting with this side, lift paper and roll, holding filling in place as you roll away from you, pressing roll gently but tightly around filling. Discard paper, wrap roll in foil; refrigerate 20 minutes. Preheat oven to hot.

4 Make tomato and mustard sauce.

5 Place roulade, still wrapped in foil, on oven tray; bake in hot oven 40 minutes. Unwrap roulade; bake on oven tray in hot oven about 15 minutes or until browned.

6 Combine radicchio and lemon in medium bowl. Serve roulade, sliced, with tomato and mustard sauce, and radicchio salad.

TOMATO AND MUSTARD SAUCE Combine ingredients in small saucepan; cook, stirring, until heated through.

SERVES 4
per serving 41.6g carbohydrate; 13.1g protein; 440kJ (440 cal); 38.8g protein

veal marsala

PREPARATION TIME 10 MINUTES   COOKING TIME 20 MINUTES

2 fresh corn cobs (800g), trimmed,
    chopped coarsely

300g frozen broad beans, peeled

8 x 100g veal schnitzels

50g butter

1 large brown onion (200g), sliced

1 tablespoon plain flour

¼ cup (60ml) marsala

¾ cup (180ml) beef stock

1 tablespoon finely chopped fresh
    flat-leaf parsley

1 Boil, steam or microwave corn and beans, separately, until tender; drain.

2 Meanwhile, cook veal in large heated oiled frying pan, in batches, until browned both sides and cooked as desired. Cover to keep warm.

3 Add butter and onion to same pan; cook, stirring, until onion softens. Add flour; cook, stirring, until mixture thickens and bubbles. Gradually stir in combined marsala and stock; stir until mixture boils and thickens. Stir in parsley. Serve veal with sauce and vegetables.

SERVES 4
per serving 37.3g carbohydrate; 15.3g fat; 2090kJ (500 cal); 52.5g protein

beef fajitas

PREPARATION TIME 20 MINUTES (PLUS REFRIGERATION TIME)   COOKING TIME 20 MINUTES

500g beef fillet, sliced thinly

¼ cup (60ml) barbecue sauce

1 teaspoon ground cumin

1 teaspoon ground coriander

½ teaspoon chilli powder

1 small red capsicum (150g),
seeded, sliced thinly

1 small green capsicum (150g),
seeded, sliced thinly

1 small yellow capsicum (150g),
seeded, sliced thinly

8 large flour tortillas

½ cup (120g) sour cream

AVOCADO TOPPING

2 small avocados (400g)

1 tablespoon lime juice

1 clove garlic, crushed

TOMATO SALSA

2 small tomatoes (180g), seeded,
chopped finely

1 small red onion (100g),
chopped finely

1 tablespoon olive oil

2 teaspoons finely chopped
fresh coriander

1 Place beef in medium bowl with sauce, cumin, coriander and chilli. Cover; refrigerate 3 hours or overnight.

2 Cook capsicum slices on heated oiled grill plate (or grill or barbecue) until browned. Cover to keep warm. Cook beef on same heated oiled grill plate until browned and cooked as desired.

3 Meanwhile, heat tortillas according to directions on packet. Make avocado topping. Make tomato salsa. Divide tortillas and beef mixture among serving plates; top with sour cream, avocado topping and salsa.

AVOCADO TOPPING Mash avocados coarsely in medium bowl with a fork; stir in juice and garlic.

TOMATO SALSA Combine ingredients in small bowl.

SERVES 4
per serving 40.3g carbohydrate; 42g fat; 2822kJ (675 cal); 34.5g protein

veal souvlakia with tomato and onion salsa

PREPARATION TIME 40 MINUTES (PLUS REFRIGERATION TIME)   COOKING TIME 10 MINUTES

1kg whole piece veal fillets

3 pitta bread, cut into

4 wedges each

MARINADE

1 small brown onion (80g),

chopped coarsely

2 cloves garlic, crushed

2 tablespoons yogurt

1 tablespoon lemon juice

1 tablespoon olive oil

¼ cup firmly packed fresh

mint leaves

3 teaspoons white wine vinegar

TOMATO AND ONION SALSA

4 small egg tomatoes (240g),

seeded, chopped finely

1 small white onion (80g),

chopped finely

2 tablespoons finely chopped

fresh mint

1 teaspoon sweet paprika

YOGURT SAUCE

¼ cup (140g) yogurt

2 teaspoons tahini

1 tablespoon hot water

1 Make marinade. Cut veal into 3cm pieces; thread onto eight skewers. Combine veal and marinade in large shallow dish. Cover; refrigerate 3 hours or overnight.

2 Cook veal on heated oiled grill plate (or grill or barbecue) until browned and cooked as desired.

3 Meanwhile, make tomato and onion salsa. Make yogurt sauce.

4 Serve veal with salsa, yogurt sauce and warm pitta bread.

MARINADE Blend or process ingredients until combined.

TOMATO AND ONION SALSA Combine ingredients in small bowl.

YOGURT SAUCE Whisk ingredients in small bowl until combined.

SERVES 4
per serving 34.7g carbohydrate; 13.9g fat; 2161kJ (517 cal); 61.9g protein
tip If using bamboo skewers, soak in water for at least 1 hour before using to avoid them splintering and scorching.

beef, pumpkin and mushroom salad with onion chutney

PREPARATION TIME 25 MINUTES   COOKING TIME 40 MINUTES

4 large egg tomatoes (360g), quartered

8 large flat mushrooms (400g),

   chopped coarsely

1 clove garlic, chopped finely

1 tablespoon olive oil

40g butter

2 tablespoons brown sugar

1 large brown onion (200g), sliced thinly

400g butternut pumpkin, sliced thinly

750g beef rump steak

2 tablespoons balsamic vinegar

100g baby rocket leaves

1. Preheat oven to moderately hot. Place tomato and mushrooms on large oven tray; sprinkle with combined garlic and oil. Bake, uncovered, in moderately hot oven about 40 minutes or until tomato is browned lightly.

2. Meanwhile, heat butter and sugar in medium saucepan, stirring, until sugar dissolves. Add onion; cook, stirring, until onion softens. Reduce heat; simmer, uncovered, about 10 minutes or until onion caramelises, stirring frequently.

3. Heat oiled medium non-stick frying pan; cook pumpkin, in batches, until browned both sides. Drain on absorbent paper.

4. Cook beef in same pan until browned all over and cooked as desired. Remove beef from pan, cover; stand 10 minutes, slice thinly.

5. Add vinegar to pan juices, reduce heat; simmer, uncovered, 2 minutes. Add onion mixture to pan; stir until chutney is heated through.

6. Divide pumpkin and mushrooms among serving plates; stack with beef, tomato, onion chutney and rocket.

SERVES 4
per serving 25.7g carbohydrate; 26.7g fat; 2295kJ (549 cal); 51.6g protein

beef with brandied walnuts and prunes

PREPARATION TIME 10 MINUTES (PLUS REFRIGERATION TIME)   COOKING TIME 50 MINUTES

650g beef butt fillet

⅓ cup (80ml) walnut oil

⅓ cup (80ml) cider vinegar

¼ cup (55g) firmly packed brown sugar

1 cup (170g) seeded prunes, halved

1 cup (100g) walnut pieces, chopped coarsely

⅓ cup (80ml) brandy

70g butter

150g mesclun

1. Place beef in large bowl with combined walnut oil, vinegar and sugar. Cover; refrigerate 3 hours or overnight.

2. Drain beef over medium bowl; reserve marinade. Cook beef on heated oiled barbecue until well browned all over. Place beef on roasting rack or basket, or in disposable baking dish. Cook in covered barbecue, using indirect heat, following manufacturer's instructions, about 40 minutes or until browned all over and cooked as desired. Remove from heat, cover; stand 10 minutes before slicing and serving.

3. Meanwhile, combine reserved marinade with prunes, nuts, brandy and butter in small saucepan; bring to a boil. Reduce heat; simmer, uncovered, 5 minutes.

4. Serve brandied walnuts and prunes with beef.

SERVES 4
per serving 29g carbohydrate; 61.4g fat; 3578kJ (856 cal); 38.5g protein

veal chops with pear relish and spinach

PREPARATION TIME 15 MINUTES   COOKING TIME 55 MINUTES

4 x 200g veal chops

40g butter

500g baby spinach leaves

PEAR RELISH

4 small pears (720g)

1 medium red onion (150g), chopped coarsely

20g butter

1 tablespoon red wine vinegar

¼ cup (55g) firmly packed brown sugar

4 cloves

¼ teaspoon ground allspice

1   Make pear relish.

2   Cook chops on heated oiled grill plate (or grill or barbecue) until browned both sides and cooked as desired.

3   Meanwhile, melt butter in large saucepan; cook spinach, tossing, until just wilted.

4   Serve chops with spinach and pear relish.

PEAR RELISH   Peel and core pears; chop coarsely. Combine pear in medium saucepan with onion, butter and vinegar; bring to a boil. Reduce heat; simmer, covered, about 20 minutes or until mixture is pulpy. Add sugar, cloves and allspice, stir over low heat until sugar dissolves; bring to a boil. Reduce heat; simmer, uncovered, stirring occasionally, about 20 minutes or until mixture thickens slightly.

SERVES 4
per serving   36.4g carbohydrate; 16.8g fat; 1777kJ (425 cal); 33.4g protein

beef steak with capsicum relish

PREPARATION TIME 10 MINUTES   COOKING TIME 20 MINUTES

3 medium red capsicums (600g)

1 teaspoon olive oil

1 large brown onion (200g), sliced thinly

2 cloves garlic, sliced thinly

2 tablespoons brown sugar

2 tablespoons sherry vinegar

3 fresh small red thai chillies, seeded, chopped finely

4 x 200g beef eye fillet steaks

300g tiny new potatoes, halved

200g broccoli

400g baby carrots

2 tablespoons finely chopped fresh flat-leaf parsley

1   Quarter capsicums; discard seeds and membranes. Roast under grill or in very hot oven, skin-side up, until skin blisters and blackens. Cover with plastic or paper for 5 minutes; peel away skin, slice thinly.

2   Heat oil in medium frying pan; cook onion and garlic, stirring, until soft. Add sugar, vinegar, chilli and capsicum; cook, stirring, 5 minutes.

3   Meanwhile, cook beef on heated oiled grill plate (or grill or barbecue) until browned and cooked as desired.

4   Boil, steam or microwave vegetables, separately, until just tender; drain.

5   Top steaks with capsicum relish; serve with vegetables, sprinkle with parsley.

SERVES 4
per serving   27.3g carbohydrate; 14.7g fat; 1885kJ (451 cal); 51.9g protein
tip   You can make the capsicum relish a day ahead; store, covered, in refrigerator. Reheat just before serving.

borscht with meatballs

PREPARATION TIME 20 MINUTES   COOKING TIME 2 HOURS

Borscht is a fresh beetroot soup, originally from Poland and Russia, made with meat or cabbage, or both. Serve it cold or hot, but always with a dollop of sour cream. Ask your butcher to cut the shanks into thirds for you.

1 tablespoon olive oil

1 small brown onion (80g),
  chopped coarsely

1 small carrot (70g),
  chopped coarsely

1 small leek (200g),
  chopped coarsely

250g cabbage, chopped coarsely

1 large tomato (250g),
  chopped coarsely

2 medium beetroots (350g), peeled,
  chopped coarsely

2 veal shanks (1.5kg), trimmed,
  cut into thirds

1.25 litres (5 cups) water

500g beef mince

½ cup (100g) medium-grain
  brown rice

1 teaspoon sweet paprika

1 small brown onion (80g),
  chopped finely

3 cloves garlic, crushed

½ cup finely chopped fresh
  flat-leaf parsley

2 eggs, beaten lightly

½ cup (120g) sour cream

2 tablespoons finely chopped
  fresh dill

1 Heat oil in large saucepan; cook coarsely chopped onion, carrot, leek, cabbage, tomato and beetroot, stirring, 15 minutes. Add shank and the water; bring to a boil. Reduce heat; simmer, covered, 1½ hours. Remove shank; remove and reserve meat from shank for another use, if desired.

2 Meanwhile, using hand, combine mince, rice, paprika, finely chopped onion, garlic, parsley and egg in large bowl; shape rounded teaspoons of the mince mixture into meatballs.

3 Return borscht to a boil; add meatballs. Reduce heat; simmer, uncovered, until meatballs are cooked through.

4 Divide borscht and meatballs among serving bowls; dollop with combined sour cream and dill.

SERVES 4
per serving 33.9g carbohydrate; 31.4g fat; 3047kJ (729 cal); 77.5g protein
tips Make the meatballs the day before; refrigerate them, uncooked, covered on a tray. Drop meatballs in reheated soup to cook. Make soup a day ahead to allow the flavours to intensify.

soupe au pistou

PREPARATION TIME 15 MINUTES (PLUS SOAKING TIME)   COOKING TIME 1 HOUR 40 MINUTES

Soupe au pistou is a classic Provençale recipe, usually made with white and green beans, and flavoured with pistou, a French spin-off of its near-neighbour Italy's pesto. Not dissimilar to Italian minestrone, this soup also benefits from being made a day in advance.

1 cup (200g) dried cannellini beans

⅓ cup (80ml) olive oil

2 veal shanks (1.5kg), trimmed

1 large leek (500g), sliced thinly

2 litres (8 cups) water

2 cups (500ml) chicken stock

2 tablespoons toasted pine nuts

1 clove garlic, quartered

¼ cup (20g) finely grated
**   parmesan cheese**

½ cup firmly packed fresh
**   basil leaves**

2 medium carrots (240g),
**   chopped coarsely**

200g green beans, trimmed,
**   chopped coarsely**

1 Cover cannellini beans with cold water in large bowl; stand, covered, overnight.

2 Heat 1 tablespoon of the oil in large saucepan; cook shanks, uncovered, until browned all over. Remove from pan. Cook leek in same pan, stirring, about 5 minutes or until just softened. Return shanks to pan with the water and stock; bring to a boil. Reduce heat; simmer, covered, 1 hour.

3 Meanwhile, blend or process nuts, garlic, cheese and remaining oil until combined. Add basil; process until pistou mixture forms a paste.

4 Remove shanks from soup. When cool enough to handle, remove meat from bones. Discard bones; chop meat coarsely. Return meat to soup with rinsed and drained cannellini beans; bring to a boil. Reduce heat; simmer, uncovered, 20 minutes. Add carrot; simmer, uncovered, 10 minutes. Add green beans and pistou; simmer, uncovered, 5 minutes.

SERVES 4
per serving 27.5g carbohydrate; 29.6g fat; 2508kJ (600 cal); 58.1g protein

mexican meatballs with guacamole

PREPARATION TIME 25 MINUTES   COOKING TIME 25 MINUTES

2 tablespoons vegetable oil

1 medium brown onion (150g),

   chopped finely

1 clove garlic, crushed

1 teaspoon ground cumin

1 teaspoon ground coriander

½ teaspoon chilli powder

750g beef mince

¼ cup (25g) packaged breadcrumbs

2 x 400g cans crushed tomatoes

425g can mexican-style beans

⅓ cup (80g) sour cream

GUACAMOLE

2 medium avocados (500g)

1 large tomato (220g), seeded, chopped finely

1 small red onion (100g), chopped finely

2 teaspoons lemon juice

1 Heat half of the oil in large frying pan; cook onion, garlic and spices, stirring, until onion softens.

2 Using hand, combine beef and onion mixture in medium bowl; using hands, roll level tablespoons into balls. Heat remaining oil in same pan; cook meatballs, in batches, until browned all over.

3 Add undrained tomato and beans to same pan; bring to a boil. Reduce heat; simmer, uncovered, about 5 minutes or until mixture thickens slightly. Return meatballs to pan; simmer, uncovered, about 10 minutes or until meatballs are cooked through.

4 Meanwhile, make guacamole.

5 Serve meatballs topped with guacamole and sour cream.

   GUACAMOLE Mash avocados with fork in medium bowl; stir in remaining ingredients.

SERVES 4
per serving 26g carbohydrate; 52.2g fat; 3189kJ (763 cal); 48g protein
tip Meatballs and sauce can be made a day ahead and refrigerated, covered separately.

veal goulash with braised red cabbage

PREPARATION TIME 20 MINUTES   COOKING TIME 1 HOUR 30 MINUTES

1 tablespoon olive oil

1 medium brown onion (150g), sliced thickly

1 medium red capsicum (200g), sliced thickly

2 cloves garlic, crushed

800g boneless veal leg, cut into 3cm cubes

1 tablespoon sweet paprika

½ teaspoon cayenne pepper

425g can crushed tomatoes

1½ cups (375ml) beef stock

¾ cup (150g) long-grain brown rice

30g butter

400g red cabbage, chopped coarsely

1 Heat oil in large saucepan; cook onion, capsicum and garlic, stirring, until onion softens. Add veal, paprika, pepper, undrained tomato and ½ cup of the stock; bring to a boil, stirring. Reduce heat; simmer, uncovered, about 1 hour or until veal is tender and sauce thickens slightly.

2 Meanwhile, cook rice in medium saucepan of boiling water until just tender; drain.

3 Melt butter in large frying pan; cook cabbage, stirring, about 5 minutes or until just softened. Add remaining stock; bring to a boil. Reduce heat; simmer, covered, 10 minutes.

4 Serve goulash with rice and braised red cabbage.

SERVES 4
per serving 39.9g carbohydrate; 16.1g fat; 2195kJ (525 cal); 54.7g protein

hoisin beef stir-fry (see page 240)

lamb shanks in five-spice, tamarind and ginger (see page 121)

mint and lime lamb with salsa

PREPARATION TIME 20 MINUTES (PLUS REFRIGERATION TIME)   COOKING TIME 10 MINUTES

½ cup (125ml) olive oil

2 cloves garlic, crushed

2 teaspoons finely grated lime rind

2 tablespoons lime juice

2 tablespoons finely chopped fresh mint

8 lamb chops

WATERMELON AND MANGO SALSA

1kg chopped watermelon

3 small mangoes (900g), chopped coarsely

2 fresh small red thai chillies, seeded, chopped

¼ cup finely shredded fresh coriander

2 tablespoons finely grated lime rind

¼ cup (60ml) raspberry vinegar

1 Combine oil, garlic, rind, juice and mint in medium bowl, add lamb; toss to coat lamb in marinade. Cover; refrigerate 3 hours or overnight.

2 Cook lamb on heated oiled grill plate (or grill or barbecue) until browned both sides and cooked as desired.

3 Meanwhile, make watermelon and mango salsa.

4 Serve lamb with salsa.

WATERMELON AND MANGO SALSA Place ingredients in large bowl; toss gently to combine.

SERVES 4
per serving 33.4g carbohydrates; 38.9g fat; 2533kJ (606 cal); 30.5g protein

curried lamb shanks

PARATION TIME 20 MINUTES   COOKING TIME 2 HOURS 15 MINUTES

To "french cut" meat is to remove the excess gristle and fat from the end of a shank, cutlet or rack to expose the bone. Ask your butcher to prepare the lamb shanks for this recipe.

8 french-cut lamb shanks (1.5kg)

¼ cup (35g) plain flour

2 tablespoons peanut oil

1 medium brown onion (150g), chopped finely

2 cloves garlic, crushed

½ cup (125g) rogan josh curry paste

2 cups (500ml) water

400g can crushed tomatoes

1 teaspoon sugar

2 cups (500ml) beef stock

400g cauliflower, chopped coarsely

400g pumpkin, chopped coarsely

½ cup (100g) red lentils

¼ cup coarsely chopped fresh coriander

1 Toss lamb in flour; shake away excess. Heat oil in large frying pan; cook lamb, in batches, until browned all over.

2 Cook onion and garlic in same pan, stirring, until onion softens. Add paste; cook, stirring, until fragrant. Return lamb to pan with the water, undrained tomatoes, sugar and stock; bring to a boil. Reduce heat; simmer, covered, 1½ hours.

3 Add cauliflower and pumpkin to curry; bring to a boil. Reduce heat; simmer, covered, 15 minutes. Stir in lentils; simmer, covered, about 10 minutes or until lentils are tender. Remove from heat; stir in coriander.

SERVES 4
per serving 31.9g carbohydrate; 40.1g fat; 3235kJ (774 cal); 71.9g protein

lemon and artichoke rack of lamb with moroccan orange and radish salad

PREPARATION TIME 20 MINUTES   COOKING TIME 40 MINUTES

2 racks of lamb with 8 cutlets each

2 medium brown onions (300g), sliced thickly

1 medium lemon (140g)

400g can artichoke hearts, drained, quartered

2 tablespoons drained capers, rinsed

30g butter

1 teaspoon brown sugar

4 medium seedless oranges (960g), sliced thinly

3 large red radishes (150g), sliced thinly

½ small red onion (50g), sliced thinly

¾ cup (135g) seeded kalamata olives

LEMON DRESSING

1 clove garlic, crushed

½ teaspoon sweet paprika

½ teaspoon ground cumin

2 tablespoons lemon juice

2 tablespoons olive oil

2 tablespoons finely chopped fresh parsley

1 teaspoon orange-flower water

½ teaspoon ground cinnamon

1   Cook lamb and onion on heated oiled barbecue plate until lamb is browned all over and onion soft.

2   Cut lemon into eight wedges. Place lamb, onion and lemon in disposable baking dish with artichoke hearts, capers, butter and sugar. Cook in covered barbecue, using indirect heat, following manufacturer's instructions, about 30 minutes or until lamb is cooked as desired.

3   Make lemon dressing.

4   Overlap alternate slices of orange and radish around edge of serving plate; overlap remaining slices in centre. Top with onion and olives; drizzle with dressing.

5   Serve lamb, vegetables and lemon with salad.

LEMON DRESSING   Place ingredients in screw-top jar; shake well.

SERVES 4
per serving   27.5g carbohydrate; 29.1g fat; 1898kJ (454 cal); 20.2g protein

mango chutney lamb with rocket snap pea salad

PREPARATION TIME 10 MINUTES   COOKING TIME 10 MINUTES

⅓ cup (80ml) yogurt

⅓ cup (80ml) mango chutney

⅓ cup (80ml) sweet chilli sauce

12 lamb cutlets (1kg)

250g sugar snap peas

150g rocket, trimmed

¼ cup (60ml) olive oil

2 tablespoons balsamic vinegar

2 large wholemeal pitta, cut into 4 wedges

1   Combine yogurt, chutney and sauce in large bowl.

2   Cook lamb on heated oiled grill plate (or grill or barbecue) until browned both sides and cooked as desired, brushing with yogurt mixture.

3   Meanwhile, boil, steam or microwave peas until just tender; drain. Rinse peas under cold water; drain. Toss peas and rocket in large bowl with combined oil and vinegar.

4   Serve salad with lamb and pitta.

SERVES 4
per serving   38.8g carbohydrate; 36g fat; 2516kJ (602 cal); 27.4g protein

lamb and haloumi kebabs

PREPARATION TIME 30 MINUTES (PLUS REFRIGERATION TIME)   COOKING TIME 15 MINUTES

1.2kg diced lamb

300g semi-dried tomatoes

600g haloumi cheese, chopped coarsely

½ cup (125ml) red wine vinegar

2 cloves garlic, crushed

⅓ cup (80ml) olive oil

150g mesclun

1   Thread lamb, tomato and cheese onto 12 skewers.

2   Place kebabs in shallow dish; pour over combined vinegar, garlic and oil. Cover; refrigerate 3 hours or overnight.

3   Drain kebabs; discard marinade. Cook kebabs on heated oiled grill plate (or grill or barbecue) until browned all over and cooked as desired.

4   Serve kebabs with mesclun.

SERVES 4
per serving 29.3g carbohydrate; 73.7g fat; 4995kJ (1195 cal); 103.2g protein
tip If using bamboo skewers, soak in water for at least 1 hour before using to avoid them splintering and scorching.

dhal with minted cucumber yogurt

PREPARATION TIME 20 MINUTES   COOKING TIME 35 MINUTES

2 cups (500ml) water

1 cup (200g) red lentils

1 teaspoon ground turmeric

1 teaspoon cumin seeds

1 teaspoon black mustard seeds

20g butter

2 green onions, sliced thinly

1 fresh small red thai chilli, chopped finely

8cm piece fresh ginger (40g), grated

1 clove garlic, crushed

1 small tomato (130g), seeded, chopped finely

1 teaspoon garam masala

1 tablespoon vegetable oil

500g lamb fillet, sliced thinly

MINTED CUCUMBER YOGURT

2 lebanese cucumbers (260g), seeded, chopped finely

1 cup (280g) yogurt

½ cup thinly sliced fresh mint

¼ cup (60ml) lime juice

1   Combine the water, lentils and turmeric in large saucepan; bring to a boil. Reduce heat; simmer, uncovered, about 15 minutes or until lentils are tender, stirring occasionally.

2   Meanwhile, make minted cucumber yogurt.

3   Cook seeds in large heated frying pan, stirring until fragrant. Add butter, onion, chilli, ginger, garlic and tomato; cook, stirring, 5 minutes. Add lentil mixture to pan; stir over low heat until heated through. Remove from heat; stir in garam masala.

4   Meanwhile, heat oil in large saucepan; cook lamb, in batches, until browned all over and cooked through.

5   Serve dhal topped with lamb and minted cucumber yogurt.

MINTED CUCUMBER YOGURT Combine ingredients in small bowl.

SERVES 4
per serving 28.9g carbohydrate; 12.6g fat; 1743kJ (417 cal); 46.5g protein

slow-roasted lamb shanks with white bean puree and caramelised red onion

PREPARATION TIME 20 MINUTES   COOKING TIME 4 HOURS 30 MINUTES

1 tablespoon olive oil

8 french-trimmed lamb shanks
  (approximately 1.2kg)

2 teaspoons sugar

1½ cups (375ml) dry red wine

2 cups (500ml) beef stock

3 cloves garlic, crushed

20g butter

1 small brown onion (80g),
  chopped finely

1 trimmed celery stalk (100g),
  chopped finely

1 tablespoon plain flour

1 tablespoon tomato paste

4 sprigs fresh rosemary,
  chopped coarsely

WHITE BEAN PUREE

2 x 400g cans cannellini beans,
  rinsed, drained

1 cup (250ml) chicken stock

4 cloves garlic, quartered

1 tablespoon lemon juice

2 tablespoons olive oil

CARAMELISED RED ONION

40g butter

2 small red onions (200g),
  sliced thinly

2 tablespoons brown sugar

¼ cup (60ml) raspberry vinegar

1   Preheat oven to slow.

2   Heat oil in large flameproof baking dish; cook shanks until browned all over. Stir in sugar, wine, stock and garlic; bring to a boil. Transfer lamb to slow oven; roast, covered, about 4 hours, turning twice during cooking.

3   Make white bean puree. Make caramelised onion.

4   Remove lamb from dish; cover to keep warm. Pour pan liquids into large heatproof jug.

5   Return dish to heat, melt butter; cook onion and celery, stirring, until celery is just tender. Stir in flour; cook, stirring, 2 minutes. Add reserved pan liquids, tomato paste and rosemary; bring to a boil. Reduce heat; simmer, uncovered, stirring until mixture boils and thickens. Strain wine sauce into large heatproof jug.

6   Serve lamb with sauce, bean puree and caramelised onion.

WHITE BEAN PUREE   Combine beans and stock in medium saucepan; bring to a boil. Reduce heat; simmer, covered, 20 minutes. Uncover; simmer, stirring occasionally, about 10 minutes or until liquid is absorbed. Blend or process beans, garlic and juice until almost smooth. With motor operating, gradually add oil in thin, steady stream until mixture forms a smooth puree.

CARAMELISED RED ONION   Melt butter in medium saucepan; cook onion, stirring, about 15 minutes or until browned and soft. Stir in sugar and vinegar; cook, stirring, about 15 minutes or until onion is caramelised.

SERVES 4
per serving 35g carbohydrate; 43.9g fat; 3674kJ (879 cal); 72.3g protein

mustard lamb cutlets with basil cream and mixed vegetables

PREPARATION TIME 25 MINUTES (PLUS REFRIGERATION TIME)   COOKING TIME 40 MINUTES

1 rack of lamb with 4 cutlets

¾ cup (180ml) olive oil

½ cup coarsely chopped fresh basil

1 clove garlic, crushed

2 medium potatoes (400g)

2 medium yellow zucchini (240g)

2 medium green zucchini (240g)

1 large red capsicum (350g)

1 large yellow capsicum (350g)

4 medium baby eggplant (240g)

4 spring onions (100g)

200g haloumi cheese, sliced thinly

1 tablespoon caraway
    seeds, toasted

1 tablespoon finely grated
    lemon rind

1 clove garlic, extra

2 teaspoons ground cumin

1 tablespoon finely chopped fresh
    lemon thyme

2 tablespoons finely chopped capers

2 tablespoons wholegrain mustard

BASIL CREAM

2 teaspoons olive oil

1 medium white onion (150g),
    sliced thinly

1 clove garlic, crushed

½ cup (125ml) dry white wine

300ml cream

½ cup coarsely chopped fresh basil

1   Cut lamb racks into double cutlets. Combine ¼ cup of the oil, basil and garlic in large shallow dish, add cutlets; toss to coat cutlets in marinade. Cover; refrigerate 3 hours or overnight.

2   Slice all vegetables thickly lengthways. Cook vegetables and cheese, in batches, on heated oiled grill plate (or grill or barbecue), uncovered, until browned both sides and tender. Transfer vegetables and cheese to large serving platter; drizzle with combined seeds, rind, extra garlic, cumin, thyme, capers and remaining oil.

3   Cook drained cutlets, uncovered, on same plate until browned all over and cooked as desired.

4   Make basil cream.

5   Spread lamb with mustard; serve lamb with basil cream and vegetables.

BASIL CREAM Heat oil in medium pan; cook onion and garlic, stirring, until onion softens. Add wine, reduce heat; simmer, uncovered, about 5 minutes or until reduced by half. Add cream; boil about 5 minutes or until sauce thickens. Remove from heat; stir in basil.

SERVES 4
per serving 28.7g carbohydrate; 99.1g fat; 4828kJ (1155 cal); 35g protein

merguez, beetroot and lentil salad

PREPARATION TIME 30 MINUTES   COOKING TIME 50 MINUTES

1 cup (200g) brown lentils

2 sprigs fresh thyme

20 baby red beetroots (500g)

20 baby golden beetroots (500g)

6 merguez sausages (640g)

1 medium brown onion (150g), chopped finely

2 teaspoons yellow mustard seeds

2 teaspoons ground cumin

1 teaspoon ground coriander

½ cup (125ml) chicken stock

500g spinach, trimmed, chopped coarsely

THYME DRESSING

1 teaspoon finely chopped fresh thyme

1 clove garlic, crushed

½ cup (125ml) red wine vinegar

¼ cup (60ml) extra virgin olive oil

1 Make thyme dressing.

2 Cook lentils with thyme sprigs, uncovered, in large saucepan of boiling water until tender; drain lentils, discard thyme sprigs. Place lentils in large bowl with half of the dressing; toss gently to combine.

3 Meanwhile, discard leaves and most of the stalk of each beetroot. Boil, steam or microwave unpeeled beetroots until just tender; drain. When cool enough to handle, peel beetroots; cut each beetroot in half.

4 Cook sausages in heated large non-stick frying pan until browned and cooked through. Cool 5 minutes; slice thickly.

5 Reheat same pan; cook onion, seeds and spices, stirring, until onion softens. Add stock; bring to a boil. Remove from heat; stir in spinach.

6 Add spinach mixture, beetroot, sausage and remaining dressing to lentil mixture; toss gently to combine.

THYME DRESSING Place ingredients in screw-top jar; shake well.

SERVES 4

per serving 35.7g carbohydrate; 41.3g fat; 2872kJ (687 cal); 44.7g protein
tips Merguez sausages, can be found at most delicatessens and sausage specialists.

tex-mex ribs with sage and bacon corn

PREPARATION TIME 10 MINUTES (PLUS REFRIGERATION TIME)   COOKING TIME 55 MINUTES

4 corn cobs (1.6kg)

5 litres (20 cups) water

¼ cup (60ml) milk

⅓ cup (80ml) barbecue sauce

1 teaspoon chilli powder

35g packet taco seasoning mix

1kg pork spareribs

2 tablespoons coarsely chopped fresh sage

2 bacon rashers (140g), sliced thinly

1 Peel husks back from corn, leaving them attached at base; remove silk, fold husks back over corn. Soak corn in combined water and milk. Cover; refrigerate 3 hours or overnight.

2 Combine sauce, chilli powder and seasoning in large bowl; add ribs, coat in mixture. Cover; refrigerate 3 hours or overnight.

3 Place ribs in disposable baking dish. Cook in covered barbecue, using indirect heat, following manufacturer's instructions, about 55 minutes or until tender, brushing ribs occasionally with pan juices.

4 Meanwhile, gently peel husk back from corn, press combined sage and bacon onto corn; tie husks with kitchen string to enclose filling. Cook in covered barbecue, using indirect heat, following manufacturer's instructions, about 40 minutes or until tender.

5 Serve corn with ribs.

SERVES 4

per serving 40.5g carbohydrate; 17.1g fat; 2065kJ (494 cal); 44.4g protein

sweet and spicy pork skewers

PREPARATION TIME 50 MINUTES (PLUS REFRIGERATION TIME)   COOKING TIME 10 MINUTES

750g pork fillets

6 cloves garlic, crushed

2 tablespoons honey

2 teaspoons hot paprika

¼ cup finely chopped fresh flat-leaf parsley

1½ cup (375ml) extra virgin olive oil

2 egg yolks

1 clove garlic, crushed, extra

1 teaspoon finely grated lemon rind

2 tablespoons lemon juice

1 teaspoon bottled horseradish

500g celeriac, trimmed, peeled

1 large red apple (200g)

2 medium carrots (240g), grated coarsely

1 cup (100g) walnuts, toasted, chopped coarsely

¼ cup coarsely chopped chopped fresh

flat-leaf parsley

1 bunch (15g) fresh chives, cut into 7cm lengths

1 Cut pork into 3cm cubes; combine with garlic, honey, paprika, finely chopped parsley and ½ cup of the oil in large bowl. Cover; refrigerate 3 hours or overnight.

2 Blend or process yolks, garlic, rind and juice until combined. With motor operating, gradually add remaining oil; process until dressing thickens and is smooth. Stir in horseradish.

3 Using mandoline or sharp knife, cut celeriac and apple into very thin slices; cut slices into matchstick-size pieces. Place in large bowl of water to prevent discolouration.

4 Thread pork onto skewers; discard marinade. Cook skewers, in batches, in heated oiled grill plate (or grill or barbecue) until browned and cooked through.

5 Place drained celeriac and apple in large bowl with carrot, nuts, coarsely chopped parsley, chives and horseradish dressing; toss gently to combine.

6 Serve pork with salad.

SERVES 4
per serving 26.3g carbohydrate; 109.9g fat; 5321kJ (1273 cal); 48.7g protein
tip Soak bamboo skewers in water for at least 1 hour before using to prevent them splintering and scorching.

pork chops valencia with roasted garlic celeriac

PREPARATION TIME 15 MINUTES   COOKING TIME 1 HOUR

1 large celeriac (1.5kg)

1 large garlic bulb, cloves separated

2 tablespoons olive oil

4 pork loin chops (800g)

½ cup (175g) orange marmalade

2 tablespoons mild chilli sauce

1 tablespoon cider vinegar

1cm piece fresh ginger (5g), grated

1 teaspoon ground cumin

3 green onions, sliced thinly

1 Peel celeriac; cut into 3cm pieces. Combine celeriac and garlic in disposable baking dish; stir in oil. Cook in covered barbecue, using indirect heat, following manufacturer's instructions, about 1 hour or until celeriac is golden brown and tender, turning occasionally during cooking.

2 Meanwhile, cook pork, uncovered, in large heated oiled frying pan until browned both sides and cooked through. Remove pork from pan; cover to keep warm.

3 Cook marmalade, sauce, vinegar, ginger and cumin in small frying pan, stirring, until sauce thickens slightly; stir onion into sauce.

4 Cut garlic in half crossways; squeeze pulp over celeriac. Toss with parsley. Drizzle pork with sauce; serve with celeriac.

SERVES 4
per serving 34g carbohydrate; 30.4g fat; 2370kJ (567 cal); 39.8g protein

pork with orange mustard sauce on kumara mash

PREPARATION TIME 10 MINUTES   COOKING TIME 30 MINUTES

4 medium pork steaks (600g)

1 clove garlic, crushed

1cm piece fresh ginger (5g), grated

1 tablespoon marmalade

1 teaspoon finely grated orange rind

2 tablespoons orange juice

2 tablespoons olive oil

700g kumara, chopped coarsely

20g butter

1 tablespoon maple syrup

50g butter, extra

2 tablespoons wholegrain mustard

½ cup (125ml) orange juice, extra

½ cup (125ml) dry white wine

¼ cup (60ml) chicken stock

¼ cup (60g) sour cream

1 Combine pork in large bowl with garlic, ginger, marmalade, rind, juice and half of the oil. Refrigerate until required.

2 Boil, steam or microwave kumara until tender; drain. Mash kumara in large bowl with butter and maple syrup; cover to keep warm.

3 Drain pork; reserve marinade. Heat remaining oil in large frying pan; cook pork, in batches, until browned both sides and cooked as desired. Cover to keep warm.

4 Heat extra butter in same frying pan, cook mustard, extra juice, wine, stock and reserved marinade; bring to a boil. Reduce heat; simmer, uncovered, about 5 minutes or until sauce reduces by half. Remove sauce from heat; stir in sour cream.

5 Serve kumara with pork; drizzle with sauce.

SERVES 4
per serving 34.4g carbohydrate; 33.7g fat; 2495kJ (597 cal); 34.8g protein

baked mustard pork with caramelised apple

PREPARATION TIME 10 MINUTES   COOKING TIME 25 MINUTES

1 medium red onion (170g), cut into
    thin wedges

1 tablespoon olive oil

750g pork fillets, trimmed

½ cup (140g) honey dijon wholegrain mustard

½ cup (125ml) apple juice

⅓ cup (80ml) vegetable stock

¼ cup coarsely chopped fresh
    flat-leaf parsley

60g butter

3 large apples (600g), peeled, cored,
    sliced thinly

1 tablespoon brown sugar

150g watercress

1 Preheat oven to very hot.

2 Combine onion and oil in large flameproof baking dish. Brush pork all over with mustard; place on onion in baking dish. Bake, uncovered, in very hot oven about 20 minutes or until cooked as desired. Remove pork from dish, cover; stand 5 minutes.

3 Place dish over heat, add juice and stock; bring to a boil. Reduce heat; simmer, uncovered, about 3 minutes or until sauce thickens slightly. Stir in parsley.

4 Meanwhile, melt butter in large frying pan; cook apple and sugar, stirring occasionally, about 10 minutes or until caramelised.

5 Slice pork thickly; serve pork with onion sauce, apple and watercress.

SERVES 4
per serving 35.4g carbohydrate; 22.6g fat; 2186kJ (523 cal); 45.6g protein

pork loin with fresh peach chutney

PREPARATION TIME 35 MINUTES   COOKING TIME 2 HOURS 15 MINUTES

1.5kg boned pork loin

1 tablespoon olive oil

½ teaspoon celery seeds

1 teaspoon sea salt

200g baby spinach leaves

FRESH PEACH CHUTNEY

1 large peach (220g), chopped coarsely

1 large brown onion (200g), chopped coarsely

1 tablespoon coarsely chopped raisins

1cm piece fresh ginger (5g), grated

½ cup (110g) sugar

½ cup (125ml) apple cider vinegar

1 cinnamon stick

¼ teaspoon ground clove

1 Make fresh peach chutney.

2 Preheat oven to hot. Remove rind from loin; reserve. Rub pork with half of the oil; sprinkle with seeds.

3 Place pork on wire rack in large baking dish; roast, uncovered, in hot oven, about 1 hour or until juices run clear when pierced with skewer. Remove from oven; place pork on board, cover to keep warm.

4 Increase oven temperature to very hot.

5 Remove excess fat from underside of reserved rind; score rind, rub with remaining oil and sea salt. Place rind, fatty-side up, on wire rack in baking dish; bake, uncovered, in very hot oven about 15 minutes or until crisp and browned. Drain on absorbent paper.

6 Serve thickly sliced pork and rind with chutney and spinach.

FRESH PEACH CHUTNEY Combine ingredients in medium saucepan, stir over heat, without boiling, until sugar dissolves; bring to a boil. Reduce heat; simmer, uncovered, stirring occasionally, about 1¾ hours or until mixture thickens.

SERVES 4
per serving 36.8g carbohydrate; 27g fat; 3482kJ (833 cal); 110g protein
tip The chutney can be made up to a week ahead. Place in a sterilised jar while still hot; seal, cool, then refrigerate until required.

pork with pear chutney and pumpkin mash

PREPARATION TIME 30 MINUTES   COOKING TIME 30 MINUTES

1 tablespoon vegetable oil

750g pork fillets

500g pumpkin, chopped coarsely

2 tablespoons milk

500g broccoli

PEAR CHUTNEY

2 small pears (450g)

1 small brown onion (80g), chopped finely

¼ cup (60ml) apple cider vinegar

2 tablespoons bourbon

¼ cup (55g) firmly packed brown sugar

1 Make pear chutney.

2 Meanwhile, heat oil in large frying pan; cook pork, in batches, over medium heat until browned all over and cooked as desired.

3 Boil, steam or microwave pumpkin until tender; drain. Mash pumpkin with milk in large bowl until smooth.

4 Separate broccoli into florets. Boil, steam or microwave until just tender; drain. Serve pork with pear chutney, pumpkin mash and broccoli.

PEAR CHUTNEY Peel, core and thinly slice pears. Combine pears with remaining ingredients in medium saucepan; bring to a boil. Reduce heat; simmer, uncovered, about 25 minutes or until liquid is almost evaporated.

SERVES 4
per serving 40.7g carbohydrate; 10.1g fat; 1860kJ (445 cal); 48.1g protein
tip For a non-alcoholic version, substitute apple juice for bourbon.

honey soy pork with spinach and snow pea salad

PREPARATION TIME 10 MINUTES (PLUS REFRIGERATION TIME)   COOKING TIME 2 HOURS

800g pork neck

2 cloves garlic, crushed

2 tablespoons olive oil

1 tablespoon brown sugar

¼ cup (90g) honey

2cm piece fresh ginger (10g), grated

2 tablespoons soy sauce

2 tablespoons lime juice

SPINACH AND SNOW PEA SALAD

200g baby spinach leaves

100g snow peas, trimmed, sliced thinly

4 green onions, sliced thinly

⅓ cup (50g) toasted pine nuts, chopped coarsely

½ cup (40g) flaked parmesan cheese

⅓ cup (80ml) olive oil

1 teaspoon finely grated lime rind

¼ cup (60ml) lime juice

1 tablespoon sugar

1   Place pork in large shallow dish; pour combined remaining ingredients over pork. Cover; refrigerate 3 hours or overnight, turning pork occasionally in marinade.

2   Preheat oven to moderate.

3   Drain pork; reserve marinade. Wrap pork in three layers of foil, securing ends tightly. Bake in moderate oven about 2 hours or until cooked as desired. Stand 10 minutes; slice thinly.

4   Meanwhile, place reserved marinade in small saucepan; bring to a boil. Reduce heat; simmer, uncovered, 5 minutes.

5   Make spinach and snow pea salad.

6   Drizzle pork with marinade; serve with salad.

SPINACH AND SNOW PEA SALAD   Place spinach, snow peas, onion, nuts and cheese in large bowl. Just before serving, add combined remaining ingredients; toss gently to combine.

SERVES 4
per serving 28.8g carbohydrate; 55.6g fat; 3394kJ (812 cal); 50.7g protein

grilled pork cutlets with green apple salad

PREPARATION TIME 20 MINUTES   COOKING TIME 10 MINUTES (PLUS COOLING TIME)

4 x 250g pork cutlets

3 medium apples (450g), sliced thinly

4 green onions, sliced thinly

2 cups loosely packed fresh mint leaves

1 cup loosely packed fresh coriander leaves

½ cup (125ml) lemon juice

¾ cup (110g) toasted unsalted cashews

PALM SUGAR DRESSING

¼ cup (65g) grated palm sugar

2 tablespoons fish sauce

2cm piece fresh ginger (10g), grated

1   Cook pork on heated oiled grill plate (or grill or barbecue) until browned both sides and cooked as desired.

2   Meanwhile, make palm sugar dressing.

3   Place apple, onion, mint, coriander and juice in large bowl; pour over half of the palm sugar dressing, toss gently to combine.

4   Divide pork among serving plates. Top with salad, sprinkle with nuts, then drizzle with remaining dressing.

PALM SUGAR DRESSING   Combine ingredients in small saucepan; bring to a boil. Remove from heat; strain. Cool 15 minutes.

SERVES 4
per serving 35.8g carbohydrate; 34.4g fat; 2437kJ (583 cal); 33.7g protein

marmalade chicken with asparagus walnut salad

PREPARATION TIME 15 MINUTES   COOKING TIME 1 HOUR 30 MINUTES

½ cup (175g) orange marmalade

2 tablespoons Grand Marnier

¼ cup (60ml) orange juice

1.6kg chicken

ASPARAGUS WALNUT SALAD

500g asparagus, trimmed, halved

¼ cup (30g) finely chopped toasted walnuts

2 teaspoons wholegrain mustard

1 tablespoon red wine vinegar

1 shallot (25g), chopped finely

¼ cup (60ml) extra virgin olive oil

100g baby rocket leaves

1   Combine marmalade, liqueur and juice in small pan; bring to a boil. Reduce heat; simmer, uncovered, about 5 minutes or until glaze thickens. Divide glaze into two portions.

2   Place chicken on roasting rack or basket; cook in covered barbecue, using indirect heat, following manufacturer's instructions, 1 hour. Brush chicken with one portion of glaze, cook a further 20 minutes or until browned all over and cooked through.

3   Make asparagus walnut salad.

4   Just before serving, brush chicken with remaining glaze. Serve with salad.

ASPARAGUS WALNUT SALAD Boil, steam or microwave asparagus until tender; drain. Blend or process half of the walnuts with mustard, vinegar, shallot and oil until smooth. Combine asparagus with dressing in large bowl, sprinkle with remaining walnuts.

SERVES 4
per serving 36.9g carbohydrate; 47.7g fat; 3198kJ (765 cal); 43.8g protein

chicken burgers with avocado cream

PREPARATION TIME 30 MINUTES   COOKING TIME 10 MINUTES

800g chicken mince

2 bacon rashers (140g), rind removed,
     chopped finely

⅓ cup (25g) finely grated parmesan cheese

3 green onions, chopped finely

1 tablespoon finely chopped fresh thyme

1 egg, beaten lightly

⅓ cup (35g) packaged breadcrumbs

4 thick slices rye bread (200g)

1 cup (55g) snow pea sprouts

2 medium tomatoes (260g), sliced thinly

1 medium carrot (120g), sliced thinly

AVOCADO CREAM

1 medium avocado (250g), chopped coarsely

125g packaged cream cheese, softened

1 tablespoon lemon juice

1   Using hand, combine chicken, bacon, cheese, onion, thyme, egg and breadcrumbs in medium bowl. Using hands, shape mixture into four patties.

2   Cook patties on heated oiled grill plate (or grill or barbecue), uncovered, until browned and cooked through.

3   Toast bread both sides.

4   Meanwhile, make avocado cream.

5   Top bread with sprouts, patties, tomato, avocado cream and carrot.

AVOCADO CREAM Place ingredients in small bowl; mash with a fork until well combined.

SERVES 4
per serving 40.4g carbohydrate; 44.2g fat; 3311kJ (792 cal); 58.4g protein

roast chicken on parsnip mash with tomato chutney

PREPARATION TIME 20 MINUTES   COOKING TIME 1 HOUR 20 MINUTES

1.8kg free-range chicken

1 tablespoon olive oil

2 teaspoons sea salt

1kg large parsnips,
chopped coarsely

2 cloves garlic, crushed

40g butter, chopped

½ cup (125ml) milk

TOMATO CHUTNEY

1 tablespoon olive oil

1 small red onion (100g),
chopped coarsely

4 small tomatoes (520g),
chopped coarsely

1 clove garlic, crushed

¼ cup (55g) firmly packed
brown sugar

1 tablespoon balsamic vinegar

1   Preheat oven to hot.

2   Wash chicken under cold water; pat dry with absorbent paper. Using kitchen scissors, cut along both sides of backbone of chicken; discard backbone. Place chicken, skin-side up, on board; using heel of hand, press down on breastbone to flatten chicken.

3   Rub oil all over chicken, sprinkle with salt; place chicken on oiled wire rack over baking dish. Roast, uncovered, in hot oven 20 minutes. Reduce oven to moderate; roast, uncovered, 1 hour or until chicken is browned and cooked through. Cover with foil halfway through cooking if chicken starts to overbrown.

4   Meanwhile, make tomato chutney.

5   Boil, steam or microwave parsnip until tender; drain. Mash parsnip in large bowl until smooth; stir in garlic, butter and milk. Push parsnip mash through fine sieve or food mill (mouli) back into same bowl. Serve mash with chicken; top with tomato chutney.

TOMATO CHUTNEY   Combine ingredients in large saucepan, stir over heat until sugar dissolves; bring to a boil. Reduce heat; simmer, uncovered, about 1 hour or until chutney is thickened, stirring occasionally.

SERVES 4
per serving   39.9g carbohydrate; 59.8g fat; 4197kJ (1004 cal); 69.8g protein

caribbean-style chicken stew

PREPARATION TIME 45 MINUTES   COOKING TIME 50 MINUTES

1kg chicken thigh fillets

2 teaspoons ground allspice

1 teaspoon ground cinnamon

1 tablespoon finely chopped fresh thyme

¼ cup (60ml) olive oil

2 medium brown onions (300g), sliced thinly

2 cloves garlic, crushed

4cm piece fresh ginger (20g), grated

5 medium tomatoes (650g), peeled, seeded,
   chopped finely

2 tablespoons brown sugar

2 teaspoons finely grated orange rind

2 tablespoons soy sauce

1 medium kumara (400g), chopped coarsely

2 fresh corn cobs, sliced thickly

125g baby spinach leaves

1   Cut chicken into 2cm strips. Toss chicken in combined spices and thyme.

2   Heat half of the oil in large saucepan; cook chicken, in batches, stirring, until browned. Drain on absorbent paper.

3   Heat remaining oil in pan; cook onion, garlic and ginger, stirring, until onion softens. Add tomato, sugar, rind, sauce, kumara, corn and chicken; cook, covered, about 15 minutes or until chicken is cooked through and vegetables are tender. Remove cover; simmer 5 minutes.

4   Remove from heat. Add spinach; stir until spinach is wilted.

SERVES 4
per serving 37.2g carbohydrate; 33g fat; 2763kJ (661 cal); 54.5g protein

baked chicken, kumara and spinach

PREPARATION TIME 15 MINUTES   COOKING TIME 45 MINUTES

250g fetta cheese

250g packet frozen spinach, thawed

2 medium kumara (800g), sliced thinly

700g chicken breast fillets, sliced thinly

1 medium brown onion (150g), chopped finely

2 teaspoons finely chopped fresh thyme

¼ cup (60ml) light sour cream

½ cup (125ml) chicken stock

2 teaspoons plain flour

1 tablespoon water

2 cups (250g) grated pizza cheese

1   Preheat oven to moderately hot. Crumble fetta into medium bowl. Using hands, squeeze excess moisture from spinach; mix spinach with fetta.

2   Boil, steam or microwave kumara until just tender; drain.

3   Meanwhile, cook chicken, in batches, in medium heated oiled frying pan until just cooked through and browned all over.

4   Cook onion and thyme in same pan, stirring, until onion softens; stir into fetta mixture. Cook sour cream, stock and blended flour and water in same pan, stirring, until mixture boils and thickens.

5   Place half of the kumara, half of the chicken and all of the fetta mixture, in layers, in oiled 3-litre (12-cup) ovenproof dish. Repeat layering with remaining kumara and chicken; pour cream mixture over the top. Sprinkle with pizza cheese; bake, uncovered, in moderately hot oven about 30 minutes or until cheese is browned lightly.

SERVES 4
per serving 28.5g carbohydrate; 41.4g fat; 3235kJ (774 cal); 72.5g protein

chicken with mushrooms and celeriac

PREPARATION TIME 35 MINUTES   COOKING TIME 1 HOUR 30 MINUTES

2 large red capsicums (700g)

8 chicken thigh cutlets (1.2kg)

¼ cup (35g) plain flour

1 tablespoon olive oil

1½ teaspoons caraway seeds

5 dried juniper berries

1 medium celeriac (630g), chopped coarsely

250g mushrooms, halved

1½ cups (375ml) chicken stock

1 tablespoon tomato paste

1 tablespoon cornflour

1 tablespoon water

1 tablespoon finely chopped fresh
    flat-leaf parsley

1   Quarter capsicums; remove seeds and membranes. Grill capsicum, skin-side up, until skin blisters and blackens. Peel away skin; slice capsicum into strips.

2   Toss chicken in flour; shake away excess flour. Heat oil in 3-litre (12-cup) flameproof casserole dish; cook chicken, in batches, until browned. Drain on absorbent paper.

3   Cook seeds, berries, celeriac and mushrooms in same dish, stirring, until mushrooms are just soft.

4   Return chicken to dish with capsicum, stock and paste. Cook, covered, in moderate oven about 45 minutes or until chicken is cooked through and tender.

5   Stir in blended cornflour and water; stir over heat until mixture boils and thickens slightly.

6   Serve sprinkled with parsley.

SERVES 4
per serving 26.4g carbohydrate; 35.9g fat; 2525kJ (604 cal); 44.2g protein

honey soy chicken salad

PREPARATION TIME 20 MINUTES   COOKING TIME 15 MINUTES

600g chicken breast fillets, sliced thinly

2 tablespoons soy sauce

⅓ cup (115g) honey

1 clove garlic, crushed

2 fresh small red thai chillies, chopped finely

300g snow peas, trimmed

1 small carrot (120g)

1 tablespoon peanut oil

2 cups (160g) finely shredded savoy cabbage

2 medium red capsicums (400g), sliced thinly

1 lebanese cucumber (130g), seeded, sliced thinly

4 green onions, sliced thinly

½ cup loosely packed fresh mint leaves

2 tablespoons lime juice

2 teaspoons sesame oil

1   Place chicken in medium bowl with sauce, honey, garlic and half of the chilli; toss to coat chicken in chilli mixture. Cover; refrigerate until required.

2   Boil, steam or microwave snow peas until just tender; drain. Rinse immediately under cold water; drain. Using vegetable peeler, slice carrot into ribbons.

3   Heat peanut oil in wok or large frying pan; stir-fry drained chicken, in batches, until browned and cooked through.

4   Place chicken, snow peas and carrot in large serving bowl with remaining ingredients and remaining chilli; toss gently to combine.

SERVES 4
per serving 33.7g carbohydrate; 15.6g fat; 1764kJ (422 cal); 37.6g protein
tip You can use a large barbecued chicken instead of the breast fillets, if you prefer; discard bones and skin, then shred meat coarsely before tossing with remaining salad ingredients.

spicy chicken legs with mango salad

PREPARATION TIME 40 MINUTES   COOKING TIME 30 MINUTES

2 teaspoons sesame oil

8 chicken drumsticks (1.2kg)

½ cup (125ml) chicken stock

3 teaspoons honey

2 tablespoons rice vinegar

1 teaspoon five-spice powder

6 cloves garlic, crushed

¼ cup (60ml) soy sauce

½ cup (125ml) water

MANGO SALAD

2 green mangoes (700g),
  sliced thinly

4 green onions, sliced thinly

1 cup loosely packed
  coriander leaves

150g snow peas, trimmed, halved

2 lebanese cucumbers (260g),
  seeded, sliced thinly

1½ cups (120g) bean sprouts

LIME AND VINEGAR DRESSING

¼ cup (60ml) lime juice

¼ cup (60ml) rice vinegar

2 teaspoon peanut oil

1 Heat oil in large deep frying pan; cook chicken, in batches, about 5 minutes or until brown all over.

2 Meanwhile, combine stock, honey, vinegar, five-spice, garlic, sauce and the water in medium jug.

3 Return chicken to pan with stock mixture; bring to a boil. Reduce heat; simmer, covered, about 20 minutes or until chicken is cooked through.

4 Meanwhile, make mango salad. Make lime and vinegar dressing.

5 Add dressing to salad; toss gently to combine. Divide salad among serving plates; top with chicken and remaining pan juices.

MANGO SALAD Combine ingredients in large bowl.

LIME AND VINEGAR DRESSING Place ingredients in screw-top jar; shake well.

SERVES 4
per serving 26g carbohydrate; 27g fat; 2132kJ (510 cal); 40.2g protein

chicken jambalaya

PREPARATION TIME 15 MINUTES   COOKING TIME 30 MINUTES

A well-known American creole dish, jambalaya is believed to have been devised when a New Orleans cook named Jean tossed together — or "balayez" in the Louisiana dialect — various leftovers and came up with such a delicious dish that diners named it "Jean Balayez".

1 tablespoon olive oil

1 medium brown onion (150g), chopped coarsely

1 medium red capsicum (200g), chopped coarsely

1 clove garlic, crushed

2 trimmed celery stalks (200g), sliced thinly

2 fresh small red thai chillies, seeded, sliced thinly

1½ cups (300g) basmati rice

½ cup (125ml) dry white wine

2½ cups (625ml) chicken stock

425g can crushed tomatoes

1 tablespoon tomato paste

700g chicken and herb sausages

⅓ cup coarsely chopped fresh coriander

1   Heat oil in large saucepan; cook onion, capsicum, garlic, celery and chilli, stirring, until vegetables soften. Stir in rice, wine, stock, undrained tomatoes and paste; bring to a boil. Reduce heat; simmer, covered, about 20 minutes or until liquid is absorbed.

2   Meanwhile, cook sausages, uncovered, in large frying pan until browned and cooked through. Drain on absorbent paper; slice thickly.

3   Stir sausage and coriander into jambalaya mixture just before serving.

SERVES 4
per serving 33g carbohydrate; 45.5g fat; 3499kJ (837 cal); 26.3g protein

oven-baked parmesan chicken

PREPARATION TIME 10 MINUTES   COOKING TIME 20 MINUTES

Curly endive, also known as frisée, is a loose-headed green vegetable having curly, ragged edged leaves and a slightly bitter flavour.

1 tablespoon plain flour

2 eggs, beaten lightly

2 cups (140g) stale breadcrumbs

⅓ cup (25g) coarsely grated parmesan cheese

2 tablespoons finely chopped fresh flat-leaf parsley

12 chicken tenderloins (900g)

1 cup firmly packed fresh basil leaves

½ cup (125ml) olive oil

¼ cup (60ml) lemon juice

1 clove garlic, quartered

¾ cup (120g) seeded kalamata olives

200g curly endive

40g baby rocket leaves

1   Preheat oven to hot.

2   Combine flour and egg in medium bowl; combine breadcrumbs, cheese and parsley in another medium bowl. Coat chicken, one piece at a time, first in flour mixture then in breadcrumb mixture. Place chicken, in single layer, on oiled oven tray; roast, uncovered, in hot oven about 15 minutes or until chicken is browned lightly and cooked through.

3   Meanwhile, blend or process basil, oil, juice and garlic until combined.

4   Serve chicken with combined olives, endive and rocket; drizzle with basil dressing.

SERVES 4
per serving 31.5g carbohydrate; 40g fat; 3085kJ (738 cal); 63g protein

pork fillet with apple and leek (see page 251)

warm chicken tabbouleh (see page 299)

green peppercorn chicken with avocado and mango salad

PREPARATION TIME 25 MINUTES   COOKING TIME 20 MINUTES

8 chicken thigh cutlets (1.2kg)

¼ cup (60g) wholegrain mustard

2 tablespoons drained green peppercorns,
chopped finely

2 cloves garlic, crushed

2 tablespoons lemon juice

¼ cup chopped fresh chives

¼ cup (60ml) olive oil

1 small brown onion (80g), chopped coarsely

1 cup (80g) mung bean sprouts

350g watercress

1 medium avocado (250g), sliced thinly

2 trimmed celery stalks (200g), sliced thinly

1 medium mango (430g), sliced thinly

CREAMY AVOCADO DRESSING

½ small avocado (100g)

½ cup (125ml) buttermilk

1 teaspoon wholegrain mustard

1 tablespoon olive oil

1 tablespoon lemon juice

1 teaspoon wasabi paste

1 Remove and discard skin from chicken; place chicken in large bowl, coat with combined mustard, peppercorns, garlic, juice, chives and 2 tablespoons of the oil.

2 Heat remaining oil in large non-stick frying pan; cook onion, stirring, until soft. Add chicken to pan; cook, brushing chicken occasionally with peppercorn mixture, until chicken is browned both sides and cooked through.

3 Meanwhile, make creamy avocado dressing.

4 Place sprouts, watercress, avocado, celery and mango in large bowl; drizzle with dressing.

5 Serve chicken with salad.

CREAMY AVOCADO DRESSING Blend or process ingredients until smooth.

SERVES 4
per serving 36.3g carbohydrate; 64.3g fat; 3825kJ (915 cal); 48.4g protein

coronation chicken

PREPARATION TIME 15 MINUTES   COOKING TIME 20 MINUTES

800g chicken breast fillets

1 cup (300g) mayonnaise

½ cup (120g) sour cream

1 teaspoon curry powder

2 cups loosely packed fresh basil leaves

5 ripe nectarines (850g), cut into wedges

1 cup (150g) toasted unsalted cashews

1 Poach chicken, covered, in large frying pan of boiling water about 10 minutes or until cooked through. Cool chicken in liquid 10 minutes; slice thinly.

2 Combine mayonnaise, cream and curry powder in large bowl. Add chicken, basil, nectarine and three-quarters of the nuts; toss gently to combine.

3 Serve salad, sprinkled with remaining nuts.

SERVES 4
per serving 40.4g carbohydrate; 66.7g fat; 4046kJ (968 cal); 52.7g protein

grilled duck liver salad with toffeed ginger and wasabi soy dressing

PREPARATION TIME 20 MINUTES (PLUS STANDING TIME)   COOKING TIME 5 MINUTES

Wasabi is a pungent root vegetable also known as Japanese horseradish, even though it's a member of the mustard family.

8 duck livers (500g)

2 cups (500ml) milk

80g fresh ginger, sliced thinly

½ cup (80g) icing sugar mixture

vegetable oil, for deep-frying

¼ cup (60ml) peanut oil

180g curly endive

125g mizuna

⅓ cup (80ml) soy sauce

2 teaspoons sesame oil

1 teaspoon wasabi paste

1   Trim and wash livers. Place in medium bowl with milk, cover; refrigerate overnight.

2   Drain livers, rinse under cold water, dry on absorbent paper; cut each liver into three pieces.

3   Coat ginger in icing sugar. Heat vegetable oil in wok or medium saucepan; deep-fry ginger, in batches, until crisp. Drain on absorbent paper.

4   Heat half of the peanut oil in large non-stick frying pan over high heat; sear liver quickly, in batches, both sides, until pieces are well browned but quite rare. Cover to keep warm.

5   Place endive and mizuna in large bowl with combined sauce, sesame oil, wasabi and remaining peanut oil; toss gently to combine. Divide salad among serving plates; top with liver and ginger.

SERVES 4
per serving 28.2g carbohydrate; 24.6g fat; 1643kJ (393 cal); 16.5g protein

chilli quail, mandarin and grape salad

PREPARATION TIME 40 MINUTES (PLUS REFRIGERATION TIME)   COOKING TIME 20 MINUTES

8 quails (1.6kg)

4 fresh small red thai chillies,
    chopped coarsely

2 cloves garlic, halved

¼ cup (60ml) olive oil

2 tablespoons lemon juice

4 medium mandarins (800g)

300g snow peas, trimmed, halved

400g watercress, trimmed

1 cup (160g) toasted
    blanched almonds

200g seedless red grapes,
    halved lengthways

1   Using kitchen scissors, cut along both sides of each quail's backbone; discard backbones. Place each quail flat, skin-side down, on chopping board; discard ribcages. Cut each quail into quarters.

2   Blend or process chilli, garlic, oil and half of the lemon juice until smooth; combine with quail pieces in large bowl. Cover; refrigerate 20 minutes.

3   Meanwhile, segment peeled mandarins over large bowl to save juice. Reserve segments with juice.

4   Cook undrained quail on heated oiled grill plate (or grill or barbecue) until browned both sides and cooked through.

5   Meanwhile, boil, steam or microwave peas until just tender; drain.

6   Place quail and peas in large bowl with mandarin segments and juice, watercress, nuts, grapes and remaining lemon juice; toss gently to combine.

SERVES 4
per serving 25.1g carbohydrate; 63.6g fat; 3833kJ (917 cal); 61.8g protein

chicken enchiladas with corn salsa

PREPARATION TIME 30 MINUTES   COOKING TIME 35 MINUTES

1 large red onion (300g), chopped finely

2 tablespoons vegetable oil

2 cloves garlic, crushed

1 tablespoon tomato paste

¼ cup (45g) drained bottled jalapeño chillies,
   chopped coarsely

400g can crushed tomatoes

1 cup (250ml) chicken stock

500g chicken breast fillets, sliced thinly

10 corn tortillas

2 cups (250g) coarsely grated cheddar cheese

½ cup (120g) sour cream

CORN SALSA

1 small red capsicum (150g), chopped finely

310g can corn kernels, drained

1 tablespoon lime juice

1 cup coarsely chopped fresh coriander

1 Reserve a quarter of the onion for the corn salsa (below). Preheat oven to moderate.

2 Heat oil in large frying pan; cook remaining onion with garlic, stirring, until onion softens. Add tomato paste, chilli, undrained tomatoes, stock and chicken; bring to a boil. Reduce heat; simmer, uncovered, until chicken is cooked through. Remove chicken from pan; cover to keep warm.

3 Soften tortillas according to manufacturer's instructions. Dip tortillas, one at a time, in tomato mixture in pan; place on board. Divide chicken and half of the cheese among tortillas, placing along edge; roll tortilla to enclose filling. Place enchiladas, seam-side down, in large oiled 3-litre (12-cup) shallow ovenproof dish; enchiladas should fit snugly, without overcrowding.

4 Pour remaining tomato mixture over enchiladas; top with sour cream, sprinkle with remaining cheese. Bake, uncovered, in moderate oven about 15 minutes or until heated through.

5 Meanwhile, make corn salsa. Divide enchiladas among serving plates; serve with corn salsa.

CORN SALSA Combine reserved onion in medium bowl with remaining ingredients.

SERVES 4
per serving 42.8g carbohydrate; 51.8g fat; 3520kJ (842 cal); 51.4g protein

waldorf salad

PREPARATION TIME 15 MINUTES   COOKING TIME 15 MINUTES

4 x 170g single chicken breast fillets

2 tablespoons lemon juice

1 tablespoon honey

2 teaspoons olive oil

4 medium red delicious apples (600g)

¼ cup (60ml) lemon juice, extra

5 trimmed celery stalks (500g)

1 cup (120g) coarsely chopped toasted walnuts

MAYONNAISE

2 egg yolks

2 teaspoons lemon juice

1 teaspoon dijon mustard

¾ cup (180ml) olive oil

1 Place chicken in large bowl with juice, honey and oil; toss to coat the chicken in mixture. Cook chicken on heated oiled grill plate (or grill or barbecue) until browned and cooked through.

2 Meanwhile, core and coarsely chop unpeeled apples. Combine apple in small bowl with extra juice. Coarsely chop celery.

3 Make mayonnaise. Combine apple, celery and walnuts in large bowl with mayonnaise. Serve salad topped with chicken.

MAYONNAISE Blend or process egg yolks, juice and mustard until smooth. With motor operating, add oil in thin, steady stream; process until mayonnaise thickens.

SERVES 4
per serving 25.5g carbohydrate; 71.1g fat; 3825kJ (915 cal); 45.7g protein

chicken with prunes and honey

PREPARATION TIME 20 MINUTES   COOKING TIME 1 HOUR

1.5kg chicken

¼ cup (60ml) olive oil

1 medium brown onion (150g), sliced thinly

1 teaspoon ground cinnamon

pinch saffron threads

¼ teaspoon ground turmeric

2 teaspoons ground ginger

1¼ cups (310ml) water

⅓ cup (120g) honey

½ cup (80g) seeded prunes

3 teaspoons sesame seeds

30g butter

½ cup (80g) blanched almonds

1 tablespoon thinly sliced preserved
    lemon rind

1 Halve chicken lengthways. Cut each half crossways through the centre; separate breasts from wings and thighs from legs. You will have eight pieces.

2 Heat oil in large deep frying pan; cook chicken, in batches, until well browned all over. Drain all but 1 tablespoon of the oil from pan.

3 Cook onion in same pan, stirring, until soft. Add spices; cook, stirring, until fragrant. Return chicken to pan; stir to coat chicken in onion mixture. Add the water; bring to a boil. Reduce heat; simmer, covered, about 30 minutes or until chicken is tender.

4 Remove chicken from pan; cover to keep warm. Add honey and prunes to pan; simmer, uncovered, about 15 minutes or until sauce thickens slightly.

5 Meanwhile, toast sesame seeds in small saucepan, stirring, until lightly browned. Remove from pan immediately.

6 Melt butter in same saucepan; cook almonds, stirring, until almonds are browned lightly. Remove from pan immediately.

7 Return chicken to frying pan; stir over heat until chicken is heated through. Divide chicken and sauce among serving plates; sprinkle with seeds, nuts and preserved lemon.

SERVES 4
per serving 34.5g carbohydrate; 60.4g fat; 3549kJ (849 cal); 44.9g protein

warm duck, orange and mushroom salad

PREPARATION TIME 25 MINUTES   COOKING TIME 15 MINUTES

2 tablespoons honey

¼ cup (60ml) orange juice

2 tablespoons soy sauce

1 clove garlic, crushed

4 duck breast fillets (600g)

300g oyster mushrooms

200g button mushrooms, sliced thickly

300g shiitake mushrooms, halved

3 large oranges (900g), segmented

100g lamb's lettuce leaves

1 Preheat oven to moderately hot.

2 Combine honey, juice, sauce and garlic in small bowl. Score each piece of duck shallowly; brush with about ¼ cup of the honey mixture.

3 Combine mushrooms with remaining honey mixture in large flameproof baking dish. Place duck on wire rack over dish; roast, uncovered, in moderately hot oven 10 minutes. Remove duck and wire rack from dish; drain mushrooms, reserving about a third of the pan juices. Place mushrooms in large bowl.

4 Replace duck on wire rack over same dish; brown under preheated grill until skin crisps. Slice duck thickly.

5 Add orange, lettuce and reserved pan juices to mushrooms; toss gently to combine. Divide salad among serving plates; top with duck slices.

SERVES 4
per serving 28.2g carbohydrate; 9g fat; 1417kJ (339 cal); 36.3g protein

salt and lemon-pepper squid with lemon mayonnaise

PREPARATION TIME 15 MINUTES   COOKING TIME 15 MINUTES

600g squid hoods

½ cup (70g) plain flour

2 teaspoons coarse cooking salt

1 tablespoon lemon pepper

vegetable oil, for deep-frying

350g mesclun

LEMON MAYONNAISE

1 cup (300g) mayonnaise

¼ cup (60ml) lemon juice

1 tablespoon boiling water

1   Halve squid hoods lengthways, score the insides in crosshatch pattern then cut each half lengthways into five pieces. Toss squid in medium bowl with combined flour, salt and pepper until coated; shake off excess.

2   Make lemon mayonnaise.

3   Heat oil in wok or large saucepan; deep-fry squid, in batches, until tender and browned lightly. Drain on absorbent paper.

4   Place mesclun with a quarter of the lemon mayonnaise in medium bowl; toss gently to combine. Serve squid and mesclun salad with remaining lemon mayonnaise.

LEMON MAYONNAISE   Whisk ingredients in small bowl until well combined.

SERVES 4
per serving 28.5g carbohydrate; 25.8g fat; 2299kJ (550 cal); 28.2g protein
tip We used whole-egg mayonnaise in this recipe.

blue cheese and green onion mini pizzas

PREPARATION TIME 20 MINUTES   COOKING TIME 10 MINUTES

335g (30cm) ready-made pizza base

2 tablespoons tomato paste

2 green onions, sliced thinly

75g danish blue cheese,
  chopped coarsely

1 Preheat oven to moderately hot.

2 Using 4.5cm-round cutter, cut rounds from pizza base.

3 Place rounds on oven trays. Divide paste evenly over rounds; top with onion and cheese. Bake, uncovered, in moderately hot oven about 5 minutes or until pizzas are heated through.

SERVES 4
per serving 41.2g carbohydrate; 9g fat; 1216kJ (291 cal); 11g protein

greek mini pizzas

PREPARATION TIME 20 MINUTES   COOKING TIME 10 MINUTES

335g (30cm) ready-made pizza base

2 tablespoons tomato paste

2 tablespoons seeded
  kalamata olives

100g fetta cheese, crumbled

24 small fresh basil leaves

1 Preheat oven to moderately hot.

2 Using 4.5cm-round cutter, cut rounds from pizza base.

3 Place rounds on oven trays. Divide paste evenly over rounds; top with olives and cheese. Bake, uncovered, in moderately hot oven about 5 minutes or until pizzas are heated through. Top with basil.

SERVES 4
per serving 42.7g carbohydrate; 8.8g fat; 1246kJ (298 cal); 11.6g protein

lamb and rocket mini pizzas

PREPARATION TIME 20 MINUTES   COOKING TIME 10 MINUTES

335g (30cm) ready-made pizza base

2 tablespoons tomato paste

70g firm goat cheese, sliced thinly

6 drained semi-dried

    tomatoes (40g), quartered

140g cooked lamb fillet, sliced thinly

24 baby rocket leaves, sliced thinly

1 Preheat oven to moderately hot.

2 Using 4.5cm-round cutter, cut rounds from pizza base.

3 Place rounds on oven trays. Divide paste evenly over rounds; top with cheese. Bake, uncovered, in moderately hot oven about 5 minutes or until pizzas are heated through. Top with tomato, lamb and rocket.

SERVES 4
per serving 41.2g carbohydrate; 10.7g fat; 1446kJ (346 cal); 20.8g protein

mascarpone and ham mini pizzas

PREPARATION TIME 20 MINUTES   COOKING TIME 10 MINUTES

335g (30cm) ready-made pizza base

2 tablespoons tomato paste

100g shaved leg ham

2 tablespoons mascarpone cheese

2 teaspoons finely chopped

    fresh chives

1 Preheat oven to moderately hot.

2 Using 4.5cm-round cutter, cut rounds from pizza base.

3 Place rounds on oven trays. Divide paste evenly over rounds; top with ham, cheese and chives. Bake, uncovered, in moderately hot oven about 5 minutes or until pizzas are heated through.

SERVES 4
per serving 41.1g carbohydrate; 9.4g fat; 1246kJ (298 cal); 11.9g protein

roast beef with caramelised onion on rye

PREPARATION TIME 20 MINUTES   COOKING TIME 30 MINUTES

250g beef fillet

1 tablespoon olive oil

1 large red onion (300g), sliced thinly

2 teaspoons brown sugar

2 teaspoons red wine vinegar

½ loaf rye bread (330g)

2 tablespoons olive oil, extra

1 tablespoon mild english mustard

20 fresh flat-leaf parsley sprigs

1   Preheat oven to moderate.

2   Cook beef in medium heated oiled frying pan until browned all over; place in small baking dish. Roast, uncovered, in moderate oven about 20 minutes or until cooked as desired. Wrap beef in foil.

3   Meanwhile, heat oil in same pan; cook onion, stirring, until soft. Add sugar and vinegar; cook, stirring, until caramelised.

4   Cut bread into 1.5cm slices; cut each slice into quarters. Brush bread both sides with extra oil; toast both sides.

5   Slice beef thinly. Spread mustard on bread; top with parsley, beef and onion. Serve at room temperature.

SERVES 4
per serving 41.1g carbohydrate; 19.5g fat; 1785kJ (427 cal); 21.9g protein

chicken tandoori pockets with raita

PREPARATION TIME 10 MINUTES   COOKING TIME 10 MINUTES

2 teaspoons lime juice

¼ cup (75g) tandoori paste

2 tablespoons yogurt

250g chicken tenderloins

4 large flour tortillas

30g snow pea tendrils

RAITA

½ cup (140g) yogurt

½ lebanese cucumber (65g), halved, seeded, chopped finely

2 teaspoons finely chopped fresh mint

1   Combine juice, paste and yogurt in medium bowl, add chicken; toss to coat chicken in mixture.

2   Cook chicken on heated oiled grill plate (or grill or barbecue) until cooked through. Stand 5 minutes; slice thickly.

3   Meanwhile, heat tortillas according to manufacturer's instructions.

4   Make raita.

5   Place equal amounts of each of the chicken, tendrils and raita on a quarter section of each tortilla; fold tortilla in half and then in half again to enclose filling and form triangle-shaped pockets.

RAITA Combine ingredients in small bowl.

SERVES 4
per serving 28.4g carbohydrate; 12.1g fat; 1308kJ (313 cal); 21.6g protein

turkey, brie and cranberry on pumpernickel rounds

PREPARATION TIME 30 MINUTES

300g brie

120g thinly sliced smoked turkey breast

24 packaged cocktail pumpernickel rounds

¼ cup (80g) whole-berry cranberry sauce

1 tablespoon coarsely chopped fresh chives

1   Cut cheese into small, thin slices.

2   Divide cheese and turkey equally among pumpernickel rounds; top each with cranberry sauce and chives.

SERVES 4
per serving 39.6g carbohydrate; 24g fat; 2027kJ (485 cal); 28.1g protein

indian chicken on naan

PREPARATION TIME 30 MINUTES (PLUS REFRIGERATION TIME)   COOKING TIME 15 MINUTES

250g chicken breast fillets

2 tablespoons tandoori paste

⅓ cup (95g) yogurt

2 tablespoons coarsely chopped fresh mint

1 tablespoon lemon juice

2 pieces naan (250g)

16 small fresh mint leaves

1   Place chicken, paste and ¼ cup of the yogurt in medium bowl; toss to coat chicken all over. Cover; refrigerate 3 hours or overnight.

2   Cook chicken on heated oiled grill plate (or grill or barbecue) until browned and cooked through; stand 10 minutes. Slice chicken; cut into small pieces.

3   Combine remaining yogurt, mint and juice in small bowl. Cut 16 x 4cm rounds from naan. Spread about ½ teaspoon of the yogurt mixture on each round; top with chicken, another ½ teaspoon of the yogurt mixture and mint leaf.

SERVES 4
per serving 34g carbohydrate; 14.9g fat; 1731kJ (414 cal); 35.3g protein

chocolate rum mini mousse

PREPARATION TIME 10 MINUTES   COOKING TIME 5 MINUTES

6 egg yolks

⅓ cup (75g) caster sugar

½ cup (125ml) dark rum, warmed

50g dark eating chocolate,
   grated finely

1   Beat egg yolks and sugar in small deep-sided heatproof bowl with electric mixer until light and fluffy.

2   Place bowl over small saucepan of simmering water; whisk egg mixture constantly while gradually adding rum. Continue to whisk until mixture is thick and creamy. Add chocolate, in two batches, whisking gently until chocolate melts between additions.

3   Pour mousse mixture into four ⅓-cup (80ml) serving glasses.

SERVES 4
per serving 26.7g carbohydrate; 25.6g fat; 1856kJ (444 cal); 12.8g protein
tip The mousse can be served chilled if desired; refrigerate about 2 hours.

ricotta and berry trifle

PREPARATION TIME 15 MINUTES (PLUS REFRIGERATION TIME)

The traditional English favourite is given a new look with this summery update. If you prefer, trifle can be served in a large glass bowl. Pavlova nests are commercially made small meringue shells sold in packages of 10.

250g raspberries

250g blueberries

250g strawberries, quartered

2 cups (400g) low-fat ricotta cheese

⅓ cup (80ml) orange juice

⅓ cup (80ml) maple-flavoured syrup

2 pavlova nests (20g), crumbled

1 tablespoon toasted flaked almonds

1   Combine berries in medium bowl.

2   Blend or process combined cheese, juice and syrup until smooth.

3   Divide a quarter of the cheese mixture among four 1-cup (250ml) dessert glasses; sprinkle with some of the berries. Repeat layering with remaining cheese mixture and berries, finishing with berries.

4   Sprinkle meringue and nuts over trifles. Refrigerate, covered, for at least 3 hours.

SERVES 4
per serving 38.8g carbohydrate; 10.7g fat; 1267kJ (303 cal); 13.3g protein

pink grapefruit granita with hazelnut wafers

PREPARATION TIME 20 MINUTES (PLUS FREEZING TIME)   COOKING TIME 10 MINUTES

You need two large pink grapefruit for this recipe.

1 cup (250ml) water

1 cup (220g) sugar

**1 cup (250ml) fresh pink
    grapefruit juice**

¼ cup (60ml) lemon juice

2 egg whites

HAZELNUT WAFERS

1 egg white

¼ cup (55g) caster sugar

2 tablespoons hazelnut meal

20g low-fat dairy-free spread, melted

1   Stir the water and sugar in small saucepan over heat, without boiling, until sugar dissolves. Bring to a boil; boil 5 minutes without stirring. Remove from heat; stir in juices, cool 15 minutes.

2   Using electric mixer, beat egg whites in small bowl until soft peaks form. Fold grapefruit syrup into egg white mixture; pour into 10cm x 24cm loaf pan. Cover; freeze 3 hours or overnight.

3   Blend or process granita until pale and creamy. Return to loaf pan, cover; freeze 3 hours or overnight.

4   Make hazelnut wafers.

5   Serve granita with hazelnut wafers.

HAZELNUT WAFERS Preheat oven to moderate. Grease two oven trays; line each with baking paper. Using electric mixer, beat egg white in small bowl until soft peaks form; gradually add sugar, beating until sugar dissolves between additions. Add hazelnut meal and spread; stir until combined. Trace 16 x 7cm circles, 2cm apart, on lined trays. Spread a teaspoon of the mixture in each circle. Bake in moderate oven about 5 minutes or until browned lightly. Cool wafers on trays before carefully peeling away paper.

SERVES 8
per serving 37g carbohydrate; 2.8g fat; 736kJ (176 cal); 2.0g protein

pears poached in cranberry syrup

PREPARATION TIME 5 MINUTES (PLUS STANDING TIME)   COOKING TIME 45 MINUTES

2 cups (500ml) cranberry juice

½ cup (125ml) dry white wine

2 cardamom pods, bruised

½ vanilla bean, halved lengthways

**4 small beurre bosc
    pears (720g), peeled**

1   Combine juice, wine, cardamom and vanilla bean in large saucepan.

2   Add pears to pan; bring to a boil. Reduce heat; simmer, covered, about 25 minutes or until tender. Cool pears in syrup.

3   Remove pears from syrup; strain syrup into medium heatproof bowl. Return 2 cups of the strained syrup to same pan (discard remaining syrup); bring to a boil. Boil, uncovered, about 15 minutes or until syrup is reduced by half. Serve pears, hot or cold, with syrup.

SERVES 4
per serving 31.2g carbohydrate; 0.7g fat; 681kJ (163 cal); 2.3g protein

fruit salad with star-anise syrup

PREPARATION TIME 30 MINUTES (PLUS COOLING TIME)   COOKING TIME 5 MINUTES

1 small honeydew melon (900g)

250g strawberries

300g cherries

3 cardamom pods

3 star anise

¼ cup (55g) caster sugar

2 tablespoons lemon juice

2 tablespoons water

1 Halve, peel and chop melon coarsely. Hull strawberries; cut in half. Seed cherries; place fruit in large bowl.

2 Bruise cardamom pods; place in small saucepan with star anise, sugar, juice and the water. Stir over heat, without boiling, until sugar dissolves.

3 Pour warm syrup over fruit; refrigerate, covered, about 30 minutes or until cold.

SERVES 4
per serving 33.4g carbohydrate; 0.7g fat; 627kJ (150 cal); 2.9g protein

yogurt and kiwi mousse

PREPARATION TIME 10 MINUTES (PLUS REFRIGERATING TIME)

85g packet mango jelly crystals

1 cup (250ml) boiling water

2 x 200g cartons low-fat
**   five-fruit yogurt**

1 medium mango (430g),
**   chopped finely**

1 medium banana (200g),
**   sliced thinly**

1 medium kiwi fruit (85g), halved,
**   sliced thinly**

1 Stir jelly crystals with the water in small heatproof bowl until dissolved; refrigerate about 20 minutes or until cold (do not allow to set).

2 Add yogurt and mango to jelly; stir to combine. Divide yogurt mixture among six 1-cup (250ml) serving glasses. Cover; refrigerate about 2 hours or until set. Just before serving, top each with equal amounts of banana and kiwi fruit.

SERVES 6
per serving 35.9g carbohydrate; 1g fat; 706kJ (169 cal;) 5.3g protein

mocha smoothie

PREPARATION TIME 5 MINUTES

1 litre (4 cups) no-fat milk

1 cup (250ml) chocolate mousse

1 cup (250ml) chocolate ice-cream

1 tablespoon instant coffee powder

½ teaspoon vanilla extract

1 Blend or process ingredients, in batches, until smooth.

SERVES 4
per serving 29.7g carbohydrate; 7.1g fat; 974kJ (233 cal); 13.8g protein

rhubarb galette

PREPARATION TIME 10 MINUTES   COOKING TIME 20 MINUTES

You need about four trimmed large stems of rhubarb for this recipe.

20g butter, melted

2½ cups (275g) coarsely
chopped rhubarb

⅓ cup (75g) firmly packed
brown sugar

1 teaspoon finely grated orange rind

1 sheet ready-rolled puff pastry

2 tablespoons almond meal

10g butter, melted, extra

1 Preheat oven to hot. Line oven tray with baking paper.

2 Combine butter, rhubarb, sugar and rind in medium bowl.

3 Cut 24cm round from pastry, place on prepared tray; sprinkle almond meal evenly over pastry. Spread rhubarb mixture over pastry, leaving a 4cm border. Fold 2cm of pastry edge up and around filling. Brush edge with extra butter. Bake galette, uncovered, in hot oven about 20 minutes or until browned lightly.

SERVES 4
per serving 34.5g carbohydrate; 18.2g fat; 1325kJ (317 cal); 4.3g protein

glossary

ALLSPICE also known as pimento or Jamaican pepper; so-named because it tastes like a combination of nutmeg, cumin, clove and cinnamon – all spices. Is available whole (a pea-size dark-brown berry) or ground, and used in both sweet and savoury dishes.

ARTICHOKES

globe large flower-bud of a member of the thistle family; having tough petal-like leaves, edible in part when cooked.

hearts tender centre of the globe artichoke, itself the large flower-bud of a member of the thistle family; having tough petal like leaves, edible in part when cooked. Artichoke hearts can be harvested fresh from the plant or purchased in brine canned or in glass jars.

jerusalem neither from Jerusalem nor an artichoke, this crunchy tuber tastes a bit like a fresh water chestnut and is related to the sunflower family.

BAKING POWDER a raising agent consisting mainly of two parts cream of tartar to one part bicarbonate of soda (baking soda).

BAMBOO SHOOTS the tender shoots of bamboo plants, available in cans; must be drained and rinsed before use.

BARBERRIES elongated bright red berries; rarely eaten raw due to their high acidity. Available from specialist food outlets.

BARLEY a nutritious grain used in soups and stews (often as a thickener) as well as in whisky- and beer-making. Hulled barley is the least processed form of barley and nutritious and high in fibre. Pearl barley has had the husk discarded and been hulled and polished, much the same as rice.

BEANS

black-eyed also known as black-eyed peas, are the dried seed of a variant of the snake or yard bean.

borlotti also known as Roman beans, they can be eaten fresh or dried. Borlotti can also substitute for pinto beans because of the similarity in appearance – both are pale pink or beige with darker red spots.

cannellini small white dried bean similar in appearance and flavour to other Phaseolus vulgaris varieties – great northern and navy or haricot beans. Sometimes sold as butter beans.

haricot similar in appearance and flavour to other small dried white beans such as great northern, navy and cannellini; sold dried, good in soups and casseroles.

mexican-style baked a canned mixture of either kidney or pinto beans cooked with tomato, peppers, onion, garlic and various spices.

mung tiny dried green beans available from Asian food stores, whole, skinned and split. A good source of fibre, protein, iron, folate, niacin and thiamin, mung beans are commonly used for sprouting.

salted black also known as Chinese black beans, these are fermented and salted soy beans available in cans and jars. Used most often in Asian cooking; chop before, or mash during cooking to release flavour.

snake long (about 40cm), thin, round, fresh green beans, Asian in origin, with a taste similar to green or French beans. Used most frequently in stir-fries, they are also called yard-long beans because of their length.

yellow string also known as wax, French, runner and (incorrectly) butter beans; basically a yellow-coloured fresh green bean.

beetroot, golden have a slightly sweeter flavour than the purple-red variety and can be found at most greengrocers.

BOK CHOY also known as bak choy, pak choi, Chinese white cabbage or Chinese chard, has a fresh, mild mustard taste; use stems and leaves, stir-fry or braised. Baby bok choy, also known as pak kat farang or Shanghai bok choy, is small and more tender than bok choy.

BROCCOLINI a cross between broccoli and Chinese kale, is milder and sweeter than broccoli. Each long stem is topped by a loose floret that closely resembles broccoli; from floret to stem, broccolini is completely edible.

BURGHUL also known as bulghur wheat; hulled steamed wheat kernels that, once dried, are crushed into various size grains. Not the same as cracked wheat. Used in Middle-Eastern dishes such as kibbeh and tabbouleh.

CAJUN SEASONING used to give an authentic USA Deep South spicy cajun flavour to food, this packaged blend of assorted herbs and spices can include paprika, basil, onion, fennel, thyme, cayenne and tarragon.

CAPERBERRIES fruit formed after the caper buds have flowered; caperberries are pickled usually with stalks intact.

CARAWAY SEEDS a member of the parsley family, available in seed or ground form and appropriate for sweet or savoury dishes.

CARDAMOM native to India and used extensively in its cuisine; can be purchased in pod, seed or ground form. Has a distinctive aromatic, sweetly rich flavour and is one of the world's most expensive spices.

CAYENNE PEPPER a thin-fleshed, long, extremely hot dried red chilli, usually purchased ground.

CELERIAC tuberous root with brown skin, white flesh and a celery-like flavour.

CHEESE

bocconcini walnut-sized, baby mozzarella, a delicate, semi-soft, white cheese traditionally made in Italy from buffalo milk. Spoils rapidly so must be kept under refrigeration, in brine, for 1 or 2 days at most.

brie Often referred to as the 'queen of cheeses', brie originated in France but is now manufactured locally. Brie has a bloomy white rind and a creamy centre which becomes runnier as it ripens.

goat made from goat milk, has an earthy, strong taste; available in both soft and firm textures, in various shapes and sizes, sometimes rolled in ash or herbs.

gorgonzola a creamy Italian blue cheese having a mild, sweet taste; good as an accompaniment to fruit or to flavour sauces.

gruyère a Swiss cheese having small holes and a nutty, slightly salty flavour.

haloumi a firm, cream-coloured sheep milk cheese matured in brine; somewhat like a minty, salty fetta in flavour, haloumi can be grilled or fried, briefly, without breaking down.

mascarpone a cultured cream product made in much the same way as yogurt. It's whitish to creamy yellow in colour, with a soft, creamy texture.

pecorino is the generic Italian name for cheeses made from sheep milk. It's a hard, white to pale yellow cheese, usually matured for eight to 12 months and known for the region in which it's produced – Romano from Rome, Sardo from Sardinia, Siciliano from Sicily and Toscano from Tuscany.

CHICKPEAS also called garbanzos, hummus or channa; an irregularly round, sandy-coloured legume used extensively in Mediterranean and Latin cooking.

CHILLI use rubber gloves when seeding and chopping chillies as they can burn your skin. Removing seeds and membranes lessens the heat.

chipotle hot, dried, smoked jalapeños, available in cans.

green generally unripened Thai chillies but sometimes different varieties that are ripe when green, such as habanero, poblano or serrano chillies.

guajillo also called travieso or cascabel; the dried form of the fresh mirasol chilli. Deep red to almost black in colour, this medium-hot chilli must be soaked in boiling water before being used.

jalapeños fairly hot green chillies, available in brine bottled or fresh from specialty greengrocers.

thai, red small, medium hot, and bright red in colour.

CHORIZO a sausage of Spanish origin, made of coarsely ground pork and highly seasoned with garlic and chillies.

CHOY SUM also known as pakaukeo or flowering cabbage, a member of the bok choy family; easy to identify with its long stems, light green leaves and yellow flowers. Is eaten, stems and all, steamed or stir-fried.

CLOVES dried flower buds of a tropical tree; can be used whole or in ground form. Have a strong scent and taste so should be used minimally.

CORNICHON French for gherkin, a very small variety of cucumber. Pickled, they are a traditional accompaniment to pâté; the Swiss always serve them with fondue (or raclette).

CUMIN also known as zeera, available in ground or seed form; can be purchased from supermarkets.

CURLY ENDIVE also known as frisee; a curly-leafed green vegetable, mainly used in salads.

CURRY PASTES some recipes in this book call for commercially prepared pastes of various strengths and flavours. Use whichever one you feel suits your spice-level tolerance best.

rogan josh a spicy paste made from fresh chillies or paprika, tomato and spices.

tandoori consisting of garlic, tamarind, ginger, coriander, chilli and spices.

tikka consisting of chilli, coriander, cumin, lentil flour, garlic, ginger, oil, turmeric, fennel, pepper, cloves, cinnamon and cardamom.

CURRY POWDER a blend of ground spices used for convenience when making Indian food. Can consist of some of the following spices: dried chilli, cinnamon, coriander, cumin, fennel, fenugreek, mace, cardamom and turmeric.

CRÈME FRAÎCHE a naturally fermented cream (minimum fat content 35%) having a velvety texture and tangy taste.

DAIKON sweet, fresh flavour. The daikon's flesh is crisp, juicy and white, while the skin can be either creamy white or black. It can range from 6 to 15 inches in length with an average diameter of 2 to 3 inches. Refrigerate, wrapped in a plastic bag, up to a week.

EGGS some recipes in this book call for raw or barely cooked eggs; exercise caution if there is a salmonella problem in your area.

FARFALLE bow-tie shaped short pasta; sometimes known as butterfly pasta.

FENUGREEK hard, dried seed usually sold ground as an astringent spice powder. Good with seafood and in chutneys, fenugreek helps mask unpleasant odours.

FIVE-SPICE POWDER a fragrant mixture of ground cinnamon, cloves, star anise, Sichuan pepper and fennel seeds.

GAI LARN also known as kanah, gai lum, Chinese broccoli and Chinese kale; appreciated more for its stems than its coarse leaves. Can be served steamed and stir-fried, in soups and noodle dishes.

GALANGAL a rhizome with a hot ginger-citrusy flavour; used similarly to ginger and garlic as a seasoning and as an ingredient. It also comes in a dried powdered form called laos. Fresh ginger can be substituted for fresh galangal but the flavour of the dish will not be the same.

GARAM MASALA a blend of spices, originating in North India; based on varying proportions of cardamom, cinnamon, cloves, coriander, fennel and cumin, roasted and ground together. Black pepper and chilli can be added for a hotter version.

GARLIC

fried also known as kratiem jiew, sold in Asian grocery stores packed in jars or in cellophane bags; used as toppings for various Thai rice and noodle dishes, and also served as condiments for a Thai meal.

pickled sweet and subtle young green bulb, packed in jars whole and unpeeled in a vinegar brine. Available from most Asian food stores.

GINGER

ground also known as powdered ginger; used as a flavouring in cakes, pies and puddings but cannot be substituted for fresh ginger.

pickled pink available, packaged, from Asian grocery stores; pickled paper-thin shavings of ginger in a mixture of vinegar, sugar and natural colouring.

GRAND MARNIER orange-flavoured liqueur.

GRAPEVINE LEAVES available fresh or cryovac-packed in brine. Can be purchased from Middle-Eastern food stores.

GREEN PEPPERCORNS soft, unripe berry of the pepper plant, usually sold packed in brine (occasionally found dried, packed in salt in health food stores and delicatessens). Has a distinctive fresh taste that goes well with mustard or cream sauces.

pickled has a fresh herbal 'green' flavour without being extremely pungent; early harvested unripe pepper that needs to be dried or pickled to avoid fermentation. We used pickled Thai green peppercorns, which are canned, still strung in clusters, but an equivalent weight from a bottle of green peppercorns in brine can be substituted.

GUAVA PASTE made from guava pulp and sugar, cooked to a paste-like consistency. Available in cans from delicatessens and specialty stores.

HAM, GYPSY rind is removed and the meat is then twice hickory smoked. Available from delicatessens.

HARISSA sauce or paste made from dried red chillies, garlic, oil and sometimes caraway seeds.

HERBS 1 teaspoon dried herbs equals 4 teaspoons (1 tablespoon) chopped fresh herbs.

chervil also known as cicily; mildly fennel-flavoured herb with curly dark-green leaves.

marjoram sweet and mild tasting, used to season meats and fish.

opal basil has large oval leaves and a sweet, almost gingery flavour.

tarragon has a strong anise-like flavour, use sparingly.

thai basil has smaller leaves and purplish stems with a slight licorice or aniseed taste.

thai mint also known as marsh mint; similar to spearmint. Its somewhat thick round leaves are usually used raw, as a flavouring sprinkled over soups and salads.

vietnamese mint not a mint at all, but a pungent and peppery narrow-leafed member of the buckwheat family.

HUMMUS a Middle-Eastern salad or dip made from softened dried chickpeas, garlic, lemon juice and tahini (sesame seed paste); can be purchased, ready-made, from most delicatessens and supermarkets.

INDIRECT METHOD a kettle barbecue cooking method where the heat beads or coals are placed around the outside perimeter of the bottom grill, surrounding the food being cooked rather than burning directly under it.

JUNIPER BERRIES dried berries of an evergreen tree; it is the main flavouring ingredient in gin.

KAFFIR LIME wrinkled, bumpy-skinned green fruit of a small citrus tree originally grown in South Africa and Southeast Asia. Gives Thai food a unique aromatic flavour; usually only the zest is used.

KAFFIR LIME LEAVES look like two glossy dark green leaves joined end to end, forming a rounded hourglass shape. Used fresh or dried in many Asian dishes and used like bay leaves or curry leaves, especially in Thai cooking.

KALONJI also known as nigella or black onion seeds, are angular seeds, black on the outside and creamy within, having a sharp nutty flavour.

KECAP MANIS a dark, thick sweet soy sauce used in most Southeast-Asian cuisines.

KIRSCH cherry-flavoured liqueur.

KUMARA Polynesian name of orange-fleshed sweet potato, often confused with yam.

LEEK, PENCIL about a quarter the size of normal mature leeks; sweet and tender they can be steamed or braised and eaten like asparagus.

LEMON GRASS a tall, clumping, lemon-smelling and tasting, sharp-edged grass; the white lower part of the stem is used, finely chopped, in cooking.

LETTUCE

coral a curly-leafed lettuce.

lamb's also known as mâche, corn salad or lamb tongue, the tender narrow dark-green leaves have a mild, almost nutty flavour.

mignonette has crisp, tightly furled leaves and a slightly bitter taste.

mizuna Japanese in origin; frizzy green salad leaf having a delicate mustard flavour.

oak leaf also known as Feville de Chene. Available in both red and green leaf.

LOW-FAT DAIRY-FREE SPREAD we used a polyunsaturated, cholesterol-free, reduced-fat diet spread made of vegetable oils, water and gelatine having 2.35g of fat per 5g.

MAPLE SYRUP a thin syrup distilled from the sap of the maple tree. Maple-flavoured syrup or pancake syrup is not an adequate substitute for the real thing.

MARSALA a sweet fortified wine originally from Sicily.

MESCLUN a salad mix of assorted young lettuce and other green leaves, including baby spinach leaves, mizuna and curly endive.

MIRIN is a Japanese champagne-coloured cooking wine made of glutinous rice and alcohol expressly for cooking and should not be confused with sake.

MIXED SPICE a blend of ground spices usually consisting of cinnamon, allspice and nutmeg.

MUSHROOMS

button small, cultivated white mushrooms with a mild flavour.

dried cloud ear also known as wood ear or dried black fungus is popular in Asian cooking. Sold dried, it's black on one side and pale grey on the other.

dried shiitake also known as donko or dried Chinese mushrooms; have a unique meaty flavour.

enoki long thin white mushrooms, with a delicate fruit flavour.

flat large, flat mushrooms with a rich earthy flavour. They are sometimes misnamed field mushrooms which are wild mushrooms.

oyster also known as abalone; grey-white mushroom shaped like a fan. Prized for their smooth texture and subtle, oyster-like flavour.

portobello mature Swiss browns. Large, dark brown mushrooms with a full-bodied flavour.

shiitake also known as Chinese black, forest or golden oak mushrooms; although cultivated, have the earthiness and taste of wild mushrooms.

swiss brown light to dark brown mushrooms with full-bodied flavour also known as Roman or cremini.

MUSTARD

dry powdered yellow mustard seeds.

powder finely ground white (yellow) mustard seeds.

seeds, black also known as brown mustard seeds; more pungent than the white (or yellow) seeds.

NAAN is that delicious leavened bread we associate with the tandoori dishes of northern India.

NOODLES

bean thread also known as cellophane or glass noodles because they are transparent when cooked. White in colour (not off-white like rice vermicelli), very delicate and fine.

rice stick especially popular Southeast Asian dried rice noodles. Come in different widths, but all should be soaked in hot water until soft.

rice vermicelli similar to bean threads, only they're longer and made with rice flour instead of mung bean starch.

NORI a type of dried seaweed used in Japanese cooking as a flavouring, garnish or for sushi. Sold in thin sheets.

OKRA also known as bamia or lady fingers, a green, ridged, oblong pod with a furry skin. Native to Africa, this vegetable is used in Indian, Middle-Eastern and southern USA cooking, and is used to thicken stews.

PANCETTA an Italian bacon cured in spices and salt. Can be purchased from delicatessens.

PAPPADUMS sun-dried wafers made from a combination of lentil and rice flours, oil and spices.

PASTRAMI a highly seasoned cured and smoked beef, usually cut from the round; ready to eat when purchased.

PATTY PAN SQUASH a round, slightly flat summer squash being yellow to pale green in colour and having a scalloped edge. It has firm white flesh and a distinct flavour.

PEA EGGPLANT slightly larger than a green pea and of similar shape and colour; sold fresh, in bunches like grapes, or pickled packed in jars. More bitter than the slightly larger Thai eggplant, which can be substituted in many Thai recipes; both can be found in Asian grocery stores.

PEPITAS dried pumpkin seeds.

PERNOD an aniseed-flavoured liqueur.

PITTA also known as Lebanese bread. This wheat-flour pocket bread is sold in large, flat pieces that separate into two thin rounds. Also available in small thick pieces called pocket pitta.

POLENTA also known as cornmeal; a flour-like cereal made of dried corn (maize) sold ground in several different textures; also the name of the dish made from it.

PRESERVED LEMON salted lemons preserved in a mixture of olive oil and lemon juice. They're available here from good food shops and delicatessens. Rinse preserved lemon well under cold water before using.

PROSCIUTTO cured, air-dried (unsmoked), pressed ham; usually sold thinly sliced. Available from most delicatessens.

RADICCHIO a member of the chicory family used in Italian cooking as well as salads. Has dark burgundy leaves and a strong bitter flavour.

RIGANI Greek oregano, is a stronger, sharper version of the familiar herb we use in Italian cooking and is available from good delicatessens and Mediterranean food stores.

SAKE Japan's favourite rice wine, is used in cooking, marinating and as part of dipping sauces. If sake is unavailable, dry sherry, vermouth or brandy can be used as a substitute.

SAMBAL OELEK also ulek or olek; Indonesian in origin, a salty paste made from ground chillies and vinegar.

SANSHO PEPPER a hot Japanese seasoning ground from the pod of the prickly ash tree. Closely related to Chinese Sichuan pepper.

SAUCES

char siu sauce a dark thick sauce made from sugar, water, salt, fermented soy bean paste, honey, soy sauce, malt syrup and spices. It can be found at most supermarkets.

chinese barbecue a thick, sweet and salty sauce made from fermented soy beans, vinegar, garlic, pepper and various spices. Available from Asian food stores.

fish made from pulverised salted fermented fish (most often anchovies); has a pungent smell and strong taste. There are many versions of varying intensity, so use according to your taste.

hoisin a thick, sweet and spicy Chinese paste made from salted fermented soy beans, onions and garlic; used as a marinade or baste, or to accent stir-fries and barbecued or roasted foods.

plum a thick, sweet and sour sauce made from plums, vinegar, sugar, chillies and spices.

SHALLOTS also called French shallots, golden shallots or eschalots; small, elongated, brown-skinned members of the onion family. Grows in tight clusters similar to garlic.

fried usually served as condiments on the Thai table or sprinkled over just-cooked dishes. Can be purchased packaged in jars or cellophane bags at all Asian grocery stores.

thai purple also known as Asian or pink shallots; used throughout South-east Asia, they are a member of the onion family but resemble garlic in that they grow in multiple-clove bulbs and are intensely flavoured.

SHERRY fortified wine consumed as an aperitif or used in cooking. Sold as fino (light, dry), amontillado (medium sweet, dark) and oloroso (full-bodied, very dark).

SICHUAN PEPPERCORNS also known as szechuan or Chinese pepper. A mildly hot spice that comes from the prickly ash tree. Although it is not related to the peppercorn family, small, red-brown aromatic Sichuan berries look like black peppercorns and have a distinctive peppery-lemon flavour and aroma.

SILVERBEET also known as Swiss chard or chard; a leafy, dark green vegetable, with thick, crisp white or red stems and ribs. The leaves, often trimmed from the stems and ribs, are used raw or cooked.

SPECK smoked pork; available from delicatessens.

STAR ANISE a dried star-shaped pod whose seeds have an astringent aniseed flavour; used to flavour stocks and marinades.

STOCK 1 cup (250ml) stock is the equivalent of 1 cup (250ml) water plus 1 crumbled stock cube (or 1 teaspoon stock powder).

SUGAR, PALM also known as nam tan pip, jaggery, jawa or gula melaka; made from the sap of the sugar palm tree. Light brown to black in colour and usually sold in rock-hard cakes; substitute it with brown sugar if unavailable.

SUMAC a purple-red, astringent spice ground from berries growing on shrubs that flourish wild around the Mediterranean; adds a tart, lemony flavour to dips and dressings and goes well with barbecued meat. Can be found in Middle-Eastern food stores.

TACO SEASONING MIX a packaged seasoning meant to duplicate the Mexican sauce made from oregano, cumin, chillies and other spices.

TAHINI sesame seed paste available from Middle-Eastern food stores; most often used in hummus, baba ghanoush and other Lebanese recipes.

TAMARIND CONCENTRATE (OR PASTE) the commercial result of the distillation of tamarind juice into a condensed, compacted paste. Thick and purple-black, it is ready-to-use, with no soaking or straining required; can be diluted with water according to taste. Use tamarind concentrate to add zing to sauces, chutneys, curries and marinades.

TARAMASALATA a Greek dip made from salted, dried roe of the grey mullet fish, olive oil, lemon juice and soaked breadcrumbs. It can be purchased from most delicatessens.

TAT SOI also known as rosette and chinese flat cabbage, a variety of bok choy, developed to grow close to the ground so it is easily protected from frost. It's used in soups, braises and stir-fries.

TOFU also known as bean curd, an off-white, custard-like product made from the 'milk' of crushed soy beans.

silken refers to the manufacturing method of straining the soy bean liquid through silk.

firm made by compressing bean curd to remove most of the water. Good used in stir-fries because it can be tossed without falling apart.

TORTILLA thin, round unleavened bread originating in Mexico; can be made at home or purchased frozen, fresh or vacuum-packed. Available in two varieties; flour and corn.

TURMERIC also known as kamin, is a rhizome related to galangal and ginger; must be grated or pounded to release its somewhat acrid aroma and pungent flavour. Known for the golden colour it imparts to the dishes, it can be substituted with the more common dried powder (use 2 teaspoons of ground turmeric plus a teaspoon of sugar for every 20g of fresh turmeric).

VIENNA LOAF also known as continental bread.

WASABI an Asian horseradish used to make the pungent, green-coloured sauce traditionally served with Japanese raw fish dishes; sold in powdered or paste form.

WATERCRESS one of the cress family, a large group of peppery greens used raw in salads, dips and sandwiches, or cooked in soups. Highly perishable, so must be used as soon as possible after purchase.

WHEAT GERM flakes milled from the embryo of wheat.

WITLOF also known as chicory or Belgian endive.

facts & figures

Wherever you live, you'll be able to use our recipes with the help of these easy-to-follow conversions. While these conversions are approximate only, the difference between an exact and the approximate conversion of various liquid and dry measures is minimal and will not affect your cooking results.

dry measures

metric	imperial
15g	½oz
30g	1oz
60g	2oz
90g	3oz
125g	4oz (¼lb)
155g	5oz
185g	6oz
220g	7oz
250g	8oz (½lb)
280g	9oz
315g	10oz
345g	11oz
375g	12oz (¾lb)
410g	13oz
440g	14oz
470g	15oz
500g	16oz (1lb)
750g	24oz (1½lb)
1kg	32oz (2lb)

liquid measures

metric	imperial
30ml	1 fluid oz
60ml	2 fluid oz
100ml	3 fluid oz
125ml	4 fluid oz
150ml	5 fluid oz (¼ pint/1 gill)
190ml	6 fluid oz
250ml	8 fluid oz
300ml	10 fluid oz (½ pint)
500ml	16 fluid oz
600ml	20 fluid oz (1 pint)
1000ml (1 litre)	1¾ pints

helpful measures

metric	imperial
3mm	⅛in
6mm	¼in
1cm	½in
2cm	¾in
2.5cm	1in
5cm	2in
6cm	2½in
8cm	3in
10cm	4in
13cm	5in
15cm	6in
18cm	7in
20cm	8in
23cm	9in
25cm	10in
28cm	11in
30cm	12in (1ft)

measuring equipment

The difference between one country's measuring cups and another's is, at most, within a 2 or 3 teaspoon variance. (For the record, one Australian metric measuring cup holds approximately 250ml.) The most accurate way of measuring dry ingredients is to weigh them. When measuring liquids, use a clear glass or plastic jug with the metric markings. (One Australian metric tablespoon holds 20ml; one Australian metric teaspoon holds 5ml.)

how to measure

When using graduated metric measuring cups, shake dry ingredients loosely into the appropriate cup. Do not tap the cup on a bench or tightly pack the ingredients unless directed to do so. Level top of measuring cups and measuring spoons with a knife. When measuring liquids, place a clear glass or plastic jug with metric markings on a flat surface to check accuracy at eye level.

Note: North America, NZ and the UK use 15ml tablespoons. All cup and spoon measurements are level. We use large eggs having an average weight of 60g.

oven temperatures

These oven temperatures are only a guide. Always check the manufacturer's manual.

	°C (Celsius)	°F (Fahrenheit)	Gas Mark
Very slow	120	250	½
Slow	140 – 150	275 – 300	1 – 2
Moderately slow	170	325	3
Moderate	180 – 190	350 – 375	4 – 5
Moderately hot	200	400	6
Hot	220 – 230	425 – 450	7 – 8
Very hot	240	475	9

index

Page numbers in italics refer to photographs